Recent Titles in the
Children's and Young Adult Literature Reference Series

Catherine Barr, Series Editor

Best Books for Middle School and Junior High Readers, Grades 6–9. 2nd Edition
Catherine Barr and John T. Gillespie

Green Reads: Best Environmental Resources for Youth, K–12
Lindsey Patrick Wesson

Best Books for Children: Preschool Through Grade 6. 9th Edition
Catherine Barr and John T. Gillespie

Literature Links to World History, K–12: Resources to Enhance and Entice
Lynda G. Adamson

A to Zoo: Subject Access to Children's Picture Books. 8th Edition
Carolyn W. Lima and Rebecca L. Thomas

Literature Links to American History, 7–12: Resources to Enhance and Entice
Lynda G. Adamson

Literature Links to American History, K–6: Resources to Enhance and Entice
Lynda G. Adamson

Celebrating Cuentos: Promoting Latino Children's Literature and Literacy in
Classrooms and Libraries
Jamie Campbell Naidoo

The Family in Literature for Young Readers: A Resource Guide for Use with
Grades 4 to 9
John T. Gillespie

Best Books for High School Readers, Grades 9–12.
Supplement to the Second Edition
Catherine Barr

Best Books for Middle School and Junior High Readers, Grades 6–9.
Supplement to the Second Edition
Catherine Barr

Rainbow Family Collections: Selecting and Using Children's Books with Lesbian,
Gay, Bisexual, Transgender, and Queer Content
Jamie Campbell Naidoo

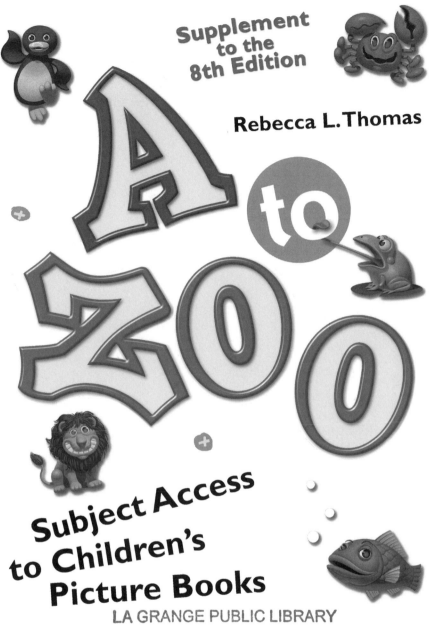

Supplement
to the
8th Edition

Rebecca L. Thomas

A to Zoo

Subject Access to Children's Picture Books

Children's and Young Adult Literature Reference
Catherine Barr, Series Editor

LIBRARIES UNLIMITED

AN IMPRINT OF ABC-CLIO, LLC
Santa Barbara, California • Denver, Colorado • Oxford, England

Library of Congress Cataloging-in-Publication Data

Thomas, Rebecca L.
 A to zoo : subject access to children's picture books. Supplement to the 8th edition / Rebecca L. Thomas.
    pages cm. — (Children's and young adult literature reference series)
 Includes bibliographical references and indexes.
 ISBN 978-1-61069-332-5 (case) — ISBN 978-1-61069-361-5 (ebook) (print) 1. Picture books for children—Indexes. I. Title.
 Z1037.L715 2010 Suppl.
 011.62—dc23   2012030256

ISBN: 978-1-61069-332-5

16 15 14 13 12   1 2 3 4 5

Libraries Unlimited
An Imprint of ABC-CLIO, LLC

ABC-CLIO, LLC
130 Cremona Drive, P.O. Box 1911
Santa Barbara, California 93116-1911

This book is printed on acid-free paper ∞
Manufactured in the United States of America

Contents

Preface

This supplement to the 8th edition of *A to Zoo* (Libraries Unlimited, 2010) provides users with subject access to picture books published in 2010 and 2011. It includes more than 1,790 titles cataloged under more than 700 subjects, and will be useful for public and school librarians developing collections, preparing bibliographies and classroom units, and for reader's advisory. Its arrangement is the same as that of the main edition, and the familiar subject headings are used.

Rebecca Thomas has been a school librarian, university teacher, and author in the field of children's literature. With this supplement, she continues the work of Carolyn W. Lima and John Lima.

HOW TO USE THIS BOOK

A to Zoo can be used to obtain information about children's picture books in two ways: to learn the titles, authors, and illustrators of books on a particular subject, such as "dragons" or "weddings"; or to ascertain the subject (or subjects) when only the title, author and title, or illustrator and title are known. For example, if the title *Knuffle Bunny Free* is known, this volume will enable the user to discover that *Knuffle Bunny Free* is written and illustrated by Mo Willems, was published by HarperCollins in 2010, and that its subject areas are Activities – traveling; Animals – rabbits; Behavior – lost & found possessions; Character traits – bravery; and Toys.

For ease and convenience of reference use, *A to Zoo* is divided into five sections:

> Subject Headings
> Subject Guide
> Bibliographic Guide
> Title Index
> Illustrator Index

SUBJECT HEADINGS: This section contains an alphabetical list of the subjects cataloged in this book. The subject headings reflect the established terms used commonly in public libraries, originally based on questions asked by parents and teachers and then modified and adapted by librarians. To facilitate reference use, and because subjects are requested in a variety of terms, the list of subject headings contains numerous cross-references. Subheadings are arranged alphabetically under each general topic, for example:

Animals (general topic)
Animals – apes *see* Animals – baboons; Animals –
 chimpanzees; Animals – gorillas; Animals –
 monkeys (cross-reference)
Animals – babies (subheading)
Animals – baboons (subheading)

SUBJECT GUIDE: This guide to more than 1,790 picture books is cataloged under more than 700 subjects. The guide reflects the arrangement in the Subject Headings, alphabetically arranged by subject heading and subheading. Many books, of course, relate to more than one subject, and this comprehensive list provides a means of identifying all those books that may contain any information or material on a particular subject.

If, for example, the user wants books on alligators (reptiles), the Subject Headings section will show that **Reptiles** is a subject classification with several subheadings. A look in the Subject Guide reveals that there are nine titles listed alphabetically by author under **Reptiles – alligators, crocodiles**.

BIBLIOGRAPHIC GUIDE: Each book is listed with full bibliographic information. This section is arranged alphabetically by author, or by title when the author is unknown, or by uniform (classic) title.

Each entry contains bibliographic information in order: author, title, illustrator, publisher and date of publication, miscellaneous notes when given, International Standard Book Number (ISBN), and subjects, listed according to the alphabetical classification in the Subject Headings section.

The user can consult the Bibliographic Guide to find complete data on each of the titles listed in the Subject Guide under the subheading of **Reptiles – alligators, crocodiles**, as for example:

Jewell, Nancy. *Alligator wedding* ill. by J. Rutland.
 Henry Holt, 2010. ISBN 978-0-8050-6819-1 Subj:
 Reptiles – alligators, crocodiles. Rhyming text.
 Swamps. Weddings.

In the case of joint authors, the second author is listed in alphabetical order, followed by the book title and the name of the primary author or main entry. The user can then locate the first-named author for complete bibliographic information. For example:

Page, Robin. *How to clean a hippopotamus: a look at
 unusual animal partnerships* (Jenkins, Steve)

Bibliographic information for this title will be found in the Bibliographic Guide section under "Jenkins, Steve."

Titles for an author who is both a single author and a joint author are interfiled alphabetically. Where the author is not known, the entry is listed alphabetically by title with complete bibliographic information following the same format as given above.

TITLE INDEX: This section contains an alphabetical list of all titles in the book with authors in parentheses, followed by the page number of the full listing in the Bibliographic Guide, such as:

A ball for Daisy (Raschka, Chris), 138

If a title has no known author, the name of the illustrator is given if available. When multiple versions of the same title are listed, the illustrator's name is given with the author's name (when known) in parentheses:

Twelve days of Christmas ill. by Rachel Isadora (The twelve days of Christmas. English folk song), 151

The twelve days of Christmas ill. by Laurel Long (The twelve days of Christmas. English folk song), 151

The twelve days of Christmas, ill. by Jane Ray (The twelve days of Christmas. English folk song), 151

ILLUSTRATOR INDEX: This section contains an alphabetical list of illustrators with titles and authors, followed by the page number of the full listing in the Bibliographic Guide. For example:

Adams, Steve. *The boy who wanted to cook* (Whelan, Gloria), 154

Titles listed under an illustrator's name appear in alphabetical sequence. When the author is the same as the illustrator, the author's name is not repeated.

Acknowledgments

The author wishes to express her thanks for the assistance provided by many people in bringing this book together. Special thanks to Barbara Ittner of Libraries Unlimited, to series editor Catherine Barr, and to Christine McNaull, who looked after the database, sorting, and typesetting and provided invaluable help with the editing.

Subject Headings

Main headings, subheadings, and cross-references are arranged alphabetically and provide a quick reference to the subjects used in the Subject Guide section, where author and title names appear under appropriate headings.

Aardvarks *see* Animals – aardvarks
ABC books
Accordion books *see* Format, unusual
Activities
Activities – babysitting
Activities – baking, cooking
Activities – ballooning
Activities – bathing
Activities – cooking *see* Activities – baking, cooking
Activities – dancing
Activities – digging
Activities – drawing
Activities – eating *see* Food
Activities – flying
Activities – gardening *see* Gardens, gardening
Activities – jumping
Activities – kissing *see* Kissing
Activities – knitting
Activities – making things
Activities – painting
Activities – photographing
Activities – picnicking
Activities – playing
Activities – reading *see* Books, reading
Activities – sewing
Activities – singing
Activities – storytelling
Activities – swimming *see* Sports – swimming
Activities – swinging
Activities – traveling
Activities – vacationing
Activities – walking
Activities – weaving
Activities – working
Activities – writing
Actors *see* Careers – actors
Adoption
Afghanistan *see* Foreign lands – Afghanistan
Africa *see* Foreign lands – Africa

African Americans *see* Ethnic groups in the U.S. – African Americans
Aged *see* Old age
Airplane pilots *see* Careers – airplane pilots
Airplanes, airports
Airports *see* Airplanes, airports
Alaska
Aliens
All Souls' Day *see* Holidays – Day of the Dead
Allergies *see* Illness – allergies
Alligators *see* Reptiles – alligators, crocodiles
Alphabet books *see* ABC books
Ambition *see* Character traits – ambition
Amusement parks *see* Parks – amusement
Anatomy
Anatomy – ears
Anatomy – eyes
Anatomy – faces
Anatomy – feet
Anatomy – fingers
Anatomy – hands
Anatomy – noses
Anatomy – skeletons
Anatomy – tails
Anatomy – teeth *see* Teeth
Anatomy – thumbs *see* Thumb sucking
Angels
Anger *see* Emotions – anger
Animals
Animals – aardvarks
Animals – anteaters
Animals – apes *see* Animals – baboons; Animals – chimpanzees; Animals – gorillas; Animals – monkeys
Animals – armadillos
Animals – babies
Animals – baboons
Animals – badgers

Animals – bats
Animals – bears
Animals – beavers
Animals – bison *see* Animals – buffaloes
Animals – brush wolves *see* Animals – coyotes
Animals – buffaloes
Animals – bulls, cows
Animals – cats
Animals – chimpanzees
Animals – chipmunks
Animals – cows *see* Animals – bulls, cows
Animals – coyotes
Animals – dogs
Animals – donkeys
Animals – elephants
Animals – endangered animals
Animals – ferrets
Animals – foxes
Animals – giraffes
Animals – goats
Animals – gorillas
Animals – groundhogs
Animals – guinea pigs
Animals – hamsters
Animals – hedgehogs
Animals – hippopotamuses
Animals – horses, ponies
Animals – hyenas
Animals – kindness to animals *see* Character traits – kindness to animals
Animals – leopards
Animals – lions
Animals – llamas
Animals – manatees
Animals – marsupials
Animals – mice
Animals – migration *see* Migration
Animals – moles
Animals – monkeys
Animals – moose
Animals – mules

Animals – octopuses *see*
    Octopuses
Animals – opossums *see*
    Animals – possums
Animals – otters
Animals – pandas
Animals – panthers *see* Animals
    – leopards
Animals – pigs
Animals – polar bears
Animals – porcupines
Animals – possums
Animals – prairie wolves *see*
    Animals – coyotes
Animals – rabbits
Animals – raccoons
Animals – rats
Animals – rhinoceros
Animals – salamanders *see*
    Reptiles – salamanders
Animals – seals
Animals – sheep
Animals – shrews
Animals – skunks
Animals – slugs
Animals – snails
Animals – snow leopards *see*
    Animals – leopards
Animals – squirrels
Animals – swine *see* Animals –
    pigs
Animals – tigers
Animals – voles
Animals – walruses
Animals – whales
Animals – wolves
Animals – wombats
Animals – woodchucks *see*
    Animals – groundhogs
Animals – worms
Animals – zebras
Antarctic *see* Foreign lands –
    Antarctic
Anteaters *see* Animals –
    anteaters
Anti-violence *see* Violence,
    nonviolence
Ants *see* Insects – ants
Apartments *see* Homes, houses
Appearance *see* Character traits
    – appearance
April Fools' Day *see* Holidays –
    April Fools' Day
Arachnids *see* Spiders
Archery *see* Sports – archery
Architects *see* Careers –
    architects
Arctic *see* Foreign lands – Arctic
Arguing *see* Behavior – fighting,
    arguing
Arithmetic *see* Counting,
    numbers

Armadillos *see* Animals –
    armadillos
Art
Artists *see* Careers – artists
Assertiveness *see* Character
    traits – assertiveness
Astrology *see* Zodiac
Astronomers *see* Careers –
    astronomers
Aunts *see* Family life – aunts,
    uncles
Australia *see* Foreign lands –
    Australia
Austria *see* Foreign lands –
    Austria
Authors *see* Careers – authors
Autism *see* Handicaps – autism
Automobiles
Autumn *see* Seasons – fall
Aztec Indians *see* Indians of
    North America – Aztec

Babies *see also* Animals – Babies
Babies, new *see* Family life – new
    sibling
Baboons *see* Animals – baboons
Babysitting *see* Activities –
    babysitting
Bad day *see* Behavior – bad day
Badgers *see* Animals – badgers
Bakers *see* Careers – bakers
Baking *see* Activities – baking,
    cooking
Ballet
Ballooning *see* Activities –
    ballooning
Balloons *see* Toys – balloons
Balls *see* Toys – balls
Bands *see* Musical instruments
    – bands
Bangladesh *see* Foreign lands –
    Bangladesh
Banjos *see* Musical instruments
    – banjos
Barbers *see* Careers – barbers
Baseball *see* Sports – baseball
Bashfulness *see* Character traits
    – shyness
Basketball *see* Sports –
    basketball
Bathing *see* Activities – bathing
Bats *see* Animals – bats
Bears *see* Animals – bears
Beasts *see* Monsters
Beauty shops
Beavers *see* Animals – beavers
Beds *see* Furniture – beds
Bedtime
Beekeepers *see* Careers –
    beekeepers
Bees *see* Insects – bees
Behavior

Behavior – bad day
Behavior – boasting
Behavior – boredom
Behavior – bossy
Behavior – bullying
Behavior – carelessness
Behavior – cheating
Behavior – collecting things
Behavior – cooperation
Behavior – dissatisfaction
Behavior – fighting, arguing
Behavior – gossip
Behavior – greed
Behavior – growing up
Behavior – hiding
Behavior – hiding things
Behavior – imitation
Behavior – indecision
Behavior – lost
Behavior – lost & found
    possessions
Behavior – lying
Behavior – messy
Behavior – misbehavior
Behavior – mistakes
Behavior – misunderstanding
Behavior – name calling
Behavior – naughty *see* Behavior
    – misbehavior
Behavior – potty training *see*
    Toilet training
Behavior – resourcefulness
Behavior – running away
Behavior – secrets
Behavior – seeking better
    things
Behavior – sharing
Behavior – solitude
Behavior – stealing
Behavior – talking to strangers
Behavior – teasing
Behavior – toilet training *see*
    Toilet training
Behavior – trickery
Behavior – wishing
Behavior – worrying
Being different *see* Character
    traits – being different
Bible *see* Religion
Bicycling *see* Sports – bicycling
Bigotry *see* Prejudice
Birds
Birds – canaries
Birds – chickens
Birds – cranes
Birds – crows
Birds – doves
Birds – ducks
Birds – eagles
Birds – geese
Birds – hawks

Birds – herons
Birds – hummingbirds
Birds – loons
Birds – nightingales
Birds – owls
Birds – parakeets, parrots
Birds – peacocks, peahens
Birds – pelicans
Birds – penguins
Birds – pigeons
Birds – puffins
Birds – ravens
Birds – robins
Birds – seagulls
Birds – sparrows
Birds – swans
Birds – turkeys
Birth
Birthdays
Bison *see* Animals – buffaloes
Black Americans *see* Ethnic
    groups in the U.S. – African
    Americans
Blizzards *see* Weather –
    blizzards
Blocks *see* Toys – blocks
Board books *see* Format,
    unusual – board books
Boasting *see* Behavior –
    boasting
Boats, ships
Boogy man *see* Monsters
Books, reading
Boredom *see* Behavior –
    boredom
Bossy *see* Behavior – bossy
Boxing *see* Sports – boxing
Bravery *see* Character traits –
    bravery
Brownies *see* Mythical creatures
    – elves
Brush wolves *see* Animals –
    coyotes
Buffaloes *see* Animals –
    buffaloes
Bugs *see* Insects
Buildings
Bulldozers *see* Machines
Bulls *see* Animals – bulls, cows
Bullying *see* Behavior – bullying
Bumble bees *see* Insects – bees
Burglars *see* Crime
Burros *see* Animals – donkeys
Buses
Butterflies *see* Insects –
    butterflies, caterpillars

Cafés *see* Restaurants
Caldecott award books
Caldecott award honor books
Camouflages *see* Disguises
Camps, camping

Canada *see* Foreign lands –
    Canada
Canaries *see* Birds – canaries
Cancer *see* Illness – cancer
Caps *see* Clothing – hats
Cardboard page books *see*
    Format, unusual – board
    books
Cards *see* Letters, cards
Careers
Careers – actors
Careers – airplane pilots
Careers – architects
Careers – artists
Careers – astronomers
Careers – authors
Careers – bakers
Careers – barbers
Careers – beekeepers
Careers – chefs, cooks
Careers – composers
Careers – conductors (music)
Careers – construction workers
Careers – cooks *see* Careers –
    chefs, cooks
Careers – custodians, janitors
Careers – detectives
Careers – doctors
Careers – explorers
Careers – farmers
Careers – firefighters
Careers – garbage collectors *see*
    Careers – sanitation workers
Careers – inventors
Careers – janitors *see* Careers –
    custodians, janitors
Careers – librarians
Careers – lumberjacks
Careers – magicians
Careers – mail carriers *see*
    Careers – postal workers
Careers – mechanics
Careers – military
Careers – musicians
Careers – painters *see* Careers
    – artists
Careers – paleontologists
Careers – photographers
Careers – physicians *see* Careers
    – doctors
Careers – poets
Careers – police officers
Careers – postal workers
Careers – principals *see* Careers
    – school principals
Careers – ranchers
Careers – salespeople
Careers – sanitation workers
Careers – school principals
Careers – scientists
Careers – shepherds
Careers – shoemakers

Careers – singers
Careers – soldiers *see* Careers –
    military
Careers – storekeepers
Careers – teachers
Careers – truck drivers
Careers – veterinarians
Careers – zookeepers
Carelessness *see* Behavior –
    carelessness
Cars *see* Automobiles
Castles
Caterpillars *see* Insects –
    butterflies, caterpillars
Cats *see* Animals – cats
Caves
Chad *see* Foreign lands – Chad
Chameleons *see* Reptiles –
    chameleons
Change *see* Concepts – change
Chanukah *see* Holidays –
    Hanukkah
Character traits
Character traits – ambition
Character traits – appearance
Character traits – assertiveness
Character traits – being
    different
Character traits – bravery
Character traits – cleanliness
Character traits – cleverness
Character traits – clumsiness
Character traits – completing
    things
Character traits –
    compromising
Character traits – confidence
Character traits – cooperation
Character traits – courage *see*
    Character traits – bravery
Character traits – cruelty to
    animals *see* Character traits –
    kindness to animals
Character traits – curiosity
Character traits – foolishness
Character traits – fortune *see*
    Character traits – luck
Character traits – freedom
Character traits – generosity
Character traits – helpfulness
Character traits – honesty
Character traits – incentive *see*
    Character traits – ambition
Character traits – individuality
Character traits – kindness
Character traits – kindness to
    animals
Character traits – laziness
Character traits – loyalty
Character traits – luck
Character traits – optimism

Character traits – ostracism *see* Character traits – being different
Character traits – patience
Character traits – perfectionism
Character traits – perseverance
Character traits – persistence
Character traits – pride
Character traits – questioning
Character traits – responsibility
Character traits – shyness
Character traits – smallness
Character traits – stubbornness
Character traits – vanity
Cheating *see* Behavior – cheating
Chefs *see* Careers – chefs, cooks
Cherubs *see* Angels
Chickens *see* Birds – chickens
Chimpanzees *see* Animals – chimpanzees
China *see* Foreign lands – China
Chinese Americans *see* Ethnic groups in the U.S. – Chinese Americans
Chinese New Year *see* Holidays – Chinese New Year
Chipmunks *see* Animals – chipmunks
Christmas *see* Holidays – Christmas
Church *see* Religion
Cinco de Mayo *see* Holidays – Cinco de Mayo
Circular tales
Circus
Cities, towns
Cleanliness *see* Character traits – cleanliness
Cleverness *see* Character traits – cleverness
Clocks, watches
Clothing
Clothing – boots
Clothing – costumes
Clothing – dresses
Clothing – gloves, mittens
Clothing – handbags, purses
Clothing – hats
Clothing – pants
Clothing – scarves
Clothing – shoes
Clothing – socks
Clothing – underwear
Clouds *see* Weather – clouds
Clubs, gangs
Clumsiness *see* Character traits – clumsiness
Cold (disease) *see* Illness – cold (disease)

Collecting things *see* Behavior – collecting things
Colombia *see* Foreign lands – Colombia
Color *see* Concepts – color
Communication
Communities, neighborhoods
Competition *see* Contests; Sibling rivalry; Sports
Completing things *see* Character traits – completing things
Composers *see* Careers – composers
Compromising *see* Character traits – compromising
Concepts
Concepts – change
Concepts – color
Concepts – counting *see* Counting, numbers
Concepts – measurement
Concepts – opposites
Concepts – self *see* Self-concept
Concepts – shape
Concepts – size
Conductors *see* Careers – conductors (music)
Confidence *see* Character traits – confidence
Conservation *see* Ecology
Construction workers *see* Careers – construction workers
Contests
Cooking *see* Activities – baking, cooking
Cooperation *see* Character traits – cooperation
Costumes *see* Clothing – costumes
Counting, numbers
Courage *see* Character traits – bravery
Cousins *see* Family life – cousins
Cowboys, cowgirls
Cows *see* Animals – bulls, cows
Coyotes *see* Animals – coyotes
Crabs *see* Crustaceans – crabs
Crafts *see* Activities – making things
Cranes (birds) *see* Birds – cranes
Creation
Crime
Crocodiles *see* Reptiles – alligators, crocodiles
Crows *see* Birds – crows
Cruelty to animals *see* Character traits – kindness to animals
Crustaceans – crabs

Crying *see* Emotions
Cuba *see* Foreign lands – Cuba
Cumulative tales
Curiosity *see* Character traits – curiosity
Currency *see* Money
Custodians *see* Careers – custodians, janitors

Dancing *see* Activities – dancing
Darkness – fear *see* Emotions – fear
Dawn *see* Morning
Day
Day care *see* School – nursery
Days of the week, months of the year
Death
Denmark *see* Foreign lands – Denmark
Desert
Detectives *see* Careers – detectives
Digging *see* Activities – digging
Diners *see* Restaurants
Dinosaurs
Disabilities *see* Handicaps
Diseases *see* Illness
Disguises
Dissatisfaction *see* Behavior – dissatisfaction
Divorce
Doctors *see* Careers – doctors
Dogs *see* Animals – dogs
Dolls *see* Toys – dolls
Donkeys *see* Animals – donkeys
Doves *see* Birds – doves
Dragons
Drawing *see* Activities – drawing
Dreams
Dresses *see* Clothing – dresses
Droughts *see* Weather – droughts
Drums *see* Musical instruments – drums
Ducks *see* Birds – ducks
Dwarfs, midgets
Dying *see* Death

Eagles *see* Birds – eagles
Ears *see* Anatomy – ears
Earth
Earthquakes
East Indian Americans *see* Ethnic groups in the U.S. – East Indian Americans
Easter *see* Holidays – Easter

Eating see Food
Ecology
Education see School
Eggs
Egypt see Foreign lands – Egypt
El Salvador see Foreign lands – El Salvador
Elderly see Old age
Elephant seals see Animals – seals
Elephants see Animals – elephants
Elves see Mythical creatures – elves
Emotions
Emotions – anger
Emotions – envy, jealousy
Emotions – fear
Emotions – grief
Emotions – happiness
Emotions – jealousy see Emotions – envy, jealousy
Emotions – loneliness
Emotions – love
Emotions – sadness
Emperors see Royalty – emperors
Endangered animals see Animals – endangered animals
England see Foreign lands – England
Entertainment see Theater
Environment see Ecology
Envy see Emotions – envy, jealousy
Ethiopia see Foreign lands – Ethiopia
Ethnic groups in the U.S. – African Americans
Ethnic groups in the U.S. – Black Americans see Ethnic groups in the U.S. – African Americans
Ethnic groups in the U.S. – Chinese Americans
Ethnic groups in the U.S. – Cuban Americans
Ethnic groups in the U.S. – East Indian Americans
Ethnic groups in the U.S. – Hispanic Americans
Ethnic groups in the U.S. – Italian Americans
Ethnic groups in the U.S. – Japanese Americans
Ethnic groups in the U.S. – Korean Americans
Ethnic groups in the U.S. – Mexican Americans
Ethnic groups in the U.S. – Pakistani Americans

Ethnic groups in the U.S. – Puerto Rican Americans
Ethnic groups in the U.S. – racially mixed
Ethnic groups in the U.S. – Tibetan Americans
Etiquette
Experiments see Science
Explorers see Careers – explorers
Extraterrestrial beings see Aliens
Eye glasses see Glasses
Eyes see Anatomy – eyes

Faces see Anatomy – faces
Fairies
Fairs, festivals
Fall see Seasons – fall
Family life
Family life – aunts, uncles
Family life – brothers
Family life – brothers & sisters
Family life – cousins
Family life – fathers
Family life – grandfathers
Family life – grandmothers
Family life – grandparents
Family life – great-grandparents
Family life – mothers
Family life – new sibling
Family life – parents
Family life – single-parent families
Family life – sisters
Family life – stepfamilies
Farmers see Careers – farmers
Farms
Fathers see Family life – fathers
Fear see Emotions – fear
Feelings see Emotions
Feet see Anatomy – feet
Ferrets see Animals – ferrets
Fighting see Behavior – fighting, arguing
Fingers see Anatomy – hands
Finishing things see Character traits – completing things
Fire
Firefighters see Careers – firefighters
Fires see Fire
Fish
Fish – sharks
Fishing see Sports – fishing
Flags
Fleas see Insects – fleas
Flies see Insects – flies
Floods see Weather – floods
Flowers
Flowers – roses

Flying see Activities – flying
Folk & fairy tales
Food
Foolishness see Character traits – foolishness
Football see Sports – football
Foreign lands – Afghanistan
Foreign lands – Africa
Foreign lands – Antarctic
Foreign lands – Arctic
Foreign lands – Australia
Foreign lands – Austria
Foreign lands – Bangladesh
Foreign lands – Canada
Foreign lands – Chad
Foreign lands – China
Foreign lands – Colombia
Foreign lands – Cuba
Foreign lands – Denmark
Foreign lands – Egypt
Foreign lands – El Salvador
Foreign lands – England
Foreign lands – Ethiopia
Foreign lands – France
Foreign lands – Germany
Foreign lands – Ghana
Foreign lands – Greece
Foreign lands – Haiti
Foreign lands – Himalayas
Foreign lands – Honduras
Foreign lands – India
Foreign lands – Indonesia
Foreign lands – Iran
Foreign lands – Ireland
Foreign lands – Israel
Foreign lands – Italy
Foreign lands – Japan
Foreign lands – Kenya
Foreign lands – Laos
Foreign lands – Mali
Foreign lands – Mexico
Foreign lands – Middle East
Foreign lands – Morocco
Foreign lands – Russia
Foreign lands – South Africa
Foreign lands – South America
Foreign lands – Spain
Foreign lands – Tanzania
Foreign lands – Tibet
Foreign lands – Turkey
Foreign lands – Vietnam
Foreign languages
Forest, woods
Format, unusual
Format, unusual – board books
Format, unusual – toy & movable books
Fortune see Character traits – luck
Fourth of July see Holidays – Fourth of July
Foxes see Animals – foxes

France *see* Foreign lands –
France
Freedom *see* Character traits –
freedom
Friendship
Frogs & toads
Furniture – beds

Games
Gangs *see* Clubs, gangs
Garbage collectors *see* Careers –
sanitation workers
Gardens, gardening
Geese *see* Birds – geese
Gender roles
Generosity *see* Character traits –
generosity
Geography
Germany *see* Foreign lands –
Germany
Ghana *see* Foreign lands –
Ghana
Ghosts
Giants
Gifts
Giraffes *see* Animals – giraffes
Glasses
Gloves *see* Clothing – gloves,
mittens
Goats *see* Animals – goats
Gorillas *see* Animals – gorillas
Gossip *see* Behavior – gossip
Grammar *see* Language
Grasshoppers *see* Insects –
grasshoppers
Greece *see* Foreign lands –
Greece
Greed *see* Behavior – greed
Grief *see* Emotions – grief
Groundhog Day *see* Holidays –
Groundhog Day
Groundhogs *see* Animals –
groundhogs
Growing up *see* Behavior –
growing up
Guinea pigs *see* Animals –
guinea pigs
Gypsies

Habits *see* Thumb sucking
Hair
Haiti *see* Foreign lands – Haiti
Halloween *see* Holidays –
Halloween
Hamsters *see* Animals –
hamsters
Handbags *see* Clothing –
handbags, purses
Handicaps
Handicaps – autism
Handicaps – blindness

Handicaps – deafness
Handicaps – physical handicaps
Hands *see* Anatomy – hands
Hanukkah *see* Holidays –
Hanukkah
Happiness *see* Emotions –
happiness
Hares *see* Animals – rabbits
Hats *see* Clothing – hats
Hawaii
Hawks *see* Birds – hawks
Health & fitness
Health & fitness – exercise
Heavy equipment *see* Machines
Hedgehogs *see* Animals –
hedgehogs
Helpfulness *see* Character traits
– helpfulness
Hens *see* Birds – chickens
Herons *see* Birds – herons
Hibernation
Hiding *see* Behavior – hiding
Hiding things *see* Behavior –
hiding things
Himalayas *see* Foreign lands –
Himalayas
Hippopotamuses *see* Animals –
hippopotamuses
Hispanic Americans *see* Ethnic
groups in the U.S. – Hispanic
Americans
Hockey *see* Sports – hockey
Hogs *see* Animals – pigs
Holidays
Holidays – April Fools' Day
Holidays – Chanukah *see*
Holidays – Hanukkah
Holidays – Chinese New Year
Holidays – Christmas
Holidays – Cinco de Mayo
Holidays – Day of the Dead
Holidays – Earth Day
Holidays – Easter
Holidays – Fourth of July
Holidays – Groundhog Day
Holidays – Halloween
Holidays – Hanukkah
Holidays – Independence Day
see Holidays – Fourth of July
Holidays – Kwanzaa
Holidays – Mother's Day
Holidays – New Year's
Holidays – Passover
Holidays – Purim
Holidays – Ramadan
Holidays – Rosh Hashanah
Holidays – St. Patrick's Day
Holidays – Sukkot
Holidays – Thanksgiving
Holidays – Valentine's Day
Holocaust
Homeless

Homes, houses
Homework
Homosexuality
Honduras *see* Foreign lands –
Honduras
Honesty *see* Character traits –
honesty
Honey bees *see* Insects – bees
Hope
Horses *see* Animals – horses,
ponies
Houses *see* Homes, houses
Hugging
Hummingbirds *see* Birds –
hummingbirds
Humor
Humorous stories
Hurricanes *see* Weather –
hurricanes
Hyenas *see* Animals – hyenas
Hygiene

Ice skating *see* Sports – ice
skating
Identity *see* Self-concept
Illness
Illness – allergies
Illness – cancer
Illness – cold (disease)
Imaginary friends *see*
Imagination – imaginary
friends
Imagination
Imagination – imaginary
friends
Imitation *see* Behavior –
imitation
Immigrants
Indecision *see* Behavior –
indecision
Independence Day *see* Holidays
– Fourth of July
India *see* Foreign lands – India
Indians of Central America –
Maya
Indians of North America
Indians of North America –
Aztec
Indians of North America –
Shoshone
Individuality *see* Character
traits – individuality
Indonesia *see* Foreign lands –
Indonesia
Insects
Insects – ants
Insects – bees
Insects – butterflies,
caterpillars
Insects – fleas
Insects – flies
Insects – grasshoppers

Insects – lady birds *see* Insects – ladybugs
Insects – ladybugs
Inventions
Inventors *see* Careers – inventors
Iran *see* Foreign lands – Iran
Ireland *see* Foreign lands – Ireland
Israel *see* Foreign lands – Israel
Italian Americans *see* Ethnic groups in the U.S. – Italian Americans
Italy *see* Foreign lands – Italy

Janitors *see* Careers – custodians, janitors
Japan *see* Foreign lands – Japan
Jealousy *see* Emotions – envy, jealousy
Jewish culture
Jobs *see* Careers
Jumping *see* Activities – jumping
Jungle

Kenya *see* Foreign lands – Kenya
Kindness *see* Character traits – kindness
Kindness to animals *see* Character traits – kindness to animals
Kings *see* Royalty – kings
Kissing
Kites
Knights
Knitting *see* Activities – knitting
Korean Americans *see* Ethnic groups in the U.S. – Korean Americans
Kwanzaa *see* Holidays – Kwanzaa

Lady birds *see* Insects – ladybugs
Ladybugs *see* Insects – ladybugs
Lakes, ponds
Language
Language – sign language *see* Sign language
Language, foreign *see* Foreign languages
Laos *see* Foreign lands – Laos
Laziness *see* Character traits – laziness
Leopards *see* Animals – leopards
Leprechauns *see* Mythical creatures – leprechauns
Letters, cards

Librarians *see* Careers – librarians
Libraries
Light, lights
Lighthouses
Lions *see* Animals – lions
Littleness *see* Character traits – smallness
Lizards *see* Reptiles – lizards
Llamas *see* Animals – llamas
Loneliness *see* Emotions – loneliness
Loons *see* Birds – loons
Losing things *see* Behavior – lost & found possessions
Lost *see* Behavior – lost
Love *see* Emotions – love
Loyalty *see* Character traits – loyalty
Luck *see* Character traits – luck
Lullabies
Lumberjacks *see* Careers – lumberjacks
Lying *see* Behavior – lying

Machines
Magic
Magicians *see* Careers – magicians
Making things *see* Activities – making things
Mali *see* Foreign lands – Mali
Manatees *see* Animals – manatees
Manners *see* Etiquette
Marionettes *see* Puppets
Markets *see* Stores
Marriages *see* Weddings
Mars *see* Planets
Marsupials *see* Animals – marsupials
Math *see* Counting, numbers
Maya Indians *see* Indians of Central America – Maya
Mazes
Measurement *see* Concepts – measurement
Mechanical men *see* Robots
Mechanics *see* Careers – mechanics
Memories, memory
Messy *see* Behavior – messy
Metamorphosis
Mexican Americans *see* Ethnic groups in the U.S. – Mexican Americans
Mexico *see* Foreign lands – Mexico
Mice *see* Animals – mice
Middle Ages
Middle East *see* Foreign lands – Middle East

Migration
Military *see* Careers – military
Mirrors
Misbehavior *see* Behavior – misbehavior
Mistakes *see* Behavior – mistakes
Misunderstanding *see* Behavior – misunderstanding
Mittens *see* Clothing – gloves, mittens
Moles *see* Animals – moles
Money
Monkeys *see* Animals – monkeys
Monsters
Monsters – vampires
Months of the year *see* Days of the week, months of the year
Moon
Moose *see* Animals – moose
Mopeds *see* Motorcycles
Morning
Morocco *see* Foreign lands – Morocco
Mother Goose *see* Nursery rhymes
Mother's Day *see* Holidays – Mother's Day
Motorcycles
Mountains
Moving
Mules *see* Animals – mules
Multiple births – twins
Muppets *see* Puppets
Museums
Music
Musical instruments
Musical instruments – bands
Musical instruments – banjos
Musical instruments – drums
Musical instruments – pianos
Musicians *see* Careers – musicians
Mythical creatures
Mythical creatures – aliens *see* Aliens
Mythical creatures – elves
Mythical creatures – leprechauns
Mythical creatures – ogres
Mythical creatures – trolls

Name calling *see* Behavior – name calling
Names
Napping *see* Sleep
Nativity *see* Religion – Nativity
Nature
Naughty *see* Behavior – misbehavior

Neighborhoods *see* Communities, neighborhoods
New Year's *see* Holidays – New Year's
Night
Nightingales *see* Birds – nightingales
No text *see* Wordless
Noah *see* Religion – Noah
Noise, sounds
Noise, sounds – snoring *see* Sleep – snoring
North Pole *see* Foreign lands – Arctic
Numbers *see* Counting, numbers
Nursery rhymes
Nursery school *see* School – nursery

Occupations *see* Careers
Octopuses
Ogres *see* Mythical creatures – ogres
Old age
Olympics *see* Sports – Olympics
Opossums *see* Animals – possums
Opposites *see* Concepts – opposites
Optimism *see* Character traits – optimism
Orphans
Otters *see* Animals – otters
Outlaws *see* Crime
Owls *see* Birds – owls

Pageants *see* Theater
Painters *see* Careers – artists
Painting *see* Activities – painting
Paleontologists *see* Careers – paleontologists
Pandas *see* Animals – pandas
Panthers *see* Animals – leopards
Pants *see* Clothing – pants
Paper
Parades
Parakeets *see* Birds – parakeets, parrots
Parks – amusement
Parrots *see* Birds – parakeets, parrots
Participation
Parties
Passover *see* Holidays – Passover
Patience *see* Character traits – patience
Peacocks, peahens *see* Birds – peacocks, peahens

Pelicans *see* Birds – pelicans
Pen pals
Penguins *see* Birds – penguins
Perfectionism *see* Character traits – perfectionism
Perseverance *see* Character traits – perseverance
Persistence *see* Character traits – persistence
Pets
Pharaohs *see* Royalty – pharaohs
Photographers *see* Careers – photographers
Photography *see* Activities – photographing
Physical handicaps *see* Handicaps – physical handicaps
Physicians *see* Careers – doctors
Pianos *see* Musical instruments – pianos
Picnics *see* Activities – picnicking
Picture puzzles
Pigeons *see* Birds – pigeons
Pigs *see* Animals – pigs
Pilots *see* Careers – airplane pilots
Pirates
Planes *see* Airplanes, airports
Planets
Plants
Playing *see* Activities – playing
Plays *see* Theater
Pockets *see* Clothing
Poetry
Poets *see* Careers – poets
Polar bears *see* Animals – polar bears
Police officers *see* Careers – police officers
Poltergeists *see* Ghosts
Ponds *see* Lakes, ponds
Ponies *see* Animals – horses, ponies
Porcupines *see* Animals – porcupines
Possums *see* Animals – possums
Post office
Postal workers *see* Careers – postal workers
Potty training *see* Toilet training
Poverty
Prairie wolves *see* Animals – coyotes
Prayers *see* Religion
Pregnancy *see* Birth
Prehistory
Prejudice
Preschool *see* School – nursery
Pride *see* Character traits – pride

Princes *see* Royalty – princes
Princesses *see* Royalty – princesses
Problem solving
Puffins *see* Birds – puffins
Puppets
Purim *see* Holidays – Purim
Purses *see* Clothing – handbags, purses
Puzzles *see also* Picture puzzles; Rebuses; Riddles & jokes

Queens *see* Royalty – queens
Questioning *see* Character traits – questioning

Rabbits *see* Animals – rabbits
Raccoons *see* Animals – raccoons
Race relations *see* Prejudice
Racing *see* Sports – racing
Railroads *see* Trains
Rain *see* Weather – rain
Ramadan *see* Holidays – Ramadan
Ranchers *see* Careers – ranchers
Rats *see* Animals – rats
Ravens *see* Birds – ravens
Reading *see* Books, reading
Rebuses
Religion
Religion – Islam
Religion – Nativity
Religion – Noah
Remembering *see* Memories, memory
Repetitive stories *see* Cumulative tales
Reptiles
Reptiles – alligators, crocodiles
Reptiles – chameleons
Reptiles – crocodiles *see* Reptiles – alligators, crocodiles
Reptiles – lizards
Reptiles – salamanders
Reptiles – snakes
Reptiles – turtles, tortoises
Resourcefulness *see* Behavior – resourcefulness
Responsibility *see* Character traits – responsibility
Rest *see* Sleep
Restaurants
Rhinoceros *see* Animals – rhinoceros
Rhyming text
Riddles & jokes
Rivers
Roads
Robbers *see* Crime

Robins *see* Birds – robins
Robots
Rocks
Roller skating *see* Sports – roller skating
Roosters *see* Birds – chickens
Rosh Hashanah *see* Holidays – Rosh Hashanah
Royalty
Royalty – emperors
Royalty – kings
Royalty – pharaohs
Royalty – princes
Royalty – princesses
Royalty – queens
Running away *see* Behavior – running away
Russia *see* Foreign lands – Russia

Sadness *see* Emotions – sadness
Safety
Sailing *see* Sports – sailing
Saint Patrick's Day *see* Holidays – St. Patrick's Day
Salamanders *see* Reptiles – salamanders
Salesmen *see* Careers – salespeople
Sand
Sandcastles *see* Sand
Sanitation workers *see* Careers – sanitation workers
Santa Claus
Scarecrows
School
School – field trips
School – first day
School – nursery
School principals *see* Careers – school principals
School teachers *see* Careers – teachers
Science
Scientists *see* Careers – scientists
Sea & seashore
Sea & seashore – beaches
Seagulls *see* Birds – seagulls
Seals *see* Animals – seals
Seasons
Seasons – fall
Seasons – spring
Seasons – summer
Seasons – winter
Secrets *see* Behavior – secrets
Seeds
Seeking better things *see* Behavior – seeking better things
Self-concept
Self-esteem *see* Self-concept
Self-image *see* Self-concept

Self-reliance *see* Character traits – confidence
Senses
Senses – sight
Sewing *see* Activities – sewing
Sex roles *see* Gender roles
Shadows
Shape *see* Concepts – shape
Sharing *see* Behavior – sharing
Sharks *see* Fish – sharks
Sheep *see* Animals – sheep
Shells
Shepherds *see* Careers – shepherds
Ships *see* Boats, ships
Shoemakers *see* Careers – shoemakers
Shopping
Shops *see* Stores
Shoshone Indians *see* Indians of North America – Shoshone
Shows *see* Theater
Shrews *see* Animals – shrews
Shyness *see* Character traits – shyness
Sibling rivalry
Sign language
Signs & signboards
Singers *see* Careers – singers
Singing *see* Activities – singing
Single-parent families *see* Family life – single-parent families
Size *see* Concepts – size
Skeletons *see* Anatomy – skeletons
Skiing *see* Sports – skiing
Skunks *see* Animals – skunks
Sky
Slavery
Sledding *see* Sports – sledding
Sleep
Sleep – snoring
Sleepovers
Sleight-of-hand *see* Magic
Slugs *see* Animals – slugs
Smallness *see* Character traits – smallness
Smiles, smiling *see* Anatomy – faces
Snails *see* Animals – snails
Snakes *see* Reptiles – snakes
Snoring *see* Sleep – snoring
Snow *see* Weather – blizzards; Weather – snow
Snow leopards *see* Animals – leopards
Snowmen
Soccer *see* Sports – soccer
Socks *see* Clothing – socks
Soldiers *see* Careers – military
Solitude *see* Behavior – solitude

Songs
Sorcerers *see* Wizards
Sounds *see* Noise, sounds
South Africa *see* Foreign lands – South Africa
South America *see* Foreign lands – South America
South Pole *see* Foreign lands – Antarctic
Space & space ships
Spain *see* Foreign lands – Spain
Sparrows *see* Birds – sparrows
Spectacles *see* Glasses
Spelunking *see* Caves
Spiders
Sports – archery
Sports – baseball
Sports – basketball
Sports – bicycling
Sports – boxing
Sports – camping *see* Camps, camping
Sports – fishing
Sports – football
Sports – hockey
Sports – ice skating
Sports – Olympics
Sports – racing
Sports – roller skating
Sports – sailing
Sports – skiing
Sports – sledding
Sports – soccer
Sports – surfing
Sports – swimming
Spring *see* Seasons – spring
Squirrels *see* Animals – squirrels
Stage *see* Theater
Stars
Stealing *see* Behavior – stealing
Steam shovels *see* Machines
Steamrollers *see* Machines
Stones *see* Rocks
Storekeepers *see* Careers – storekeepers
Stores
Stories in rhyme *see* Rhyming text
Storms *see* Weather – storms
Storytelling *see* Activities – storytelling
Strangers *see* Behavior – talking to strangers
Streams *see* Rivers
Streets *see* Roads
String
Stubbornness *see* Character traits – stubbornness
Submarines *see* Boats, ships
Sukkot *see* Holidays – Sukkot
Summer *see* Seasons – summer
Sun

Surfing *see* Sports – surfing
Swamps
Swans *see* Birds – swans
Swimming *see* Sports –
  swimming
Swinging *see* Activities –
  swinging

Tails *see* Anatomy – tails
Talent shows *see* Theater
Talking to strangers *see*
  Behavior – talking to
  strangers
Tall tales
Tanzania *see* Foreign lands –
  Tanzania
Teachers *see* Careers – teachers
Teasing *see* Behavior – teasing
Teddy bears *see* Toys – bears
Teeth
Television
Telling stories *see* Activities –
  storytelling
Temper tantrums *see* Emotions
  – anger
Texas
Textless *see* Wordless
Thanksgiving *see* Holidays –
  Thanksgiving
Theater
Thieves *see* Crime
Thumb sucking
Tibet *see* Foreign lands – Tibet
Tigers *see* Animals – tigers
Time
Toilet training
Tongue twisters
Tools
Tornadoes *see* Weather –
  tornadoes
Tortoises *see* Reptiles – turtles,
  tortoises
Towns *see* Cities, towns
Toys
Toys – balloons
Toys – balls
Toys – bears
Toys – blocks
Toys – dolls
Toys – pandas *see* Toys – bears
Toys – teddy bears *see* Toys –
  bears

Toys – wagons
Tractors
Trains
Transportation
Traveling *see* Activities –
  traveling
Trees
Trickery *see* Behavior – trickery
Tricks *see* Magic
Trolls *see* Mythical creatures –
  trolls
Truck drivers *see* Careers –
  truck drivers
Trucks
Turkey *see* Foreign lands –
  Turkey
Turkeys *see* Birds – turkeys
Turtles *see* Reptiles – turtles,
  tortoises
TV *see* Television
Twins *see* Multiple births – twins

U.S. history
U.S. history – frontier &
  pioneer life
Umbrellas
Uncles *see* Family life – aunts,
  uncles
Unusual format *see* Format,
  unusual

Vacationing *see* Activities –
  vacationing
Valentine's Day *see* Holidays –
  Valentine's Day
Vampires *see* Monsters –
  vampires
Vanity *see* Character traits –
  vanity
Veterinarians *see* Careers –
  veterinarians
Vietnam *see* Foreign lands –
  Vietnam
Vikings
Violence, nonviolence
Volcanoes
Voles *see* Animals – voles

Wagons *see* Toys – wagons
Walking *see* Activities – walking

Walruses *see* Animals – walruses
War
Washing machines *see* Machines
Watches *see* Clocks, watches
Water
Weather
Weather – blizzards
Weather – clouds
Weather – droughts
Weather – floods
Weather – hurricanes
Weather – rain
Weather – snow *see also*
  Snowmen
Weather – storms
Weather – tornadoes
Weather – wind
Weaving *see* Activities – weaving
Weddings
Weekdays *see* Days of the week,
  months of the year
Whales *see* Animals – whales
Wheelchairs *see* Handicaps –
  physical handicaps
Wind *see* Weather – wind
Winter *see* Seasons – winter
Wishing *see* Behavior – wishing
Witches
Wizards
Wolves *see* Animals – wolves
Wombats *see* Animals –
  wombats
Woodchucks *see* Animals –
  groundhogs
Woods *see* Forest, woods
Word games *see* Language
Wordless
World
Worms *see* Animals – worms
Worrying *see* Behavior –
  worrying
Wrecking machines *see*
  Machines
Writing *see* Activities – writing
Writing letters *see* Letters, cards

Zebras *see* Animals – zebras
Zodiac
Zookeepers *see* Careers –
  zookeepers
Zoos

Subject Guide

This is a subject-arranged guide to picture books. Under appropriate subject headings and subheadings, titles appear alphabetically by author name, or by title when author is unknown. Complete bibliographic information for each title cited will be found in the Bibliographic Guide.

Aardvarks *see* Animals – aardvarks

ABC books

Archer, Peggy. *Name that dog!*
Baker, Keith. *LMNO peas*
Basher, Simon. *ABC kids*
Bottner, Barbara. *An annoying ABC*
Brown, Margaret Wise. *Goodnight moon ABC*
    Sleepy ABC
Czekaj, Jef. *A call for a new alphabet*
DeRubertis, Barbara. *Alexander Anteater's amazing act*
    Bobby Baboon's banana be-bop
    Dilly Dog's dizzy dancing
Downing, Johnette. *Amazon alphabet*
Fleming, Denise. *Shout! Shout it out!*
Frasier, Debra. *A fabulous fair alphabet*
Fuge, Charles. *Astonishing animal ABC*
Geisert, Arthur. *Country road ABC*
Green, Dan. *Wild alphabet*
Herzog, Brad. *G is for gold medal*
Hudes, Quiara Alegría. *Welcome to my neighborhood!*
Joubert, Beverly. *African animal alphabet*
Kabakov, Vladimir. *R is for Russia*
Katz, Susan B. *ABC, baby me!*
Kontis, Alethea. *AlphaOops!*
Lawlor, Laurie. *Muddy as a duck puddle and other American similes*
Lichtenheld, Tom. *E-mergency!*
Maass, Robert. *A is for autumn*
McAarthur, Meher. *An ABC of what art can be*
McGuirk, Leslie. *If rocks could sing*
Murray, Alison. *Apple pie ABC*
O'Connell, Rebecca. *Danny is done with diapers*
Parker, Marjorie Blain. *A paddling of ducks*
Rodriguez, Sonia. *T is for tutu*
Rosenthal, Amy Krouse. *Al Pha's bet*
Siddals, Mary McKenna. *Compost stew*
Smith, Marie. *S is for Smithsonian*

Spradlin, Michael P. *Baseball from A to Z*
Thurlby, Paul. *Paul Thurlby's alphabet*
Verstraete, Larry. *S is for scientists*
Watterson, Carol. *An edible alphabet*
Wishinsky, Frieda. *Where are you, Bear?*

Accordion books *see* Format, unusual

Activities

Hop a little, jump a little!
Johnson, Angela. *Lottie Paris lives here*
Mayo, Margaret. *Stomp, dinosaur, stomp!*
Numeroff, Laura. *What puppies do best*

Activities – babysitting

Butler, M. Christina. *The special blankie*
Hughes, Shirley. *Don't want to go!*
Urbanovic, Jackie. *Sitting duck*

Activities – baking, cooking

Argueta, Jorge. *Arroz con leche / Rice pudding*
Bastianich, Lidia. *Nonna tell me a story*
Best, Cari. *Easy as pie*
Cartaya, Pablo. *Tina Cocolina*
Compestine, Ying Chang. *The runaway wok*
Emberley, Ed. *The red hen*
Goldin, Barbara Diamond. *Cakes and miracles*
Hassett, Ann. *Too many frogs!*
Iwai, Melissa. *Soup day*
Jackson, Kathryn. *Pantaloon*
Kneen, Maggie. *Chocolate moose*
Krause, Ute. *Oscar and the very hungry dragon*
The little red hen. *The Little Red Hen and the Passover matzah*
McMullan, Kate. *Bulldog's big day*
Meadows, Michelle. *Piggies in the kitchen*
Mother Goose. *Pat-a-cake*
Muir, Leslie. *The little bitty bakery*
Murray, Alison. *Apple pie ABC*
Parish, Herman. *Amelia Bedelia's first apple pie*
Parkhurst, Carolyn. *Cooking with Henry and Elliebelly*
Platt, Cynthia. *A little bit of love*
Rosenthal, Amy Krouse. *One smart cookie*
Rossell, Judith. *Ruby and Leonard and the great big surprise*
Schubert, Leda. *The Princess of Borscht*
Sylver, Adrienne. *Hot diggity dog*

Vamos, Samantha R. *The cazuela that the farm maiden stirred*
Wheeler, Lisa. *Ugly pie*
Whelan, Gloria. *The boy who wanted to cook*
Zia, F. *Hot, hot roti for Dada-ji*

Activities – ballooning

Huneck, Stephen. *Sally's great balloon adventure*
Jahn-Clough, Lisa. *Felicity and Cordelia*

Activities – bathing

Andres, Kristina. *Elephant in the bathtub*
Barner, Bob. *Animal baths*
Brown, Alan James. *Love-a-Duck*
Coffelt, Nancy. *Catch that baby!*
Jenkins, Steve. *Time for a bath*
Patricelli, Leslie. *Tubby*
Postgate, Daniel. *Smelly Bill*
Segal, John. *Pirates don't take baths*
Wilson, Karma. *Hogwash!*

Activities – cooking *see* Activities – baking, cooking

Activities – dancing

Bansch, Helga. *Brava, mimi!*
Benzwie, Teresa. *Numbers on the move*
Bonwill, Ann. *Naughty toes*
Craig, Lindsey. *Dancing feet!*
DeRubertis, Barbara. *Dilly Dog's dizzy dancing*
Greenberg, Jan. *Ballet for Martha*
Grimm, Jacob. *Twelve dancing princesses*
Hoffmann, E. T. A. *The nutcracker*
Hudson, Cheryl Willis. *My friend Maya loves to dance*
Hueston, M. P. *The all-American jump and jive jig*
Janni, Rebecca. *Every cowgirl needs dancing boots*
Krosoczka, Jarrett J. *Ollie the purple elephant*
Lynn, Sarah. *Tip-tap pop*
Maccarone, Grace. *Miss Lina's ballerinas and the prince*
Silverman, Erica. *The Hanukkah hop!*
Stutson, Caroline. *Cats' night out*
Tucker, Lindy. *Porkelia*
Witte, Anna. *Lola's fandango*

Activities – digging

Gay, Marie-Louise. *Roslyn Rutabaga and the biggest hole on earth!*

Activities – drawing

Banks, Kate. *The eraserheads*
Collins, Ross. *Doodleday*
Lichtenheld, Tom. *Bridget's beret*
O'Connor, Jane. *Fancy Nancy*
Roslonek, Steve. *The shape song swingalong*
Thomson, Bill. *Chalk*
Tierney, Fiona. *Lion's lunch?*
Watt, Mélanie. *Chester's masterpiece*
Williams, Karen Lynn. *A beach tail*

Activities – eating *see* Food

Activities – flying

Berne, Jennifer. *Calvin can't fly*
Bildner, Phil. *The hallelujah flight*
Brown, Tami Lewis. *Soar, Elinor!*
James, Simon. *George flies south*
Jeffers, Oliver. *Up and down*
Kroll, Steven. *Super-dragon*
Meade, Holly. *If I never forever endeavor*
Spinelli, Eileen. *Buzz*

Activities – gardening *see* Gardens, gardening

Activities – jumping

Fischer, Scott M. *Jump!*

Activities – kissing *see* Kissing

Activities – knitting

Barnett, Mac. *Extra yarn*
Clifton-Brown, Holly. *Annie Hoot and the knitting extravaganza*
Mortimer, Rachael. *The three Billy Goats Fluff*
Webster, Sheryl. *Noodle's knitting*

Activities – making things

Bastin, Marjolein. *Christmas with Vera*

Activities – painting

Carle, Eric. *The artist who painted a blue horse*
Engle, Margarita. *Summer birds*
Freedman, Deborah. *Blue chicken*
Knapp, Ruthie. *Who stole Mona Lisa?*
Wiesner, David. *Art and Max*
Ziefert, Harriet. *My dog thinks I'm a genius*

Activities – photographing

Davis, Jill. *Orangutans are ticklish*

Activities – picnicking

Harper, Charise Mericle. *Pink me up*

Activities – playing

Alda, Arlene. *Lulu's piano lesson*
Aliki. *Push button*
Alko, Selina. *Every-day dress-up*
Allen, Joy. *Princess Palooza*
Bently, Peter. *King Jack and the dragon*
Bergman, Mara. *Lively Elizabeth!*
Bloom, Suzanne. *What about Bear?*
Clarke, Jane. *Gilbert the hero*
Crews, Nina. *Sky-high Guy*
Durand, Hallie. *Mitchell's license*
Gammell, Stephen. *Mudkin*
Gibala-Broxholm, Scott. *Maddie's monster dad*
Gudeon, Adam. *Me and Meow*
Guy, Ginger Foglesong. *¡Bravo!*
Hines, Anna Grossnickle. *I am a backhoe*
Hubbell, Patricia. *Snow happy!*
Joosse, Barbara. *Sleepover at Gramma's house*
Liwska, Renata. *Red wagon*

McQuinn, Anna. *Lola loves stories*
Onyefulu, Ifeoma. *Omer's favorite place*
Patricelli, Leslie. *Tubby*
Portis, Antoinette. *Princess Super Kitty*
Rayner, Catherine. *Solomon Crocodile*
Roode, Daniel. *Little Bea and the snowy day*
Rylant, Cynthia. *Brownie and Pearl get dolled up*
Scheffler, Axel. *The super scooter*
Sheridan, Sara. *I'm me!*
Shields, Gillian. *Library Lily*
Slegers, Liesbet. *Playing*
Soman, David. *The amazing adventures of Bumblebee Boy*
   Ladybug Girl and the Bug Squad
Wewer, Iris. *My wild sister and me*
Wishinsky, Frieda. *You're mean, Lily Jean!*
Young, Ned. *Zoomer*

Activities – reading *see* Books, reading

Activities – sewing

Ashburn, Boni. *I had a favorite dress*
Johnston, Tony. *Levi Strauss gets a bright idea*
Masini, Beatrice. *Here comes the bride*

Activities – singing

Cunnane, Kelly. *Chirchir is singing*
Gray, Luli. *Ant and Grasshopper*
Litwin, Eric. *Pete the cat*
Ljungkvist, Laura. *Pepi sings a new song*
Mitchell, Margaree King. *When Grandmama sings*

Activities – storytelling

Fleming, Candace. *Clever Jack takes the cake*
Kroll, Steven. *The Tyrannosaurus game*
LaRochelle, David. *The haunted hamburger and other ghostly stories*
McQuinn, Anna. *Lola loves stories*
Mortimer, Rachael. *Song for a princess*
Muth, Jon J. *Zen ghosts*
Sierra, Judy. *Tell the truth, B.B. Wolf*
Sullivan, Sarah. *Once upon a baby brother*
Yeh, Kat. *The magic brush*

Activities – swimming *see* Sports – swimming

Activities – swinging

Tusa, Tricia. *Follow me*

Activities – traveling

Bart, Kathleen. *Town Teddy and Country Bear go global*
Clifton-Brown, Holly. *Annie Hoot and the knitting extravaganza*
Cora, Cat. *A suitcase surprise for Mommy*
Deacon, Alexis. *A place to call home*
Egan, Tim. *Dodsworth in Rome*
Elissa, Barbara. *The remarkable journey of Josh's kippah*
Foreman, Michael. *Fortunately, unfortunately*
Gaiman, Neil. *Instructions*
Hawkes, Kevin. *The wicked big toddlah goes to New York*

Holmes, Mary Tavener. *A giraffe goes to Paris*
Jahn-Clough, Lisa. *Felicity and Cordelia*
Kirk, Daniel. *Honk honk! Beep beep!*
London, Jonathan. *Froggy goes to Hawaii*
Loth, Sebastian. *Clementine*
McPhail, David. *Pig Pig returns*
Moss, Miriam. *Matty takes off!*
Ramsey, Calvin Alexander. *Ruth and the Green Book*
Siegel, Randy. *Grandma's smile*
Stead, Philip C. *Jonathan and the big blue boat*
Suen, Anastasia. *Road work ahead*
Verburg, Bonnie. *The kiss box*
Willems, Mo. *Knuffle Bunny free*

Activities – vacationing

Cousins, Lucy. *Maisy goes on vacation*
Falconer, Ian. *Olivia goes to Venice*
Korda, Lerryn. *It's vacation time*
Teague, Mark. *LaRue across America*
Thomas, Shelley Moore. *A Good Knight's rest*

Activities – walking

Waber, Bernard. *Lyle walks the dogs*
White, Kathryn. *Ruby's school walk*

Activities – weaving

Hurd, Thacher. *The weaver*
Perrow, Angeli. *Many hands*
Schubert, Leda. *Feeding the sheep*

Activities – working

Gray, Luli. *Ant and Grasshopper*
Levine, Arthur A. *Monday is one day*
Warwick, Dionne. *Little Man*
Wells, Rosemary. *Love waves*
Yu, Li-Qiong. *A New Year's reunion*

Activities – writing

Asch, Frank. *The Daily Comet*
Banks, Kate. *The eraserheads*
Christelow, Eileen. *The desperate dog writes again*
Crimi, Carolyn. *Dear Tabby*
French, Jackie. *Diary of a baby wombat*
Gorbachev, Valeri. *What's the big idea, Molly?*
Hopkins, Lee Bennett. *Full moon and star*
Long, Ethan. *The book that Zack wrote*
Look, Lenore. *Polka Dot Penguin Pottery*
Murphy, Stuart J. *Write on, Carlos!*
O'Connor, Jane. *Fancy Nancy*
O'Malley, Kevin. *Once upon a royal superbaby*
Pulver, Robin. *Thank you, Miss Doover*
Schubert, Leda. *Reading to Peanut*
Solheim, James. *Born yesterday*
Stein, David Ezra. *Love, Mouserella*
Sullivan, Sarah. *Once upon a baby brother*
Sutton, Jane. *Don't call me Sidney*
Taback, Simms. *Postcards from camp*
Teague, Mark. *LaRue across America*
Tonatiuh, Duncan. *Dear Primo*
Watt, Mélanie. *Chester's masterpiece*
Yeh, Kat. *The magic brush*

Actors *see* Careers – actors

Adoption

Clark, Karen Henry. *Sweet moon baby*
Foggo, Cheryl. *Dear baobab*
Lewis, Rose. *Orange Peel's pocket*
López, Susana. *The best family in the world*
McDonnell, Christine. *Goyangi means cat*
Pettitt, Linda. *Yafi's family*
Rotner, Shelley. *I'm adopted!*
Thisdale, François. *Nini*

Afghanistan *see* Foreign lands – Afghanistan

Africa *see* Foreign lands – Africa

African Americans *see* Ethnic groups in the U.S. – African Americans

Aged *see* Old age

Airplane pilots *see* Careers – airplane pilots

Airplanes, airports

Buzzeo, Toni. *Lighthouse Christmas*
Ford, Gilbert. *Flying lessons*
London, Jonathan. *A plane goes ka-zoom!*
Reynolds, Peter H. *I'm here*
Williams, Treat. *Air show!*

Airports *see* Airplanes, airports

Alaska

Blake, Robert J. *Painter and Ugly*
Crummel, Susan Stevens. *Ten-Gallon Bart beats the heat*
McCarthy, Meghan. *The incredible life of Balto*

Aliens

Donovan, Sandy. *Bob the Alien discovers the Dewey Decimal System*
McNamara, Margaret. *The three little aliens and the big bad robot*
Schories, Pat. *When Jack goes out*
Smallcomb, Pam. *Earth to Clunk*

All Souls' Day *see* Holidays – Day of the Dead

Allergies *see* Illness – allergies

Alligators *see* Reptiles – alligators, crocodiles

Alphabet books *see* ABC books

Ambition *see* Character traits – ambition

Amusement parks *see* Parks – amusement

Anatomy

Barnett, Mac. *Mustache!*
Bauer, Marion Dane. *Thank you for me!*
Bennett, Artie. *The butt book*
Harper, Charise Mericle. *Henry's heart*
Harris, Robie H. *Who has what?*
Menchin, Scott. *What if everything had legs?*

Anatomy – ears

Slegers, Liesbet. *Funny ears*

Anatomy – eyes

Fielding, Beth. *Animal eyes*
Lyon, George Ella. *The pirate of kindergarten*

Anatomy – faces

Hodgkinson, Leigh. *Smile!*
Siegel, Randy. *Grandma's smile*

Anatomy – feet

Gow, Nancy. *Ten big toes and a prince's nose*
Hulbert, Laura. *Who has these feet?*
Slegers, Liesbet. *Funny feet*

Anatomy – fingers

Hendra, Sue. *Barry, the fish with fingers*

Anatomy – hands

Clements, Andrew. *The handiest things in the world*
Mason, Margaret H. *These hands*

Anatomy – noses

Conway, David. *Errol and his extraordinary nose*
Gow, Nancy. *Ten big toes and a prince's nose*
Lucke, Deb. *Sneezenesia*

Anatomy – skeletons

Rohmann, Eric. *Bone dog*

Anatomy – tails

Fielding, Beth. *Animal tails*
Slegers, Liesbet. *Funny tails*

Anatomy – teeth *see* Teeth

Anatomy – thumbs *see* Thumb sucking

Angels

Kleven, Elisa. *The friendship wish*
Randall, Angel. *Snow angels*

Anger *see* Emotions – anger

Animals

Adler, Victoria. *Baby, come away*
Agee, Jon. *Mr. Putney's quacking dog*

Alter, Anna. *Disappearing Desmond*
Anderson, Derek. *Story county*
Animal I spy
Animal 123
Arnosky, Jim. *At this very moment*
Averbeck, Jim. *Except if*
Barner, Bob. *Animal baths*
Bartoletti, Susan Campbell. *Naamah and the ark at night*
Battut, Eric. *The fox and the hen*
    Little Mouse's big secret
Beaumont, Karen. *No sleep for the sheep!*
Berkes, Marianne. *Animalogy*
    Going home
Blackstone, Stella. *Octopus opposites*
Bolam, Emily. *Animals talk*
Bond, Felicia. *Big hugs, little hugs*
Boyle, Bob. *Hugo and the really, really, really long string*
Brett, Jan. *The three little dassies*
Broach, Elise. *Gumption!*
Brown, Margaret Wise. *The fathers are coming home*
Browne, Eileen. *Handa's hen*
Bunting, Eve. *Hey diddle diddle*
Butler, M. Christina. *The smiley snowman*
Callery, Sean. *Hide and seek in the jungle*
Carle, Eric. *The artist who painted a blue horse*
Carlson, Nancy. *Henry and the bully*
Chaconas, Dori. *Don't slam the door!*
Chichester Clark, Emma. *Little Miss Muffet counts to ten*
Chin, Oliver. *The year of the tiger*
Chivers, Natalie. *Rhino's great big itch!*
Comden, Betty. *What's new at the zoo?*
Costello, David Hyde. *I can help*
Cousins, Lucy. *I'm the best*
    Maisy's amazing big book of learning
    Maisy's book of things that go
Craig, Lindsey. *Dancing feet!*
    Farmyard beat
Crimi, Carolyn. *Dear Tabby*
Cummings, Phil. *Boom bah!*
Davis, Jill. *Orangutans are ticklish*
Dempsey, Kristy. *Mini racer*
DePalma, Mary Newell. *The perfect gift*
DiTerlizzi, Angela. *Say what?*
Dodd, Emma. *Meow said the cow*
Donaldson, Julia. *What the ladybug heard*
Dylan, Bob. *Man gave names to all the animals*
Edwards, Pamela Duncan. *While the world is sleeping*
Egan, Tim. *Dodsworth in Rome*
Ehlert, Lois. *Lots of spots*
Elliott, David. *In the wild*
Elliot, Laura Malone. *A string of hearts*
Elya, Susan Middleton. *No more, por favor*
Emberley, Ed. *The red hen*
    Where's my sweetie pie?
Fearnley, Jan. *Arthur and the meanies*
Felix, Monique. *The rumor*
Fernandes, Eugenie. *Kitten's winter*
Fielding, Beth. *Animal eyes*
    Animal tails
Fischer, Scott M. *Jump!*
Fitzsimmons, David. *Curious critters*
Fleming, Denise. *Sleepy, oh so sleepy*
Foley, Greg. *Purple little bird*
Fuge, Charles. *Astonishing animal ABC*

Gershator, Phillis. *Moo, moo, brown cow! Have you any milk?*
    Who's awake in springtime?
    Who's in the forest?
Gibbs, Edward. *I spy with my little eye*
Goembel, Ponder. *Animal fair*
Gorbachev, Valeri. *What's the big idea, Molly?*
Gore, Leonid. *The wonderful book*
    Worms for lunch
Gottfried, Maya. *Our farm*
Green, Alison. *The fox in the dark*
Green, Dan. *Wild alphabet*
Grey, Mini. *Three by the sea*
Haas, Rick de. *Peter and the winter sleepers*
Hacohen, Dean. *Tuck me in!*
Hall, Michael. *My heart is like a zoo*
Hill, Susanna Leonard. *Can't sleep without sheep*
Hodgkinson, Leigh. *Limelight Larry*
Horowitz, Dave. *Buy my hats!*
Hruby, Emily. *Counting in the garden*
Hulbert, Laura. *Who has these feet?*
Huling, Jan. *Ol' Bloo's boogie-woogie band and blues ensemble*
Ichikawa, Satomi. *My little train*
Isop, Laurie. *How do you hug a porcupine?*
Jenkins, Steve. *How to clean a hippopotamus*
    Time for a bath
    Time to eat
    Time to sleep
Joubert, Beverly. *African animal alphabet*
Juan, Ana. *The pet shop revolution*
Judge, Lita. *Red sled*
Kelly, Irene. *Even an octopus needs a home*
Kelly, Mij. *A bed of your own!*
Korda, Lerryn. *Into the wild*
    It's vacation time
Krebs, Laurie. *We're roaming in the rainforest*
Krensky, Stephen. *Mother's Day surprise*
    Noah's bark
Krilanovich, Nadia. *Chicken, chicken, duck!*
    Moon child
Landa, Norbert. *The great monster hunt*
Lester, Helen. *Wodney Wat's wobot*
Lewis, Kevin. *Not inside this house!*
Little old lady who swallowed a fly. *There was an old monkey who swallowed a frog*
The little red hen. *The Little Red Hen and the Passover matzah*
Liwska, Renata. *Red wagon*
McDonnell, Patrick. *Me . . . Jane*
Marino, Gianna. *One too many*
Meadows, Michelle. *Hibernation station*
Messner, Kate. *Over and under the snow*
Miller, Pat. *Squirrel's New Year's resolution*
Minor, Wendell. *My farm friends*
Moore, Inga. *A house in the woods*
Murphy, Stuart J. *Freda is found*
    Write on, Carlos!
Na, Il Sung. *Snow rabbit, spring rabbit*
Norman, Kim. *Ten on the sled*
Numeroff, Laura. *The Jellybeans and the big book bonanza*
    The Jellybeans and the big camp kickoff
O'Malley, Kevin. *Animal crackers fly the coop*
Parker, Marjorie Blain. *A paddling of ducks*
Patten, Brian. *The big snuggle-up*
Perrin, Martine. *Look who's there!*
Petersen, David. *Snowy Valentine*
Pittau, Francisco. *Out of sight*

Plourde, Lynn. *Only cows allowed!*
Regan, Dian Curtis. *The Snow Blew Inn*
Riphagen, Loes. *Animals home alone*
Robinson, Fiona. *What animals really like*
Rosen, Michael. *Tiny little fly*
Roth, Carol. *Will you still love me?*
Sabuda, Robert. *Beauty and the beast*
Sauer, Tammi. *Mr. Duck means business*
Sayre, April Pulley. *If you're hoppy*
Schaefer, Lola. *Just one bite*
Shaskan, Stephen. *A dog is a dog*
Sierra, Judy. *We love our school!*
    Zoozical
Slack, Michael. *Monkey truck*
Slegers, Liesbet. *Funny ears*
    Funny feet
    Funny tails
Smith, Lane. *It's a book*
Srinivasan, Divya. *Little Owl's night*
Stead, Philip C. *A sick day for Amos McGee*
Sutton, Jane. *Don't call me Sidney*
Symes, Sally. *Yawn*
Taback, Simms. *Simms Taback's farm animals*
Tafuri, Nancy. *All kinds of kisses*
Tebbs, Victoria. *Noah's Ark story*
Thimmesh, Catherine. *Friends*
Thompson, Lauren. *One starry night*
Tillman, Nancy. *The crown on your head*
The tree house
Underwood, Deborah. *The quiet book*
Vamos, Samantha R. *The cazuela that the farm
    maiden stirred*
Van Fleet, Matthew. *Heads*
    Moo
Vestergaard, Hope. *Potty animals*
Von Konigslow, Andrea Wayne. *How do you read to
    a rabbit?*
Waldron, Kevin. *Mr. Peek and the misunderstanding
    at the zoo*
Willis, Jeanne. *That's not funny!*
Yaccarino, Dan. *Lawn to lawn*
Zelch, Patti R. *Ready, set . . . wait!*
Ziefert, Harriet. *Wiggle like an octopus*

Animals – aardvarks

Brown, Marc. *Arthur turns green*

Animals – anteaters

DeRubertis, Barbara. *Alexander Anteater's amazing
    act*
Dewdney, Anna. *Roly Poly pangolin*

Animals – apes *see* Animals – baboons; Animals
    – chimpanzees; Animals – gorillas; Animals
    – monkeys

Animals – armadillos

Brimner, Larry Dane. *Trick or treat, Old Armadillo*

Animals – babies

Bauer, Marion Dane. *The cutest critter*
Cowen-Fletcher, Jane. *Hello, puppy!*
Evans, Lezlie. *Who loves the little lamb?*
Falwell, Cathryn. *Pond babies*
Fernandes, Eugenie. *Kitten's spring*

French, Jackie. *Diary of a baby wombat*
Genechten, Guido van. *Kai-Mook*
Heos, Bridget. *What to expect when you're expecting
    joeys*
Holt, Sharon. *Did my mother do that?*
Hulme, Joy N. *Easter babies*
Joosse, Barbara. *Higgledy-piggledy chicks*
Kimmelman, Leslie. *The three bully goats*
London, Jonathan. *Little penguin*
McAllister, Angela. *Little Mist*
Numeroff, Laura. *What puppies do best*
Nyeu, Tao. *Bunny days*
O'Hair, Margaret. *My kitten*
Reasoner, Charles. *Animal babies!*
Rostoker-Gruber, Karen. *Bandit's surprise*
Thompson, Lauren. *Wee little bunny*
Wilson, Karma. *What's in the egg, Little Pip?*
Zenz, Aaron. *Chuckling ducklings and baby animal
    friends*

Animals – baboons

DeRubertis, Barbara. *Bobby Baboon's banana be-bop*

Animals – badgers

Saunders, Karen. *Baby Badger's wonderful night*

Animals – bats

Dyer, Sarah. *Batty*
Gerber, Carole. *Little red bat*
Lies, Brian. *Bats at the ballgame*

Animals – bears

Barner, Bob. *Bears! bears! bears!*
Becker, Bonny. *A bedtime for Bear*
    The sniffles for Bear
Blackstone, Stella. *Bear's birthday*
Bloom, Suzanne. *What about Bear?*
Bonwill, Ann. *Bug and Bear*
Brown, Peter. *Children make terrible pets*
    You will be my friend!
Browne, Anthony. *Me and you*
Bruins, David. *The call of the cowboy*
Cusimano, Maryann K. *You are my wish*
DeRubertis, Barbara. *Corky Cub's crazy caps*
Doodler, Todd H. *Bear in long underwear*
Dunrea, Olivier. *Old Bear and his cub*
Elya, Susan Middleton. *Rubia and the three osos*
Foley, Greg. *I miss you Mouse*
Guiberson, Brenda Z. *Moon bear*
Hayes, Karel. *The summer visitors*
Helquist, Brett. *Bedtime for Bear*
Hillenbrand, Will. *Spring is here*
Ketteman, Helen. *If Beaver had a fever*
Klassen, Jon. *I want my hat back*
Kornell, Max. *Bear with me*
Lamb, Albert. *The abandoned lighthouse*
    Tell me the day backwards
McGinness, Suzanne. *My bear Griz*
Melling, David. *Don't worry, Douglas!*
    Hugless Douglas
Merlin, Christophe. *Under the hood*
Monari, Manuela. *Zero kisses for me!*
Moss, Miriam. *Matty in a mess!*
    Matty takes off!
Nesbitt, Kenn. *More bears!*

Numeroff, Laura. *Otis and Sydney and the best birthday ever*
Nyeu, Tao. *Bunny days*
Pamintuan, Macky. *Twelve haunted rooms of Halloween*
Rayner, Catherine. *The bear who shared*
Rueda, Claudia. *No*
Schoenherr, Ian. *Don't spill the beans!*
Shoulders, Michael. *Goodnight Baby Bear*
Taylor, Sean. *The grizzly bear with the frizzly hair*
The three bears. *Goldilocks and the three bears*, ill. by Emma Chichester Clark
   Goldilocks and the three bears, ill. by Gerda Muller
van Lieshout, Maria. *Tumble!*
Verburg, Bonnie. *The kiss box*
Wallace, Nancy Elizabeth. *Pond walk*
Wargin, Kathy-jo. *Scare a bear*
Wheeler, Lisa. *Ugly pie*
Wilson, Karma. *Bear's loose tooth*
Wright, Maureen. *Sneeze, Big Bear, sneeze*
Yolen, Jane. *Sister Bear*

Animals – beavers

Cooper, Elisha. *Beaver is lost*
Oldland, Nicholas. *The busy beaver*

Animals – bison *see* Animals – buffaloes

Animals – brush wolves *see* Animals – coyotes

Animals – buffaloes

George, Jean Craighead. *The buffalo are back*
Vernick, Audrey. *Is your buffalo ready for kindergarten?*
   Teach your buffalo to play drums

Animals – bulls, cows

Baehr, Patricia. *Boo Cow*
Helakoski, Leslie. *Fair cow*
Himmelman, John. *Cows to the rescue*
Ohi, Ruth. *Chicken, pig, cow and the class pet*
   Chicken, pig, cow, horse around
Plourde, Lynn. *Only cows allowed!*
Ross, Fiona. *Chilly Milly Moo*
Souders, Taryn. *Whole-y cow!*
Thomas, Jan. *Is everyone ready for fun?*
Wilson, Karma. *The cow loves cookies*

Animals – cats

Baeten, Lieve. *Happy birthday, Little Witch!*
Bailey, Linda. *Stanley's little sister*
Boyer, Cécile. *Woof meow tweet-tweet*
Brown, Ruth. *Gracie the lighthouse cat*
Bruel, Nick. *A Bad Kitty Christmas*
Crimi, Carolyn. *Dear Tabby*
Czekaj, Jef. *Cat secrets*
Dahl, Michael. *Nap time for Kitty*
Davis, Anne. *No dogs allowed!*
Dodd, Emma. *I don't want a cool cat!*
Esbaum, Jill. *Tom's tweet*
Fernandes, Eugenie. *Kitten's spring*
   Kitten's winter
Fletcher, Ashlee. *My dog, my cat*
Fuller, Sandy F. *My cat, coon cat*

Gay, Marie-Louise. *Caramba and Henry*
Godwin, Laura. *One moon, two cats*
Gorbachev, Valeri. *The best cat*
Gudeon, Adam. *Me and Meow*
Harper, Charise Mericle. *The best birthday ever!*
Harris, Trudy. *Tally cat keeps track*
Henrichs, Wendy. *I am Tama, lucky cat*
Jackson, Shelley. *Mimi's Dada Catifesto*
Jarka, Jeff. *Love that kitty!*
Krasnesky, Thad. *That cat can't stay*
Krauss, Ruth. *And I love you*
Krosoczka, Jarrett J. *Ollie the purple elephant*
Lewin, Betsy. *Where is Tippy Toes?*
Lewis, J. Patrick. *Kindergarten cat*
Lindbergh, Reeve. *Homer the library cat*
Litwin, Eric. *Pete the cat*, ill. by James Dean
   Pete the cat, ill. by James Dean
Lobel, Anita. *Nini lost and found*
Lord, Janet. *Where is Catkin?*
Luxbacher, Irene. *Mattoo, let's play!*
McCarty, Peter. *Henry in love*
McDonnell, Christine. *Goyangi means cat*
Martin, Bill, Jr. *Kitty Cat, Kitty Cat, are you going to sleep?*
Mortimer, Anne. *Pumpkin cat*
Moss, Miriam. *Matty in a mess!*
   Matty takes off!
Nelson-Schmidt, Michelle. *Cats, cats!*
O'Hair, Margaret. *My kitten*
Pelley, Kathleen T. *Raj the bookstore tiger*
Perrault, Charles. *Puss in boots*
Peters, Lisa Westberg. *Frankie works the night shift*
Pinkney, Jerry. *Three little kittens*
Prap, Lila. *Doggy whys*
Protopopescu, Orel. *Thelonious Mouse*
Pulver, Robin. *Christmas kitten, home at last*
Regan, Dian Curtis. *The Snow Blew Inn*
Ritz, Karen. *Windows with birds*
Root, Phyllis. *Scrawny cat*
Rose, Deborah Lee. *All the seasons of the year*
Rosenthal, Eileen. *I must have Bobo!*
Rostoker-Gruber, Karen. *Bandit's surprise*
   Ferret fun
Rubin, Adam. *Those darn squirrels and the cat next door*
Rylant, Cynthia. *Brownie and Pearl get dolled up*
   Brownie and Pearl grab a bite
   Brownie and Pearl hit the hay
   Brownie and Pearl see the sights
   Brownie and Pearl take a dip
Samuels, Barbara. *The trucker*
Schachner, Judy. *Skippyjon Jones class action*
Schoonmaker, Elizabeth. *Square cat*
Schwarz, Viviane. *There are no cats in this book*
Scotton, Rob. *Splish, splash, Splat!*
Spinelli, Eileen. *Do you have a cat?*
Stutson, Caroline. *Cats' night out*
Teague, Mark. *LaRue across America*
Tillman, Nancy. *Tumford the terrible*
Vischer, Frans. *Fuddles*
Voake, Charlotte. *Ginger and the mystery visitor*
Wahman, Wendy. *A cat like that*
Wardlaw, Lee. *Won Ton*
Watt, Mélanie. *Chester's masterpiece*
Wiviott, Meg. *Benno and the night of broken glass*
Yolen, Jane. *The day Tiger Rose said goodbye*

Animals – chimpanzees

McDonnell, Patrick. *Me . . . Jane*
Winter, Jeanette. *The watcher*

Animals – chipmunks

Taylor, Jane. *Twinkle, twinkle, little star*

Animals – cows *see* Animals – bulls, cows

Animals – coyotes

Puttock, Simon. *Little lost cowboy*

Animals – dogs

Archer, Peggy. *Name that dog!*
Bailey, Linda. *Stanley's little sister*
Beaumont, Karen. *Where's my t-r-u-c-k?*
Belton, Robyn. *Herbert*
Blake, Robert J. *Painter and Ugly*
Bliss, Harry. *Bailey*
Blumenthal, Deborah. *The blue house dog*
Boyer, Cécile. *Woof meow tweet-tweet*
Bunting, Eve. *My dog Jack is fat*
Burleigh, Robert. *Good-bye, Sheepie*
Cabrera, Jane. *Here we go round the mulberry bush*
Chall, Marsha Wilson. *One pup's up*
    Pick a pup
Christelow, Eileen. *The desperate dog writes again*
Cousins, Lucy. *I'm the best*
Cowen-Fletcher, Jane. *Hello, puppy!*
Crosby, Jeff. *Wiener Wolf*
Crummel, Susan Stevens. *Ten-Gallon Bart beats the heat*
Davis, Anne. *No dogs allowed!*
Desrosiers, Sylvie. *Hocus pocus*
Drummond, Ree. *Charlie the ranch dog*
Ehlert, Lois. *Rrralph*
Fletcher, Ashlee. *My dog, my cat*
Franco, Betsy. *A dazzling display of dogs*
Furstinger, Nancy. *Maggie's second chance*
Gal, Susan. *Please take me for a walk*
Gardner, Carol. *Princess Zelda and the frog*
George, Lindsay Barrett. *Maggie's ball*
    That pup!
Goodrich, Carter. *Say hello to Zorro!*
Gormley, Greg. *Dog in boots*
Gravett, Emily. *Dogs*
Grogan, John. *Trick or treat, Marley!*
Harper, Charise Mericle. *Henry's heart*
Hill, Meggan. *Nico and Lola*
Hills, Tad. *How Rocket learned to read*
Himmelman, John. *10 little hot dogs*
Hubbell, Patricia. *Shaggy dogs, waggy dogs*
Huneck, Stephen. *Sally's great balloon adventure*
Jackson, Kathryn. *Pantaloon*
Jennings, Sharon. *C'mere, boy!*
Joosse, Barbara. *Dog parade*
Katz, Bobbi. *Nothing but a dog*
Katz, Jon. *Meet the dogs of Bedlam Farm*
Kerby, Johanna. *Little pink pup*
King, Stephen Michael. *You*
Kirk, Katie. *Eli, no!*
Kleven, Elisa. *The friendship wish*
Kumin, Maxine. *What color is Caesar?*
Lendroth, Susan. *Calico Dorsey*
Lord, Cynthia. *Hot rod Hamster*

Lyon, Tammie. *Olive and Snowflake*
McCarthy, Meghan. *The incredible life of Balto*
McCue, Lisa. *Quiet Bunny and Noisy Puppy*
McMullan, Kate. *Bulldog's big day*
Macomber, Debbie. *The yippy, yappy Yorkie in the green doggy sweater*
Marcus, Kimberly. *Scritch-scratch a perfect match*
Meadows, Michelle. *Traffic pups*
Meddaugh, Susan. *Martha says it with flowers*
Monroe, Chris. *Sneaky sheep*
Murray, Alison. *Apple pie ABC*
Nelson, Marilyn. *Snook alone*
Nelson-Schmidt, Michelle. *Dogs, dogs!*
North, Sherry. *Champ's story*
Noullet, Georgette. *Bed hog*
Numeroff, Laura. *If you give a dog a donut*
    What puppies do best
Patricelli, Leslie. *The Patterson puppies and the midnight monster party*
Peters, Bernadette. *Stella is a star!*
Pfister, Marcus. *Snow puppy*
Pinkwater, Daniel. *I am the dog*
Postgate, Daniel. *Smelly Bill*
Prap, Lila. *Doggy whys*
Raschka, Chris. *A ball for Daisy*
    Hip Hop Dog
Rohmann, Eric. *Bone dog*
Rubinger, Ami. *Dog number 1 dog number 10*
Sattler, Jennifer. *Chick 'n' Pug*
Schachner, Judy. *Skippyjon Jones class action*
Schories, Pat. *When Jack goes out*
Schubert, Ingrid. *The umbrella*
Schubert, Leda. *Reading to Peanut*
Shaskan, Stephen. *A dog is a dog*
Singer, Marilyn. *What is your dog doing?*
Slater, Teddy. *Smooch your pooch*
Smith, Linda. *The inside tree*
Snicket, Lemony. *13 words*
Spinelli, Eileen. *Do you have a dog?*
Staake, Bob. *The first pup*
Stephens, Helen. *Fleabag*
Stuve-Bodeen, Stephanie. *A small brown dog with a wet pink nose*
Teague, Mark. *Firehouse!*
    LaRue across America
Urbanovic, Jackie. *Sitting duck*
Van Dusen, Chris. *Learning to ski with Mr. Magee*
Waber, Bernard. *Lyle walks the dogs*
Wild, Margaret. *Harry and Hopper*
Willems, Mo. *City dog, country frog*
Yates, Louise. *Dog loves books*
Young, Ned. *Zoomer*
    Zoomer's summer snowstorm
Ziefert, Harriet. *My dog thinks I'm a genius*

Animals – donkeys

Brown, Monica. *Waiting for the Biblioburro*
Mandell, Muriel. *A donkey reads*
Newton, Jill. *Crash bang donkey!*
Winter, Jeanette. *Biblioburro*

Animals – elephants

Andres, Kristina. *Elephant in the bathtub*
Badescu, Ramona. *Pomelo begins to grow*
Bunting, Eve. *Tweak tweak*
Clarke, Jane. *Trumpet*
Conway, David. *Errol and his extraordinary nose*

Cowcher, Helen. *Desert elephants*
Fearnley, Jan. *Arthur and the meanies*
Genechten, Guido van. *Kai-Mook*
Henrichs, Wendy. *When Anju loved being an elephant*
Joosse, Barbara. *Sleepover at Gramma's house*
Kleven, Elisa. *Welcome home, Mouse*
Krosoczka, Jarrett J. *Ollie the purple elephant*
McKee, David. *Elmer and Rose*
    Elmer and the hippos
    Elmer's Christmas
Monroe, Chris. *Monkey with a tool belt and the seaside shenanigans*
Muir, Leslie. *The little bitty bakery*
Na, Il Sung. *The thingamabob*
Rubinger, Ami. *I dream of an elephant*
van Lieshout, Maria. *Hopper and Wilson*
Wells, Robert E. *Why do elephants need the sun?*

Animals – endangered animals

Barry, Frances. *Let's save the animals*
Beard, Alex. *Crocodile's tears*
Dewdney, Anna. *Roly Poly pangolin*
George, Jean Craighead. *The buffalo are back*
Guiberson, Brenda Z. *Moon bear*
Hatkoff, Craig et al. *Leo the snow leopard*
Jenkins, Martin. *Can we save the tiger?*
Markle, Sandra. *Family pack*
Martin, Jacqueline Briggs. *The chiru of High Tibet*
Slade, Suzanne. *What's the difference?*

Animals – ferrets

Rostoker-Gruber, Karen. *Ferret fun*

Animals – foxes

Battut, Eric. *The fox and the hen*
Blackaby, Susan. *Brownie Groundhog and the February Fox*
Bloom, Suzanne. *What about Bear?*
Ernst, Lisa Campbell. *The Gingerbread Girl goes animal crackers*
Liwska, Renata. *Red wagon*
Rave, Friederike. *Outfoxing the fox*
Rawlinson, Julia. *Fletcher and the snowflake Christmas*
Rodriguez, Béatrice. *The chicken thief*
    Fox and hen together
Smith, Alex T. *Foxy and Egg*
Spinelli, Eileen. *Miss Fox's class earns a field trip*
    Miss Fox's class shapes up
Tompert, Ann. *Little Fox goes to the end of the world*

Animals – giraffes

Bracken, Beth. *Too shy for show-and-tell*
Cronin, Doreen. *Rescue bunnies*
Holmes, Mary Tavener. *A giraffe goes to Paris*

Animals – goats

Fox, Mem. *Let's count goats!*
Hale, Dean. *Scapegoat*
Kimmelman, Leslie. *The three bully goats*
Mortimer, Rachael. *The three Billy Goats Fluff*
Taylor, Sean. *Huck runs amuck!*
Waddell, Martin. *Captain Small Pig*

Animals – gorillas

Adams, Sarah. *Gary and Ray*
Durango, Julia. *Go-go gorillas*
Gibbons, Gail. *Gorillas*
Rex, Michael. *Furious George goes bananas*

Animals – groundhogs

Blackaby, Susan. *Brownie Groundhog and the February Fox*
Hill, Susanna Leonard. *April Fool, Phyllis!*
Olson, Julie. *Tickle, tickle! itch, twitch!*

Animals – guinea pigs

Cuyler, Margery. *Guinea pigs add up*
McGinty, Alice B. *Eliza's kindergarten pet*
Middleton, Charlotte. *Nibbles*

Animals – hamsters

Deacon, Alexis. *A place to call home*
Lord, Cynthia. *Happy birthday, Hamster*
    Hot rod Hamster
Ohi, Ruth. *Chicken, pig, cow and the class pet*

Animals – hedgehogs

Butler, M. Christina. *The special blankie*
Falkenstern, Lisa. *A dragon moves in*
Sutton, Benn. *Hedgehug*

Animals – hippopotamuses

Fliess, Sue. *Shoes for me!*
McKee, David. *Elmer and the hippos*
Pfister, Marcus. *Happy birthday, Bertie!*
    Questions, questions
Shea, Bob. *Oh, Daddy!*
Wild, Margaret. *Hush, hush!*

Animals – horses, ponies

Cantrell, Charlie. *A friend for Einstein*
Dockray, Tracy. *The lost and found pony*
Havill, Juanita. *Call the horse lucky*
Hobbie, Holly. *Everything but the horse*
Hubbell, Patricia. *Horses*
Isaacs, Anne. *Dust Devil*
Kay, Verla. *Whatever happened to the Pony Express?*
Kumin, Maxine. *Oh, Harry!*
Lester, Alison. *Running with the horses*
McCully, Emily Arnold. *Wonder horse*
Numeroff, Laura. *Ponyella*
Ohi, Ruth. *Chicken, pig, cow, horse around*
Yolen, Jane. *Hush, little horsie*

Animals – hyenas

Willis, Jeanne. *That's not funny!*

Animals – kindness to animals *see* Character traits – kindness to animals

Animals – leopards

Hatkoff, Craig et al. *Leo the snow leopard*
McAllister, Angela. *Little Mist*

Orr, Wendy. *The princess and her panther*

Animals – lions

Aesop. *Mouse and lion*
Richardson, Justin. *Christian, the hugging lion*
Tierney, Fiona. *Lion's lunch?*

Animals – llamas

Dewdney, Anna. *Llama Llama home with Mama*

Animals – manatees

Arnosky, Jim. *Slow down for manatees*

Animals – marsupials

Heos, Bridget. *What to expect when you're expecting joeys*

Animals – mice

Aesop. *Mouse and lion*
Bansch, Helga. *Brava, mimi!*
Bastin, Marjolein. *Christmas with Vera*
Battut, Éric. *Little Mouse's big secret*
Becker, Bonny. *A bedtime for Bear*
   The sniffles for Bear
Braun, Sebastien. *Back to bed, Ed!*
Carlson, Nancy. *Henry and the bully*
Church, Caroline Jayne. *One more hug for Madison*
Cousins, Lucy. *Maisy goes on vacation*
   Maisy's amazing big book of learning
   Maisy's book of things that go
Cox, Judy. *Cinco de Mouse-o!*
   Haunted house, haunted mouse
Fleming, Denise. *Shout! Shout it out!*
Foley, Greg. *I miss you Mouse*
Frederick, Heather Vogel. *Hide and squeak*
Gorbachev, Valeri. *What's the big idea, Molly?*
Hoffmann, E. T. A. *The nutcracker*
Holabird, Katharine. *Angelina and the royal wedding*
Kirk, Daniel. *Library mouse*
Kleven, Elisa. *Welcome home, Mouse*
Kneen, Maggie. *Chocolate moose*
Kolanovic, Dubravka. *Everyone needs a friend*
Lord, Cynthia. *Hot rod Hamster*
Morrissey, Dean. *The wizard mouse*
Mortimer, Anne. *Pumpkin cat*
Moser, Lisa. *Perfect soup*
Muir, Leslie. *The little bitty bakery*
Olson, Julie. *Tickle, tickle! itch, twitch!*
Platt, Cynthia. *A little bit of love*
Protopopescu, Orel. *Thelonious Mouse*
Rayner, Catherine. *The bear who shared*
Riddell, Chris. *Wendel's workshop*
Rossell, Judith. *Ruby and Leonard and the great big surprise*
Scheffler, Axel. *The little puddle*
   The super scooter
Spinelli, Eileen. *Now it is summer*
Stein, David Ezra. *Love, Mouserella*
Taylor, Thomas. *Little Mouse and the big cupcake*
Thomas, Jan. *Pumpkin trouble*
van Lieshout, Maria. *Hopper and Wilson*
Walsh, Ellen Stoll. *Balancing act*
Webster, Sheryl. *Noodle's knitting*
Yamashita, Haruo. *Seven little mice go to school*
   Seven little mice have fun on the ice

Animals – migration *see* Migration

Animals – moles

Crimi, Carolyn. *Rock 'n' roll Mole*
Hillenbrand, Will. *Spring is here*
Villeneuve, Anne. *The red scarf*

Animals – monkeys

Black, Michael Ian. *The purple kangaroo*
Christelow, Eileen. *Five little monkeys reading in bed*
Franco, Betsy. *Double play!*
McDermott, Gerald. *Monkey*
Metzger, Steve. *The dancing clock*
Monroe, Chris. *Monkey with a tool belt and the seaside shenanigans*
Myers, Walter Dean. *Looking for the easy life*
Patricelli, Leslie. *Be quiet, Mike!*
Peet, Mal. *Cloud tea monkeys*
Sayre, April Pulley. *Meet the howlers!*
Slack, Michael. *Monkey truck*
Vere, Ed. *Banana!*

Animals – moose

Kneen, Maggie. *Chocolate moose*
Oldland, Nicholas. *Making the moose out of life*
Rayner, Catherine. *Ernest, the moose who doesn't fit*

Animals – mules

Ramsey, Calvin Alexander. *Belle, the last mule at Gee's Bend*

Animals – octopuses *see* Octopuses

Animals – opossums *see* Animals – possums

Animals – otters

Berger, Samantha. *Martha doesn't share!*
Casanova, Mary. *Utterly otterly night*
Ohora, Zachariah. *Stop snoring, Bernard!*

Animals – pandas

Muth, Jon J. *Zen ghosts*
Perry, Phyllis J. *Pandas' earthquake escape*

Animals – panthers *see* Animals – leopards

Animals – pigs

Alexander, Claire. *Small Florence*
Asch, Frank. *Happy birthday, Big Bad Wolf*
Bardhan-Quallen, Sudipta. *Hampire!*
Bendall-Brunello, Tiziana. *I wish I could read!*
Black, Michael Ian. *A pig parade is a terrible idea*
Costello, David Hyde. *Little Pig joins the band*
Côté, Geneviève. *Without you*
Edwards, Pamela Duncan. *Princess Pigtoria and the pea*
Ernst, Lisa Campbell. *Sylvia Jean, scout supreme*
Falconer, Ian. *Olivia goes to Venice*
Geisert, Arthur. *Ice*
Guarnaccia, Steven. *The three little pigs*

Himmelman, John. *Pigs to the rescue*
Kerby, Johanna. *Little pink pup*
Kinney, Jessica. *The pig scramble*
McPhail, David. *Pig Pig returns*
Meadows, Michelle. *Piggies in the kitchen*
Ohi, Ruth. *Chicken, pig, cow and the class pet*
  Chicken, pig, cow, horse around
Palatini, Margie. *Hogg, Hogg, and Hog*
Peterson, Mary. *Piggies in the pumpkin patch*
Ruddell, Deborah. *Who said coo?*
Sattler, Jennifer. *Pig kahuna*
Segal, John. *Pirates don't take baths*
Sendak, Maurice. *Bumble-ardy*
Shaw, Natalie. *Olivia plans a tea party*
Snyder, Laurel. *Baxter, the pig who wanted to be kosher*
Sutton, Jane. *Don't call me Sidney*
Thomas, Jan. *Pumpkin trouble*
Thurman, Kathryn K. *A garden for Pig*
Tucker, Lindy. *Porkelia*
Twohy, Mike. *Poindexter makes a friend*
Waddell, Martin. *Captain Small Pig*
Wilson, Karma. *Hogwash!*
Wood, Audrey. *Piggy Pie Po*
Yamaguchi, Kristi. *Dream big, little pig!*

Animals – polar bears

Brooks, Erik. *Polar opposites*
De Beer, Hans. *Little Polar Bear and the submarine*
Genechten, Guido van. *Because you are my friend*
Steven, Kenneth. *The biggest thing in the world*
Thomson, Sarah L. *Where do polar bears live?*
Wilson, Karma. *Mama, why?*

Animals – porcupines

LaReau, Kara. *Mr. Prickles*
Schmid, Paul. *Hugs from Pearl*
Underwood, Deborah. *A balloon for Isabel*

Animals – possums

deGroat, Diane. *Ants in your pants, worms in your plants!*

Animals – prairie wolves *see* Animals – coyotes

Animals – rabbits

Battersby, Katherine. *Squish Rabbit*
Berger, Carin. *Forever friends*
Bianco, Margery Williams. *The velveteen rabbit*
Boelts, Maribeth. *Sweet dreams, little bunny!*
Brett, Jan. *The Easter egg*
Brown, Margaret Wise. *Goodnight moon ABC*
Carrer, Chiara. *Otto Carrotto*
Côté, Geneviève. *Without you*
Cronin, Doreen. *Rescue bunnies*
Czekaj, Jef. *Hip and Hop, don't stop!*
D'Amico, Carmela. *Suki the very loud bunny*
Desrosiers, Sylvie. *Hocus pocus*
Falkenstern, Lisa. *A dragon moves in*
Gay, Marie-Louise. *Roslyn Rutabaga and the biggest hole on earth!*
Genechten, Guido van. *Ricky and the squirrel*
  Ricky is brave
Glaser, Linda. *Hoppy Passover!*

Gravett, Emily. *The rabbit problem*
Harper, Charise Mericle. *Pink me up*
Hayes, Geoffrey. *The bunny's night-light*
Henkes, Kevin. *Little white rabbit*
Jackson, Ellen. *The seven seas*
Jahn-Clough, Lisa. *Felicity and Cordelia*
Kaplan, Michael B. *Betty Bunny loves chocolate cake*
Klise, Kate. *Little Rabbit and the Meanest Mother on Earth*
McCarty, Peter. *Henry in love*
McCue, Lisa. *Quiet Bunny and Noisy Puppy*
Martin, David. *Little Bunny and the magic Christmas tree*
Morrison, Toni. *The tortoise or the hare*
Mortimer, Anne. *Bunny's Easter egg*
Na, Il Sung. *Snow rabbit, spring rabbit*
Nyeu, Tao. *Bunny days*
O'Malley, Kevin. *The great race*
Palatini, Margie. *Goldie and the three hares*
  Stuff
Petersen, David. *Snowy Valentine*
Rand, Betseygail. *Big Bunny*
Russell, Natalie. *Brown Rabbit in the city*
Russo, Marisabina. *A very big bunny*
Ruzzier, Sergio. *Hey, rabbit!*
Ryan, Candace. *Ribbit rabbit*
Sakai, Komako. *Mad at Mommy*
Scheffler, Axel. *The little puddle*
  The super scooter
Shields, Gillian. *When the world was waiting for you*
Smee, Nicola. *What's the matter, Bunny Blue?*
Stalder, Päivi. *Ernest's first Easter*
Stiegemeyer, Julie. *Seven little bunnies*
Taylor, Sean. *The grizzly bear with the frizzly hair*
Thompson, Lauren. *Wee little bunny*
Wallace, Nancy Elizabeth. *Planting seeds*
  Ready, set, 100th day!
Washington, Donna L. *Li'l Rabbit's Kwanzaa*
Watson, Wendy. *Bedtime bunnies*
Watt, Mélanie. *You're finally here!*
Wells, Rosemary. *Love waves*
  Max and Ruby's bedtime book
Willems, Mo. *Knuffle Bunny free*
Ziefert, Harriet. *Bunny's lessons*

Animals – raccoons

McPhail, David. *Waddles*
Modarressi, Mitra. *Taking care of Mama*
Penn, Audrey. *A bedtime kiss for Chester Raccoon*
Rayner, Catherine. *The bear who shared*
Shaw, Hannah. *School for bandits*

Animals – rats

Lester, Helen. *Wodney Wat's wobot*

Animals – rhinoceros

Agee, Jon. *My rhinoceros*
Chivers, Natalie. *Rhino's great big itch!*

Animals – salamanders *see* Reptiles – salamanders

Animals – seals

Seeger, Laura Vaccaro. *What if?*

Animals – sheep

Alborough, Jez. *The gobble gobble moooooo tractor book*
Beaty, Andrea. *Hide and sheep*
Beaumont, Karen. *No sleep for the sheep!*
De Sève, Randall. *Mathilda and the orange balloon*
Goodings, Christina. *Lost sheep story*
Hale, Sarah Josepha Buell. *Mary had a little lamb*
Hill, Susanna Leonard. *Can't sleep without sheep*
Levine, Gail Carson. *Betsy Red Hoodie*
McQuinn, Anna. *The sleep sheep*
Monroe, Chris. *Sneaky sheep*
Moses, Will. *Mary and her little lamb*
Schubert, Leda. *Feeding the sheep*

Animals – shrews

Weiss, Ellen. *The taming of Lola*

Animals – skunks

Schmid, Paul. *A pet for Petunia*

Animals – slugs

Pearson, Susan. *How to teach a slug to read*

Animals – snails

Base, Graeme. *The legend of the Golden Snail*
Foley, Greg. *Willoughby and the moon*
Loth, Sebastian. *Clementine*

Animals – snow leopards *see* Animals – leopards

Animals – squirrels

Freeman, Don. *One more acorn*
Genechten, Guido van. *Ricky and the squirrel*
George, Lindsay Barrett. *That pup!*
Glass, Beth Raisner. *Blue-ribbon dad*
Guthrie, James. *Last song*
Iwamura, Kazuo. *Bedtime in the forest*
    Hooray for summer!
Miller, Pat. *Squirrel's New Year's resolution*
Rubin, Adam. *Those darn squirrels and the cat next door*
Vainio, Pirkko. *Who hid the Easter eggs?*
Watt, Mélanie. *Scaredy Squirrel has a birthday party*

Animals – swine *see* Animals – pigs

Animals – tigers

Chin, Oliver. *The year of the tiger*
Fore, S. J. *Read to tiger*
Rumford, James. *Tiger and turtle*

Animals – voles

Schwartz, Roslyn. *The Vole brothers*

Animals – walruses

Savage, Stephen. *Where's Walrus?*

Animals – whales

Lunde, Darrin. *Hello, baby beluga*

Animals – wolves

Asch, Frank. *Happy birthday, Big Bad Wolf*
Brun-Cosme, Nadine. *Big Wolf and Little Wolf, such a beautiful orange!*
Crosby, Jeff. *Wiener Wolf*
Felix, Monique. *The rumor*
Grimm, Jacob. *Little Red Riding Hood*
    The story of Little Red Riding Hood
Guarnaccia, Steven. *The three little pigs*
Kolanovic, Dubravka. *Everyone needs a friend*
Levine, Gail Carson. *Betsy Red Hoodie*
Machado, Ana Maria. *Wolf wanted*
Markle, Sandra. *Family pack*
Ramos, Mario. *I am so strong*
Shireen, Nadia. *Good little wolf*
Sierra, Judy. *Tell the truth, B.B. Wolf*
Teckentrup, Britta. *Little Wolf's song*
Yum, Hyewon. *There are no scary wolves*

Animals – wombats

French, Jackie. *Diary of a baby wombat*

Animals – woodchucks *see* Animals – groundhogs

Animals – worms

French, Vivian. *Yucky worms*
Runton, Andy. *Owly and Wormy*
Scanlon, Liz Garton. *Noodle and Lou*

Animals – zebras

Walker, Anna. *I love birthdays*
    I love my dad
    I love my mom

Antarctic *see* Foreign lands – Antarctic

Anteaters *see* Animals – anteaters

Anti-violence *see* Violence, nonviolence

Ants *see* Insects – ants

Apartments *see* Homes, houses

Appearance *see* Character traits – appearance

April Fools' Day *see* Holidays – April Fools' Day

Arachnids *see* Spiders

Archery *see* Sports – archery

Architects *see* Careers – architects

Arctic *see* Foreign lands – Arctic

Arguing *see* Behavior – fighting, arguing

Arithmetic *see* Counting, numbers

Armadillos *see* Animals – armadillos

Art

Carle, Eric. *The artist who painted a blue horse*
Engle, Margarita. *Summer birds*
Falken, Linda. *Can you find it?*
Friedland, Katy. *Art museum opposites*
Hartland, Jessie. *How the sphinx got to the museum*
Harvey, Jeanne Walker. *My hands sing the blues*
Hill, Laban Carrick. *Dave the potter*
Jackson, Shelley. *Mimi's Dada Catifesto*
Johnson, D. B. *Palazzo inverso*
Knapp, Ruthie. *Who stole Mona Lisa?*
McAarthur, Meher. *An ABC of what art can be*
McCully, Emily Arnold. *The secret cave*
Maltbie, P. I. *Claude Monet*
Micklethwait, Lucy. *In the picture*
O'Connor, Jane. *Fancy Nancy*
Shapiro, J. H. *Magic trash*
Tonatiuh, Duncan. *Diego Rivera*
Velasquez, Eric. *Grandma's gift*
Wahl, Jan. *The art collector*
Wiesner, David. *Art and Max*
Yolleck, Joan. *Paris in the spring with Picasso*
Zuffi, Stefano. *Art 123*

Artists *see* Careers – artists

Assertiveness *see* Character traits – assertiveness

Astrology *see* Zodiac

Astronomers *see* Careers – astronomers

Aunts *see* Family life – aunts, uncles

Australia *see* Foreign lands – Australia

Austria *see* Foreign lands – Austria

Authors *see* Careers – authors

Autism *see* Handicaps – autism

Automobiles

Harper, Jamie. *Miles to go*

Kirk, Daniel. *Honk honk! Beep beep!*
LaReau, Kara. *Otto*
Lord, Cynthia. *Hot rod Hamster*
Medina, Meg. *Tía Isa wants a car*
Merlin, Christophe. *Under the hood*
Stein, Peter. *Cars galore*

Autumn *see* Seasons – fall

Aztec Indians *see* Indians of North America – Aztec

Babies *see also* Animals – babies

Adler, Victoria. *Baby, come away*
American babies
Appelt, Kathi. *Brand-new baby blues*
Banks, Kate. *This baby*
Bunting, Eve. *Will it be a baby brother?*
Burell, Sarah. *Diamond Jim Dandy and the sheriff*
Burningham, John. *There's going to be a baby*
Coffelt, Nancy. *Catch that baby!*
Crum, Shutta. *Mine!*
Diesen, Deborah. *The barefooted, bad-tempered baby brigade*
Doerrfeld, Cori. *Penny loves pink*
Elkin, Mark. *Samuel's baby*
Feiffer, Kate. *But I wanted a baby brother!*
Fleming, Candace. *Seven hungry babies*
Frazee, Marla. *The boss baby*
Frederick, Heather Vogel. *Babyberry pie*
Hawkes, Kevin. *The wicked big toddlah goes to New York*
Hop a little, jump a little!
Janovitz, Marilyn. *Baby, baby, baby!*
Katz, Karen. *The babies on the bus*
Katz, Susan B. *ABC, baby me!*
Macken, JoAnn Early. *Baby says "moo!"*
MacLachlan, Patricia. *Before you came*
Novak, Matt. *A wish for you*
O'Malley, Kevin. *Once upon a royal superbaby*
Sartell, Debra. *Time for bed, Baby Ted*
Solheim, James. *Born yesterday*
Stanley, Malaika Rose. *Baby Ruby bawled*
Stevens, April. *Edwin speaks up*
Tafolla, Carmen. *Fiesta babies*
Waiting for baby
Walton, Rick. *Baby's first year!*
Wild, Margaret. *Itsy-bitsy babies*
Woodson, Jacqueline. *Pecan pie baby*

Babies, new *see* Family life – new sibling

Baboons *see* Animals – baboons

Babysitting *see* Activities – babysitting

Bad day *see* Behavior – bad day

Badgers *see* Animals – badgers

Bakers *see* Careers – bakers

Baking *see* Activities – baking, cooking

Ballet

Bansch, Helga. *Brava, mimi!*
Bonwill, Ann. *Naughty toes*
Capucilli, Alyssa Satin. *My first ballet class*
Greenberg, Jan. *Ballet for Martha*
Hoffmann, E. T. A. *The nutcracker*
Howe, James. *Brontorina*
Maccarone, Grace. *Miss Lina's ballerinas*
    Miss Lina's ballerinas and the prince
Mayhew, James. *Ella Bella ballerina and Swan Lake*
Newman, Lesléa. *Miss Tutu's star*
Peters, Bernadette. *Stella is a star!*
Rodriguez, Sonia. *T is for tutu*
Singer, Marilyn. *Tallulah's tutu*
Skeers, Linda. *Tutus aren't my style*

Ballooning *see* Activities – ballooning

Balloons *see* Toys – balloons

Balls *see* Toys – balls

Bands *see* Musical instruments – bands

Bangladesh *see* Foreign lands – Bangladesh

Banjos *see* Musical instruments – banjos

Barbers *see* Careers – barbers

Baseball *see* Sports – baseball

Bashfulness *see* Character traits – shyness

Basketball *see* Sports – basketball

Bathing *see* Activities – bathing

Bats *see* Animals – bats

Bears *see* Animals – bears

Beasts *see* Monsters

Beauty shops

Daly, Niki. *A song for Jamela*
O'Connor, Jane. *Fancy Nancy*

Beavers *see* Animals – beavers

Beds *see* Furniture – beds

Bedtime

Allen, Elanna. *Itsy Mitsy runs away*
Bardhan-Quallen, Sudipta. *Chicks run wild*
Beaumont, Karen. *No sleep for the sheep!*
Becker, Bonny. *A bedtime for Bear*
Blackall, Sophie. *Are you awake?*
Boelts, Maribeth. *Sweet dreams, little bunny!*
Braun, Sebastien. *Back to bed, Ed!*
Brown, Margaret Wise. *Goodnight moon ABC*
    Sleepy ABC
Burnell, Heather Ayris. *Bedtime monster / ¡A dormir, pequeño monstruo!*
Christelow, Eileen. *Five little monkeys reading in bed*
Church, Caroline Jayne. *One more hug for Madison*
Craig, Lindsey. *Farmyard beat*
Crimi, Carolyn. *Principal Fred won't go to bed*
Cushman, Doug. *Christmas Eve good night*
    Halloween good night
Durand, Hallie. *Mitchell's license*
Edwards, Pamela Duncan. *While the world is sleeping*
Egielski, Richard. *The sleepless little vampire*
Fleming, Denise. *Sleepy, oh so sleepy*
Frederick, Heather Vogel. *Babyberry pie*
    Hide and squeak
Genechten, Guido van. *No ghost under my bed*
Geringer, Laura. *Boom boom go away!*
Gershator, Phillis. *Moo, moo, brown cow! Have you any milk?*
    Who's awake in springtime?
Guthrie, James. *Last song*
Hacohen, Dean. *Tuck me in!*
Hayes, Geoffrey. *The bunny's night-light*
Hill, Susanna Leonard. *Can't sleep without sheep*
Holt, Sharon. *Did my mother do that?*
Hoppe, Paul. *The woods*
Howland, Naomi. *Princess says goodnight*
Iwamura, Kazuo. *Bedtime in the forest*
Jadoul, Émile. *Good night, Chickie*
Kelly, Mij. *A bed of your own!*
Kempter, Christa. *When Mama can't sleep*
Ketteman, Helen. *Goodnight, Little Monster*
Kramer, Andrew. *Pajama pirates*
Krilanovich, Nadia. *Moon child*
Lamb, Albert. *Tell me the day backwards*
LaRochelle, David. *The haunted hamburger and other ghostly stories*
McQuinn, Anna. *The sleep sheep*
Martin, Bill, Jr. *Kitty Cat, Kitty Cat, are you going to sleep?*
Meng, Cece. *I will not read this book*
Meserve, Jessica. *Bedtime without Arthur*
Monari, Manuela. *Zero kisses for me!*
Patricelli, Leslie. *The Patterson puppies and the midnight monster party*

Penn, Audrey. *A bedtime kiss for Chester Raccoon*
Perlman, Willa. *Good night, world*
Reidy, Jean. *Light up the night*
Rinker, Sherri Duskey. *Goodnight, goodnight, construction site*
Rosenthal, Amy Krouse. *Bedtime for Mommy*
Ross, Tony. *I want my light on!*
Ruddell, Deborah. *Who said coo?*
Rueda, Claudia. *No*
Rylant, Cynthia. *Brownie and Pearl hit the hay*
Sartell, Debra. *Time for bed, Baby Ted*
Schaefer, Carole Lexa. *Who's there?*
Shea, Bob. *Race you to bed*
Shoulders, Michael. *Goodnight Baby Bear*
Snyder, Betsy. *Sweet dreams lullaby*
Stanley, Malaika Rose. *Baby Ruby bawled*
Stein, David Ezra. *Interrupting chicken*
Stiegemeyer, Julie. *Seven little bunnies*
Symes, Sally. *Yawn*
Taylor, Sean. *The world champion of staying awake*
Teague, David. *Franklin's big dreams*
Watson, Wendy. *Bedtime bunnies*
Wild, Margaret. *Hush, hush!*
Wilson, Karma. *Mama, why?*
Wolfe, Myra. *Charlotte Jane battles bedtime*
Yolen, Jane. *Creepy monsters, sleepy monsters* *Hush, little horsie*

Beekeepers *see* Careers – beekeepers

Bees *see* Insects – bees

Behavior

Bennett, Kelly. *Your daddy was just like you*
Doyle, Malachy. *Get happy*
Javernick, Ellen. *What if everybody did that?*
Johnson, Angela. *Lottie Paris lives here*
Reidy, Jean. *Too pickley!*
Rosenthal, Amy Krouse. *One smart cookie* *This plus that*
Torrey, Richard. *Because*
Ziefert, Harriet. *Bunny's lessons*

Behavior – bad day

Hodgkinson, Leigh. *Smile!*

Behavior – boasting

Cousins, Lucy. *I'm the best*
Hodgkinson, Leigh. *Limelight Larry*
Ludwig, Trudy. *Better than you*
Van Dusen, Chris. *King Hugo's huge ego*
Wortche, Allison. *Rosie Sprout's time to shine*

Behavior – boredom

Donovan, Sandy. *Bored Bella learns about fiction and nonfiction*

Behavior – bossy

Frazee, Marla. *The boss baby*

Behavior – bullying

Carlson, Nancy. *Henry and the bully*

Docherty, Thomas. *Big scary monster*
Eaton, Maxwell, III. *Two dumb ducks*
Fearnley, Jan. *Arthur and the meanies*
Finlay, Lizzie. *Little Croc's purse*
Javaherbin, Mina. *Goal!*
Kilodavis, Cheryl. *My princess boy*
Kimmelman, Leslie. *The three bully goats*
Kling, Kevin. *Big little brother*
Lester, Helen. *Wodney Wat's wobot*
Ramos, Mario. *I am so strong*
Tierney, Fiona. *Lion's lunch?*

Behavior – carelessness

Bergman, Mara. *Lively Elizabeth!*
Oldland, Nicholas. *The busy beaver*

Behavior – cheating

Cuyler, Margery. *I repeat, don't cheat!*
Fox, Kathleen. *The pirates of plagiarism*

Behavior – collecting things

DiPucchio, Kelly. *Alfred Zector, book collector*
Palatini, Margie. *Stuff*
Reid, Margarette S. *Lots and lots of coins*
Wahl, Jan. *The art collector*

Behavior – cooperation

Cohen, Caron Lee. *Broom, zoom!*
Conahan, Carolyn. *The big wish*
Cowcher, Helen. *Desert elephants*
Fraser, Mary Ann. *Pet shop follies*
Gainer, Cindy. *I'm like you, you're like me*
Geisert, Arthur. *Ice*
Grey, Mini. *Three by the sea*
Heide, Florence Parry. *Always listen to your mother*
Hopkins, Lee Bennett. *Full moon and star*
McKee, David. *Elmer and the hippos*
Otoshi, Kathryn. *Zero*
Reid, Barbara. *Perfect snow*
Ruddell, Deborah. *Who said coo?*
Soman, David. *Ladybug Girl and the Bug Squad*
Stevens, Janet. *The little red pen*
Wallace, Nancy Elizabeth. *Ready, set, 100th day!*

Behavior – dissatisfaction

Crosby, Jeff. *Wiener Wolf*
Kornell, Max. *Bear with me*
Laminack, Lester L. *Three hens and a peacock*

Behavior – fighting, arguing

Burg, Sarah Emmanuelle. *Do you still love me?*
Côté, Geneviève. *Without you*
Rumford, James. *Tiger and turtle*

Behavior – gossip

Felix, Monique. *The rumor*

Behavior – greed

Kasbarian, Lucine. *The greedy sparrow*

Behavior – growing up

Badescu, Ramona. *Pomelo begins to grow*
Carluccio, Maria. *I'm 3! Look what I can do*
Harris, Teresa E. *Summer Jackson*
James, Simon. *George flies south*
Milgrim, David. *How you got so smart*
Oud, Pauline. *Ian's new potty*
Shea, Susan A. *Do you know which one will grow?*
Stott, Ann. *I'll be there*
Teckentrup, Britta. *Little Wolf's song*
Vande Griek, Susan. *Loon*

Behavior – hiding

Alter, Anna. *Disappearing Desmond*

Behavior – hiding things

Vainio, Pirkko. *Who hid the Easter eggs?*

Behavior – imitation

Chou, Yih-Fen. *Mimi loves to mimic*

Behavior – indecision

Reidy, Jean. *Too purpley!*

Behavior – lost

Baeten, Lieve. *Happy birthday, Little Witch!*
Brown, Ruth. *Gracie the lighthouse cat*
Browne, Anthony. *Me and you*
Cooper, Elisha. *Beaver is lost*
D'Amico, Carmela. *Suki the very loud bunny*
Davis, Jerry. *Little Chicken's big day*
Goodings, Christina. *Lost sheep story*
Grimm, Jacob. *Hansel and Gretel*
Haughton, Chris. *Little Owl lost*
Hawkes, Kevin. *The wicked big toddlah goes to New York*
Holt, Kimberly Willis. *The adventures of Granny Clearwater and Little Critter*
Kato, Yukiko. *In the meadow*
McMullan, Kate. *I'm big!*
Murphy, Stuart J. *Freda is found*
Pfister, Marcus. *Snow puppy*
Pinkwater, Daniel. *Beautiful Yetta*
Puttock, Simon. *Little lost cowboy*
Ramsden, Ashley. *Seven fathers*
Root, Phyllis. *Scrawny cat*
Smee, Nicola. *What's the matter, Bunny Blue?*
Stead, Philip C. *Jonathan and the big blue boat*
Uhlberg, Myron. *A storm called Katrina*
Vischer, Frans. *Fuddles*

Behavior – lost & found possessions

Beaumont, Karen. *Where's my t-r-u-c-k?*
Brown, Alan James. *Love-a-Duck*
Butler, M. Christina. *The special blankie*
Crimi, Carolyn. *Principal Fred won't go to bed*
Diesen, Deborah. *The pout-pout fish in the big-big dark*
George, Lindsay Barrett. *Maggie's ball*
Hodgkinson, Leigh. *Smile!*
Holmes, Janet A. *Have you seen Duck?*
Hoppe, Paul. *The woods*
Klassen, Jon. *I want my hat back*

Lobel, Anita. *Nini lost and found*
McDonnell, Christine. *Goyangi means cat*
McGinty, Alice B. *Eliza's kindergarten pet*
Meserve, Jessica. *Bedtime without Arthur*
Meyers, Susan. *Bear in the air*
Moss, Miriam. *Matty takes off!*
Pinkney, Jerry. *Three little kittens*
Polacco, Patricia. *Bun Bun Button*
Rosenthal, Eileen. *I must have Bobo!*
Siegel, Randy. *Grandma's smile*
Simhaee, Rebeka. *Sara finds a mitzva*
Villeneuve, Anne. *The red scarf*
Willems, Mo. *Knuffle Bunny free*

Behavior – lying

Cuyler, Margery. *I repeat, don't cheat!*
Hale, Dean. *Scapegoat*
Latimer, Alex. *The boy who cried ninja*

Behavior – messy

Brennan, Eileen. *Dirtball Pete*
Killen, Nicola. *Not me!*
Klise, Kate. *Little Rabbit and the Meanest Mother on Earth*
Moss, Miriam. *Matty in a mess!*
Waldman, Debby. *Room enough for Daisy*

Behavior – misbehavior

Bardhan-Quallen, Sudipta. *Chicks run wild*
Bottner, Barbara. *An annoying ABC*
Bruel, Nick. *A Bad Kitty Christmas*
Buzzeo, Toni. *No T. Rex in the library*
Collins, Ross. *Doodleday*
DePalma, Mary Newell. *Uh-oh!*
Devlin, Jane. *Hattie the bad*
Gassman, Julie. *Crabby pants*
Heide, Florence Parry. *Always listen to your mother*
Isol. *Petit, the monster*
Kaplan, Bruce Eric. *Monsters eat whiny children*
Kirk, Katie. *Eli, no!*
Kumin, Maxine. *Oh, Harry!*
Monroe, Chris. *Sneaky sheep*
Palatini, Margie. *Goldie and the three hares*
Pearce, Clemency. *Frangoline and the midnight dream*
Pinfold, Levi. *The Django*
Shannon, Molly. *Tilly the trickster*
Shaw, Hannah. *School for bandits*
Tillman, Nancy. *Tumford the terrible*
Urdahl, Catherine. *Polka-dot fixes kindergarten*
Watt, Mélanie. *You're finally here!*
Weiss, Ellen. *The taming of Lola*
Wells, Rosemary. *Hands off, Harry!*
    Yoko's show-and-tell

Behavior – mistakes

Scheffler, Axel. *The little puddle*

Behavior – misunderstanding

Waldron, Kevin. *Mr. Peek and the misunderstanding at the zoo*

Behavior – name calling

Eaton, Maxwell, III. *Two dumb ducks*

Behavior – naughty *see* Behavior – misbehavior

Behavior – potty training *see* Toilet training

Behavior – resourcefulness

Bouler, Olivia. *Olivia's birds*
Button, Lana. *Willow's whispers*
Foreman, Michael. *Fortunately, unfortunately*
Juster, Norton. *Neville*
Medina, Meg. *Tía Isa wants a car*
Rayner, Catherine. *Ernest, the moose who doesn't fit*
Rees, Douglas. *Jeannette Claus saves Christmas*
Stuve-Bodeen, Stephanie. *A small brown dog with a wet pink nose*
Young, Cybèle. *A few blocks*

Behavior – running away

Allen, Elanna. *Itsy Mitsy runs away*
Brett, Jan. *Home for Christmas*
Cadow, Kenneth M. *Alfie runs away*
Ernst, Lisa Campbell. *The Gingerbread Girl goes animal crackers*
The gingerbread boy. *The gingerbread man loose in the school*
     The Library Gingerbread Man
Johnson, Angela. *The day Ray got away*
Macomber, Debbie. *The yippy, yappy Yorkie in the green doggy sweater*
Rand, Betseygail. *Big Bunny*
Savage, Stephen. *Where's Walrus?*

Behavior – secrets

Battut, Éric. *Little Mouse's big secret*
Lehman, Barbara. *The secret box*
Schoenherr, Ian. *Don't spill the beans!*

Behavior – seeking better things

Adler, David A. *A picture book of Cesar Chavez*
Myers, Walter Dean. *Looking for the easy life*

Behavior – sharing

Battut, Éric. *Little Mouse's big secret*
Berger, Samantha. *Martha doesn't share!*
Crum, Shutta. *Mine!*
Emberley, Ed. *The red hen*
Grimm, Jacob. *The star child*
Kirsch, Vincent X. *Forsythia and me*
The little red hen. *The Little Red Hen and the Passover matzah*
Orloff, Karen Kaufman. *I wanna new room*
Patten, Brian. *The big snuggle-up*
Ransome, James. *New red bike!*
Rayner, Catherine. *The bear who shared*
Rosenthal, Amy Krouse. *Plant a kiss*
Rostoker-Gruber, Karen. *Bandit's surprise*
Seeger, Laura Vaccaro. *What if?*
Taylor, Thomas. *Little Mouse and the big cupcake*
Toscano, Charles. *Papa's pastries*
van Lieshout, Maria. *Tumble!*
Vere, Ed. *Banana!*
Waldman, Debby. *Room enough for Daisy*
Yum, Hyewon. *The twins' blanket*

Behavior – solitude

Underwood, Deborah. *The quiet book*

Behavior – stealing

Bromley, Anne C. *The lunch thief*

Behavior – talking to strangers

Grimm, Jacob. *Little Red Riding Hood*
     The story of Little Red Riding Hood

Behavior – teasing

Alexander, Claire. *Small Florence*
Diggs, Taye. *Chocolate me!*
Hilton, Perez. *The boy with pink hair*
Schaefer, Lola. *Frankie Stein starts school*
Teckentrup, Britta. *Little Wolf's song*

Behavior – toilet training *see* Toilet training

Behavior – trickery

Blackaby, Susan. *Brownie Groundhog and the February Fox*
Davis, David. *Fandango stew*
Kasbarian, Lucine. *The greedy sparrow*
Krause, Ute. *Oscar and the very hungry dragon*
McDermott, Gerald. *Monkey*
Smith, Alex T. *Foxy and Egg*
Taylor, Sean. *The grizzly bear with the frizzly hair*

Behavior – wishing

Conahan, Carolyn. *The big wish*
Davis, Aubrey. *Kishka for Koppel*
Fagan, Cary. *Ella May and the wishing stone*
Holub, Joan. *Twinkle, star of the week*
Kimmel, Eric A. *Joha makes a wish*
Washington, Ned. *When you wish upon a star*

Behavior – worrying

Brun-Cosme, Nadine. *Big Wolf and Little Wolf, such a beautiful orange!*
Burg, Sarah Emmanuelle. *Do you still love me?*
Corey, Dorothy. *You go away*
George, Lucy M. *Back to school Tortoise*
Griffin, Molly Beth. *Loon baby*
Jadoul, Émile. *Good night, Chickie*
Johnson, Neil. *The falling raindrop*
Kempter, Christa. *When Mama can't sleep*
Lyon, Tammie. *Olive and Snowflake*
McGinty, Alice B. *Eliza's kindergarten pet*
McPhail, David. *Pig Pig returns*
Pett, Mark. *The girl who never made mistakes*
Quackenbush, Robert. *First grade jitters*
Ray, Jane. *The dollhouse fairy*
Waldron, Kevin. *Mr. Peek and the misunderstanding at the zoo*

Being different *see* Character traits – being different

Bible *see* Religion

Bicycling *see* Sports – bicycling

Bigotry *see* Prejudice

Birds

Adams, Sarah. *Gary and Ray*
Baker, Keith. *No two alike*
Berger, Carin. *Forever friends*
Berne, Jennifer. *Calvin can't fly*
Bouler, Olivia. *Olivia's birds*
Boyer, Cécile. *Woof meow tweet-tweet*
Chivers, Natalie. *Rhino's great big itch!*
Dunning, Joan. *Seabird in the forest*
Esbaum, Jill. *Tom's tweet*
Fleming, Candace. *Seven hungry babies*
Foley, Greg. *Purple little bird*
Frazier, Craig. *Bee and bird*
Hills, Tad. *How Rocket learned to read*
James, Simon. *George flies south*
King, Stephen Michael. *You*
Krilanovich, Nadia. *Chicken, chicken, duck!*
Long, Ethan. *Bird and Birdie in a fine day*
Malnor, Carol L. *The Blues go birding across America*
Meade, Holly. *If I never forever endeavor*
Melvin, Alice. *Counting birds*
Mortimer, Rachael. *Song for a princess*
Munro, Roxie. *Hatch!*
Perry, Andrea. *The Bicklebys' birdbath*
Reed, Lynn Rowe. *Basil's birds*
Robey, Katharine Crawford. *Where's the party?*
Rubin, Adam. *Those darn squirrels and the cat next door*
Runton, Andy. *Owly and Wormy*
Scanlon, Liz Garton. *Noodle and Lou*
Snicket, Lemony. *13 words*
Stileman, Kali. *Roly-poly egg*
Stockdale, Susan. *Bring on the birds*
Thong, Roseanne. *Fly free!*
Timmers, Leo. *Crow*
Young, Cybèle. *Ten birds*

Birds – canaries

Yolen, Jane. *Elsie's bird*

Birds – chickens

Alexander, Kwame. *Acoustic Rooster and his barnyard band*
Baehr, Patricia. *Boo Cow*
Bardhan-Quallen, Sudipta. *Chicks run wild*
Battut, Eric. *The fox and the hen*
Browne, Eileen. *Handa's hen*
Davis, Jerry. *Little Chicken's big day*
Emberley, Ed. *The red hen*
Franceschelli, Christopher. *(Oliver)*
Freedman, Deborah. *Blue chicken*
Graves, Keith. *Chicken Big*
Helakoski, Leslie. *Big chickens go to town*
Jadoul, Émile. *Good night, Chickie*
Joosse, Barbara. *Higgledy-piggledy chicks*
Kimmel, Eric A. *Medio Pollito*
Knudsen, Michelle. *Argus*
Laminack, Lester L. *Three hens and a peacock*
The little red hen. *The Little Red Hen and the Passover matzah*
Ohi, Ruth. *Chicken, pig, cow and the class pet*

Chicken, pig, cow, horse around
Perl, Erica S. *Chicken Butt's back!*
Pinkwater, Daniel. *Beautiful Yetta*
Rave, Friederike. *Outfoxing the fox*
Rodriguez, Béatrice. *The chicken thief*
　　Fox and hen together
Sattler, Jennifer. *Chick 'n' Pug*
Stampler, Ann Redisch. *The rooster prince of Breslov*
Stein, David Ezra. *Interrupting chicken*
Stoeke, Janet Morgan. *The Loopy Coop hens*
Stuchner, Joan Betty. *Can hens give milk?*
Thomas, Jan. *Is everyone ready for fun?*
Vere, Ed. *Chick*

Birds – cranes

Say, Allen. *The boy in the garden*

Birds – crows

Raschka, Chris. *Little black crow*
Timmers, Leo. *Crow*

Birds – doves

Ford, Gilbert. *Flying lessons*

Birds – ducks

Abrahams, Peter. *Quacky baseball*
Andersen, Hans Christian. *The ugly duckling*, ill. by Sebastien Braun
　　The ugly duckling, ill. by Roberta Wilson
Bardhan-Quallen, Sudipta. *Hampire!*
Berry, Lynne. *Ducking for apples*
Brown, Alan James. *Love-a-Duck*
Costello, David Hyde. *I can help*
Eaton, Maxwell, III. *Two dumb ducks*
Egan, Tim. *Dodsworth in Rome*
Holmes, Janet A. *Have you seen Duck?*
McPhail, David. *Waddles*
Milgrim, David. *Santa Duck and his merry helpers*
Roberton, Fiona. *Wanted: the perfect pet*
Salzano, Tammi. *One rainy day*
Sauer, Tammi. *Mr. Duck means business*
Stewart, Amber. *Puddle's new school*
Thomas, Jan. *Pumpkin trouble*
Urbanovic, Jackie. *Sitting duck*

Birds – eagles

Brett, Jan. *The three little dassies*

Birds – geese

Bloom, Suzanne. *What about Bear?*
Dunrea, Olivier. *Ollie's Easter eggs*
　　Ollie's Halloween
Greenstein, Elaine. *The goose man*
Loth, Sebastian. *Remembering Crystal*

Birds – hawks

Kimura, Ken. *999 tadpoles*

Birds – herons

Yolen, Jane. *An egret's day*

Birds – hummingbirds

Sill, Cathryn. *About hummingbirds*
Yahgulanaas, Michael Nicoll. *The little hummingbird*

Birds – loons

Griffin, Molly Beth. *Loon baby*
Vande Griek, Susan. *Loon*

Birds – nightingales

Andersen, Hans Christian. *The nightingale*

Birds – owls

Ainsworth, Kimberly. *Hootenanny!*
Clifton-Brown, Holly. *Annie Hoot and the knitting extravaganza*
Corderoy, Tracey. *The little white owl*
Edwards, Pamela Duncan. *While the world is sleeping*
Haughton, Chris. *Little Owl lost*
Iwamura, Kazuo. *Bedtime in the forest*
Ruddell, Deborah. *Who said coo?*
Srinivasan, Divya. *Little Owl's night*

Birds – parakeets, parrots

DePalma, Mary Newell. *The perfect gift*
Harris, Trudy. *Say something, Perico*
Javaherbin, Mina. *The secret message*
Ljungkvist, Laura. *Pepi sings a new song*
Pinkwater, Daniel. *Beautiful Yetta*

Birds – peacocks, peahens

Hodgkinson, Leigh. *Limelight Larry*
Laminack, Lester L. *Three hens and a peacock*

Birds – pelicans

Reed, Lynn Rowe. *Roscoe and the pelican rescue*

Birds – penguins

Brooks, Erik. *Polar opposites*
Dodd, Emma. *I am small*
Genechten, Guido van. *No ghost under my bed*
Harper, Lee. *The Emperor's cool clothes*
Jeffers, Oliver. *Up and down*
Lester, Helen. *Tacky's Christmas*
London, Jonathan. *Little penguin*
Marzollo, Jean. *Pierre the penguin*
Ryan, Pam Muñoz. *Tony Baloney*
Wilson, Karma. *What's in the egg, Little Pip?*

Birds – pigeons

Ruddell, Deborah. *Who said coo?*

Birds – puffins

Soltis, Sue. *Nothing like a puffin*

Birds – ravens

Bansch, Helga. *Odd bird out*

Birds – robins

Mackall, Dandi Daley. *The story of the Easter robin*

Birds – seagulls

Eaton, Maxwell, III. *Two dumb ducks*

Birds – sparrows

Kasbarian, Lucine. *The greedy sparrow*
Lee, YJ. *The little moon princess*

Birds – swans

Andersen, Hans Christian. *The ugly duckling*, ill. by Sebastien Braun
   The ugly duckling, ill. by Roberta Wilson

Birds – turkeys

Cole, Brock. *The money we'll save*
Falwell, Cathryn. *Gobble gobble*
Sturgis, Brenda Reeves. *10 turkeys in the road*
Waddell, Martin. *Captain Small Pig*
White, Linda. *Too many turkeys*

Birth

Holt, Sharon. *Did my mother do that?*
Waiting for baby

Birthdays

Allen, Nancy Kelly. *"Happy Birthday"*
Asch, Frank. *Happy birthday, Big Bad Wolf*
Avraham, Kate Aver. *What will you be, Sara Mee?*
Baeten, Lieve. *Happy birthday, Little Witch!*
Bertrand, Diane Gonzales. *The party for Papa Luis / La fiesta para Papa Luis*
Blackstone, Stella. *Bear's birthday*
Clarke, Jane. *Trumpet*
Fleming, Candace. *Clever Jack takes the cake*
Gorbachev, Valeri. *What's the big idea, Molly?*
Harper, Charise Mericle. *The best birthday ever!*
Hobbie, Holly. *Everything but the horse*
Huget, Jennifer LaRue. *The best birthday party ever*
Janni, Rebecca. *Every cowgirl needs a horse*
Khan, Rukhsana. *Big red lollipop*
Levine, Gail Carson. *Betsy Red Hoodie*
Lord, Cynthia. *Happy birthday, Hamster*
McClatchy, Lisa. *Dear Tyrannosaurus Rex*
Mackintosh, David. *Marshall Armstrong is new to our school*
Meddaugh, Susan. *Martha says it with flowers*
Milord, Susan. *Happy 100th day!*
Muir, Leslie. *The little bitty bakery*
Numeroff, Laura. *Otis and Sydney and the best birthday ever*
O'Connor, Jane. *Fancy Nancy*
Pfister, Marcus. *Happy birthday, Bertie!*
Rim, Sujean. *Birdie's big-girl dress*
Ross, Tony. *I want two birthdays!*
Rossell, Judith. *Ruby and Leonard and the great big surprise*
Schoenherr, Ian. *Don't spill the beans!*
Sendak, Maurice. *Bumble-ardy*
Stevens, April. *Edwin speaks up*
Walker, Anna. *I love birthdays*
Watt, Mélanie. *Scaredy Squirrel has a birthday party*

Witte, Anna. *Lola's fandango*

Bison *see* Animals – buffaloes

Black Americans *see* Ethnic groups in the U.S. – African Americans

Blizzards *see* Weather – blizzards

Blocks *see* Toys – blocks

Board books *see* Format, unusual – board books

Boasting *see* Behavior – boasting

Boats, ships

Bartoletti, Susan Campbell. *Naamah and the ark at night*
Base, Graeme. *The legend of the Golden Snail*
De Beer, Hans. *Little Polar Bear and the submarine*
Krensky, Stephen. *Noah's bark*
Lamb, Albert. *The abandoned lighthouse*
Stead, Philip C. *Jonathan and the big blue boat*
Steggall, Susan. *Busy boats*
Tebbs, Victoria. *Noah's Ark story*
Waddell, Martin. *Captain Small Pig*
Wick, Walter. *Can you see what I see? treasure ship*
Winter, Jonah. *Here comes the garbage barge!*

Boogy man *see* Monsters

Books, reading

Amado, Elisa. *What are you doing?*
Bendall-Brunello, Tiziana. *I wish I could read!*
Berne, Jennifer. *Calvin can't fly*
Bottner, Barbara. *Miss Brooks loves books! (and I don't)*
Brown, Monica. *Waiting for the Biblioburro*
Buzzeo, Toni. *Penelope Popper book doctor*
Casanova, Mary. *The day Dirk Yeller came to town*
Chin, Jason. *Coral reefs*
Christelow, Eileen. *Five little monkeys reading in bed*
de Las Casas, Dianne. *There's a dragon in the library*
DePalma, Mary Newell. *The perfect gift*
DiPucchio, Kelly. *Alfred Zector, book collector*
Donovan, Sandy. *Bob the Alien discovers the Dewey Decimal System*
　Bored Bella learns about fiction and nonfiction
　Karl and Carolina uncover the parts of a book
　Pingpong Perry experiences how a book is made
Fore, S. J. *Read to tiger*
Fox, Kathleen. *The pirates of plagiarism*
Gore, Leonid. *The wonderful book*
Hector, Julian. *The gentleman bug*
Hills, Tad. *How Rocket learned to read*
Houston, Gloria. *Miss Dorothy and her bookmobile*
Hubbell, Patricia. *Check it out!*
Long, Ethan. *The book that Zack wrote*
McQuinn, Anna. *Lola loves stories*
Meng, Cece. *I will not read this book*
Milord, Susan. *Happy 100th day!*

Numeroff, Laura. *The Jellybeans and the big book bonanza*
Pearson, Susan. *How to teach a slug to read*
Schubert, Leda. *Reading to Peanut*
Shields, Gillian. *Library Lily*
Shoulders, Michael. *Goodnight Baby Bear*
Smith, Lane. *It's a book*
Staake, Bob. *Look! A book!*
Twohy, Mike. *Poindexter makes a friend*
Von Konigslow, Andrea Wayne. *How do you read to a rabbit?*
Watt, Mélanie. *You're finally here!*
Winter, Jeanette. *Biblioburro*
Yates, Louise. *Dog loves books*

Boredom *see* Behavior – boredom

Bossy *see* Behavior – bossy

Boxing *see* Sports – boxing

Bravery *see* Character traits – bravery

Brownies *see* Mythical creatures – elves

Brush wolves *see* Animals – coyotes

Buffaloes *see* Animals – buffaloes

Bugs *see* Insects

Buildings

Hill, Isabel. *Building stories*
Johnson, D. B. *Palazzo inverso*

Bulldozers *see* Machines

Bulls *see* Animals – bulls, cows

Bullying *see* Behavior – bullying

Bumble bees *see* Insects – bees

Burglars *see* Crime

Burros *see* Animals – donkeys

Buses

Cabrera, Jane. *The wheels on the bus*
Grandits, John. *Ten rules you absolutely must not break if you want to survive the school bus*
Katz, Karen. *The babies on the bus*

Butterflies *see* Insects – butterflies, caterpillars

Cafés *see* Restaurants

Caldecott award books

Raschka, Chris. *A ball for Daisy*
Stead, Philip C. *A sick day for Amos McGee*

Caldecott award honor books

Hill, Laban Carrick. *Dave the potter*
McDonnell, Patrick. *Me . . . Jane*
Rocco, John. *Blackout*
Smith, Lane. *Grandpa Green*
Stein, David Ezra. *Interrupting chicken*

Camouflages *see* Disguises

Camps, camping

Genechten, Guido van. *Ricky is brave*
Jules, Jacqueline. *Picnic at Camp Shalom*
Korda, Lerryn. *Into the wild*
Numeroff, Laura. *The Jellybeans and the big camp kickoff*
Orr, Wendy. *The princess and her panther*
Ross, Tony. *I want to do it myself!*
Taback, Simms. *Postcards from camp*

Canada *see* Foreign lands – Canada

Canaries *see* Birds – canaries

Cancer *see* Illness – cancer

Caps *see* Clothing – hats

Cardboard page books *see* Format, unusual – board books

Cards *see* Letters, cards

Careers

Baker, Keith. *LMNO peas*
Karas, G. Brian. *The village garage*
Lloyd-Jones, Sally. *How to get a job—by me, the boss*
McMullan, Kate. *Bulldog's big day*
Spinelli, Jerry. *I can be anything!*
Swinburne, Stephen R. *Whose shoes?*
Yankovic, Al. *When I grow up*

Careers – actors

LaChanze. *Little diva*
McLean, Dirk. *Curtain up!*

Careers – airplane pilots

Bildner, Phil. *The hallelujah flight*
Brown, Tami Lewis. *Soar, Elinor!*

Careers – architects

Guarnaccia, Steven. *The three little pigs*

Careers – artists

Browning, Diane. *Signed, Abiah Rose*
Carle, Eric. *The artist who painted a blue horse*
Domney, Alexis. *Splish, splat!*
Freedman, Deborah. *Blue chicken*
Harvey, Jeanne Walker. *My hands sing the blues*
Johnson, D. B. *Palazzo inverso*
Lichtenheld, Tom. *Bridget's beret*
Maltbie, P. I. *Claude Monet*
Shapiro, J. H. *Magic trash*
Tonatiuh, Duncan. *Diego Rivera*
Wiesner, David. *Art and Max*

Careers – astronomers

Gerber, Carole. *Annie Jump Cannon, astronomer*

Careers – authors

Nesbitt, Kenn. *More bears!*
Yaccarino, Dan. *All the way to America*

Careers – bakers

Jackson, Kathryn. *Pantaloon*
Kneen, Maggie. *Chocolate moose*
McMullan, Kate. *Bulldog's big day*

Careers – barbers

McElligott, Matthew. *Even monsters need haircuts*

Careers – beekeepers

Nargi, Lela. *The honeybee man*

Careers – chefs, cooks

Whelan, Gloria. *The boy who wanted to cook*

Careers – composers

Robinson, Fiona. *What animals really like*

Careers – conductors (music)

Costello, David Hyde. *Little Pig joins the band*
Devernay, Laetitia. *The conductor*
Robinson, Fiona. *What animals really like*

Careers – construction workers

Clement, Nathan. *Job site*
Dale, Penny. *Dinosaur dig!*
Mandel, Peter. *Jackhammer Sam*
Meltzer, Lynn. *The construction crew*

Careers – cooks *see* Careers – chefs, cooks

Careers – custodians, janitors

Reed, Lynn Rowe. *Basil's birds*

Careers – detectives

Biedrzycki, David. *Ace Lacewing, bug detective*
Metzger, Steve. *Detective Blue*

Careers – doctors

Ketteman, Helen. *If Beaver had a fever*
Oelschlager, Vanita. *Bonyo Bonyo*
Slegers, Liesbet. *Katie goes to the doctor*

Careers – explorers

Kirk, Daniel. *Library mouse*

Careers – farmers

Sturgis, Brenda Reeves. *10 turkeys in the road*

Careers – firefighters

Miller, Edward. *Fireboy to the rescue!*
Nolan, Janet. *The firehouse light*
Teague, Mark. *Firehouse!*

Careers – garbage collectors *see* Careers – sanitation workers

Careers – inventors

Brown, Don. *A wizard from the start*
Kulling, Monica. *All aboard!*

Careers – janitors *see* Careers – custodians, janitors

Careers – librarians

King, M. G. *Librarian on the roof!*

Careers – lumberjacks

Bateman, Teresa. *Paul Bunyan vs. Hals Halson*

Careers – magicians

Villeneuve, Anne. *The red scarf*

Careers – mail carriers *see* Careers – postal workers

Careers – mechanics

Merlin, Christophe. *Under the hood*

Careers – military

Brisson, Pat. *Sometimes we were brave*
Hardin, Melinda. *Hero dad*
Nadel, Carolina. *Daddy's home*

Careers – musicians

Alexander, Kwame. *Acoustic Rooster and his barnyard band*
Celenza, Anna Harwell. *Duke Ellington's Nutcracker Suite*
Huling, Jan. *Ol' Bloo's boogie-woogie band and blues ensemble*
Ingalls, Ann. *The little piano girl*
Manders, John. *The really awful musicians*

Careers – painters *see* Careers – artists

Careers – paleontologists

Hartland, Jessie. *How the dinosaur got to the museum*

Careers – photographers

Alter, Anna. *A photo for Greta*
Davis, Jill. *Orangutans are ticklish*

Careers – physicians *see* Careers – doctors

Careers – poets

Malaspina, Ann. *Phillis sings out freedom*

Careers – police officers

Meadows, Michelle. *Traffic pups*

Careers – postal workers

Kay, Verla. *Whatever happened to the Pony Express?*
Lendroth, Susan. *Calico Dorsey*
Spradlin, Michael P. *Off like the wind!*

Careers – principals *see* Careers – school principals

Careers – ranchers

Drummond, Ree. *Charlie the ranch dog*
Lawson, Dorie McCullough. *Tex*
Parish, Herman. *Go west, Amelia Bedelia!*

Careers – salespeople

Horowitz, Dave. *Buy my hats!*

Careers – sanitation workers

Winter, Jonah. *Here comes the garbage barge!*

Careers – school principals

Crimi, Carolyn. *Principal Fred won't go to bed*

Careers – scientists

Greenstein, Elaine. *The goose man*
McDonnell, Patrick. *Me . . . Jane*
Marzollo, Jean. *The little plant doctor*
Offill, Jenny. *11 experiments that failed*
Verstraete, Larry. *S is for scientists*
Winter, Jeanette. *The watcher*

Careers – shepherds

Levine, Gail Carson. *Betsy Red Hoodie*

Careers – shoemakers

Barrett, Mary Brigid. *Shoebox Sam*
Tegen, Katherine. *The story of the leprechaun*

Careers – singers

Orgill, Roxane. *Skit-scat raggedy cat*

Careers – soldiers *see* Careers – military

Careers – storekeepers

Yorinks, Arthur. *The invisible man*

Careers – teachers

Cook, Lisa Broadie. *Peanut butter and homework sandwiches*
Gall, Chris. *Substitute creacher*
George, Lucy M. *Back to school Tortoise*
Polacco, Patricia. *The junkyard wonders*
Primavera, Elise. *Louise the big cheese and the back-to-school smarty-pants*
Spinelli, Eileen. *Miss Fox's class shapes up*

Careers – truck drivers

London, Jonathan. *I'm a truck driver*

Careers – veterinarians

McCully, Emily Arnold. *Wonder horse*

Careers – zookeepers

Savage, Stephen. *Where's Walrus?*

Carelessness *see* Behavior – carelessness

Cars *see* Automobiles

Castles

Ashburn, Boni. *Over at the castle*

Caterpillars *see* Insects – butterflies, caterpillars

Cats *see* Animals – cats

Caves

McCully, Emily Arnold. *The secret cave*

Chad *see* Foreign lands – Chad

Chameleons *see* Reptiles – chameleons

Change *see* Concepts – change

Chanukah *see* Holidays – Hanukkah

Character traits

Javernick, Ellen. *What if everybody did that?*
Lee, Spike. *Giant steps to change the world*
Obama, Barack. *Of thee I sing*
Rosenthal, Amy Krouse. *One smart cookie*
Yahgulanaas, Michael Nicoll. *The little hummingbird*

Character traits – ambition

Palatini, Margie. *Hogg, Hogg, and Hog*
Primavera, Elise. *Louise the big cheese and the back-to-school smarty-pants*
Tucker, Lindy. *Porkelia*
Yamaguchi, Kristi. *Dream big, little pig!*

Character traits – appearance

Andersen, Hans Christian. *The ugly duckling*, ill. by Sebastien Braun
  The ugly duckling, ill. by Roberta Wilson
Barnett, Mac. *Mustache!*
Beaumont, Karen. *Shoe-la-la!*
Harper, Charise Mericle. *Cupcake*
Harper, Lee. *The Emperor's cool clothes*
Hosford, Kate. *Big bouffant*
Kochan, Vera. *What if your best friend were blue?*
Langen, Annette. *I won't comb my hair!*
Long, Ethan. *Chamelia*
Primavera, Elise. *Louise the big cheese and the la-di-da shoes*
Reidy, Jean. *Too purpley!*
Rylant, Cynthia. *Brownie and Pearl get dolled up*
Sabuda, Robert. *Beauty and the beast*
Skeers, Linda. *Tutus aren't my style*

Character traits – assertiveness

Chou, Yih-Fen. *Mimi says no*
Dunklee, Annika. *My name is Elizabeth!*
Meade, Holly. *If I never forever endeavor*
Milgrim, David. *Eddie gets ready for school*
Urdahl, Catherine. *Polka-dot fixes kindergarten*

Character traits – being different

Al Abdullah, Rania. *The sandwich swap*
Andersen, Hans Christian. *The ugly duckling*, ill. by Sebastien Braun
  The ugly duckling, ill. by Roberta Wilson
Bansch, Helga. *Odd bird out*
Corderoy, Tracey. *The little white owl*
Dyer, Sarah. *Batty*
Ford, Gilbert. *Flying lessons*
Graves, Keith. *Chicken Big*
Hilton, Perez. *The boy with pink hair*
Hovland, Henrik. *John Jensen feels different*
Kilodavis, Cheryl. *My princess boy*
Klise, Kate. *Stand straight, Ella Kate*
Kochan, Vera. *What if your best friend were blue?*
McAllister, Angela. *Yuck! That's not a monster*
McKee, David. *Elmer and Rose*
Maclear, Kyo. *Spork*
Reynolds, Peter H. *I'm here*
Ross, Fiona. *Chilly Milly Moo*
Russo, Marisabina. *A very big bunny*
Sauer, Tammi. *Mostly monsterly*

Schaefer, Lola. *Frankie Stein starts school*
Smith, Cynthia Leitich. *Holler Loudly*
Spires, Ashley. *Small Saul*
Timmers, Leo. *Crow*
Underwood, Deborah. *A balloon for Isabel*
Yorinks, Arthur. *The invisible man*
Young, Amy. *The mud fairy*

Character traits – bravery

Danticat, Edwidge. *Eight days*
Genechten, Guido van. *Ricky is brave*
Griffin, Kitty. *The ride*
Hoppe, Paul. *The woods*
Kirk, Daniel. *Library mouse*
Lester, Alison. *Running with the horses*
Meade, Holly. *If I never forever endeavor*
Rappaport, Doreen. *Jack's path of courage*
Reynolds, Aaron. *Back of the bus*
Van Allsburg, Chris. *Queen of the falls*
Weitzman, Jacqueline Preiss. *Superhero Joe*
Willems, Mo. *Knuffle Bunny free*

Character traits – cleanliness

Bradford, Wade. *Why do I have to make my bed?*
Brennan, Eileen. *Dirtball Pete*
Cohen, Caron Lee. *Broom, zoom!*
Huget, Jennifer LaRue. *How to clean your room in 10 easy steps*
Moss, Miriam. *Matty in a mess!*
Riddell, Chris. *Wendel's workshop*
Wilson, Karma. *Hogwash!*

Character traits – cleverness

Birtha, Becky. *Lucky beans*
Davis, David. *Fandango stew*
Desrosiers, Sylvie. *Hocus pocus*
Geisert, Arthur. *Ice*
Guarnaccia, Steven. *The three little pigs*
Krause, Ute. *Oscar and the very hungry dragon*
McDermott, Gerald. *Monkey*
Mandell, Muriel. *A donkey reads*
Perrault, Charles. *Puss in boots*
Taylor, Sean. *The grizzly bear with the frizzly hair*
Yamashita, Haruo. *Seven little mice go to school*

Character traits – clumsiness

Kleven, Elisa. *Welcome home, Mouse*

Character traits – completing things

Alda, Arlene. *Lulu's piano lesson*

Character traits – compromising

Janni, Rebecca. *Every cowgirl needs dancing boots*
Sauer, Tammi. *Mr. Duck means business*

Character traits – confidence

Alexander, Claire. *Small Florence*
Milgrim, David. *Eddie gets ready for school*

Character traits – cooperation

Numeroff, Laura. *The Jellybeans and the big camp kickoff*

Character traits – courage *see* Character traits – bravery

Character traits – cruelty to animals *see* Character traits – kindness to animals

Character traits – curiosity

Bunting, Eve. *Tweak tweak*
Chou, Yih-Fen. *Mimi loves to mimic*
Henkes, Kevin. *Little white rabbit*
Lewis, Kevin. *Not inside this house!*
Torrey, Richard. *Why?*

Character traits – foolishness

Davis, Aubrey. *Kishka for Koppel*

Character traits – fortune *see* Character traits – luck

Character traits – freedom

Andersen, Hans Christian. *The nightingale*
Evans, Shane W. *Underground*
Walker, Sally M. *Freedom song*

Character traits – generosity

Barrett, Mary Brigid. *Shoebox Sam*
Blackwood, Freya. *Ivy loves to give*
Bouler, Olivia. *Olivia's birds*
Grimm, Jacob. *The star child*
Heller, Linda. *How Dalia put a big yellow comforter inside a tiny blue box*
McGinley, Phyllis. *The year without a Santa Claus*
O'Connor, Jane. *Fancy Nancy and the fabulous fashion boutique*
Patten, Brian. *The big snuggle-up*
Sacre, Antonio. *A mango in the hand*
Toscano, Charles. *Papa's pastries*
Villnave, Erica Pelton. *Sophie's lovely locks*
Williams, Laura E. *The can man*

Character traits – helpfulness

Aesop. *Mouse and lion*
Bouler, Olivia. *Olivia's birds*
Brett, Jan. *Home for Christmas*
Costello, David Hyde. *I can help*
Cunnane, Kelly. *Chirchir is singing*
Emberley, Ed. *The red hen*
Ernst, Lisa Campbell. *Sylvia Jean, scout supreme*
Freedman, Deborah. *Blue chicken*
Garland, Sarah. *Eddie's toolbox and how to make and mend things*
Himmelman, John. *Pigs to the rescue*
Jackson, Kathryn. *Pantaloon*
Kirsch, Vincent X. *Forsythia and me*
Melling, David. *Don't worry, Douglas!*
Miller, Pat. *Squirrel's New Year's resolution*
Randall, Angel. *Snow angels*
Shaw, Hannah. *School for bandits*
Slack, Michael. *Monkey truck*
Verdick, Elizabeth. *On-the-go time*

Character traits – honesty

Cocca-Leffler, Maryann. *Princess Kim and too much truth*
Cuyler, Margery. *I repeat, don't cheat!*
Finlay, Lizzie. *Little Croc's purse*
Latimer, Alex. *The boy who cried ninja*
Sierra, Judy. *Tell the truth, B.B. Wolf*

Character traits – incentive *see* Character traits – ambition

Character traits – individuality

Baker, Keith. *No two alike*
Battut, Éric. *The little pea*
Brooks, Erik. *Polar opposites*
Carrer, Chiara. *Otto Carrotto*
Cartaya, Pablo. *Tina Cocolina*
Diggs, Taye. *Chocolate me!*
Evans, Kristina. *What's special about me, Mama?*
Gainer, Cindy. *I'm like you, you're like me*
Hall, Michael. *Perfect square*
Helakoski, Leslie. *Fair cow*
Hosford, Kate. *Big bouffant*
Hovland, Henrik. *John Jensen feels different*
Kilodavis, Cheryl. *My princess boy*
Long, Ethan. *Chamelia*
McAllister, Angela. *Yuck! That's not a monster*
McKee, David. *Elmer and Rose*
Mackintosh, David. *Marshall Armstrong is new to our school*
Maclear, Kyo. *Spork*
Morrison, Toni. *Little Cloud and Lady Wind*
Moss, Peggy. *One of us*
Sauer, Tammi. *Mostly monsterly*
Schoonmaker, Elizabeth. *Square cat*
Shireen, Nadia. *Good little wolf*
Skeers, Linda. *Tutus aren't my style*
Smallcomb, Pam. *I'm not*
Tillman, Nancy. *The crown on your head*
Yolen, Jane. *Not all princesses dress in pink*
Yum, Hyewon. *The twins' blanket*

Character traits – kindness

Aesop. *Mouse and lion*
Barrett, Mary Brigid. *Shoebox Sam*
Bromley, Anne C. *The lunch thief*
Gainer, Cindy. *I'm like you, you're like me*
Juster, Norton. *The odious ogre*
Say, Allen. *The boy in the garden*
Schwartz, Howard. *Gathering sparks*
Thong, Roseanne. *Fly free!*
Toscano, Charles. *Papa's pastries*

Character traits – kindness to animals

Arnosky, Jim. *Slow down for manatees*
Chall, Marsha Wilson. *Pick a pup*
Cowcher, Helen. *Desert elephants*
Davis, Anne. *No dogs allowed!*
Dockray, Tracy. *The lost and found pony*
Furstinger, Nancy. *Maggie's second chance*
Gottfried, Maya. *Our farm*
Havill, Juanita. *Call the horse lucky*
Henrichs, Wendy. *When Anju loved being an elephant*
Hill, Meggan. *Nico and Lola*
Juan, Ana. *The pet shop revolution*

Lamstein, Sarah Marwil. *Big night for salamanders*
Marzollo, Jean. *Pierre the penguin*
Numeroff, Laura. *If you give a dog a donut*
Peet, Mal. *Cloud tea monkeys*
Reed, Lynn Rowe. *Roscoe and the pelican rescue*
Sayre, April Pulley. *Turtle, turtle, watch out!*
Wardlaw, Lee. *Won Ton*

Character traits – laziness

The little red hen. *The Little Red Hen and the Passover matzah*

Character traits – loyalty

Lester, Alison. *Running with the horses*
Nelson, Marilyn. *Snook alone*
Sabuda, Robert. *Beauty and the beast*

Character traits – luck

Polacco, Patricia. *Bun Bun Button*

Character traits – optimism

Cocca-Leffler, Maryann. *Rain brings frogs*

Character traits – ostracism *see* Character traits – being different

Character traits – patience

Kaplan, Michael B. *Betty Bunny loves chocolate cake*

Character traits – perfectionism

Pett, Mark. *The girl who never made mistakes*

Character traits – perseverance

Lee, Spike. *Giant steps to change the world*
Schubert, Leda. *Reading to Peanut*
Singer, Marilyn. *Tallulah's tutu*
Warwick, Dionne. *Little Man*

Character traits – persistence

Daly, Cathleen. *Prudence wants a pet*
Poydar, Nancy. *No fair science fair*
Ramsden, Ashley. *Seven fathers*
Van Allsburg, Chris. *Queen of the falls*
Yamaguchi, Kristi. *Dream big, little pig!*

Character traits – pride

Andersen, Hans Christian. *The emperor's new clothes*
Cousins, Lucy. *I'm the best*

Character traits – questioning

Adler, David A. *A little at a time*
Blackall, Sophie. *Are you awake?*
Brown, Calef. *Boy wonders*
McClure, Nikki. *Mama, is it summer yet?*
Menchin, Scott. *What if everything had legs?*
Munro, Roxie. *Hatch!*
Offill, Jenny. *11 experiments that failed*
Pfister, Marcus. *Questions, questions*
Raschka, Chris. *Little black crow*

Steven, Kenneth. *The biggest thing in the world*
Torrey, Richard. *Why?*
Wilson, Karma. *Mama, why?*

Character traits – responsibility

Johnson, Jen Cullerton. *Seeds of change*
Killen, Nicola. *Not me!*
Napoli, Donna Jo. *Mama Miti*
Schwartz, Howard. *Gathering sparks*

Character traits – shyness

Adams, Sarah. *Dave and Violet*
Alter, Anna. *Disappearing Desmond*
Bracken, Beth. *Too shy for show-and-tell*
Button, Lana. *Willow's whispers*
Choldenko, Gennifer. *A giant crush*
Maccarone, Grace. *Miss Lina's ballerinas and the prince*
Newman, Jeff. *The boys*
Twohy, Mike. *Poindexter makes a friend*

Character traits – smallness

Andersen, Hans Christian. *Sylvia Long's Thumbelina*
Balouch, Kristen. *The little little girl with the big big voice*
Battersby, Katherine. *Squish Rabbit*
Cantrell, Charlie. *A friend for Einstein*
Costello, David Hyde. *Little Pig joins the band*
Dodd, Emma. *I am small*
Lichtenheld, Tom. *Cloudette*
Martin, David. *Little Bunny and the magic Christmas tree*
Spires, Ashley. *Small Saul*
Symes, Ruth. *Little Rex, big brother*

Character traits – stubbornness

Chou, Yih-Fen. *Mimi says no*
Langen, Annette. *I won't comb my hair!*

Character traits – vanity

Andersen, Hans Christian. *The emperor's new clothes*
Barnett, Mac. *Mustache!*
Cousins, Lucy. *I'm the best*
Harper, Lee. *The Emperor's cool clothes*
Primavera, Elise. *Louise the big cheese and the la-di-da shoes*

Cheating *see* Behavior – cheating

Chefs *see* Careers – chefs, cooks

Cherubs *see* Angels

Chickens *see* Birds – chickens

Chimpanzees *see* Animals – chimpanzees

China *see* Foreign lands – China

Chinese Americans *see* Ethnic groups in the U.S. – Chinese Americans

Chinese New Year *see* Holidays – Chinese New Year

Chipmunks *see* Animals – chipmunks

Christmas *see* Holidays – Christmas

Church *see* Religion

Cinco de Mayo *see* Holidays – Cinco de Mayo

Circular tales

Numeroff, Laura. *If you give a dog a donut*
Shaskan, Stephen. *A dog is a dog*

Circus

Coerr, Eleanor. *Circus day in Japan*
Dockray, Tracy. *The lost and found pony*
Henrichs, Wendy. *When Anju loved being an elephant*
Klise, Kate. *Little Rabbit and the Meanest Mother on Earth*
Krosoczka, Jarrett J. *Ollie the purple elephant*
MacDonald, Suse. *Circus opposites*
Sturgis, Brenda Reeves. *10 turkeys in the road*
Villeneuve, Anne. *The red scarf*

Cities, towns

Brown, Tameka Fryer. *Around our way on Neighbors' Day*
Browne, Anthony. *Me and you*
Godwin, Laura. *One moon, two cats*
Helakoski, Leslie. *Big chickens go to town*
Hodge, Deborah. *Watch me grow!*
Isadora, Rachel. *Say hello!*
Jack and the beanstalk. *Jack and the beanstalk*
Karas, G. Brian. *The village garage*
Kenney, Sean. *Cool city*
Niemann, Christoph. *Subway*
Palatini, Margie. *Hogg, Hogg, and Hog*
Pinkwater, Daniel. *Beautiful Yetta*
Russell, Natalie. *Brown Rabbit in the city*
Shapiro, J. H. *Magic trash*
Stutson, Caroline. *Cats' night out*
Watson, Renée. *A place where hurricanes happen*

Cleanliness *see* Character traits – cleanliness

Cleverness *see* Character traits – cleverness

Clocks, watches

Metzger, Steve. *The dancing clock*

Clothing

Alko, Selina. *Every-day dress-up*
Andersen, Hans Christian. *The emperor's new clothes*

Harper, Lee. *The Emperor's cool clothes*
Lewis, Rose. *Orange Peel's pocket*
Long, Ethan. *Chamelia*
Reidy, Jean. *Too purpley!*
Wright, Maureen. *Sneezy the snowman*

Clothing – boots

Olson-Brown, Ellen. *Ooh la la polka-dot boots*

Clothing – costumes

Demas, Corinne. *Halloween surprise*
Joosse, Barbara. *Dog parade*

Clothing – dresses

Ashburn, Boni. *I had a favorite dress*
Masini, Beatrice. *Here comes the bride*
Rim, Sujean. *Birdie's big-girl dress*

Clothing – gloves, mittens

Pinkney, Jerry. *Three little kittens*

Clothing – handbags, purses

Finlay, Lizzie. *Little Croc's purse*

Clothing – hats

DeRubertis, Barbara. *Corky Cub's crazy caps*
Horowitz, Dave. *Buy my hats!*
Klassen, Jon. *I want my hat back*
Könnecke, Ole. *Anton can do magic*
Langdo, Bryan. *Tornado Slim and the magic cowboy hat*
Lichtenheld, Tom. *Bridget's beret*
Melling, David. *Don't worry, Douglas!*
Savage, Stephen. *Where's Walrus?*

Clothing – pants

Gassman, Julie. *Crabby pants*
Gilani-Williams, Fawzia. *Nabeel's new pants*
Johnston, Tony. *Levi Strauss gets a bright idea*

Clothing – scarves

Villeneuve, Anne. *The red scarf*

Clothing – shoes

Barrett, Mary Brigid. *Shoebox Sam*
Beaumont, Karen. *Shoe-la-la!*
Colato Laínez, René. *My shoes and I*
Fliess, Sue. *Shoes for me!*
Gormley, Greg. *Dog in boots*
Litwin, Eric. *Pete the cat*, ill. by James Dean
   Pete the cat, ill. by James Dean
Primavera, Elise. *Louise the big cheese and the la-di-da shoes*
Rosenthal, Betsy R. *Which shoes would you choose?*
Swinburne, Stephen R. *Whose shoes?*

Clothing – socks

Dormer, Frank W. *Socksquatch*

Clothing – underwear

Freedman, Claire. *Dinosaurs love underpants*
Sendelbach, Brian. *The underpants zoo*

Clouds *see* Weather – clouds

Clubs, gangs

Ernst, Lisa Campbell. *Sylvia Jean, scout supreme*

Clumsiness *see* Character traits – clumsiness

Cold (disease) *see* Illness – cold (disease)

Collecting things *see* Behavior – collecting things

Colombia *see* Foreign lands – Colombia

Color *see* Concepts – color

Communication

de Lestrade, Agnès. *Phileas's fortune*
Felix, Monique. *The rumor*
Mortimer, Rachael. *Song for a princess*

Communities, neighborhoods

Brown, Tameka Fryer. *Around our way on Neighbors' Day*
Garland, Sarah. *Eddie's toolbox and how to make and mend things*
Hudes, Quiara Alegría. *Welcome to my neighborhood!*
Isadora, Rachel. *Say hello!*
Rose, Naomi C. *Tashi and the Tibetan flower cure*
Sís, Peter. *Madlenka, soccer star*
Watson, Renée. *A place where hurricanes happen*

Competition *see* Contests; Sibling rivalry; Sports

Completing things *see* Character traits – completing things

Composers *see* Careers – composers

Compromising *see* Character traits – compromising

Concepts

Cousins, Lucy. *Maisy's amazing big book of learning*
Fisher, Valorie. *Everything I need to know before I'm five*
Maloney, Peter. *One foot two feet*
Rosenthal, Amy Krouse. *This plus that*
Walsh, Ellen Stoll. *Balancing act*

Concepts – change

Shea, Susan A. *Do you know which one will grow?*

Concepts – color

Alda, Arlene. *Except the color grey*
Anderson, Brian. *The prince's new pet*
Barnes, Brynne. *Colors of me*
Barnett, Mac. *Extra yarn*
Brocket, Jane. *Ruby, violet, lime*
Carle, Eric. *The artist who painted a blue horse*
Doerrfeld, Cori. *Penny loves pink*
Foley, Greg. *Purple little bird*
Freedman, Deborah. *Blue chicken*
Gibbs, Edward. *I spy with my little eye*
Gonyea, Mark. *A book about color*
Gravett, Emily. *Blue chameleon*
Harper, Charise Mericle. *Pink me up*
Jackson, Ellen. *The seven seas*
Jay, Alison. *Red green blue*
Kumin, Maxine. *What color is Caesar?*
Litwin, Eric. *Pete the cat*
Macdonald, Maryann. *The pink party*
McGrath, Barbara Barbieri. *Teddy bear counting*
Reasoner, Charles. *One blue fish*
Reed, Lynn Rowe. *Color chaos!*
Rubinger, Ami. *I dream of an elephant*
Salzano, Tammi. *One rainy day*
Smith, Danna. *Pirate nap*
Tusa, Tricia. *Follow me*

Concepts – counting *see* Counting, numbers

Concepts – measurement

Pelley, Kathleen T. *Magnus Maximus, a marvelous measurer*

Concepts – opposites

Blackstone, Stella. *Octopus opposites*
Brooks, Erik. *Polar opposites*
Friedland, Katy. *Art museum opposites*
Intriago, Patricia. *Dot*
MacDonald, Suse. *Circus opposites*
Siminovich, Lorena. *I like vegetables*

Concepts – self *see* Self-concept

Concepts – shape

Basher, Simon. *Go! Go! Bobo*
Frazier, Craig. *Lots of dots*
Gravett, Emily. *Blue chameleon*
Hall, Michael. *My heart is like a zoo*
    Perfect square
Loth, Sebastian. *Clementine*
McGrath, Barbara Barbieri. *Teddy bear counting*
Ray, Mary Lyn. *Stars*
Roslonek, Steve. *The shape song swingalong*
Schoonmaker, Elizabeth. *Square cat*
Sidman, Joyce. *Swirl by swirl*

Concepts – size

Docherty, Thomas. *Big scary monster*
Graves, Keith. *Chicken Big*

Howe, James. *Brontorina*
Jenkins, Emily. *Small medium large*
Klise, Kate. *Stand straight, Ella Kate*
Lichtenheld, Tom. *Cloudette*
Rand, Betseygail. *Big Bunny*
Rayner, Catherine. *Ernest, the moose who doesn't fit*
Russo, Marisabina. *A very big bunny*

Conductors *see* Careers – conductors (music)

Confidence *see* Character traits – confidence

Conservation *see* Ecology

Construction workers *see* Careers – construction workers

Contests

Alexander, Kwame. *Acoustic Rooster and his barnyard band*
Barton, Chris. *Shark vs. train*
Bateman, Teresa. *Paul Bunyan vs. Hals Halson*
Birtha, Becky. *Lucky beans*
Brett, Jan. *The Easter egg*
Calvert, Pam. *Princess Peepers picks a pet*
Cartaya, Pablo. *Tina Cocolina*
Conahan, Carolyn. *The big wish*
Czekaj, Jef. *Hip and Hop, don't stop!*
Helmore, Jim. *Oh no, monster tomato!*
Kinney, Jessica. *The pig scramble*
Kroll, Steven. *Super-dragon*
Quattlebaum, Mary. *Pirate vs. pirate*
Rosen, Michael J. *Night of the pumpkinheads*

Cooking *see* Activities – baking, cooking

Cooperation *see* Character traits – cooperation

Costumes *see* Clothing – costumes

Counting, numbers

Ainsworth, Kimberly. *Hootenanny!*
Animal 123
Ashburn, Boni. *Over at the castle*
Beaty, Andrea. *Hide and sheep*
Benzwie, Teresa. *Numbers on the move*
Berkes, Marianne. *Over in Australia*
Birtha, Becky. *Lucky beans*
Blackstone, Stella. *Bear's birthday*
Browne, Eileen. *Handa's hen*
Chall, Marsha Wilson. *One pup's up*
Chichester Clark, Emma. *Little Miss Muffet counts to ten*
Cuyler, Margery. *Guinea pigs add up*
Dale, Penny. *Dinosaur dig!*
Degman, Lori. *1 zany zoo*
DeRubertis, Barbara. *Bobby Baboon's banana be-bop*
Donaldson, Julia. *One mole digging a hole*
Emberley, Rebecca. *Ten little beasties*
Fisher, Valorie. *Everything I need to know before I'm five*

Five little pumpkins
Fleming, Candace. *Seven hungry babies*
Fleming, Denise. *Shout! Shout it out!*
Formento, Alison. *This tree counts!*
   This tree, 1, 2, 3
Fox, Mem. *Let's count goats!*
Franco, Betsy. *Double play!*
Gravett, Emily. *The rabbit problem*
Harris, Trudy. *Tally cat keeps track*
Hill, Susanna Leonard. *Can't sleep without sheep*
Himmelman, John. *10 little hot dogs*
Hruby, Emily. *Counting in the garden*
Hulme, Joy N. *Easter babies*
Jane, Pamela. *Little goblins ten*
Jocelyn, Marthe. *Ones and twos*
Kerr, Judith. *One night in the zoo*
Larochelle, David. *1+1=5*
Levine, Arthur A. *Monday is one day*
Long, Ethan. *One drowsy dragon*
Maccarone, Grace. *Miss Lina's ballerinas*
McGrath, Barbara Barbieri. *Teddy bear counting*
McQuinn, Anna. *The sleep sheep*
Maloney, Peter. *One foot two feet*
Marino, Gianna. *One too many*
Martin, Bill, Jr. *Ten little caterpillars*
Marzollo, Jean. *Help me learn numbers 0-20*
Melvin, Alice. *Counting birds*
Milord, Susan. *Happy 100th day!*
Norman, Kim. *Ten on the sled*
Otoshi, Kathryn. *Zero*
Pamintuan, Macky. *Twelve haunted rooms of Halloween*
Pelley, Kathleen T. *Magnus Maximus, a marvelous measurer*
Peters, Lisa Westberg. *Frankie works the night shift*
Reasoner, Charles. *One blue fish*
Reid, Margarette S. *Lots and lots of coins*
Roop, Peter. *Down east in the ocean*
Rosenthal, Amy Krouse. *This plus that*
Rubinger, Ami. *Dog number 1 dog number 10*
Salzano, Tammi. *One little blueberry*
Schulman, Janet. *10 Easter egg hunters*
   10 Valentine friends
Sebe, Masayuki. *Let's count to 100!*
Siminovich, Lorena. *I like bugs*
Slade, Suzanne. *What's the difference?*
Souders, Taryn. *Whole-y cow!*
Spinelli, Eileen. *Miss Fox's class earns a field trip*
Stickland, Paul. *A number of dinosaurs*
Stiegemeyer, Julie. *Seven little bunnies*
Sturgis, Brenda Reeves. *10 turkeys in the road*
Waber, Bernard. *Lyle walks the dogs*
Wallace, Nancy Elizabeth. *Planting seeds*
   Ready, set, 100th day!
Young, Cybèle. *Ten birds*
Ziefert, Harriet. *Counting chickens*
Zuffi, Stefano. *Art 123*

Courage *see* Character traits – bravery

Cousins *see* Family life – cousins

Cowboys, cowgirls

Bruins, David. *The call of the cowboy*
Janni, Rebecca. *Every cowgirl needs a horse*
   Every cowgirl needs dancing boots

Langdo, Bryan. *Tornado Slim and the magic cowboy hat*
Lawson, Dorie McCullough. *Tex*
Montijo, Rhode. *The Halloween Kid*

Cows *see* Animals – bulls, cows

Coyotes *see* Animals – coyotes

Crabs *see* Crustaceans – crabs

Crafts *see* Activities – making things

Cranes (birds) *see* Birds – cranes

Creation

dePaola, Tomie. *Let the whole earth sing praise*
Goodings, Christina. *Creation story*

Crime

Agee, Jon. *My rhinoceros*
Base, Graeme. *The Jewel Fish of Karnak*
Biedrzycki, David. *Ace Lacewing, bug detective*
Casanova, Mary. *The day Dirk Yeller came to town*
Huling, Jan. *Ol' Bloo's boogie-woogie band and blues ensemble*
Knapp, Ruthie. *Who stole Mona Lisa?*

Crocodiles *see* Reptiles – alligators, crocodiles

Crows *see* Birds – crows

Cruelty to animals *see* Character traits – kindness to animals

Crustaceans – crabs

Mason, Janeen. *Ocean commotion*

Crying *see* Emotions

Cuba *see* Foreign lands – Cuba

Cumulative tales

Bertrand, Diane Gonzales. *The party for Papa Luis / La fiesta para Papa Luis*
Chaconas, Dori. *Don't slam the door!*
de Las Casas, Dianne. *The house that Witchy built*
Downing, Johnette. *There was an old lady who swallowed some bugs*
Egielski, Richard. *The sleepless little vampire*
Emberley, Ed. *The red hen*
Ernst, Lisa Campbell. *The Gingerbread Girl goes animal crackers*
Gershator, Phillis. *Who's awake in springtime?*
The gingerbread boy. *The gingerbread man loose in the school*
   The Library Gingerbread Man

House, Catherine. *A stork in a baobab tree*
Little old lady who swallowed a fly. *There was an old monkey who swallowed a frog*
Long, Ethan. *The book that Zack wrote*
Melvin, Alice. *The high street*
Moser, Lisa. *Perfect soup*
Perry, Andrea. *The Bicklebys' birdbath*
Reidy, Jean. *Light up the night*
Root, Phyllis. *Creak! said the bed*
Taylor, Sean. *The ring went zing!*
The twelve days of Christmas. English folk song. *Twelve days of Christmas*, ill. by Rachel Isadora
The twelve days of Christmas, ill. by Jane Ray
The twelve days of Christmas, ill. by Laurel Long
Vamos, Samantha R. *The cazuela that the farm maiden stirred*
Vasilovich, Guy. *The 13 nights of Halloween*

Curiosity *see* Character traits – curiosity

Currency *see* Money

Custodians *see* Careers – custodians, janitors

Dancing *see* Activities – dancing

Darkness – fear *see* Emotions – fear

Dawn *see* Morning

Day

Bernhard, Durga. *While you are sleeping*
Johnson, Angela. *Lottie Paris lives here*
Lamb, Albert. *Tell me the day backwards*
Martin, Ruth. *Moon dreams*
Munro, Roxie. *Desert days, desert nights*
Underwood, Deborah. *The loud book!*

Day care *see* School – nursery

Days of the week, months of the year

Elya, Susan Middleton. *A year full of holidays*
Gravett, Emily. *The rabbit problem*
Levine, Arthur A. *Monday is one day*
McGowan, Michael. *Sunday is for God*
Newman, Jeff. *The boys*

Death

Blumenthal, Deborah. *The blue house dog*
Burleigh, Robert. *Good-bye, Sheepie*

Castellucci, Cecil. *Grandma's gloves*
Genechten, Guido van. *Ricky and the squirrel*
Jeffers, Oliver. *The heart and the bottle*
Loth, Sebastian. *Remembering Crystal*
Moundlic, Charlotte. *The scar*
Murphy, Sally. *Pearl verses the world*
Rohmann, Eric. *Bone dog*
Wild, Margaret. *Harry and Hopper*
Wood, Douglas. *Aunt Mary's rose*
Yeh, Kat. *The magic brush*
Yolen, Jane. *The day Tiger Rose said goodbye*

Denmark *see* Foreign lands – Denmark

Desert

Brett, Jan. *The three little dassies*
Munro, Roxie. *Desert days, desert nights*

Detectives *see* Careers – detectives

Digging *see* Activities – digging

Diners *see* Restaurants

Dinosaurs

Barry, Frances. *Let's look at dinosaurs*
Buzzeo, Toni. *No T. Rex in the library*
Cyrus, Kurt. *The voyage of turtle Rex*
Dale, Penny. *Dinosaur dig!*
DePalma, Mary Newell. *Uh-oh!*
Drehsen, Britta. *Flip-o-storic*
Freedman, Claire. *Dinosaurs love underpants*
Hartland, Jessie. *How the dinosaur got to the museum*
Hines, Anna Grossnickle. *I am a Tyrannosaurus*
Howe, James. *Brontorina*
Kroll, Steven. *The Tyrannosaurus game*
McClatchy, Lisa. *Dear Tyrannosaurus Rex*
McMullan, Kate. *I'm big!*
Mayer, Mercer. *Too many dinosaurs*
Mayo, Margaret. *Stomp, dinosaur, stomp!*
Mitton, Tony. *Rumble, roar, dinosaur!*
Plourde, Lynn. *Dino pets go to school*
Prap, Lila. *Dinosaurs?!*
Rosenberg, Liz. *Tyrannosaurus dad*
Shea, Bob. *Dinosaur vs. the library*
Dinosaur vs. the potty
Stickland, Paul. *A number of dinosaurs*
Symes, Ruth. *Little Rex, big brother*
Wheeler, Lisa. *Dino-baseball*
Dino-basketball
Willis, Jeanne. *I'm sure I saw a dinosaur*
Wing, Natasha. *How to raise a dinosaur*
Zoehfeld, Kathleen Weidner. *Where did dinosaurs come from?*

Disabilities *see* Handicaps

Diseases *see* Illness

Disguises

Ehlert, Lois. *Lots of spots*

Ernst, Lisa Campbell. *Sylvia Jean, scout supreme*
Fenton, Joe. *Boo!*
Peters, Bernadette. *Stella is a star!*
Roberton, Fiona. *Wanted: the perfect pet*
Savage, Stephen. *Where's Walrus?*
Shaskan, Stephen. *A dog is a dog*

Dissatisfaction *see* Behavior – dissatisfaction

Divorce

Cook, Julia. *The "D" word*
Portnoy, Mindy Avra. *A tale of two seders*

Doctors *see* Careers – doctors

Dogs *see* Animals – dogs

Dolls *see* Toys – dolls

Donkeys *see* Animals – donkeys

Doves *see* Birds – doves

Dragons

Adams, Sarah. *Dave and Violet*
Ashburn, Boni. *Over at the castle*
Biedrzycki, David. *Me and my dragon*
Calvert, Pam. *Princess Peepers picks a pet*
de Las Casas, Dianne. *There's a dragon in the library*
Falkenstern, Lisa. *A dragon moves in*
Kaufman, Jeanne. *Young Henry and the dragon*
Knudsen, Michelle. *Argus*
Krause, Ute. *Oscar and the very hungry dragon*
Kroll, Steven. *Super-dragon*
Long, Ethan. *One drowsy dragon*
Moore, Jodi. *When a dragon moves in*
Ramos, Mario. *I am so strong*
Smallman, Steve. *Dragon stew*
Sperring, Mark. *The sunflower sword*
Thomas, Shelley Moore. *A Good Knight's rest*

Drawing *see* Activities – drawing

Dreams

Hurd, Thacher. *The weaver*
Lawson, Dorie McCullough. *Tex*
Martin, Ruth. *Moon dreams*
Teague, David. *Franklin's big dreams*
Washington, Ned. *When you wish upon a star*
Zalben, Jane Breskin. *Baby shower*

Dresses *see* Clothing – dresses

Droughts *see* Weather – droughts

Drums *see* Musical instruments – drums

Ducks *see* Birds – ducks

Dwarfs, midgets

Grimm, Jacob. *Snow White*

Dying *see* Death

Eagles *see* Birds – eagles

Ears *see* Anatomy – ears

Earth

Guiberson, Brenda Z. *Earth*
Munro, Roxie. *Ecomazes*
Parr, Todd. *The earth book*

Earthquakes

Danticat, Edwidge. *Eight days*
Perry, Phyllis J. *Pandas' earthquake escape*
Watson, Jesse Joshua. *Hope for Haiti*

East Indian Americans *see* Ethnic groups in
    the U.S. – East Indian Americans

Easter *see* Holidays – Easter

Eating *see* Food

Ecology

Beard, Alex. *Crocodile's tears*
Brown, Marc. *Arthur turns green*
Chin, Jason. *Coral reefs*
Cole, Henry. *The littlest evergreen*
Cole, Joanna. *The magic school bus and the climate
    challenge*
deGroat, Diane. *Ants in your pants, worms in your
    plants!*
Glaser, Linda. *Garbage helps our garden grow*
Guiberson, Brenda Z. *Earth*
Johnson, Jen Cullerton. *Seeds of change*
Lamstein, Sarah Marwil. *Big night for salamanders*
Middleton, Charlotte. *Nibbles*
Muldrow, Diane. *We planted a tree*
Munro, Roxie. *Desert days, desert nights*
    Ecomazes
Napoli, Donna Jo. *Mama Miti*
Parr, Todd. *The earth book*
Reed, Lynn Rowe. *Roscoe and the pelican rescue*
Root, Phyllis. *Big belching bog*

Rotner, Shelley. *The buzz on bees*
Seven, John. *The ocean story*
Siddals, Mary McKenna. *Compost stew*
Stewart, Melissa. *A place for frogs*
Yahgulanaas, Michael Nicoll. *The little hummingbird*
Yezerski, Thomas F. *Meadowlands*

Education *see* School

Eggs

Averbeck, Jim. *Except if*
Battut, Eric. *The fox and the hen*
Brett, Jan. *The Easter egg*
Dunrea, Olivier. *Ollie's Easter eggs*
Franceschelli, Christopher. *(Oliver)*
Mortimer, Anne. *Bunny's Easter egg*
Mother Goose. *Humpty Dumpty*
Munro, Roxie. *Hatch!*
Rand, Betseygail. *Big Bunny*
Schulman, Janet. *10 Easter egg hunters*
Smith, Alex T. *Foxy and Egg*
Stalder, Päivi. *Ernest's first Easter*
Stileman, Kali. *Roly-poly egg*
Vainio, Pirkko. *Who hid the Easter eggs?*
Wilson, Karma. *What's in the egg, Little Pip?*

Egypt *see* Foreign lands – Egypt

El Salvador *see* Foreign lands – El Salvador

Elderly *see* Old age

Elephant seals *see* Animals – seals

Elephants *see* Animals – elephants

Elves *see* Mythical creatures – elves

Emotions

Brisson, Pat. *Sometimes we were brave*
Hall, Michael. *My heart is like a zoo*
Harper, Charise Mericle. *Henry's heart*
Hodgkinson, Leigh. *Smile!*
Nemiroff, Marc A. *Shy spaghetti and excited eggs*
Stanley, Malaika Rose. *Baby Ruby bawled*
Ziefert, Harriet. *Bunny's lessons*

Emotions – anger

Burnell, Heather Ayris. *Bedtime monster / ¡A dormir, pequeño monstruo!*
Clarke, Jane. *Trumpet*
Gassman, Julie. *Crabby pants*
Hughes, Shirley. *Don't want to go!*
Nadel, Carolina. *Daddy's home*
Perl, Erica S. *Dotty*
Sakai, Komako. *Mad at Mommy*
Weiss, Ellen. *The taming of Lola*

Emotions – envy, jealousy

Grimm, Jacob. *Snow White*
Macdonald, Maryann. *The pink party*
Wewer, Iris. *My wild sister and me*
Wortche, Allison. *Rosie Sprout's time to shine*

Emotions – fear

Bently, Peter. *King Jack and the dragon*
Crimi, Carolyn. *Rock 'n' roll Mole*
Danneberg, Julie. *The big test*
Day, Nancy Raines. *On a windy night*
Dewdney, Anna. *Roly Poly pangolin*
Diesen, Deborah. *The pout-pout fish in the big-big dark*
Foley, Greg. *Willoughby and the moon*
Genechten, Guido van. *No ghost under my bed
 Ricky is brave*
Grandits, John. *Ten rules you absolutely must not
 break if you want to survive the school bus*
Green, Alison. *The fox in the dark*
Helakoski, Leslie. *Big chickens go to town*
Hoppe, Paul. *The woods*
Hughes, Shirley. *Don't want to go!*
Kirk, Daniel. *Library mouse*
Landa, Norbert. *The great monster hunt*
Meserve, Jessica. *Bedtime without Arthur*
Newman, Lesléa. *Miss Tutu's star*
Patricelli, Leslie. *The Patterson puppies and the
 midnight monster party*
Penn, Audrey. *A bedtime kiss for Chester Raccoon*
Ross, Tony. *I want my light on!*
Sattler, Jennifer. *Pig kahuna*
Saunders, Karen. *Baby Badger's wonderful night*
Schaefer, Carole Lexa. *Who's there?*
Scotton, Rob. *Splish, splash, Splat!*
Shea, Bob. *I'm a shark*
Soman, David. *Ladybug Girl at the beach*
Watt, Mélanie. *Scaredy Squirrel has a birthday party*
Weitzman, Jacqueline Preiss. *Superhero Joe*
Yum, Hyewon. *There are no scary wolves*

Emotions – grief

Blumenthal, Deborah. *The blue house dog*
Jeffers, Oliver. *The heart and the bottle*
Moundlic, Charlotte. *The scar*
Murphy, Sally. *Pearl verses the world*
Wild, Margaret. *Harry and Hopper*

Emotions – happiness

Doyle, Malachy. *Get happy*
Emberley, Rebecca. *If you're a monster and you know
 it*
Hall, Michael. *Perfect square*

Emotions – jealousy *see* Emotions – envy, jealousy

Emotions – loneliness

Battersby, Katherine. *Squish Rabbit*
DiPucchio, Kelly. *Zombie in love*
Esbaum, Jill. *Tom's tweet*
Foggo, Cheryl. *Dear baobab*
Janni, Rebecca. *Every cowgirl needs dancing boots*
Jeffers, Oliver. *The heart and the bottle*

Juster, Norton. *Neville*
Kleven, Elisa. *The friendship wish*
Kolanovic, Dubravka. *Everyone needs a friend*
LaReau, Kara. *Mr. Prickles*
Lerch. *Swim! swim!*
McDonnell, Christine. *Goyangi means cat*
Mortimer, Rachael. *Song for a princess*
Murphy, Sally. *Pearl verses the world*
Root, Phyllis. *Scrawny cat*
Yolen, Jane. *Elsie's bird*

Emotions – love

Bianco, Margery Williams. *The velveteen rabbit*
Clark, Julie Aigner. *You are the best medicine*
Dunrea, Olivier. *Old Bear and his cub*
Evans, Kristina. *What's special about me, Mama?*
Evans, Lezlie. *Who loves the little lamb?*
Jordan, Deloris. *Baby blessings*
Krauss, Ruth. *And I love you*
McCarty, Peter. *Henry in love*
Marley, Cedella. *One love*
Pham, LeUyen. *All the things I love about you*
Quattlebaum, Mary. *Pirate vs. pirate*
Rose, Deborah Lee. *All the seasons of the year*
Rosenthal, Amy Krouse. *Plant a kiss*
Roth, Carol. *Will you still love me?*
Sabuda, Robert. *Beauty and the beast*
Saltzberg, Barney. *Kisses*
Steven, Kenneth. *The biggest thing in the world*
Stott, Ann. *I'll be there*
Tillman, Nancy. *Wherever you are*
Verburg, Bonnie. *The kiss box*
Wells, Rosemary. *Love waves*

Emotions – sadness

Cora, Cat. *A suitcase surprise for Mommy*

Emperors *see* Royalty – emperors

Endangered animals *see* Animals – endangered animals

England *see* Foreign lands – England

Entertainment *see* Theater

Environment *see* Ecology

Envy *see* Emotions – envy, jealousy

Ethiopia *see* Foreign lands – Ethiopia

Ethnic groups in the U.S. – African Americans

Armand, Glenda. *Love twelve miles long*
Bandy, Michael S. *White water*
Barrett, Mary Brigid. *Shoebox Sam*
Bauer, Marion Dane. *Harriet Tubman*
Bildner, Phil. *The hallelujah flight*
Birtha, Becky. *Lucky beans*

Celenza, Anna Harwell. *Duke Ellington's Nutcracker Suite*
Diggs, Taye. *Chocolate me!*
Evans, Kristina. *What's special about me, Mama?*
Evans, Shane W. *Underground*
Grigsby, Susan. *In the garden with Dr. Carver*
Harris, Teresa E. *Summer Jackson*
Harvey, Jeanne Walker. *My hands sing the blues*
Hill, Laban Carrick. *Dave the potter*
Hoffman, Mary. *Grace at Christmas*
Hudson, Cheryl Willis. *My friend Maya loves to dance*
Ingalls, Ann. *The little piano girl*
Johnson, Angela. *Lottie Paris lives here*
Johnson, Dinah. *Black magic*
Jordan, Deloris. *Baby blessings*
Kittinger, Jo S. *Rosa's bus*
Krensky, Stephen. *Play ball, Jackie!*
Kulling, Monica. *All aboard!*
McCully, Emily Arnold. *Wonder horse*
McGowan, Michael. *Sunday is for God*
McQuinn, Anna. *Lola loves stories*
Malaspina, Ann. *Phillis sings out freedom*
Marzollo, Jean. *The little plant doctor*
Mason, Margaret H. *These hands*
Michelson, Richard. *Busing Brewster*
Mitchell, Margaree King. *When Grandmama sings*
Myers, Walter Dean. *Muhammad Ali*
Nash, Sarah. *Purrfect!*
Orgill, Roxane. *Skit-scat raggedy cat*
Peete, Holly Robinson. *My brother Charlie*
Peña, Matt de la. *A nation's hope*
Pinkney, Andrea Davis. *Sit-in*
Ramsey, Calvin Alexander. *Belle, the last mule at Gee's Bend*
 Ruth and the Green Book
Reynolds, Aaron. *Back of the bus*
Shapiro, J. H. *Magic trash*
Slade, Suzanne. *Climbing Lincoln's steps*
Tavares, Matt. *Henry Aaron's dream*
Uhlberg, Myron. *A storm called Katrina*
Vernick, Audrey. *She loved baseball*
Walker, Sally M. *Freedom song*
Warwick, Dionne. *Little Man*
Watkins, Angela Farris. *My Uncle Martin's big heart*
 My Uncle Martin's words for America
Weatherford, Carole Boston. *The Beatitudes*
Williams, Karen Lynn. *A beach tail*
Woodson, Jacqueline. *Pecan pie baby*

Ethnic groups in the U.S. – Black Americans *see* Ethnic groups in the U.S. – African Americans

Ethnic groups in the U.S. – Chinese Americans

Compestine, Ying Chang. *Crouching tiger*
Lewis, Rose. *Orange Peel's pocket*
Lin, Grace. *Thanking the moon*
Look, Lenore. *Polka Dot Penguin Pottery*
Yeh, Kat. *The magic brush*

Ethnic groups in the U.S. – Cuban Americans

Sacre, Antonio. *La Noche Buena*

Ethnic groups in the U.S. – East Indian Americans

Zia, F. *Hot, hot roti for Dada-ji*

Ethnic groups in the U.S. – Hispanic Americans

Dorros, Arthur. *Mama and me*
Hudes, Quiara Alegría. *Welcome to my neighborhood!*
Medina, Meg. *Tía Isa wants a car*
Witte, Anna. *Lola's fandango*

Ethnic groups in the U.S. – Italian Americans

Akin, Sara Laux. *Three scoops and a fig*
Bastianich, Lidia. *Nonna tell me a story*
Yaccarino, Dan. *All the way to America*

Ethnic groups in the U.S. – Japanese Americans

Wells, Rosemary. *Yoko's show-and-tell*

Ethnic groups in the U.S. – Korean Americans

Avraham, Kate Aver. *What will you be, Sara Mee?*
McDonnell, Christine. *Goyangi means cat*

Ethnic groups in the U.S. – Mexican Americans

Bertrand, Diane Gonzales. *The party for Papa Luis / La fiesta para Papa Luis*
Brown, Monica. *Chavela and the magic bubble*
   Side by side / Lado a lado
Colato Laínez, René. *The Tooth Fairy meets El Ratón Pérez*
Cox, Judy. *Carmen learns English*
Price, Mara. *Grandma's chocolate / El chocolate de Abuelita*
Tafolla, Carmen. *Fiesta babies*
Tonatiuh, Duncan. *Dear Primo*

Ethnic groups in the U.S. – Pakistani Americans

Khan, Rukhsana. *Big red lollipop*

Ethnic groups in the U.S. – Puerto Rican Americans

Velasquez, Eric. *Grandma's gift*

Ethnic groups in the U.S. – racially mixed

Washington, Kathy Gates. *Three colors of Katie*

Ethnic groups in the U.S. – Tibetan Americans

Rose, Naomi C. *Tashi and the Tibetan flower cure*

Etiquette

Ainslie, Tamsin. *I can say please*
   I can say thank you
Harper, Charise Mericle. *The best birthday ever!*
Manners mash-up
Shaw, Hannah. *School for bandits*
Vestergaard, Hope. *Potty animals*
Watt, Mélanie. *You're finally here!*

Experiments *see* Science

Explorers *see* Careers – explorers

Extraterrestrial beings *see* Aliens

Eye glasses *see* Glasses

Eyes *see* Anatomy – eyes

Faces *see* Anatomy – faces

Fairies

Colato Laínez, René. *The Tooth Fairy meets El Ratón Pérez*
Graham, Bob. *April and Esme, tooth fairies*
Kann, Victoria. *Silverlicious*
MacDonald, Margaret Read. *Too many fairies*
Numeroff, Laura. *Ponyella*
Ray, Jane. *The dollhouse fairy*
Young, Amy. *The mud fairy*

Fairs, festivals

Chaconas, Dori. *Hurry down to Derry Fair*
Fraser, Mary Ann. *Heebie-Jeebie Jamboree*
Frasier, Debra. *A fabulous fair alphabet*
Goembel, Ponder. *Animal fair*
Helakoski, Leslie. *Fair cow*
Himmelman, John. *Cows to the rescue*
Kinney, Jessica. *The pig scramble*
Lin, Grace. *Thanking the moon*
Tafolla, Carmen. *Fiesta babies*

Fall *see* Seasons – fall

Family life

Akin, Sara Laux. *Three scoops and a fig*
Avraham, Kate Aver. *What will you be, Sara Mee?*
Brisson, Pat. *Sometimes we were brave*
Chaconas, Dori. *Hurry down to Derry Fair*
Cole, Brock. *The money we'll save*
Corey, Dorothy. *You go away*
Cunnane, Kelly. *Chirchir is singing*
Dodd, Emma. *I am small*
Foggo, Cheryl. *Dear baobab*

Gilani-Williams, Fawzia. *Nabeel's new pants*
Harris, Teresa E. *Summer Jackson*
Hodgkinson, Leigh. *Smile!*
Hoffman, Mary. *Grace at Christmas*
Jarka, Jeff. *Love that kitty!*
Kempter, Christa. *When Mama can't sleep*
King, Dedie. *I see the sun in Afghanistan*
Kornell, Max. *Bear with me*
Krauss, Ruth. *And I love you*
Krosoczka, Jarrett J. *Ollie the purple elephant*
Levine, Arthur A. *Monday is one day*
Lin, Grace. *Thanking the moon*
López, Susana. *The best family in the world*
McAllister, Angela. *Yuck! That's not a monster*
McGowan, Michael. *Sunday is for God*
Meltzer, Amy. *The Shabbat Princess*
Meng, Cece. *I will not read this book*
Novak, Matt. *A wish for you*
Onyefulu, Ifeoma. *Omer's favorite place*
Orloff, Karen Kaufman. *I wanna new room*
Portnoy, Mindy Avra. *A tale of two seders*
Rocco, John. *Blackout*
Root, Phyllis. *Creak! said the bed*
Sacre, Antonio. *A mango in the hand*
Safran, Sheri. *All kinds of families*
Shoulders, Michael. *Goodnight Baby Bear*
Spinelli, Eileen. *Now it is summer*
    The perfect Christmas
Stanley, Malaika Rose. *Baby Ruby bawled*
Wallace, Nancy Elizabeth. *Ready, set, 100th day!*
Washington, Kathy Gates. *Three colors of Katie*
Whelan, Gloria. *The boy who wanted to cook*

Family life – aunts, uncles

Broach, Elise. *Gumption!*
Foggo, Cheryl. *Dear baobab*
Garland, Michael. *Super snow day seek and find*
Medina, Meg. *Tía Isa wants a car*
Parish, Herman. *Go west, Amelia Bedelia!*
Sheridan, Sara. *I'm me!*
Watkins, Angela Farris. *My Uncle Martin's big heart*
Wood, Douglas. *Aunt Mary's rose*

Family life – brothers

Banks, Kate. *Max's castle*
Borden, Louise. *Big brothers don't take naps*
Clarke, Jane. *Gilbert the hero*
Crews, Nina. *Sky-high Guy*
Gay, Marie-Louise. *Caramba and Henry*
Gorbachev, Valeri. *Shhh!*
Grandits, John. *Ten rules you absolutely must not break if you want to survive the school bus*
Kirsch, Vincent X. *Two little boys from Toolittle Toys*
Kling, Kevin. *Big little brother*
Lehman-Wilzig, Tami. *Nathan blows out the Hanukkah candles*
Schwartz, Roslyn. *The Vole brothers*
Soman, David. *The amazing adventures of Bumblebee Boy*
Symes, Ruth. *Little Rex, big brother*

Family life – brothers & sisters

Birdsall, Jeanne. *Flora's very windy day*
Brown, Marc. *Arthur turns green*
Buzzeo, Toni. *Lighthouse Christmas*
Child, Lauren. *I really, really need actual ice skates*
    My best, best friend

Doerrfeld, Cori. *Penny loves pink*
Elliott, Rebecca. *Just because*
Feiffer, Kate. *But I wanted a baby brother!*
Fraser, Mary Ann. *Heebie-Jeebie Jamboree*
Gorbachev, Valeri. *The best cat*
Heller, Linda. *How Dalia put a big yellow comforter inside a tiny blue box*
Jalali, Reza. *Moon watchers*
Kann, Victoria. *Silverlicious*
Kaplan, Bruce Eric. *Monsters eat whiny children*
LaRochelle, David. *The haunted hamburger and other ghostly stories*
Mair, Samia J. *The perfect gift*
Meserve, Jessica. *Bedtime without Arthur*
Milgrim, David. *Santa Duck and his merry helpers*
Muth, Jon J. *Zen ghosts*
Parkhurst, Carolyn. *Cooking with Henry and Elliebelly*
Peete, Holly Robinson. *My brother Charlie*
Rossell, Judith. *Ruby and Leonard and the great big surprise*
Ryan, Pam Muñoz. *Tony Baloney*
Smallcomb, Pam. *Earth to Clunk*
Wells, Rosemary. *Max and Ruby's bedtime book*
Wewer, Iris. *My wild sister and me*
Young, Cybèle. *A few blocks*

Family life – cousins

Tonatiuh, Duncan. *Dear Primo*
Weiss, Ellen. *The taming of Lola*

Family life – fathers

Allen, Elanna. *Itsy Mitsy runs away*
Alter, Anna. *A photo for Greta*
Bennett, Kelly. *Dad and Pop*
    Your daddy was just like you
Brown, Margaret Wise. *The fathers are coming home*
Bruchac, Joseph. *My father is taller than a tree*
Burleigh, Robert. *Good-bye, Sheepie*
Colato Laínez, René. *My shoes and I*
Dunrea, Olivier. *A Christmas tree for Pyn*
    Old Bear and his cub
Durand, Hallie. *Mitchell's license*
Dyer, Sarah. *Monster day at work*
Feiffer, Kate. *My side of the car*
Frederick, Heather Vogel. *Hide and squeak*
Galbraith, Kathryn O. *Arbor Day square*
Gay, Marie-Louise. *Roslyn Rutabaga and the biggest hole on earth!*
Gibala-Broxholm, Scott. *Maddie's monster dad*
Glass, Beth Raisner. *Blue-ribbon dad*
Greene, Rhonda Gowler. *Daddy is a cozy hug*
Hardin, Melinda. *Hero dad*
Harper, Charise Mericle. *Pink me up*
Johnson, Angela. *Lottie Paris lives here*
Keane, Dave. *Daddy adventure day*
Long, Ethan. *My dad, my hero*
Moore, Genevieve. *Catherine's story*
Nadel, Carolina. *Daddy's home*
Niemann, Christoph. *Subway*
North, Sherry. *Because I am your daddy*
Oelschlager, Vanita. *A tale of two daddies*
Park, Linda Sue. *The third gift*
Plecas, Jennifer. *Pretend*
Ray, Jane. *The dollhouse fairy*
Rosenberg, Liz. *Tyrannosaurus dad*
Saunders, Karen. *Baby Badger's wonderful night*

Shea, Bob. *Oh, Daddy!*
Walker, Anna. *I love my dad*
Yolen, Jane. *My father knows the names of things*
Yu, Li-Qiong. *A New Year's reunion*

Family life – grandfathers

Adler, David A. *A little at a time*
Compestine, Ying Chang. *Crouching tiger*
Garland, Michael. *Grandpa's tractor*
Lynn, Sarah. *Tip-tap pop*
Mason, Margaret H. *These hands*
Rose, Naomi C. *Tashi and the Tibetan flower cure*
Schwartz, Howard. *Gathering sparks*
Yeh, Kat. *The magic brush*
Zia, F. *Hot, hot roti for Dada-ji*

Family life – grandmothers

Addasi, Maha. *Time to pray*
Brown, Monica. *Chavela and the magic bubble*
Castellucci, Cecil. *Grandma's gloves*
DePalma, Mary Newell. *The perfect gift*
French, Vivian. *Yucky worms*
Hartt-Sussman, Heather. *Nana's getting married*
Hassett, Ann. *Too many frogs!*
Holt, Kimberly Willis. *The adventures of Granny
    Clearwater and Little Critter*
Joosse, Barbara. *Sleepover at Gramma's house*
Levine, Gail Carson. *Betsy Red Hoodie*
Mackall, Dandi Daley. *The story of the Easter robin*
MacLachlan, Patricia. *Your moon, my moon*
Meddaugh, Susan. *Martha says it with flowers*
Mitchell, Margaree King. *When Grandmama sings*
Murphy, Sally. *Pearl verses the world*
Onyefulu, Ifeoma. *Grandma comes to stay*
Perrow, Angeli. *Many hands*
Polacco, Patricia. *Bun Bun Button*
Price, Mara. *Grandma's chocolate / El chocolate de
    Abuelita*
Russo, Marisabina. *I will come back for you*
Sacre, Antonio. *La Noche Buena*
Schubert, Leda. *The Princess of Borscht*
Siegel, Randy. *Grandma's smile*
Simhaee, Rebeka. *Sara finds a mitzva*
Smee, Nicola. *What's the matter, Bunny Blue?*
Stein, David Ezra. *Love, Mouserella*
Velasquez, Eric. *Grandma's gift*
Weiss, Ellen. *The taming of Lola*
Wells, Rosemary. *Max and Ruby's bedtime book*

Family life – grandparents

Ajmera, Maya et al. *Our grandparents*
Child, Lydia Maria. *Over the river and through the
    wood*
Cusimano, Maryann K. *You are my wish*
Horrocks, Anita. *Silas' seven grandparents*
Look, Lenore. *Polka Dot Penguin Pottery*
Parish, Herman. *Amelia Bedelia's first apple pie*
Ziefert, Harriet. *Grandma's wedding album*

Family life – great-grandparents

Smith, Lane. *Grandpa Green*

Family life – mothers

Andreae, Giles. *I love my mommy*
Armand, Glenda. *Love twelve miles long*

Bardhan-Quallen, Sudipta. *Chicks run wild*
Blackall, Sophie. *Are you awake?*
Bradford, Wade. *Why do I have to make my bed?*
Brisson, Pat. *Sometimes we were brave*
Bunting, Eve. *Pirate boy*
    Tweak tweak
Cadow, Kenneth M. *Alfie runs away*
Church, Caroline Jayne. *One more hug for Madison*
Clark, Julie Aigner. *You are the best medicine*
Collins, Ross. *Doodleday*
Cora, Cat. *A suitcase surprise for Mommy*
Cronin, Doreen. *M.O.M. (Mom Operating Manual)*
Curtis, Jamie Lee. *My mommy hung the moon*
Davis, Jerry. *Little Chicken's big day*
de Las Casas, Dianne. *Mama's bayou*
dePaola, Tomie. *My mother is so smart*
Dewdney, Anna. *Llama Llama home with Mama*
Diggs, Taye. *Chocolate me!*
Dorros, Arthur. *Mama and me*
Evans, Kristina. *What's special about me, Mama?*
Evans, Lezlie. *Who loves the little lamb?*
Fleming, Denise. *Sleepy, oh so sleepy*
Genechten, Guido van. *Because you are my friend*
Greene, Rhonda Gowler. *Mommy is a soft, warm kiss*
Iwai, Melissa. *Soup day*
Jadoul, Émile. *Good night, Chickie*
Ketteman, Helen. *If Beaver had a fever*
Klise, Kate. *Little Rabbit and the Meanest Mother on
    Earth*
Kuskin, Karla. *A boy had a mother who bought him a
    hat*
LaChanze. *Little diva*
Lamb, Albert. *Tell me the day backwards*
Lawler, Janet. *A mother's song*
McAllister, Angela. *My mom has x-ray vision*
Macken, JoAnn Early. *Waiting out the storm*
MacLachlan, Patricia. *Before you came*
    Lala salama
Matthies, Janna. *The goodbye cancer garden*
Modarressi, Mitra. *Taking care of Mama*
Moundlic, Charlotte. *The scar*
Newman, Lesléa. *Donovan's big day*
    Just like Mama
Oelschlager, Vanita. *A tale of two mommies*
Peet, Mal. *Cloud tea monkeys*
Pham, LeUyen. *All the things I love about you*
Platt, Cynthia. *A little bit of love*
Rose, Deborah Lee. *All the seasons of the year*
Rosenthal, Amy Krouse. *Bedtime for Mommy*
Roth, Carol. *Will you still love me?*
Sakai, Komako. *Mad at Mommy*
Schubert, Leda. *Feeding the sheep*
Steven, Kenneth. *The biggest thing in the world*
Stott, Ann. *I'll be there*
Tafuri, Nancy. *All kinds of kisses*
Thompson, Lauren. *Leap back home to me*
Tompert, Ann. *Little Fox goes to the end of the world*
Verburg, Bonnie. *The kiss box*
Walker, Anna. *I love my mom*
White, Kathryn. *Ruby's school walk*
Witte, Anna. *Lola's fandango*
Yamashita, Haruo. *Seven little mice go to school*
    Seven little mice have fun on the ice

Family life – new sibling

Appelt, Kathi. *Brand-new baby blues*
Banks, Kate. *This baby*
Borden, Louise. *Big brothers don't take naps*

Bradman, Tony. *The perfect baby*
Bunting, Eve. *Will it be a baby brother?*
Burningham, John. *There's going to be a baby*
Cole, Joanna. *I'm a big sister*
Doerrfeld, Cori. *Penny loves pink*
Elkin, Mark. *Samuel's baby*
My new baby
Roth, Carol. *Will you still love me?*
Shields, Gillian. *When the world was waiting for you*
Sullivan, Sarah. *Once upon a baby brother*
Wilson, Karma. *What's in the egg, Little Pip?*
Woodson, Jacqueline. *Pecan pie baby*
You and me

Family life – parents

Burg, Sarah Emmanuelle. *Do you still love me?*
Elya, Susan Middleton. *No more, por favor*
Jordan, Deloris. *Baby blessings*
Proimos, James. *Todd's TV*
Rosenberg, Liz. *Nobody*
Wadham, Tim. *The queen of France*
Wells, Rosemary. *Love waves*

Family life – single-parent families

Moore, Genevieve. *Catherine's story*
Woodson, Jacqueline. *Pecan pie baby*

Family life – sisters

Alexander, Claire. *Small Florence*
Bonwill, Ann. *Naughty toes*
Cole, Joanna. *I'm a big sister*
Cox, Judy. *Carmen learns English*
George, Kristine O'Connell. *Emma dilemma*
Graham, Bob. *April and Esme, tooth fairies*
Khan, Rukhsana. *Big red lollipop*
O'Connor, Jane. *Fancy Nancy and the fabulous fashion boutique*
Orr, Wendy. *The princess and her panther*
Tuck, Justin. *Home-field advantage*
Wishinsky, Frieda. *You're mean, Lily Jean!*
Yum, Hyewon. *The twins' blanket*

Family life – stepfamilies

Bennett, Kelly. *Dad and Pop*
Horrocks, Anita. *Silas' seven grandparents*
Manna, Anthony L. *The orphan*
Shaskan, Trisha Speed. *Seriously, Cinderella is so annoying!*

Farmers *see* Careers – farmers

Farms

Adler, David A. *A picture book of Cesar Chavez*
Alborough, Jez. *The gobble gobble moooooo tractor book*
Anderson, Derek. *Story county*
Battut, Eric. *The fox and the hen*
Beaumont, Karen. *No sleep for the sheep!*
Child, Lydia Maria. *Over the river and through the wood*
Cooper, Elisha. *Farm*
Craig, Lindsey. *Farmyard beat*
Dodd, Emma. *Meow said the cow*
Donaldson, Julia. *What the ladybug heard*

Fernandes, Eugenie. *Kitten's spring*
Garland, Michael. *Grandpa's tractor*
Geisert, Arthur. *Country road ABC*
Gershator, Phillis. *Moo, moo, brown cow! Have you any milk?*
Godwin, Laura. *One moon, two cats*
Gottfried, Maya. *Our farm*
Himmelman, John. *Cows to the rescue*
Pigs to the rescue
Hobbie, Holly. *Everything but the horse*
Hulme, Joy N. *Easter babies*
Joosse, Barbara. *Higgledy-piggledy chicks*
Kalz, Jill. *An a-maze-ing farm adventure*
Katz, Jon. *Meet the dogs of Bedlam Farm*
Kelly, Mij. *A bed of your own!*
Krilanovich, Nadia. *Chicken, chicken, duck!*
Laminack, Lester L. *Three hens and a peacock*
Landman, Tanya. *Mary's penny*
Long, Loren. *Otis and the tornado*
Minor, Wendell. *My farm friends*
Moses, Will. *Mary and her little lamb*
Moulton, Mark Kimball. *The very best pumpkin*
Newton, Jill. *Crash bang donkey!*
Parish, Herman. *Amelia Bedelia's first field trip*
Peterson, Mary. *Piggies in the pumpkin patch*
Plourde, Lynn. *Field trip day*
Only cows allowed!
Schubert, Leda. *Feeding the sheep*
Stoeke, Janet Morgan. *The Loopy Coop hens*
Stuchner, Joan Betty. *Can hens give milk?*
Taback, Simms. *Simms Taback's farm animals*
Vamos, Samantha R. *The cazuela that the farm maiden stirred*
Van Fleet, Matthew. *Moo*
Watterson, Carol. *An edible alphabet*
White, Linda. *Too many turkeys*
Wilson, Karma. *The cow loves cookies*
Hogwash!

Fathers *see* Family life – fathers

Fear *see* Emotions – fear

Feelings *see* Emotions

Feet *see* Anatomy – feet

Ferrets *see* Animals – ferrets

Fighting *see* Behavior – fighting, arguing

Fingers *see* Anatomy – hands

Finishing things *see* Character traits – completing things

Fire

Jacobs, Paul Dubois. *Fire drill*
Kaufman, Jeanne. *Young Henry and the dragon*
Nolan, Janet. *The firehouse light*

Firefighters *see* Careers – firefighters

Fires *see* Fire

Fish

Bunting, Eve. *Finn McCool and the great fish*
Diesen, Deborah. *The pout-pout fish in the big-big dark*
DiPucchio, Kelly. *Gilbert goldfish wants a pet*
Hendra, Sue. *Barry, the fish with fingers*
Lerch. *Swim! swim!*

Fish – sharks

Barton, Chris. *Shark vs. train*
Clarke, Jane. *Gilbert the hero*
Shea, Bob. *I'm a shark*

Fishing *see* Sports – fishing

Flags

White, Becky. *Betsy Ross*

Fleas *see* Insects – fleas

Flies *see* Insects – flies

Floods *see* Weather – floods

Flowers

Taylor, Sean. *Huck runs amuck!*

Flowers – roses

Wood, Douglas. *Aunt Mary's rose*

Flying *see* Activities – flying

Folk & fairy tales

Aesop. *Aesop's fables*, ill. by Piet Grobler
    Aesop's fables, ill. by Fulvio Testa
    Mouse and lion
Alley, Zoe. *There's a princess in the palace*
Andersen, Hans Christian. *The emperor's new clothes*
    The nightingale
    Sylvia Long's Thumbelina
    The ugly duckling, ill. by Sebastien Braun
    The ugly duckling, ill. by Roberta Wilson
Bianco, Margery Williams. *The velveteen rabbit*
Braun, Eric. *Trust me, Jack's beanstalk stinks*
Brett, Jan. *The three little dassies*
Browne, Anthony. *Me and you*
Bunting, Eve. *Finn McCool and the great fish*
Davis, Aubrey. *Kishka for Koppel*
Davis, David. *Fandango stew*
de Las Casas, Dianne. *Blue frog*
Downing, Johnette. *There was an old lady who swallowed some bugs*
Edwards, Pamela Duncan. *Princess Pigtoria and the pea*

Elya, Susan Middleton. *Rubia and the three osos*
Emberley, Ed. *The red hen*
Fleming, Candace. *Clever Jack takes the cake*
The gingerbread boy. *The gingerbread man loose in the school*
Gray, Luli. *Ant and Grasshopper*
Grimm, Jacob. *Hansel and Gretel*
    Little Red Riding Hood
    Rapunzel
    Snow White
    The star child
    The story of Little Red Riding Hood
    Twelve dancing princesses
Guarnaccia, Steven. *The three little pigs*
Harper, Lee. *The Emperor's cool clothes*
Henrichs, Wendy. *I am Tama, lucky cat*
Hoffmann, E. T. A. *The nutcracker*
Huling, Jan. *Ol' Bloo's boogie-woogie band and blues ensemble*
Jack and the beanstalk. *Jack and the beanstalk*
    Jacques and de beanstalk
Javaherbin, Mina. *The secret message*
Kasbarian, Lucine. *The greedy sparrow*
Kimmel, Eric A. *Joseph and the Sabbath fish*
    Medio Pollito
Lewis, Jill. *Don't read this book!*
Little old lady who swallowed a fly. *There was an old monkey who swallowed a frog*
The little red hen. *The Little Red Hen and the Passover matzah*
McDermott, Gerald. *Monkey*
MacDonald, Margaret Read. *Too many fairies*
Machado, Ana Maria. *Wolf wanted*
McLeod, Heather. *Kiss me!*
Mandell, Muriel. *A donkey reads*
Manna, Anthony L. *The orphan*
Morrison, Toni. *The tortoise or the hare*
Noble, Trinka Hakes. *A Christmas spider's miracle*
Numeroff, Laura. *Ponyella*
O'Malley, Kevin. *The great race*
Perrault, Charles. *Puss in boots*
Ramsden, Ashley. *Seven fathers*
Sabuda, Robert. *Beauty and the beast*
San Souci, Robert D. *Robin Hood and the golden arrow*
Shaskan, Trisha Speed. *Seriously, Cinderella is so annoying!*
Sierra, Judy. *Tell the truth, B.B. Wolf*
Stampler, Ann Redisch. *The rooster prince of Breslov*
Sylvester, Kevin. *Splinters*
The three bears. *Goldilocks and the three bears*, ill. by Emma Chichester Clark
    Goldilocks and the three bears, ill. by Gerda Muller
Yahgulanaas, Michael Nicoll. *The little hummingbird*
Yolen, Jane. *Sister Bear*

Food

Akin, Sara Laux. *Three scoops and a fig*
Al Abdullah, Rania. *The sandwich swap*
Argueta, Jorge. *Arroz con leche / Rice pudding*
Baker, Keith. *LMNO peas*
Bardhan-Quallen, Sudipta. *Hampire!*
Berry, Lynne. *Ducking for apples*
Best, Cari. *Easy as pie*
Bloch, Serge. *You are what you eat*
Bloom, Suzanne. *Feeding friendsies*
Brokamp, Elizabeth. *The picky little witch*
Butterworth, Chris. *How did that get in my lunchbox?*

Carrer, Chiara. *Otto Carrotto*
Cartaya, Pablo. *Tina Cocolina*
Davis, David. *Fandango stew*
de Las Casas, Dianne. *Blue frog*
Elya, Susan Middleton. *No more, por favor*
Ernst, Lisa Campbell. *The Gingerbread Girl goes animal crackers*
Fleming, Candace. *Clever Jack takes the cake*
Friedman, Caitlin. *How do you feed a hungry giant?*
The gingerbread boy. *The gingerbread man loose in the school*
　The Library Gingerbread Man
Gore, Leonid. *Worms for lunch?*
Gourley, Robbin. *First garden*
Harper, Charise Mericle. *Cupcake*
Iwai, Melissa. *Soup day*
Jenkins, Steve. *Time to eat*
Kaplan, Michael B. *Betty Bunny loves chocolate cake*
Lin, Grace. *Thanking the moon*
Marshall, Linda Elovitz. *Talia and the rude vegetables*
Milway, Katie Smith. *The good garden*
Moser, Lisa. *Perfect soup*
Reidy, Jean. *Too pickley!*
Rockwell, Anne. *Apples and pumpkins*
Rosenthal, Amy Krouse. *One smart cookie*
Rylant, Cynthia. *Brownie and Pearl grab a bite*
Salzano, Tammi. *One little blueberry*
Sayre, April Pulley. *Rah, rah, radishes!*
Schaefer, Lola. *Just one bite*
Schwartz, Roslyn. *The Vole brothers*
Siminovich, Lorena. *I like vegetables*
Sylver, Adrienne. *Hot diggity dog*
Taylor, Thomas. *Little Mouse and the big cupcake*
Thompson, Lauren. *Chew, chew, gulp!*
Thurman, Kathryn K. *A garden for Pig*
Toscano, Charles. *Papa's pastries*
Vamos, Samantha R. *The cazuela that the farm maiden stirred*
Van Camp, Katie. *CookieBot!*
Wheeler, Lisa. *Ugly pie*
Wilson, Karma. *The cow loves cookies*
Wright, Michael. *Jake goes peanuts*
Zia, F. *Hot, hot roti for Dada-ji*

Foolishness *see* Character traits – foolishness

Football *see* Sports – football

Foreign lands – Afghanistan

King, Dedie. *I see the sun in Afghanistan*

Foreign lands – Africa

Aesop. *Aesop's fables*
Beard, Alex. *Crocodile's tears*
Brett, Jan. *The three little dassies*
Cabrera, Jane. *The wheels on the bus*
Faundez, Anne. *The day the rains fell*
Foggo, Cheryl. *Dear baobab*
House, Catherine. *A stork in a baobab tree*
Joubert, Beverly. *African animal alphabet*
MacLachlan, Patricia. *Your moon, my moon*
Moss, Miriam. *This is the mountain*

Foreign lands – Antarctic

Brooks, Erik. *Polar opposites*
London, Jonathan. *Little penguin*

Foreign lands – Arctic

Brooks, Erik. *Polar opposites*
Thomson, Sarah L. *Where do polar bears live?*

Foreign lands – Australia

Baker, Jeannie. *Mirror*
Berkes, Marianne. *Over in Australia*
Markle, Sandra. *Hip-pocket papa*
Pettitt, Linda. *Yafi's family*

Foreign lands – Austria

Greenstein, Elaine. *The goose man*
Lester, Alison. *Running with the horses*

Foreign lands – Bangladesh

Malaspina, Ann. *Yasmin's hammer*

Foreign lands – Canada

Wishinsky, Frieda. *Where are you, Bear?*

Foreign lands – Chad

Rumford, James. *Rain school*

Foreign lands – China

Andersen, Hans Christian. *The nightingale*
Clark, Karen Henry. *Sweet moon baby*
Compestine, Ying Chang. *The runaway wok*
Marx, Trish. *Kindergarten day USA and China*
Perry, Phyllis J. *Pandas' earthquake escape*
Thisdale, François. *Nini*
Yu, Li-Qiong. *A New Year's reunion*

Foreign lands – Colombia

Brown, Monica. *Waiting for the Biblioburro*
Winter, Jeanette. *Biblioburro*

Foreign lands – Cuba

Sacre, Antonio. *A mango in the hand*

Foreign lands – Denmark

Drummond, Allan. *Energy island*

Foreign lands – Egypt

Base, Graeme. *The Jewel Fish of Karnak*
Hartland, Jessie. *How the sphinx got to the museum*

Foreign lands – El Salvador

Colato Laínez, René. *My shoes and I*

Foreign lands – England

Hopkinson, Deborah. *The humblebee hunter*
Richardson, Justin. *Christian, the hugging lion*

San Souci, Robert D. *Robin Hood and the golden arrow*

Foreign lands – Ethiopia

Onyefulu, Ifeoma. *Omer's favorite place*
Pettitt, Linda. *Yafi's family*

Foreign lands – France

Demi. *Joan of Arc*
Holmes, Mary Tavener. *A giraffe goes to Paris*
Whelan, Gloria. *The boy who wanted to cook*
Yolleck, Joan. *Paris in the spring with Picasso*

Foreign lands – Germany

Ungerer, Tomi. *Otto*
Wiviott, Meg. *Benno and the night of broken glass*

Foreign lands – Ghana

Onyefulu, Ifeoma. *Deron goes to nursery school*
   Grandma comes to stay

Foreign lands – Greece

Manna, Anthony L. *The orphan*

Foreign lands – Haiti

Danticat, Edwidge. *Eight days*
Watson, Jesse Joshua. *Hope for Haiti*

Foreign lands – Himalayas

Peet, Mal. *Cloud tea monkeys*

Foreign lands – Honduras

Milway, Katie Smith. *The good garden*

Foreign lands – India

Kostecki-Shaw, Jenny Sue. *Same, same but different*
McDermott, Gerald. *Monkey*

Foreign lands – Indonesia

Henrichs, Wendy. *When Anju loved being an elephant*

Foreign lands – Iran

Javaherbin, Mina. *The secret message*

Foreign lands – Ireland

Bunting, Eve. *Finn McCool and the great fish*

Foreign lands – Israel

Herman, Charlotte. *First rain*

Foreign lands – Italy

Egan, Tim. *Dodsworth in Rome*
Falconer, Ian. *Olivia goes to Venice*
Nivola, Claire A. *Orani*
Russo, Marisabina. *I will come back for you*

Foreign lands – Japan

Coerr, Eleanor. *Circus day in Japan*
Henrichs, Wendy. *I am Tama, lucky cat*
Parot, Annelore. *Kimonos*
Say, Allen. *The boy in the garden*

Foreign lands – Kenya

Browne, Eileen. *Handa's hen*
Cunnane, Kelly. *Chirchir is singing*
Johnson, Jen Cullerton. *Seeds of change*
Napoli, Donna Jo. *Mama Miti*
Oelschlager, Vanita. *Bonyo Bonyo*
Richardson, Justin. *Christian, the hugging lion*

Foreign lands – Laos

Youme. *Mali under the night sky*

Foreign lands – Mali

Cowcher, Helen. *Desert elephants*

Foreign lands – Mexico

Amado, Elisa. *What are you doing?*
de Las Casas, Dianne. *Blue frog*
Tonatiuh, Duncan. *Dear Primo*
   Diego Rivera

Foreign lands – Middle East

Addasi, Maha. *Time to pray*
Kimmel, Eric A. *Joha makes a wish*

Foreign lands – Morocco

Baker, Jeannie. *Mirror*

Foreign lands – Russia

Kabakov, Vladimir. *R is for Russia*

Foreign lands – South Africa

Daly, Niki. *A song for Jamela*
Javaherbin, Mina. *Goal!*

Foreign lands – South America

Downing, Johnette. *Amazon alphabet*
Yahgulanaas, Michael Nicoll. *The little hummingbird*

Foreign lands – Spain

Kimmel, Eric A. *Medio Pollito*

Foreign lands – Tanzania

MacLachlan, Patricia. *Lala salama*
Winter, Jeanette. *The watcher*

Foreign lands – Tibet

Martin, Jacqueline Briggs. *The chiru of High Tibet*

Foreign lands – Turkey

Gilani-Williams, Fawzia. *Nabeel's new pants*
Mandell, Muriel. *A donkey reads*

Foreign lands – Vietnam

Thong, Roseanne. *Fly free!*

Foreign languages

Ada, Alma Flor. *¡Muu, moo!*
Addasi, Maha. *Time to pray*
Argueta, Jorge. *Arroz con leche / Rice pudding*
Barner, Bob. *The Day of the Dead / El Día de los Muertos*
Brimner, Larry Dane. *Trick or treat, Old Armadillo*
Brown, Monica. *Side by side / Lado a lado*
Burnell, Heather Ayris. *Bedtime monster / ¡A dormir, pequeño monstruo!*
Coerr, Eleanor. *Circus day in Japan*
Cox, Judy. *Carmen learns English*
Dorros, Arthur. *Mama and me*
Elya, Susan Middleton. *No more, por favor*
    Rubia and the three osos
Gollub, Matthew. *Jazz Fly 2*
Guy, Ginger Foglesong. *¡Bravo!*
Harris, Trudy. *Say something, Perico*
Henderson, Kathy. *Hush, baby, hush!*
Hudes, Quiara Alegría. *Welcome to my neighborhood!*
Isadora, Rachel. *Say hello!*
King, Dedie. *I see the sun in Afghanistan*
Ljungkvist, Laura. *Pepi sings a new song*
Pinkwater, Daniel. *Beautiful Yetta*
Price, Mara. *Grandma's chocolate / El chocolate de Abuelita*
Sacre, Antonio. *A mango in the hand*
Vamos, Samantha R. *The cazuela that the farm maiden stirred*
Velasquez, Eric. *Grandma's gift*
Wu, Faye-Lynn. *Chinese and English nursery rhymes*
Yeh, Kat. *The magic brush*

Forest, woods

Gershator, Phillis. *Who's in the forest?*
Gore, Leonid. *The wonderful book*
Grimm, Jacob. *Hansel and Gretel*

Format, unusual

Baeten, Lieve. *The curious little witch*
Budnitz, Paul. *The hole in the middle*
Capucilli, Alyssa Satin. *My first soccer game*
Chedru, Delphine. *Spot it again!*
Franceschelli, Christopher. *(Oliver)*
Gibbs, Edward. *I spy with my little eye*
Gore, Leonid. *Worms for lunch?*
Johnson, D. B. *Palazzo inverso*
Long, Ethan. *The book that Zack wrote*
Loth, Sebastian. *Clementine*
Marx, Trish. *Kindergarten day USA and China*
Nelson-Schmidt, Michelle. *Cats, cats!*
    Dogs, dogs!
Olson-Brown, Ellen. *Ooh la la polka-dot boots*
Siminovich, Lorena. *I like vegetables*
Taback, Simms. *Postcards from camp*
Tullet, Hervé. *The book with a hole*
    Press here
Ziefert, Harriet. *Counting chickens*

Format, unusual – board books

American babies
Animal I spy

Animal 123
Basher, Simon. *Go! Go! Bobo*
Beaton, Clare. *Clare Beaton's action rhymes*
    Clare Beaton's nursery rhymes
Boelts, Maribeth. *Sweet dreams, little bunny!*
Bolam, Emily. *Animals talk*
    I go potty
Callery, Sean. *Hide and seek in the jungle*
Dahl, Michael. *Nap time for Kitty*
Emberley, Ed. *Where's my sweetie pie?*
Five little pumpkins
Formento, Alison. *This tree, 1, 2, 3*
Hop a little, jump a little!
Janovitz, Marilyn. *Baby, baby, baby!*
Katz, Susan B. *ABC, baby me!*
Kim, Sue. *How does a seed grow?*
Logan, Bob. *Rocket town*
Look at me!
Mother Goose. *Humpty Dumpty*
    Pat-a-cake
My big book of trucks and diggers
My new baby
Penn, Audrey. *A bedtime kiss for Chester Raccoon*
Salzano, Tammi. *One rainy day*
Siminovich, Lorena. *I like bugs*
Slegers, Liesbet. *Funny ears*
    Funny feet
    Funny tails
    Playing
Verdick, Elizabeth. *On-the-go time*
Waiting for baby
Yoon, Salina. *At the beach*
You and me
Ziefert, Harriet. *Wiggle like an octopus*

Format, unusual – toy & movable books

Baeten, Lieve. *Happy birthday, Little Witch!*
Baker, Jeannie. *Mirror*
Barry, Frances. *Let's look at dinosaurs*
    Let's save the animals
Bernhard, Durga. *While you are sleeping*
Capucilli, Alyssa Satin. *My first ballet class*
Comden, Betty. *What's new at the zoo?*
Cousins, Lucy. *Maisy's amazing big book of learning*
    Maisy's book of things that go
Crowther, Robert. *Amazing pop-up trucks*
Drehsen, Britta. *Flip-o-storic*
Emberley, Ed. *Where's my sweetie pie?*
Foley, Greg. *I miss you Mouse*
Friedman, Caitlin. *How do you feed a hungry giant?*
Gravett, Emily. *The rabbit problem*
Green, Dan. *Wild alphabet*
Hacohen, Dean. *Tuck me in!*
Hamilton, Libby. *The monstrous book of monsters*
Lewin, Betsy. *Where is Tippy Toes?*
Lewis, Anne Margaret. *What am I? Christmas*
MacDonald, Suse. *Circus opposites*
Martin, Ruth. *Santa's on his way*
Merlin, Christophe. *Under the hood*
Mitton, Tony. *Rumble, roar, dinosaur!*
Parot, Annelore. *Kimonos*
Perrin, Martine. *Look who's there!*
Pittau, Francisco. *Out of sight*
Rayner, Catherine. *Ernest, the moose who doesn't fit*
Reasoner, Charles. *One blue fish*
Reinhart, Matthew. *Gods and heroes*
Rosen, Michael J. *Chanukah lights*
Sabuda, Robert. *Beauty and the beast*

Safran, Sheri. *All kinds of families*
Saltzberg, Barney. *Kisses*
Santoro, Lucio. *Wild oceans*
Schwarz, Viviane. *There are no cats in this book*
Seder, Rufus Butler. *The Wizard of Oz*
Sharratt, Nick. *What's in the witch's kitchen?*
Shea, Susan A. *Do you know which one will grow?*
Steele, Philip. *Trains*
Stickland, Paul. *A number of dinosaurs*
Stileman, Kali. *Roly-poly egg*
Taback, Simms. *Simms Taback's farm animals*
Van Fleet, Matthew. *Heads*
    Moo
Wing, Natasha. *How to raise a dinosaur*

Fortune *see* Character traits – luck

Fourth of July *see* Holidays – Fourth of July

Foxes *see* Animals – foxes

France *see* Foreign lands – France

Freedom *see* Character traits – freedom

Friendship

Adams, Sarah. *Dave and Violet*
    Gary and Ray
Al Abdullah, Rania. *The sandwich swap*
Armstrong, Matthew S. *Jane and Mizmow*
Bailey, Linda. *Stanley's little sister*
Battersby, Katherine. *Squish Rabbit*
Becker, Bonny. *A bedtime for Bear*
    The sniffles for Bear
Bendall-Brunello, Tiziana. *I wish I could read!*
Berger, Carin. *Forever friends*
Blackaby, Susan. *Brownie Groundhog and the*
    February Fox
Blake, Robert J. *Painter and Ugly*
Bloom, Suzanne. *What about Bear?*
Bonwill, Ann. *Bug and Bear*
Brown, Peter. *You will be my friend!*
Bruins, David. *The call of the cowboy*
Brun-Cosme, Nadine. *Big Wolf and Little Wolf, such*
    a beautiful orange!
Budnitz, Paul. *The hole in the middle*
Child, Lauren. *My best, best friend*
Cohen, Caron Lee. *Broom, zoom!*
Corderoy, Tracey. *The little white owl*
Côté, Geneviève. *Without you*
Cousins, Lucy. *I'm the best*
Coyle, Carmela LaVigna. *Do princesses have best*
    friends forever?
Cuyler, Margery. *I repeat, don't cheat!*
Davis, Anne. *No dogs allowed!*
DeRubertis, Barbara. *Corky Cub's crazy caps*
Dewdney, Anna. *Roly Poly pangolin*
Elliot, Laura Malone. *A string of hearts*
Esbaum, Jill. *Tom's tweet*
Fagan, Cary. *Ella May and the wishing stone*
Fearnley, Jan. *Arthur and the meanies*
Foley, Greg. *I miss you Mouse*

Garland, Sarah. *Eddie's toolbox and how to make and*
    mend things
Genechten, Guido van. *Because you are my friend*
Gleeson, Libby. *Clancy and Millie and the very fine*
    house
Gray, Luli. *Ant and Grasshopper*
Grey, Mini. *Three by the sea*
Harper, Charise Mericle. *Cupcake*
Harris, Trudy. *Tally cat keeps track*
Hopkins, Lee Bennett. *Full moon and star*
Horowitz, Dave. *Buy my hats!*
Jahn-Clough, Lisa. *Felicity and Cordelia*
Janni, Rebecca. *Every cowgirl needs dancing boots*
Javaherbin, Mina. *Goal!*
Jeffers, Oliver. *Up and down*
Jocelyn, Marthe. *Ones and twos*
Joosse, Barbara. *Friends (mostly)*
Jules, Jacqueline. *Picnic at Camp Shalom*
Jurmain, Suzanne Tripp. *Worst of friends*
King, Stephen Michael. *You*
Kirk, Daniel. *Library mouse*
Kirsch, Vincent X. *Forsythia and me*
Kleven, Elisa. *The friendship wish*
    Welcome home, Mouse
Kochan, Vera. *What if your best friend were blue?*
Kolanovic, Dubravka. *Everyone needs a friend*
Korda, Lerryn. *Into the wild*
    It's vacation time
Kostecki-Shaw, Jenny Sue. *Same, same but different*
LaReau, Kara. *Mr. Prickles*
Lerch. *Swim! swim!*
Light, Steve. *The Christmas giant*
Long, Ethan. *Bird and Birdie in a fine day*
Ludwig, Trudy. *Better than you*
McCue, Lisa. *Quiet Bunny and Noisy Puppy*
Macdonald, Maryann. *The pink party*
McGhee, Alison. *Making a friend*
McPhail, David. *Waddles*
Moss, Peggy. *One of us*
Moulton, Mark Kimball. *The very best pumpkin*
Nelson, Marilyn. *Snook alone*
Numeroff, Laura. *The Jellybeans and the big book*
    bonanza
    The Jellybeans and the big camp kickoff
    Otis and Sydney and the best birthday ever
Oldland, Nicholas. *Making the moose out of life*
Palatini, Margie. *Stuff*
Rawlinson, Julia. *Fletcher and the snowflake*
    Christmas
Rayner, Catherine. *The bear who shared*
    Solomon Crocodile
Reynolds, Peter H. *I'm here*
Ritz, Karen. *Windows with birds*
Rodriguez, Béatrice. *Fox and hen together*
Rumford, James. *Tiger and turtle*
Runton, Andy. *Owly and Wormy*
Russell, Natalie. *Brown Rabbit in the city*
Russo, Marisabina. *A very big bunny*
Ruzzier, Sergio. *Hey, rabbit!*
Ryan, Candace. *Ribbit rabbit*
Scanlon, Liz Garton. *Noodle and Lou*
Schaefer, Lola. *Frankie Stein starts school*
Scheffler, Axel. *The super scooter*
Scotton, Rob. *Splish, splash, Splat!*
Seeger, Laura Vaccaro. *What if?*
Shields, Gillian. *Library Lily*
Smallcomb, Pam. *I'm not*
Soman, David. *Ladybug Girl and the Bug Squad*

Sperring, Mark. *The sunflower sword*
Thimmesh, Catherine. *Friends*
Thomas, Shelley Moore. *A Good Knight's rest*
Twohy, Mike. *Poindexter makes a friend*
Urdahl, Catherine. *Polka-dot fixes kindergarten*
van Lieshout, Maria. *Hopper and Wilson*
Willems, Mo. *City dog, country frog*
Wishinsky, Frieda. *You're mean, Lily Jean!*
Ziefert, Harriet. *Bunny's lessons*

Frogs & toads

Downing, Johnette. *There was an old lady who swallowed some bugs*
Fitzsimmons, David. *Curious critters*
Gardner, Carol. *Princess Zelda and the frog*
Hassett, Ann. *Too many frogs!*
Kimura, Ken. *999 tadpoles*
Little old lady who swallowed a fly. *There was an old monkey who swallowed a frog*
London, Jonathan. *Froggy goes to Hawaii*
Long, Ethan. *The croaky pokey!*
McLeod, Heather. *Kiss me!*
Markle, Sandra. *Hip-pocket papa*
Ryan, Candace. *Ribbit rabbit*
Stewart, Melissa. *A place for frogs*
Thompson, Lauren. *Leap back home to me*
Willems, Mo. *City dog, country frog*
Young, Amy. *The mud fairy*

Furniture – beds

Root, Phyllis. *Creak! said the bed*

Games

Agee, Jon. *Mr. Putney's quacking dog*
Beaton, Clare. *Clare Beaton's action rhymes*
Krilanovich, Nadia. *Chicken, chicken, duck!*
Kroll, Steven. *The Tyrannosaurus game*

Gangs *see* Clubs, gangs

Garbage collectors *see* Careers – sanitation workers

Gardens, gardening

Castellucci, Cecil. *Grandma's gloves*
Donaldson, Julia. *One mole digging a hole*
Fine, Edith Hope. *Water, weed, and wait*
French, Vivian. *Yucky worms*
Glaser, Linda. *Garbage helps our garden grow*
Gourley, Robbin. *First garden*
Grigsby, Susan. *In the garden with Dr. Carver*

Helmore, Jim. *Oh no, monster tomato!*
Henkes, Kevin. *My garden*
Hodge, Deborah. *Watch me grow!*
Hruby, Emily. *Counting in the garden*
Marshall, Linda Elovitz. *Talia and the rude vegetables*
Matthies, Janna. *The goodbye cancer garden*
Middleton, Charlotte. *Nibbles*
Milway, Katie Smith. *The good garden*
Mortimer, Anne. *Pumpkin cat*
Moulton, Mark Kimball. *The very best pumpkin*
Peterson, Cris. *Seed soil sun*
Say, Allen. *The boy in the garden*
Siminovich, Lorena. *I like vegetables*
Smith, Lane. *Grandpa Green*
Thurman, Kathryn K. *A garden for Pig*
Voake, Steve. *Insect detective*
Wallace, Nancy Elizabeth. *Planting seeds*
White, Linda. *Too many turkeys*
Wood, Douglas. *Aunt Mary's rose*
Wortche, Allison. *Rosie Sprout's time to shine*

Geese *see* Birds – geese

Gender roles

Brown, Tami Lewis. *Soar, Elinor!*
Browning, Diane. *Signed, Abiah Rose*
Codell, Esmé Raji. *The basket ball*
Gerber, Carole. *Annie Jump Cannon, astronomer*
Kilodavis, Cheryl. *My princess boy*
Landman, Tanya. *Mary's penny*
Vernick, Audrey. *She loved baseball*
Yolen, Jane. *Not all princesses dress in pink*

Generosity *see* Character traits – generosity

Geography

Jackson, Ellen. *The seven seas*

Germany *see* Foreign lands – Germany

Ghana *see* Foreign lands – Ghana

Ghosts

Baehr, Patricia. *Boo Cow*
Fenton, Joe. *Boo!*
LaRochelle, David. *The haunted hamburger and other ghostly stories*
Muth, Jon J. *Zen ghosts*
Ross, Tony. *I want my light on!*

Giants

Braun, Eric. *Trust me, Jack's beanstalk stinks*
Bunting, Eve. *Finn McCool and the great fish*
Friedman, Caitlin. *How do you feed a hungry giant?*
Hawkes, Kevin. *The wicked big toddlah goes to New York*
Jack and the beanstalk. *Jack and the beanstalk Jacques and de beanstalk*
Klise, Kate. *Stand straight, Ella Kate*
Light, Steve. *The Christmas giant*

Gifts

Blackwood, Freya. *Ivy loves to give*
DePalma, Mary Newell. *The perfect gift*
Dunrea, Olivier. *A Christmas tree for Pyn*
Gorbachev, Valeri. *What's the big idea, Molly?*
Krensky, Stephen. *Mother's Day surprise*
McGinley, Phyllis. *The year without a Santa Claus*
Mair, Samia J. *The perfect gift*
Meddaugh, Susan. *Martha says it with flowers*
Price, Mara. *Grandma's chocolate / El chocolate de Abuelita*
Velasquez, Eric. *Grandma's gift*
Wells, Rosemary. *Yoko's show-and-tell*

Giraffes *see* Animals – giraffes

Glasses

Calvert, Pam. *Princess Peepers picks a pet*

Gloves *see* Clothing – gloves, mittens

Goats *see* Animals – goats

Gorillas *see* Animals – gorillas

Gossip *see* Behavior – gossip

Grammar *see* Language

Grasshoppers *see* Insects – grasshoppers

Greece *see* Foreign lands – Greece

Greed *see* Behavior – greed

Grief *see* Emotions – grief

Groundhog Day *see* Holidays – Groundhog Day

Groundhogs *see* Animals – groundhogs

Growing up *see* Behavior – growing up

Guinea pigs *see* Animals – guinea pigs

Gypsies

Pinfold, Levi. *The Django*

Habits *see* Thumb sucking

Hair

Fox, Lee. *Ella Kazoo will not brush her hair*
Grimm, Jacob. *Rapunzel*
Hilton, Perez. *The boy with pink hair*
Hosford, Kate. *Big bouffant*
Krull, Kathleen. *Big wig*
Langen, Annette. *I won't comb my hair!*
Tuck, Justin. *Home-field advantage*
Villnave, Erica Pelton. *Sophie's lovely locks*

Haiti *see* Foreign lands – Haiti

Halloween *see* Holidays – Halloween

Hamsters *see* Animals – hamsters

Handbags *see* Clothing – handbags, purses

Handicaps

Lester, Helen. *Wodney Wat's wobot*
Polacco, Patricia. *The junkyard wonders*

Handicaps – autism

Amenta, Charles A., III. *Russell's world*
Lehman-Wilzig, Tami. *Nathan blows out the Hanukkah candles*
Peete, Holly Robinson. *My brother Charlie*
Reynolds, Peter H. *I'm here*

Handicaps – blindness

Goldin, Barbara Diamond. *Cakes and miracles*

Handicaps – deafness

Domney, Alexis. *Splish, splat!*
Nijssen, Elfi. *Laurie*

Handicaps – physical handicaps

Elliott, Rebecca. *Just because*
Hudson, Cheryl Willis. *My friend Maya loves to dance*
Moore, Genevieve. *Catherine's story*

Hands *see* Anatomy – hands

Hanukkah *see* Holidays – Hanukkah

Happiness *see* Emotions – happiness

Hares *see* Animals – rabbits

Hats *see* Clothing – hats

Hawaii

London, Jonathan. *Froggy goes to Hawaii*

Hawks *see* Birds – hawks

Health & fitness

Bunting, Eve. *My dog Jack is fat*
Butterworth, Chris. *How did that get in my lunchbox?*
Harper, Charise Mericle. *Henry's heart*

Health & fitness – exercise

Spinelli, Eileen. *Miss Fox's class shapes up*

Heavy equipment *see* Machines

Hedgehogs *see* Animals – hedgehogs

Helpfulness *see* Character traits – helpfulness

Hens *see* Birds – chickens

Herons *see* Birds – herons

Hibernation

Gerber, Carole. *Little red bat*
Helquist, Brett. *Bedtime for Bear*
Meadows, Michelle. *Hibernation station*
Messner, Kate. *Over and under the snow*
Rueda, Claudia. *No*

Hiding *see* Behavior – hiding

Hiding things *see* Behavior – hiding things

Himalayas *see* Foreign lands – Himalayas

Hippopotamuses *see* Animals – hippopotamuses

Hispanic Americans *see* Ethnic groups in the U.S. – Hispanic Americans

Hockey *see* Sports – hockey

Hogs *see* Animals – pigs

Holidays

dePaola, Tomie. *Strega Nona's gift*
Elya, Susan Middleton. *A year full of holidays*
Galbraith, Kathryn O. *Arbor Day square*
Lin, Grace. *Thanking the moon*
Mair, Samia J. *The perfect gift*

Holidays – April Fools' Day

Hill, Susanna Leonard. *April Fool, Phyllis!*
Morton, Carlene. *The library pages*

Holidays – Chanukah *see* Holidays – Hanukkah

Holidays – Chinese New Year

Compestine, Ying Chang. *Crouching tiger*
The runaway wok
Yu, Li-Qiong. *A New Year's reunion*

Holidays – Christmas

Bastianich, Lidia. *Nonna tell me a story*
Bastin, Marjolein. *Christmas with Vera*
Bible. New Testament. Gospels. *The story of Christmas*
Brett, Jan. *Home for Christmas*
Bruel, Nick. *A Bad Kitty Christmas*
Buck, Nola. *A Christmas goodnight*
Buzzeo, Toni. *Lighthouse Christmas*
Cole, Brock. *The money we'll save*
Cole, Henry. *The littlest evergreen*
Cushman, Doug. *Christmas Eve good night*
Dunrea, Olivier. *A Christmas tree for Pyn*
Hoffman, Mary. *Grace at Christmas*
Hoffmann, E. T. A. *The nutcracker*
House, Catherine. *A stork in a baobab tree*
Hughes, Shirley. *The Christmas Eve ghost*
Lester, Helen. *Tacky's Christmas*
Lewis, Anne Margaret. *What am I? Christmas*
Light, Steve. *The Christmas giant*
Lloyd-Jones, Sally. *Song of the stars*
McGinley, Phyllis. *The year without a Santa Claus*
McKee, David. *Elmer's Christmas*
Martin, David. *Little Bunny and the magic Christmas tree*
Martin, Ruth. *Santa's on his way*
Milgrim, David. *Santa Duck and his merry helpers*
Moore, Clement Clarke. *'Twas the night before Christmas*
Noble, Trinka Hakes. *A Christmas spider's miracle*
Park, Linda Sue. *The third gift*
Pulver, Robin. *Christmas kitten, home at last*
Rawlinson, Julia. *Fletcher and the snowflake Christmas*
Rees, Douglas. *Jeannette Claus saves Christmas*
Sacre, Antonio. *La Noche Buena*
Slegers, Liesbet. *The child in the manger*

Spinelli, Eileen. *The perfect Christmas*
Thompson, Lauren. *One starry night*
The twelve days of Christmas. English folk song.
    Twelve days of Christmas
    The twelve days of Christmas, ill. by Jane Ray
    The twelve days of Christmas, ill. by Laurel Long
Velasquez, Eric. *Grandma's gift*
Yolen, Jane. *Sister Bear*

Holidays – Cinco de Mayo

Cox, Judy. *Cinco de Mouse-o!*

Holidays – Day of the Dead

Barner, Bob. *The Day of the Dead / El Día de los Muertos*

Holidays – Earth Day

deGroat, Diane. *Ants in your pants, worms in your plants!*

Holidays – Easter

Brett, Jan. *The Easter egg*
Dunrea, Olivier. *Ollie's Easter eggs*
Hulme, Joy N. *Easter babies*
Mackall, Dandi Daley. *The story of the Easter robin*
Marciano, John Bemelmans. *Madeline at the White House*
Mortimer, Anne. *Bunny's Easter egg*
Rand, Betseygail. *Big Bunny*
Schulman, Janet. *10 Easter egg hunters*
Stalder, Päivi. *Ernest's first Easter*
Vainio, Pirkko. *Who hid the Easter eggs?*

Holidays – Fourth of July

Malnor, Carol L. *The Blues go birding across America*

Holidays – Groundhog Day

Blackaby, Susan. *Brownie Groundhog and the February Fox*

Holidays – Halloween

Brimner, Larry Dane. *Trick or treat, Old Armadillo*
Brokamp, Elizabeth. *The picky little witch*
Brown, Lisa. *Vampire boy's good night*
Christian, Cheryl. *Witches*
Cox, Judy. *Haunted house, haunted mouse*
Cushman, Doug. *Halloween good night*
Day, Nancy Raines. *On a windy night*
de Las Casas, Dianne. *The house that Witchy built*
Demas, Corinne. *Halloween surprise*
Dunrea, Olivier. *Ollie's Halloween*
Five little pumpkins
Fraser, Mary Ann. *Heebie-Jeebie Jamboree*
Grogan, John. *Trick or treat, Marley!*
Jane, Pamela. *Little goblins ten*
Kontis, Alethea. *AlphaOops!*
Montijo, Rhode. *The Halloween Kid*
Mortimer, Anne. *Pumpkin cat*
Muth, Jon J. *Zen ghosts*
Pamintuan, Macky. *Twelve haunted rooms of Halloween*
Rockwell, Anne. *Apples and pumpkins*
Rohmann, Eric. *Bone dog*

Rosen, Michael J. *Night of the pumpkinheads*
Thomas, Jan. *Pumpkin trouble*
Vasilovich, Guy. *The 13 nights of Halloween*

Holidays – Hanukkah

Adler, David A. *The story of Hanukkah*
Edwards, Michelle. *The Hanukkah trike*
Lehman-Wilzig, Tami. *Nathan blows out the Hanukkah candles*
Melmed, Laura Krauss. *Eight winter nights*
Rosen, Michael J. *Chanukah lights*
Silverman, Erica. *The Hanukkah hop!*

Holidays – Independence Day *see* Holidays – Fourth of July

Holidays – Kwanzaa

Washington, Donna L. *Li'l Rabbit's Kwanzaa*

Holidays – Mother's Day

Krensky, Stephen. *Mother's Day surprise*

Holidays – New Year's

Miller, Pat. *Squirrel's New Year's resolution*

Holidays – Passover

Glaser, Linda. *Hoppy Passover!*
The little red hen. *The Little Red Hen and the Passover matzah*
Portnoy, Mindy Avra. *A tale of two seders*

Holidays – Purim

Goldin, Barbara Diamond. *Cakes and miracles*

Holidays – Ramadan

Gilani-Williams, Fawzia. *Nabeel's new pants*
Jalali, Reza. *Moon watchers*

Holidays – Rosh Hashanah

Marshall, Linda Elovitz. *Talia and the rude vegetables*
Schnur, Susan. *Tashlich at Turtle Rock*

Holidays – St. Patrick's Day

Rockwell, Anne. *St. Patrick's Day*

Holidays – Sukkot

Korngold, Jamie S. *Sadie's sukkah breakfast*

Holidays – Thanksgiving

Child, Lydia Maria. *Over the river and through the wood*

Holidays – Valentine's Day

Choldenko, Gennifer. *A giant crush*
Elliot, Laura Malone. *A string of hearts*
Friedman, Laurie. *Ruby Valentine saves the day*
Petersen, David. *Snowy Valentine*

Schulman, Janet. *10 Valentine friends*
Sutton, Benn. *Hedgehug*

Holocaust

Russo, Marisabina. *I will come back for you*
Ungerer, Tomi. *Otto*
Wiviott, Meg. *Benno and the night of broken glass*

Homeless

Barrett, Mary Brigid. *Shoebox Sam*
Bromley, Anne C. *The lunch thief*
Williams, Laura E. *The can man*

Homes, houses

Brett, Jan. *The three little dassies*
Deacon, Alexis. *A place to call home*
Falkenstern, Lisa. *A dragon moves in*
Foley, Greg. *Purple little bird*
Gleeson, Libby. *Clancy and Millie and the very fine house*
Kelly, Irene. *Even an octopus needs a home*
Kleven, Elisa. *Welcome home, Mouse*
Laroche, Giles. *If you lived here*
Moore, Inga. *A house in the woods*
Orloff, Karen Kaufman. *I wanna new room*
Ritz, Karen. *Windows with birds*
Siegel, Mark. *Moving house*
Smith, Linda. *The inside tree*
The tree house

Homework

Cook, Lisa Broadie. *Peanut butter and homework sandwiches*

Homosexuality

Newman, Lesléa. *Donovan's big day*
Oelschlager, Vanita. *A tale of two daddies*
A tale of two mommies

Honduras *see* Foreign lands – Honduras

Honesty *see* Character traits – honesty

Honey bees *see* Insects – bees

Hope

Cocca-Leffler, Maryann. *Rain brings frogs*
Watson, Jesse Joshua. *Hope for Haiti*

Horses *see* Animals – horses, ponies

Houses *see* Homes, houses

Hugging

Bond, Felicia. *Big hugs, little hugs*
Church, Caroline Jayne. *One more hug for Madison*
Isop, Laurie. *How do you hug a porcupine?*
Macdonald, Maryann. *How to hug*
Melling, David. *Hugless Douglas*

Schmid, Paul. *Hugs from Pearl*
Sutton, Benn. *Hedgehug*

Hummingbirds *see* Birds – hummingbirds

Humor

Diesen, Deborah. *The barefooted, bad-tempered baby brigade*

Humorous stories

Andersen, Hans Christian. *The emperor's new clothes*
Asch, Frank. *The Daily Comet*
Bardhan-Quallen, Sudipta. *Hampire!*
Barnett, Mac. *Extra yarn*
   Oh no!
Black, Michael Ian. *A pig parade is a terrible idea*
   The purple kangaroo
Bloch, Serge. *You are what you eat*
Braun, Eric. *Trust me, Jack's beanstalk stinks*
Brown, Peter. *Children make terrible pets*
Chaconas, Dori. *Don't slam the door!*
Christelow, Eileen. *The desperate dog writes again*
Coffelt, Nancy. *Catch that baby!*
Cronin, Doreen. *M.O.M. (Mom Operating Manual)*
Czekaj, Jef. *A call for a new alphabet*
   Cat secrets
DiPucchio, Kelly. *Zombie in love*
Edwards, Pamela Duncan. *Princess Pigtoria and the pea*
Ehlert, Lois. *Rrralph*
Harper, Lee. *The Emperor's cool clothes*
Hawkes, Kevin. *The wicked big toddlah goes to New York*
Heide, Florence Parry. *Always listen to your mother*
Himmelman, John. *Cows to the rescue*
Huget, Jennifer LaRue. *How to clean your room in 10 easy steps*
Jeffers, Oliver. *Stuck*
Jennings, Sharon. *C'mere, boy!*
Könnecke, Ole. *Anton can do magic*
LaReau, Kara. *Otto*
Lewis, Kevin. *Not inside this house!*
Lichtenheld, Tom. *E-mergency!*
Lucke, Deb. *Sneezenesia*
McAllister, Angela. *My mom has x-ray vision*
McNamara, Margaret. *The three little aliens and the big bad robot*
Metzger, Steve. *Detective Blue*
Milgrim, David. *Eddie gets ready for school*
Nesbitt, Kenn. *More bears!*
O'Malley, Kevin. *Animal crackers fly the coop*
Parish, Herman. *Amelia Bedelia's first apple pie*
   Amelia Bedelia's first field trip
   Go west, Amelia Bedelia!
Perl, Erica S. *Chicken Butt's back!*
Pinkwater, Daniel. *I am the dog*
Plourde, Lynn. *Only cows allowed!*
Primavera, Elise. *Thumb love*
Rausch, Molly. *My cold went on vacation*
Rex, Michael. *Furious George goes bananas*
Robinson, Fiona. *What animals really like*
Shaskan, Trisha Speed. *Seriously, Cinderella is so annoying!*
Sierra, Judy. *Tell the truth, B.B. Wolf*
Smith, Alex T. *Foxy and Egg*
Smith, Lane. *It's a book*
Smith, Linda. *The inside tree*

Solheim, James. *Born yesterday*
Stein, David Ezra. *Interrupting chicken*
Stevens, Janet. *The little red pen*
Stuchner, Joan Betty. *Can hens give milk?*
Taxali, Gary. *This is silly!*
Taylor, Sean. *The ring went zing!*
Thomas, Jan. *Is everyone ready for fun?*
Willis, Jeanne. *That's not funny!*

Hurricanes *see* Weather – hurricanes

Hyenas *see* Animals – hyenas

Hygiene

Brennan, Eileen. *Dirtball Pete*
Fox, Lee. *Ella Kazoo will not brush her hair*
Vestergaard, Hope. *Potty animals*

Ice skating *see* Sports – ice skating

Identity *see* Self-concept

Illness

Dewdney, Anna. *Llama Llama home with Mama*
Ketteman, Helen. *If Beaver had a fever*
Modarressi, Mitra. *Taking care of Mama*
Peet, Mal. *Cloud tea monkeys*
Ray, Jane. *The dollhouse fairy*
Rees, Douglas. *Jeannette Claus saves Christmas*
Rose, Naomi C. *Tashi and the Tibetan flower cure*
Schubert, Leda. *The Princess of Borscht*
Stead, Philip C. *A sick day for Amos McGee*

Illness – allergies

Pulver, Robin. *Christmas kitten, home at last*

Illness – cancer

Clark, Julie Aigner. *You are the best medicine*
Matthies, Janna. *The goodbye cancer garden*
North, Sherry. *Champ's story*

Illness – cold (disease)

Becker, Bonny. *The sniffles for Bear*
Rausch, Molly. *My cold went on vacation*

Imaginary friends *see* Imagination –
    imaginary friends

Imagination

Alko, Selina. *Every-day dress-up*
Allen, Joy. *Princess Palooza*
Andersen, Hans Christian. *The emperor's new clothes*
Banks, Kate. *The eraserheads*
    Max's castle
Barnett, Mac. *Extra yarn*
Base, Graeme. *The legend of the Golden Snail*
Bently, Peter. *King Jack and the dragon*
Black, Michael Ian. *The purple kangaroo*
Bloom, Suzanne. *Feeding friendsies*
Bunting, Eve. *Pirate boy*
Chin, Jason. *Coral reefs*
Daly, Cathleen. *Prudence wants a pet*
Devernay, Laetitia. *The conductor*
Gammell, Stephen. *Mudkin*
Gibala-Broxholm, Scott. *Maddie's monster dad*
Gleeson, Libby. *Clancy and Millie and the very fine
    house*
Harper, Charise Mericle. *The best birthday ever!*
Harper, Jamie. *Miles to go*
Henkes, Kevin. *Little white rabbit*
    My garden
Hines, Anna Grossnickle. *I am a backhoe*
    I am a Tyrannosaurus
Hoffmann, E. T. A. *The nutcracker*
Husband, Amy. *Dear teacher*
Ichikawa, Satomi. *My little train*
Jackson, Ellen. *The seven seas*
Janni, Rebecca. *Every cowgirl needs a horse*
Jarka, Jeff. *Love that kitty!*
Johnson, Angela. *Lottie Paris lives here*
Joyce, William. *The Man in the Moon*
Kirk, Daniel. *Honk honk! Beep beep!*
Kroll, Steven. *The Tyrannosaurus game*
Landa, Norbert. *The great monster hunt*
Larochelle, David. *1+1=5*
Lawson, Dorie McCullough. *Tex*
Lee, Suzy. *Shadow*
Lehman, Barbara. *The secret box*
Liwska, Renata. *Red wagon*
McQuinn, Anna. *Lola loves stories*
Melanson, Luc. *Topsy-Turvy Town*
Menchin, Scott. *What if everything had legs?*
Moore, Jodi. *When a dragon moves in*
Na, Il Sung. *The thingamabob*
Niemann, Christoph. *That's how!*
Orr, Wendy. *The princess and her panther*
Parkhurst, Carolyn. *Cooking with Henry and
    Elliebelly*
Plecas, Jennifer. *Pretend*
Portis, Antoinette. *Princess Super Kitty*
Raschka, Chris. *Little black crow*
Reidy, Jean. *Light up the night*
Roberts, Victoria. *The best pet ever*
Ruzzier, Sergio. *Hey, rabbit!*
Segal, John. *Pirates don't take baths*
Sheridan, Sara. *I'm me!*
Sís, Peter. *Madlenka, soccer star*
Slate, Jenny. *Marcel the shell with shoes on*
Soman, David. *The amazing adventures of Bumblebee
    Boy*
    Ladybug Girl and the Bug Squad
Tompert, Ann. *Little Fox goes to the end of the world*
Tullet, Hervé. *The book with a hole*
    Press here

Tusa, Tricia. *Follow me*
Van Camp, Katie. *CookieBot!*
Wadham, Tim. *The queen of France*
Weitzman, Jacqueline Preiss. *Superhero Joe*
White, Kathryn. *Ruby's school walk*
Young, Cybèle. *A few blocks*
Young, Ned. *Zoomer*
    Zoomer's summer snowstorm
Yum, Hyewon. *There are no scary wolves*

Imagination – imaginary friends

Perl, Erica S. *Dotty*
Pinfold, Levi. *The Django*
Rosenberg, Liz. *Nobody*

Imitation *see* Behavior – imitation

Immigrants

Colato Laínez, René. *My shoes and I*
Yaccarino, Dan. *All the way to America*

Indecision *see* Behavior – indecision

Independence Day *see* Holidays – Fourth of
    July

India *see* Foreign lands – India

Indians of Central America – Maya

Price, Mara. *Grandma's chocolate / El chocolate de
    Abuelita*

Indians of North America

Perrow, Angeli. *Many hands*

Indians of North America – Aztec

de Las Casas, Dianne. *Blue frog*

Indians of North America – Shoshone

Napoli, Donna Jo. *The crossing*

Individuality *see* Character traits – individuality

Indonesia *see* Foreign lands – Indonesia

Insects

Biedrzycki, David. *Ace Lacewing, bug detective*
Bonwill, Ann. *Bug and Bear*
Cyrus, Kurt. *Big rig bugs*
Dodd, Emma. *I love bugs!*
Downing, Johnette. *There was an old lady who
    swallowed some bugs*
Glaser, Linda. *Not a buzz to be found*
Hector, Julian. *The gentleman bug*
Salzano, Tammi. *One little blueberry*
Siminovich, Lorena. *I like bugs*

Voake, Steve. *Insect detective*

Insects – ants

Gray, Luli. *Ant and Grasshopper*

Insects – bees

Frazier, Craig. *Bee and bird*
Hopkinson, Deborah. *The humblebee hunter*
Morales, Melita. *Jam and honey*
Nargi, Lela. *The honeybee man*
Roode, Daniel. *Little Bea and the snowy day*
Rotner, Shelley. *The buzz on bees*
Spinelli, Eileen. *Buzz*

Insects – butterflies, caterpillars

Aston, Dianna Hutts. *A butterfly is patient*
Engle, Margarita. *Summer birds*
Markle, Sandra. *Butterfly tree*
Martin, Bill, Jr. *Ten little caterpillars*
Runton, Andy. *Owly and Wormy*
Singer, Marilyn. *Caterpillars*

Insects – fleas

Marcus, Kimberly. *Scritch-scratch a perfect match*

Insects – flies

Gollub, Matthew. *Jazz Fly 2*
Rosen, Michael. *Tiny little fly*

Insects – grasshoppers

Gray, Luli. *Ant and Grasshopper*

Insects – lady birds *see* Insects – ladybugs

Insects – ladybugs

Donaldson, Julia. *What the ladybug heard*

Inventions

Kulling, Monica. *All aboard!*
Polacco, Patricia. *The junkyard wonders*
Riddell, Chris. *Wendel's workshop*

Inventors *see* Careers – inventors

Iran *see* Foreign lands – Iran

Ireland *see* Foreign lands – Ireland

Israel *see* Foreign lands – Israel

Italian Americans *see* Ethnic groups in the
    U.S. – Italian Americans

Italy *see* Foreign lands – Italy

Janitors *see* Careers – custodians, janitors

Japan *see* Foreign lands – Japan

Jealousy *see* Emotions – envy, jealousy

Jewish culture

Adler, David A. *The story of Hanukkah*
Davis, Aubrey. *Kishka for Koppel*
Edwards, Michelle. *The Hanukkah trike*
Elissa, Barbara. *The remarkable journey of Josh's kippah*
Glaser, Linda. *Hoppy Passover!*
Goldin, Barbara Diamond. *Cakes and miracles*
Heller, Linda. *How Dalia put a big yellow comforter inside a tiny blue box*
Herman, Charlotte. *First rain*
Jules, Jacqueline. *Picnic at Camp Shalom*
Kimmel, Eric A. *Joseph and the Sabbath fish*
Korngold, Jamie S. *Sadie's sukkah breakfast*
Lehman-Wilzig, Tami. *Nathan blows out the Hanukkah candles*
The little red hen. *The Little Red Hen and the Passover matzah*
Melmed, Laura Krauss. *Eight winter nights*
Meltzer, Amy. *The Shabbat Princess*
Russo, Marisabina. *I will come back for you*
Schnur, Susan. *Tashlich at Turtle Rock*
Schubert, Leda. *The Princess of Borscht*
Schwartz, Howard. *Gathering sparks*
Silverman, Erica. *The Hanukkah hop!*
Simhaee, Rebeka. *Sara finds a mitzva*
Snyder, Laurel. *Baxter, the pig who wanted to be kosher*
Stampler, Ann Redisch. *The rooster prince of Breslov*
Stuchner, Joan Betty. *Can hens give milk?*
Ungerer, Tomi. *Otto*
Waldman, Debby. *Room enough for Daisy*
Wiviott, Meg. *Benno and the night of broken glass*

Jobs *see* Careers

Jumping *see* Activities – jumping

Jungle

Balouch, Kristen. *The little little girl with the big big voice*
Broach, Elise. *Gumption!*
Callery, Sean. *Hide and seek in the jungle*

Downing, Johnette. *Amazon alphabet*
Elya, Susan Middleton. *No more, por favor*
Gollub, Matthew. *Jazz Fly 2*
Krebs, Laurie. *We're roaming in the rainforest*
Rosen, Michael. *Tiny little fly*
Slack, Michael. *Monkey truck*
Tierney, Fiona. *Lion's lunch?*

Kenya *see* Foreign lands – Kenya

Kindness *see* Character traits – kindness

Kindness to animals *see* Character traits – kindness to animals

Kings *see* Royalty – kings

Kissing

McLeod, Heather. *Kiss me!*
Monari, Manuela. *Zero kisses for me!*
Rosenthal, Amy Krouse. *Plant a kiss*
Saltzberg, Barney. *Kisses*
Tafuri, Nancy. *All kinds of kisses*
Tarpley, Todd. *How about a kiss for me?*
Verburg, Bonnie. *The kiss box*
Walsh, Joanna. *The biggest kiss*

Kites

Jeffers, Oliver. *Stuck*

Knights

Banks, Kate. *Max's castle*
Sperring, Mark. *The sunflower sword*
Thomas, Shelley Moore. *A Good Knight's rest*

Knitting *see* Activities – knitting

Korean Americans *see* Ethnic groups in the U.S. – Korean Americans

Kwanzaa *see* Holidays – Kwanzaa

Lady birds *see* Insects – ladybugs

Ladybugs *see* Insects – ladybugs

Lakes, ponds

Falwell, Cathryn. *Pond babies*
Quattlebaum, Mary. *Jo MacDonald saw a pond*
Wallace, Nancy Elizabeth. *Pond walk*

Language

Banks, Kate. *Max's castle*
Basher, Simon. *ABC kids*
Berkes, Marianne. *Animalogy*
Bertrand, Diane Gonzales. *The party for Papa Luis / La fiesta para Papa Luis*
Bloch, Serge. *You are what you eat*
Brocket, Jane. *Ruby, violet, lime*
de Lestrade, Agnès. *Phileas's fortune*
Fleming, Denise. *Shout! Shout it out!*
Guy, Ginger Foglesong. *¡Bravo!*
Jenkins, Emily. *Small medium large*
Lawlor, Laurie. *Muddy as a duck puddle and other American similes*
Mortimer, Rachael. *Song for a princess*
O'Connor, Jane. *Fancy Nancy*, ill. by Robin Preiss Glasser
   Fancy Nancy, ill. by Robin Preiss Glasser
   Fancy Nancy and the fabulous fashion boutique
O'Malley, Kevin. *Animal crackers fly the coop*
Parker, Marjorie Blain. *A paddling of ducks*
Perl, Erica S. *Chicken Butt's back!*
Pulver, Robin. *Happy endings*
Rosenthal, Amy Krouse. *Al Pha's bet*
Snicket, Lemony. *13 words*

Language – sign language *see* Sign language

Language, foreign *see* Foreign languages

Laos *see* Foreign lands – Laos

Laziness *see* Character traits – laziness

Leopards *see* Animals – leopards

Leprechauns *see* Mythical creatures – leprechauns

Letters, cards

Christelow, Eileen. *The desperate dog writes again*
Crimi, Carolyn. *Dear Tabby*
Husband, Amy. *Dear teacher*
McClatchy, Lisa. *Dear Tyrannosaurus Rex*
Orloff, Karen Kaufman. *I wanna new room*
Pulver, Robin. *Thank you, Miss Doover*
Stein, David Ezra. *Love, Mouserella*
Taback, Simms. *Postcards from camp*
Teague, Mark. *LaRue across America*
Tonatiuh, Duncan. *Dear Primo*

Librarians *see* Careers – librarians

Libraries

Bottner, Barbara. *Miss Brooks loves books! (and I don't)*
Brown, Monica. *Waiting for the Biblioburro*
Buzzeo, Toni. *No T. Rex in the library*
   Penelope Popper book doctor
Casanova, Mary. *The day Dirk Yeller came to town*
Chapman, Susan Margaret. *Too much noise in the library*
de Las Casas, Dianne. *There's a dragon in the library*
Fox, Kathleen. *The pirates of plagiarism*
The gingerbread boy. *The Library Gingerbread Man*
Houston, Gloria. *Miss Dorothy and her bookmobile*
Hubbell, Patricia. *Check it out!*
King, M. G. *Librarian on the roof!*
Kirk, Daniel. *Library mouse*
Lindbergh, Reeve. *Homer the library cat*
Middleton, Charlotte. *Nibbles*
Morton, Carlene. *The library pages*
Numeroff, Laura. *The Jellybeans and the big book bonanza*
Shea, Bob. *Dinosaur vs. the library*
Shields, Gillian. *Library Lily*
Slegers, Liesbet. *Kevin goes to the library*
Twohy, Mike. *Poindexter makes a friend*
Winter, Jeanette. *Biblioburro*

Light, lights

Hayes, Geoffrey. *The bunny's night-light*
Rocco, John. *Blackout*

Lighthouses

Brown, Ruth. *Gracie the lighthouse cat*
Buzzeo, Toni. *Lighthouse Christmas*
Haas, Rick de. *Peter and the winter sleepers*
Lamb, Albert. *The abandoned lighthouse*

Lions *see* Animals – lions

Littleness *see* Character traits – smallness

Lizards *see* Reptiles – lizards

Llamas *see* Animals – llamas

Loneliness *see* Emotions – loneliness

Loons *see* Birds – loons

Losing things *see* Behavior – lost & found possessions

Lost *see* Behavior – lost

Love *see* Emotions – love

Loyalty *see* Character traits – loyalty

Luck *see* Character traits – luck

Lullabies

de Las Casas, Dianne. *Mama's bayou*
Guthrie, James. *Last song*
Henderson, Kathy. *Hush, baby, hush!*
MacLachlan, Patricia. *Lala salama*
Snyder, Betsy. *Sweet dreams lullaby*

Lumberjacks *see* Careers – lumberjacks

Lying *see* Behavior – lying

Machines

Clement, Nathan. *Job site*
Hines, Anna Grossnickle. *I am a backhoe*
Meltzer, Lynn. *The construction crew*
My big book of trucks and diggers
Niemann, Christoph. *That's how!*

Magic

Base, Graeme. *The Jewel Fish of Karnak*
Bianco, Margery Williams. *The velveteen rabbit*
Brown, Monica. *Chavela and the magic bubble*
Buehner, Caralyn. *Snowmen all year*
Compestine, Ying Chang. *The runaway wok*
dePaola, Tomie. *Strega Nona's gift*
Dodd, Emma. *Meow said the cow*
Grimm, Jacob. *Snow White*
Kimmel, Eric A. *Joha makes a wish*
Könnecke, Ole. *Anton can do magic*
Langdo, Bryan. *Tornado Slim and the magic cowboy hat*
Morrissey, Dean. *The wizard mouse*
Sabuda, Robert. *Beauty and the beast*

Thomson, Bill. *Chalk*
Van Dusen, Chris. *King Hugo's huge ego*

Magicians *see* Careers – magicians

Making things *see* Activities – making things

Mali *see* Foreign lands – Mali

Manatees *see* Animals – manatees

Manners *see* Etiquette

Marionettes *see* Puppets

Markets *see* Stores

Marriages *see* Weddings

Mars *see* Planets

Marsupials *see* Animals – marsupials

Math *see* Counting, numbers

Maya Indians *see* Indians of Central America – Maya

Mazes

Kalz, Jill. *An a-maze-ing amusement park adventure*
An a-maze-ing farm adventure
An a-maze-ing school adventure
An a-maze-ing zoo adventure

Measurement *see* Concepts – measurement

Mechanical men *see* Robots

Mechanics *see* Careers – mechanics

Memories, memory

Garland, Michael. *Grandpa's tractor*
Lucke, Deb. *Sneezenesia*
Lynn, Sarah. *Tip-tap pop*
Nivola, Claire A. *Orani*
Smith, Lane. *Grandpa Green*

Messy *see* Behavior – messy

Metamorphosis

Aston, Dianna Hutts. *A butterfly is patient*
Martin, Bill, Jr. *Ten little caterpillars*

Runton, Andy. *Owly and Wormy*

Mexican Americans *see* Ethnic groups in the U.S. – Mexican Americans

Mexico *see* Foreign lands – Mexico

Mice *see* Animals – mice

Middle Ages

Ashburn, Boni. *Over at the castle*
Kaufman, Jeanne. *Young Henry and the dragon*

Middle East *see* Foreign lands – Middle East

Migration

Berkes, Marianne. *Going home*
Berne, Jennifer. *Calvin can't fly*
Cowcher, Helen. *Desert elephants*
Gerber, Carole. *Little red bat*
Lamstein, Sarah Marwil. *Big night for salamanders*
Markle, Sandra. *Butterfly tree*
Sayre, April Pulley. *Turtle, turtle, watch out!*

Military *see* Careers – military

Mirrors

Baker, Jeannie. *Mirror*
Lee, Suzy. *Mirror*

Misbehavior *see* Behavior – misbehavior

Mistakes *see* Behavior – mistakes

Misunderstanding *see* Behavior – misunderstanding

Mittens *see* Clothing – gloves, mittens

Moles *see* Animals – moles

Money

Child, Lauren. *I really, really need actual ice skates*
Finlay, Lizzie. *Little Croc's purse*
Medina, Meg. *Tía Isa wants a car*
O'Connor, Jane. *Fancy Nancy and the fabulous fashion boutique*
Reid, Margarette S. *Lots and lots of coins*
Warwick, Dionne. *Little Man*

Monkeys *see* Animals – monkeys

Monsters

Armstrong, Matthew S. *Jane and Mizmow*

Burnell, Heather Ayris. *Bedtime monster / ¡A dormir, pequeño monstruo!*
Cohen, Caron Lee. *Broom, zoom!*
Cushman, Doug. *Halloween good night*
DiPucchio, Kelly. *Zombie in love*
Docherty, Thomas. *Big scary monster*
Dormer, Frank W. *Socksquatch*
Dyer, Sarah. *Monster day at work*
Emberley, Rebecca. *If you're a monster and you know it*
    Ten little beasties
Gall, Chris. *Substitute creacher*
Gibala-Broxholm, Scott. *Maddie's monster dad*
Hamilton, Libby. *The monstrous book of monsters*
Jane, Pamela. *Little goblins ten*
Kaplan, Bruce Eric. *Monsters eat whiny children*
Ketteman, Helen. *Goodnight, Little Monster*
McAllister, Angela. *Yuck! That's not a monster*
McElligott, Matthew. *Even monsters need haircuts*
MacHale, D. J. *The monster princess*
Patricelli, Leslie. *The Patterson puppies and the midnight monster party*
Sauer, Tammi. *Mostly monsterly*
Schaefer, Lola. *Frankie Stein starts school*
Yolen, Jane. *Creepy monsters, sleepy monsters*

Monsters – vampires

Bardhan-Quallen, Sudipta. *Hampire!*
Brown, Lisa. *Vampire boy's good night*
Egielski, Richard. *The sleepless little vampire*

Months of the year *see* Days of the week, months of the year

Moon

Brown, Margaret Wise. *Goodnight moon ABC*
Carroll, James Christopher. *The boy and the moon*
Clark, Karen Henry. *Sweet moon baby*
Foley, Greg. *Willoughby and the moon*
Joyce, William. *The Man in the Moon*
Krilanovich, Nadia. *Moon child*
Lin, Grace. *Thanking the moon*
Loth, Sebastian. *Clementine*
Martin, Ruth. *Moon dreams*
Pearce, Clemency. *Frangoline and the midnight dream*

Moose *see* Animals – moose

Mopeds *see* Motorcycles

Morning

Rosenberg, Liz. *Nobody*
Sedaka, Neil. *Waking up is hard to do*

Morocco *see* Foreign lands – Morocco

Mother Goose *see* Nursery rhymes

Mother's Day *see* Holidays – Mother's Day

Motorcycles

Meadows, Michelle. *Traffic pups*

Mountains

Moss, Miriam. *This is the mountain*

Moving

Denise, Anika. *Bella and Stella come home*
Gleeson, Libby. *Clancy and Millie and the very fine house*
Hallowell, George. *Wagons ho!*
Hobbie, Holly. *Everything but the horse*
Juster, Norton. *Neville*
Kleven, Elisa. *The friendship wish*
Lorenz, Albert. *The exceptionally, extraordinarily ordinary first day of school*
Macomber, Debbie. *The yippy, yappy Yorkie in the green doggy sweater*
Moss, Peggy. *One of us*
Ritz, Karen. *Windows with birds*
Siegel, Mark. *Moving house*
Stephens, Helen. *Fleabag*
Yaccarino, Dan. *Lawn to lawn*
Yolen, Jane. *Elsie's bird*

Mules *see* Animals – mules

Multiple births – twins

Peete, Holly Robinson. *My brother Charlie*
Tuck, Justin. *Home-field advantage*
Yum, Hyewon. *The twins' blanket*

Muppets *see* Puppets

Museums

Friedland, Katy. *Art museum opposites*
Hartland, Jessie. *How the dinosaur got to the museum*
 How the sphinx got to the museum
Smith, Marie. *S is for Smithsonian*

Music

Cabrera, Jane. *The wheels on the bus*
Celenza, Anna Harwell. *Duke Ellington's Nutcracker Suite*
Crimi, Carolyn. *Rock 'n' roll Mole*
Cummings, Phil. *Boom bah!*
Czekaj, Jef. *Hip and Hop, don't stop!*
Dylan, Bob. *Blowin' in the wind*
Gollub, Matthew. *Jazz Fly 2*
Greenberg, Jan. *Ballet for Martha*
Hale, Sarah Josepha Buell. *Mary had a little lamb*
Harris, John. *Jingle bells*
House, Catherine. *A stork in a baobab tree*
Ingalls, Ann. *The little piano girl*
Katz, Karen. *The babies on the bus*
Manders, John. *The really awful musicians*
Mayhew, James. *Ella Bella ballerina and Swan Lake*
Orgill, Roxane. *Skit-scat raggedy cat*
Protopopescu, Orel. *Thelonious Mouse*
Raschka, Chris. *Hip Hop Dog*

Titcomb, Gordon. *The last train*
The twelve days of Christmas. English folk song.
 Twelve days of Christmas
 The twelve days of Christmas, ill. by Jane Ray
 The twelve days of Christmas, ill. by Laurel Long

Musical instruments

Bunting, Eve. *Hey diddle diddle*
Cummings, Phil. *Boom bah!*
Geringer, Laura. *Boom boom go away!*
Newton, Jill. *Crash bang donkey!*
Uhlberg, Myron. *A storm called Katrina*

Musical instruments – bands

Alexander, Kwame. *Acoustic Rooster and his barnyard band*
Costello, David Hyde. *Little Pig joins the band*

Musical instruments – banjos

Pinfold, Levi. *The Django*

Musical instruments – drums

Guidone, Thea. *Drum city*
Patricelli, Leslie. *Be quiet, Mike!*
Vernick, Audrey. *Teach your buffalo to play drums*
Warwick, Dionne. *Little Man*

Musical instruments – pianos

Alda, Arlene. *Lulu's piano lesson*
Ingalls, Ann. *The little piano girl*

Musicians *see* Careers – musicians

Mythical creatures

Duddle, Jonny. *The pirate cruncher*
Jane, Pamela. *Little goblins ten*
Reinhart, Matthew. *Gods and heroes*

Mythical creatures – aliens *see* Aliens

Mythical creatures – elves

Light, Steve. *The Christmas giant*

Mythical creatures – leprechauns

Tegen, Katherine. *The story of the leprechaun*

Mythical creatures – ogres

Juster, Norton. *The odious ogre*
Kimmelman, Leslie. *The three bully goats*

Mythical creatures – trolls

Brett, Jan. *Home for Christmas*
Mortimer, Rachael. *The three Billy Goats Fluff*
Yolen, Jane. *Sister Bear*

Name calling *see* Behavior – name calling

Names

Dunklee, Annika. *My name is Elizabeth!*
Murphy, Stuart J. *Write on, Carlos!*
Sutton, Jane. *Don't call me Sidney*

Napping *see* Sleep

Nativity *see* Religion – Nativity

Nature

Alexander, Cecil Frances. *All things bright and
    beautiful*
Arnosky, Jim. *At this very moment*
Fitzsimmons, David. *Curious critters*
Formento, Alison. *This tree counts!*
    This tree, 1, 2, 3
Frisch, Aaron. *The lonely pine*
Galbraith, Kathryn O. *Planting the wild garden*
Jenkins, Martin. *Can we save the tiger?*
Jenkins, Steve. *How to clean a hippopotamus*
    Just a second
Kato, Yukiko. *In the meadow*
Lamstein, Sarah Marwil. *Big night for salamanders*
Lawler, Janet. *A mother's song*
Lewis, Kevin. *Not inside this house!*
McDonnell, Patrick. *Me . . . Jane*
Messner, Kate. *Over and under the snow*
Paterson, Katherine. *Brother Sun, Sister Moon*
Pfister, Marcus. *Questions, questions*
Robey, Katharine Crawford. *Where's the party?*
Sidman, Joyce. *Ubiquitous*
Snyder, Betsy. *Sweet dreams lullaby*
Winter, Jeanette. *The watcher*
Wood, Douglas. *No one but you*
    Where the sunrise begins
Yezerski, Thomas F. *Meadowlands*

Naughty *see* Behavior – misbehavior

Neighborhoods *see* Communities,
    neighborhoods

New Year's *see* Holidays – New Year's

Night

Bartoletti, Susan Campbell. *Naamah and the ark at
    night*

Bernhard, Durga. *While you are sleeping*
Blackall, Sophie. *Are you awake?*
Brown, Margaret Wise. *The fathers are coming home*
Carroll, James Christopher. *The boy and the moon*
Casanova, Mary. *Utterly otterly night*
De Roo, Elena. *The rain train*
Edwards, Pamela Duncan. *While the world is
    sleeping*
Martin, Ruth. *Moon dreams*
Munro, Roxie. *Desert days, desert nights*
Pearce, Clemency. *Frangoline and the midnight
    dream*
Peters, Lisa Westberg. *Frankie works the night shift*
Ray, Mary Lyn. *Stars*
Rocco, John. *Blackout*
Saunders, Karen. *Baby Badger's wonderful night*
Srinivasan, Divya. *Little Owl's night*
Stutson, Caroline. *Cats' night out*
Teague, David. *Franklin's big dreams*

Nightingales *see* Birds – nightingales

No text *see* Wordless

Noah *see* Religion – Noah

Noise, sounds

Balouch, Kristen. *The little little girl with the big big
    voice*
Beaumont, Karen. *No sleep for the sheep!*
Bolam, Emily. *Animals talk*
Bruins, David. *The call of the cowboy*
Chapman, Susan Margaret. *Too much noise in the
    library*
Craig, Lindsey. *Farmyard beat*
Cummings, Phil. *Boom bah!*
DiTerlizzi, Angela. *Say what?*
Dodd, Emma. *Meow said the cow*
Donaldson, Julia. *What the ladybug heard*
Garcia, Emma. *Tap tap bang bang*
Gorbachev, Valeri. *Shhh!*
Krensky, Stephen. *Noah's bark*
Krilanovich, Nadia. *Chicken, chicken, duck!*
Lucke, Deb. *Sneezenesia*
Macken, JoAnn Early. *Baby says "moo!"*
Newton, Jill. *Crash bang donkey!*
Patricelli, Leslie. *Be quiet, Mike!*
Teckentrup, Britta. *Little Wolf's song*
Underwood, Deborah. *The loud book!*
    The quiet book
Vernick, Audrey. *Teach your buffalo to play drums*

Noise, sounds – snoring *see* Sleep – snoring

North Pole *see* Foreign lands – Arctic

Numbers *see* Counting, numbers

Nursery rhymes

Ada, Alma Flor. *¡Muu, moo!*

Beaton, Clare. *Clare Beaton's nursery rhymes*
Chichester Clark, Emma. *Little Miss Muffet counts to ten*
Cummings, Troy. *The Eensy Weensy Spider freaks out! (big-time!)*
Hale, Sarah Josepha Buell. *Mary had a little lamb*
Hillenbrand, Will. *Mother Goose picture puzzles*
Jay, Alison. *Red green blue*
Metzger, Steve. *Detective Blue*
Morris, Jackie. *The cat and the fiddle*
Mother Goose. *Humpty Dumpty Pat-a-cake*
Pinkney, Jerry. *Three little kittens*
Taylor, Jane. *Twinkle, twinkle, little star*
Trapani, Iza. *Rufus and friends*
Wu, Faye-Lynn. *Chinese and English nursery rhymes*

Nursery school *see* School – nursery

Occupations *see* Careers

Octopuses

Mayer, Mercer. *Octopus soup*

Ogres *see* Mythical creatures – ogres

Old age

Huling, Jan. *Ol' Bloo's boogie-woogie band and blues ensemble*
Newman, Jeff. *The boys*
Ramsden, Ashley. *Seven fathers*
Rubin, Adam. *Those darn squirrels and the cat next door*
Smith, Lane. *Grandpa Green*
Stead, Philip C. *A sick day for Amos McGee*

Olympics *see* Sports – Olympics

Opossums *see* Animals – possums

Opposites *see* Concepts – opposites

Optimism *see* Character traits – optimism

Orphans

Manna, Anthony L. *The orphan*
Marciano, John Bemelmans. *Madeline at the White House*

Otters *see* Animals – otters

Outlaws *see* Crime

Owls *see* Birds – owls

Pageants *see* Theater

Painters *see* Careers – artists

Painting *see* Activities – painting

Paleontologists *see* Careers – paleontologists

Pandas *see* Animals – pandas

Panthers *see* Animals – leopards

Pants *see* Clothing – pants

Paper

Reynolds, Peter H. *I'm here*

Parades

Black, Michael Ian. *A pig parade is a terrible idea*
Guidone, Thea. *Drum city*
Johnson, Angela. *The day Ray got away*
Joosse, Barbara. *Dog parade*
Sweet, Melissa. *Balloons over Broadway*

Parakeets *see* Birds – parakeets, parrots

Parks – amusement

Kalz, Jill. *An a-maze-ing amusement park adventure*

Parrots *see* Birds – parakeets, parrots

Participation

Tullet, Hervé. *The book with a hole*
    Press here
Ziefert, Harriet. *Wiggle like an octopus*

Parties

Allen, Joy. *Princess Palooza*
Avraham, Kate Aver. *What will you be, Sara Mee?*
Bertrand, Diane Gonzales. *The party for Papa Luis / La fiesta para Papa Luis*
Blackstone, Stella. *Bear's birthday*
Brown, Tameka Fryer. *Around our way on Neighbors' Day*
Clarke, Jane. *Trumpet*
Friedman, Laurie. *Ruby Valentine saves the day*
Huget, Jennifer LaRue. *The best birthday party ever*
Khan, Rukhsana. *Big red lollipop*
Levine, Gail Carson. *Betsy Red Hoodie*
Lord, Cynthia. *Happy birthday, Hamster*
McClatchy, Lisa. *Dear Tyrannosaurus Rex*
Mackintosh, David. *Marshall Armstrong is new to our school*
Numeroff, Laura. *Otis and Sydney and the best birthday ever*
Pfister, Marcus. *Happy birthday, Bertie!*
Rim, Sujean. *Birdie's big-girl dress*
Ross, Tony. *I want a party!*
Sendak, Maurice. *Bumble-ardy*
Shaw, Natalie. *Olivia plans a tea party*
Walker, Anna. *I love birthdays*
Watt, Mélanie. *Scaredy Squirrel has a birthday party*
Yolleck, Joan. *Paris in the spring with Picasso*
Zalben, Jane Breskin. *Baby shower*

Passover *see* Holidays – Passover

Patience *see* Character traits – patience

Peacocks, peahens *see* Birds – peacocks, peahens

Pelicans *see* Birds – pelicans

Pen pals

Kostecki-Shaw, Jenny Sue. *Same, same but different*
Smallcomb, Pam. *Earth to Clunk*

Penguins *see* Birds – penguins

Perfectionism *see* Character traits – perfectionism

Perseverance *see* Character traits – perseverance

Persistence *see* Character traits – persistence

Pets

Agee, Jon. *My rhinoceros*
Anderson, Brian. *The prince's new pet*
Ashman, Linda. *No dogs allowed*
Biedrzycki, David. *Me and my dragon*
Brown, Peter. *Children make terrible pets*
Burleigh, Robert. *Good-bye, Sheepie*

Castillo, Lauren. *Melvin and the boy*
Chall, Marsha Wilson. *Pick a pup*
Cowen-Fletcher, Jane. *Hello, puppy!*
Cuyler, Margery. *Guinea pigs add up*
Daly, Cathleen. *Prudence wants a pet*
DiPucchio, Kelly. *Gilbert goldfish wants a pet*
Fraser, Mary Ann. *Pet shop follies*
Gorbachev, Valeri. *The best cat*
Harper, Charise Mericle. *Henry's heart*
Jarka, Jeff. *Love that kitty!*
Juan, Ana. *The pet shop revolution*
Katz, Bobbi. *Nothing but a dog*
Kerby, Johanna. *Little pink pup*
Lyon, Tammie. *Olive and Snowflake*
Mayer, Mercer. *Too many dinosaurs*
Nelson-Schmidt, Michelle. *Cats, cats! Dogs, dogs!*
Plourde, Lynn. *Dino pets go to school*
Prap, Lila. *Doggy whys*
Rickards, Lynne. *Jacob O'Reilly wants a pet*
Roberton, Fiona. *Wanted: the perfect pet*
Roberts, Victoria. *The best pet ever*
Rostoker-Gruber, Karen. *Ferret fun*
Schmid, Paul. *A pet for Petunia*
Staake, Bob. *The first pup*
Stuve-Bodeen, Stephanie. *A small brown dog with a wet pink nose*
Wing, Natasha. *How to raise a dinosaur*
Zalben, Jane Breskin. *Baby shower*

Pharaohs *see* Royalty – pharaohs

Photographers *see* Careers – photographers

Photography *see* Activities – photographing

Physical handicaps *see* Handicaps – physical handicaps

Physicians *see* Careers – doctors

Pianos *see* Musical instruments – pianos

Picnics *see* Activities – picnicking

Picture puzzles

Animal I spy
Animal 123
Chedru, Delphine. *Spot it again!*
Falken, Linda. *Can you find it?*
Garland, Michael. *Super snow day seek and find*
Herzog, Brad. *I spy with my little eye*
Hillenbrand, Will. *Mother Goose picture puzzles*
Jay, Alison. *Red green blue*
Ljungkvist, Laura. *Follow the line to school*
Marino, Gianna. *One too many*
Micklethwait, Lucy. *In the picture*
Munro, Roxie. *Ecomazes*
Pamintuan, Macky. *Twelve haunted rooms of Halloween*
Raczka, Bob. *Fall mixed up*
Staake, Bob. *Look! A book!*

Trapani, Iza. *Rufus and friends*
Wick, Walter. *Can you see what I see? toyland express*
  Can you see what I see? treasure ship

Pigeons *see* Birds – pigeons

Pigs *see* Animals – pigs

Pilots *see* Careers – airplane pilots

Pirates

Bunting, Eve. *Pirate boy*
Demas, Corinne. *Pirates go to school*
Duddle, Jonny. *The pirate cruncher*
Fox, Kathleen. *The pirates of plagiarism*
Kramer, Andrew. *Pajama pirates*
Preller, James. *A pirate's guide to first grade*
Quattlebaum, Mary. *Pirate vs. pirate*
Smith, Danna. *Pirate nap*
Spires, Ashley. *Small Saul*
Wolfe, Myra. *Charlotte Jane battles bedtime*

Planes *see* Airplanes, airports

Planets

McNamara, Margaret. *The three little aliens and the big bad robot*

Plants

Braun, Eric. *Trust me, Jack's beanstalk stinks*
Five little pumpkins
Gourley, Robbin. *First garden*
Grigsby, Susan. *In the garden with Dr. Carver*
Helmore, Jim. *Oh no, monster tomato!*
Jack and the beanstalk. *Jack and the beanstalk*
  Jacques and de beanstalk
Kim, Sue. *How does a seed grow?*
Mair, Samia J. *The perfect gift*
Peterson, Cris. *Seed soil sun*
Wortche, Allison. *Rosie Sprout's time to shine*

Playing *see* Activities – playing

Plays *see* Theater

Pockets *see* Clothing

Poetry

Archer, Peggy. *Name that dog!*
Argueta, Jorge. *Arroz con leche / Rice pudding*
Elliott, David. *In the wild*
Florian, Douglas. *Poetrees*
Franco, Betsy. *A dazzling display of dogs*
George, Kristine O'Connell. *Emma dilemma*
Glaser, Linda. *Emma's poem*
Gottfried, Maya. *Our farm*
Guthrie, James. *Last song*

Moore, Clement Clarke. *'Twas the night before Christmas*
Murphy, Sally. *Pearl verses the world*
O'Connor, Jane. *Fancy Nancy*
Peters, Lisa Westberg. *Volcano wakes up!*
Prelutsky, Jack. *There's no place like school*
Raczka, Bob. *Guyku*
Sidman, Joyce. *Ubiquitous*
Wardlaw, Lee. *Won Ton*
Yolen, Jane. *An egret's day*

Poets *see* Careers – poets

Polar bears *see* Animals – polar bears

Police officers *see* Careers – police officers

Poltergeists *see* Ghosts

Ponds *see* Lakes, ponds

Ponies *see* Animals – horses, ponies

Porcupines *see* Animals – porcupines

Possums *see* Animals – possums

Post office

Lendroth, Susan. *Calico Dorsey*

Postal workers *see* Careers – postal workers

Potty training *see* Toilet training

Poverty

Toscano, Charles. *Papa's pastries*

Prairie wolves *see* Animals – coyotes

Prayers *see* Religion

Pregnancy *see* Birth

Prehistory

McCully, Emily Arnold. *The secret cave*

Prejudice

Bandy, Michael S. *White water*
Bauer, Marion Dane. *Harriet Tubman*
Hughes, Shirley. *The Christmas Eve ghost*
Kittinger, Jo S. *Rosa's bus*
Kochan, Vera. *What if your best friend were blue?*
Krensky, Stephen. *Play ball, Jackie!*

McCully, Emily Arnold. *Wonder horse*
Mason, Margaret H. *These hands*
Michelson, Richard. *Busing Brewster*
Mitchell, Margaree King. *When Grandmama sings*
Myers, Walter Dean. *Muhammad Ali*
Pinkney, Andrea Davis. *Sit-in*
Ramsey, Calvin Alexander. *Ruth and the Green Book*
Reynolds, Aaron. *Back of the bus*
Slade, Suzanne. *Climbing Lincoln's steps*
Tavares, Matt. *Henry Aaron's dream*
Vernick, Audrey. *She loved baseball*
Watkins, Angela Farris. *My Uncle Martin's words for America*
Weatherford, Carole Boston. *The Beatitudes*

Preschool *see* School – nursery

Pride *see* Character traits – pride

Princes *see* Royalty – princes

Princesses *see* Royalty – princesses

Problem solving

Chivers, Natalie. *Rhino's great big itch!*
Maccarone, Grace. *Miss Lina's ballerinas*
McKee, David. *Elmer and the hippos*
Schmid, Paul. *Hugs from Pearl*
Wells, Rosemary. *Hands off, Harry!*
Young, Cybèle. *Ten birds*

Puffins *see* Birds – puffins

Puppets

Sweet, Melissa. *Balloons over Broadway*

Purim *see* Holidays – Purim

Purses *see* Clothing – handbags, purses

Puzzles *see also* Picture puzzles; Rebuses; Riddles & jokes

Base, Graeme. *The Jewel Fish of Karnak*

Queens *see* Royalty – queens

Questioning *see* Character traits – questioning

Rabbits *see* Animals – rabbits

Raccoons *see* Animals – raccoons

Race relations *see* Prejudice

Racing *see* Sports – racing

Railroads *see* Trains

Rain *see* Weather – rain

Ramadan *see* Holidays – Ramadan

Ranchers *see* Careers – ranchers

Rats *see* Animals – rats

Ravens *see* Birds – ravens

Reading *see* Books, reading

Rebuses

Lewis, J. Patrick. *The fantastic 5 and 10¢ store*
Sierra, Judy. *We love our school!*

Religion

Addasi, Maha. *Time to pray*
Adler, David A. *The story of Hanukkah*
Alexander, Cecil Frances. *All things bright and beautiful*
Bartoletti, Susan Campbell. *Naamah and the ark at night*
Buck, Nola. *A Christmas goodnight*
Demi. *Joan of Arc*
dePaola, Tomie. *Let the whole earth sing praise*
Gadot, A. S. *Tower of Babel*
Gilani-Williams, Fawzia. *Nabeel's new pants*
Goodings, Christina. *Creation story*
    Lost sheep story
Hughes, Shirley. *The Christmas Eve ghost*
Jalali, Reza. *Moon watchers*
Jordan, Deloris. *Baby blessings*
Kimmel, Eric A. *Joseph and the Sabbath fish*
McGowan, Michael. *Sunday is for God*
Mackall, Dandi Daley. *The story of the Easter robin*

Nelson, Marilyn. *Snook alone*
Park, Linda Sue. *The third gift*
Paterson, Katherine. *Brother Sun, Sister Moon*
Piper, Sophie. *I can say a prayer*
Schwartz, Howard. *Gathering sparks*
Slegers, Liesbet. *The child in the manger*
Tebbs, Victoria. *Noah's Ark story*
Thong, Roseanne. *Fly free!*
Warren, Rick. *The Lord's prayer*
Weatherford, Carole Boston. *The Beatitudes*

Religion – Islam

Mair, Samia J. *The perfect gift*

Religion – Nativity

Bible. New Testament. Gospels. *The story of Christmas*
Lloyd-Jones, Sally. *Song of the stars*
Thompson, Lauren. *One starry night*

Religion – Noah

Krensky, Stephen. *Noah's bark*

Remembering *see* Memories, memory

Repetitive stories *see* Cumulative tales

Reptiles

Fitzsimmons, David. *Curious critters*

Reptiles – alligators, crocodiles

Beard, Alex. *Crocodile's tears*
Finlay, Lizzie. *Little Croc's purse*
Gibbons, Gail. *Alligators and crocodiles*
Hovland, Henrik. *John Jensen feels different*
Jewell, Nancy. *Alligator wedding*
Rayner, Catherine. *Solomon Crocodile*
Sedaka, Neil. *Waking up is hard to do*
Waber, Bernard. *Lyle walks the dogs*
Wells, Rosemary. *Hands off, Harry!*

Reptiles – chameleons

Gravett, Emily. *Blue chameleon*
Long, Ethan. *Chamelia*

Reptiles – crocodiles *see* Reptiles – alligators, crocodiles

Reptiles – lizards

Wiesner, David. *Art and Max*

Reptiles – salamanders

Lamstein, Sarah Marwil. *Big night for salamanders*

Reptiles – snakes

Burell, Sarah. *Diamond Jim Dandy and the sheriff*
Krensky, Stephen. *Mother's Day surprise*

Reptiles – turtles, tortoises

Castillo, Lauren. *Melvin and the boy*
Cyrus, Kurt. *The voyage of turtle Rex*
Czekaj, Jef. *Hip and Hop, don't stop!*
George, Lucy M. *Back to school Tortoise*
Loth, Sebastian. *Remembering Crystal*
Morrison, Toni. *The tortoise or the hare*
Oldland, Nicholas. *Making the moose out of life*
O'Malley, Kevin. *The great race*
Rumford, James. *Tiger and turtle*
Sayre, April Pulley. *Turtle, turtle, watch out!*

Resourcefulness *see* Behavior – resourcefulness

Responsibility *see* Character traits – responsibility

Rest *see* Sleep

Restaurants

Ashman, Linda. *No dogs allowed*
Krause, Ute. *Oscar and the very hungry dragon*
Whelan, Gloria. *The boy who wanted to cook*

Rhinoceros *see* Animals – rhinoceros

Rhyming text

Alexander, Kwame. *Acoustic Rooster and his barnyard band*
Aliki. *Push button*
Allen, Joy. *Princess Palooza*
Andreae, Giles. *I love my mommy*
Appelt, Kathi. *Brand-new baby blues*
Ashburn, Boni. *Over at the castle*
Ashman, Linda. *Samantha on a roll*
Baker, Keith. *No two alike*
Bardhan-Quallen, Sudipta. *Chicks run wild*
Barner, Bob. *Bears! bears! bears!*
Barnes, Brynne. *Colors of me*
Bauer, Marion Dane. *In like a lion out like a lamb*
    Thank you for me!
Beaty, Andrea. *Hide and sheep*
Beaumont, Karen. *No sleep for the sheep!*
    Shoe-la-la!
Bennett, Artie. *The butt book*
Berkes, Marianne. *Over in Australia*
Berry, Lynne. *Ducking for apples*
Blackstone, Stella. *Bear's birthday*
    Octopus opposites
Bolam, Emily. *I go potty*
Brown, Calef. *Boy wonders*
Brown, Margaret Wise. *Sleepy ABC*
Brown, Tameka Fryer. *Around our way on Neighbors' Day*
Bruchac, Joseph. *My father is taller than a tree*
Bruel, Nick. *A Bad Kitty Christmas*
Buck, Nola. *A Christmas goodnight*
Buehner, Caralyn. *Snowmen all year*
Bunting, Eve. *Hey diddle diddle*
Caswell, Deanna. *Train trip*
Chaconas, Dori. *Don't slam the door!*
    Hurry down to Derry Fair

Chall, Marsha Wilson. *One pup's up*

Chichester Clark, Emma. *Little Miss Muffet counts to ten*

Christelow, Eileen. *Five little monkeys reading in bed*

Christian, Cheryl. *Witches*

Clements, Andrew. *The handiest things in the world*

Coyle, Carmela LaVigna. *Do princesses have best friends forever?*

Craig, Lindsey. *Dancing feet!*
    Farmyard beat

Crimi, Carolyn. *Principal Fred won't go to bed*

Curtis, Jamie Lee. *My mommy hung the moon*

Cushman, Doug. *Christmas Eve good night*
    Halloween good night

Cusimano, Maryann K. *You are my wish*

Cuyler, Margery. *Guinea pigs add up*

Cyrus, Kurt. *Big rig bugs*
    The voyage of turtle Rex

de Las Casas, Dianne. *Mama's bayou*

Degman, Lori. *1 zany zoo*

Demas, Corinne. *Pirates go to school*

Dempsey, Kristy. *Mini racer*

Dewdney, Anna. *Llama Llama home with Mama*
    Roly Poly pangolin

Diesen, Deborah. *The barefooted, bad-tempered baby brigade*
    The pout-pout fish in the big-big dark

DiPucchio, Kelly. *Alfred Zector, book collector*

DiTerlizzi, Angela. *Say what?*

Dodd, Emma. *I don't want a cool cat!*
    I love bugs!

Donaldson, Julia. *One mole digging a hole*
    What the ladybug heard

Doyle, Malachy. *Get happy*

Duddle, Jonny. *The pirate cruncher*

Durango, Julia. *Go-go gorillas*

Edwards, Pamela Duncan. *While the world is sleeping*

Ehlert, Lois. *Lots of spots*

Elya, Susan Middleton. *No more, por favor*
    Rubia and the three osos
    A year full of holidays

Evans, Lezlie. *Who loves the little lamb?*

Falwell, Cathryn. *Gobble gobble*

Fernandes, Eugenie. *Kitten's spring*

Fischer, Scott M. *Jump!*

Five little pumpkins

Fleming, Candace. *Seven hungry babies*

Fliess, Sue. *Shoes for me!*

Fox, Lee. *Ella Kazoo will not brush her hair*

Fox, Mem. *Let's count goats!*

Franco, Betsy. *Double play!*

Frazier, Craig. *Lots of dots*

Frederick, Heather Vogel. *Babyberry pie*
    Hide and squeak

Freedman, Claire. *Dinosaurs love underpants*

Friedman, Laurie. *Ruby Valentine saves the day*

Fuge, Charles. *Astonishing animal ABC*

Gall, Chris. *Substitute creacher*

Geringer, Laura. *Boom boom go away!*

Gershator, Phillis. *Moo, moo, brown cow! Have you any milk?*
    Who's awake in springtime?
    Who's in the forest?

Ghigna, Charles. *I see winter*

The gingerbread boy. *The gingerbread man loose in the school*

Glass, Beth Raisner. *Blue-ribbon dad*

Godwin, Laura. *One moon, two cats*

Goembel, Ponder. *Animal fair*

Gollub, Matthew. *Jazz Fly 2*

Gow, Nancy. *Ten big toes and a prince's nose*

Greene, Rhonda Gowler. *Daddy is a cozy hug*
    Mommy is a soft, warm kiss

Guidone, Thea. *Drum city*

Hall, Michael. *My heart is like a zoo*

Hill, Isabel. *Building stories*

Hop a little, jump a little!

Hosford, Kate. *Big bouffant*

Howland, Naomi. *Princess says goodnight*

Hubbell, Patricia. *Check it out!*
    Horses
    Shaggy dogs, waggy dogs
    Snow happy!

Hudes, Quiara Alegría. *Welcome to my neighborhood!*

Hudson, Cheryl Willis. *My friend Maya loves to dance*

Hueston, M. P. *The all-American jump and jive jig*

Hulme, Joy N. *Easter babies*

Isop, Laurie. *How do you hug a porcupine?*

Jack and the beanstalk. *Jacques and de beanstalk*

Jackson, Ellen. *The seven seas*

Jacobs, Paul Dubois. *Fire drill*

Jay, Alison. *Red green blue*

Jewell, Nancy. *Alligator wedding*

Jocelyn, Marthe. *Ones and twos*

Kaufman, Jeanne. *Young Henry and the dragon*

Kay, Verla. *Hornbooks and inkwells*
    Whatever happened to the Pony Express?

Kelly, Mij. *A bed of your own!*

Kerr, Judith. *One night in the zoo*

Ketteman, Helen. *Goodnight, Little Monster*
    If Beaver had a fever

Kirk, Daniel. *Honk honk! Beep beep!*

Kramer, Andrew. *Pajama pirates*

Krasnesky, Thad. *That cat can't stay*

Krebs, Laurie. *We're roaming in the rainforest*

Kumin, Maxine. *Oh, Harry!*

Kuskin, Karla. *A boy had a mother who bought him a hat*

Lawler, Janet. *A mother's song*

Levine, Arthur A. *Monday is one day*

Lewin, Betsy. *Where is Tippy Toes?*

Lewis, J. Patrick. *The fantastic 5 and 10¢ store*
    Kindergarten cat

Lewis, Kevin. *Not inside this house!*

Lies, Brian. *Bats at the ballgame*

Lindbergh, Reeve. *Homer the library cat*

Little old lady who swallowed a fly. *There was an old monkey who swallowed a frog*

Litwin, Eric. *Pete the cat*

London, Jonathan. *I'm a truck driver*
    A plane goes ka-zoom!

McArthur, Meher. *An ABC of what art can be*

Maccarone, Grace. *Miss Lina's ballerinas*
    Miss Lina's ballerinas and the prince

McGinley, Phyllis. *The year without a Santa Claus*

McGrath, Barbara Barbieri. *Teddy bear counting*

Macken, JoAnn Early. *Baby says "moo!"*
    Waiting out the storm

Mandel, Peter. *Jackhammer Sam*

Marcus, Kimberly. *Scritch-scratch a perfect match*

Martin, Bill, Jr. *Kitty Cat, Kitty Cat, are you going to sleep?*
    Ten little caterpillars

Marzollo, Jean. *Pierre the penguin*

Mayer, Lynne. *Newton and me*

Mayo, Margaret. *Stomp, dinosaur, stomp!*

Meade, Holly. *If I never forever endeavor*
Meadows, Michelle. *Hibernation station*
   Piggies in the kitchen
Melmed, Laura Krauss. *Eight winter nights*
Meltzer, Lynn. *The construction crew*
Melvin, Alice. *Counting birds*
Meyers, Susan. *Bear in the air*
Milgrim, David. *How you got so smart*
Minor, Wendell. *My farm friends*
Morales, Melita. *Jam and honey*
Mother Goose. *Humpty Dumpty*
   Pat-a-cake
Muir, Leslie. *The little bitty bakery*
Nevius, Carol. *Soccer hour*
Newman, Lesléa. *Just like Mama*
Niemann, Christoph. *Subway*
Norman, Kim. *Ten on the sled*
North, Sherry. *Because I am your daddy*
Novak, Matt. *A wish for you*
O'Hair, Margaret. *My kitten*
Olson-Brown, Ellen. *Ooh la la polka-dot boots*
Owen, Karen. *I could be, you could be*
Pamintuan, Macky. *Twelve haunted rooms of*
   Halloween
Patten, Brian. *The big snuggle-up*
Pearce, Clemency. *Frangoline and the midnight*
   dream
Penn, Audrey. *A bedtime kiss for Chester Raccoon*
Perlman, Willa. *Good night, world*
Perry, Andrea. *The Bicklebys' birdbath*
Pfister, Marcus. *Questions, questions*
Plourde, Lynn. *Dino pets go to school*
Postgate, Daniel. *Smelly Bill*
Raczka, Bob. *Fall mixed up*
Raschka, Chris. *Hip Hop Dog*
   Little black crow
Reidy, Jean. *Light up the night*
   Too pickley!
   Too purpley!
Reynolds, Aaron. *Snowbots*
Rickards, Lynne. *Jacob O'Reilly wants a pet*
Roode, Daniel. *Little Bea and the snowy day*
Root, Phyllis. *Creak! said the bed*
Rose, Deborah Lee. *All the seasons of the year*
Rosenthal, Betsy R. *Which shoes would you choose?*
Roth, Carol. *Will you still love me?*
Rubinger, Ami. *Dog number 1 dog number 10*
   I dream of an elephant
Saltzberg, Barney. *All around the seasons*
   Kisses
Santoro, Scott. *Which way to witch school?*
Sartell, Debra. *Time for bed, Baby Ted*
Sayre, April Pulley. *If you're hoppy*
   Rah, rah, radishes!
Schoenherr, Ian. *Don't spill the beans!*
Schubert, Leda. *Feeding the sheep*
Schulman, Janet. *10 Easter egg hunters*
   10 Valentine friends
Sendak, Maurice. *Bumble-ardy*
Sendelbach, Brian. *The underpants zoo*
Sharratt, Nick. *What's in the witch's kitchen?*
Shaskan, Stephen. *A dog is a dog*
Shea, Bob. *Race you to bed*
Shea, Susan A. *Do you know which one will grow?*
Shields, Gillian. *When the world was waiting for you*
Siddals, Mary McKenna. *Compost stew*
Sierra, Judy. *We love our school!*
   Zoozical
Silverman, Erica. *The Hanukkah hop!*

Singer, Marilyn. *What is your dog doing?*
Slack, Michael. *Monkey truck*
Slater, Teddy. *Smooch your pooch*
Smallman, Steve. *Dragon stew*
Smee, Nicola. *What's the matter, Bunny Blue?*
Smith, Danna. *Pirate nap*
Snyder, Betsy. *Sweet dreams lullaby*
Souders, Taryn. *Whole-y cow!*
Spinelli, Eileen. *Do you have a cat?*
   Do you have a dog?
   The perfect Christmas
Spinelli, Jerry. *I can be anything!*
Staake, Bob. *Look! A book!*
Stein, Peter. *Cars galore*
Stiegemeyer, Julie. *Seven little bunnies*
Stockdale, Susan. *Bring on the birds*
Sturgis, Brenda Reeves. *10 turkeys in the road*
Stutson, Caroline. *Cats' night out*
Suen, Anastasia. *Road work ahead*
Tafolla, Carmen. *Fiesta babies*
Tarpley, Todd. *How about a kiss for me?*
Taxali, Gary. *This is silly!*
Thompson, Lauren. *Chew, chew, gulp!*
   Leap back home to me
Tillman, Nancy. *The crown on your head*
   Tumford the terrible
   Wherever you are
Tucker, Lindy. *Porkelia*
Van Dusen, Chris. *King Hugo's huge ego*
   Learning to ski with Mr. Magee
Vasilovich, Guy. *The 13 nights of Halloween*
Vestergaard, Hope. *Potty animals*
Walker, Anna. *I love birthdays*
   I love my dad
   I love my mom
Walsh, Joanna. *The biggest kiss*
Walton, Rick. *Baby's first year!*
Wargin, Kathy-jo. *Scare a bear*
Wells, Rosemary. *Love waves*
Wheeler, Lisa. *Dino-basketball*
White, Becky. *Betsy Ross*
White, Kathryn. *Ruby's school walk*
Wick, Walter. *Can you see what I see? treasure ship*
Wild, Margaret. *Itsy-bitsy babies*
Willis, Jeanne. *I'm sure I saw a dinosaur*
Wilson, Karma. *Bear's loose tooth*
   The cow loves cookies
   Hogwash!
   Mama, why?
Wood, Audrey. *Piggy Pie Po*
Wright, Maureen. *Sneeze, Big Bear, sneeze*
Wright, Michael. *Jake goes peanuts*
Yankovic, Al. *When I grow up*
Yolen, Jane. *Creepy monsters, sleepy monsters*
   Hush, little horsie
   My father knows the names of things
   Not all princesses dress in pink
Ziefert, Harriet. *Wiggle like an octopus*
Zuffi, Stefano. *Art 123*

Riddles & jokes

Agee, Jon. *Mr. Putney's quacking dog*
Krull, Kathleen. *Lincoln tells a joke*
Wick, Walter. *Can you see what I see? treasure ship*

Rivers

Downing, Johnette. *Amazon alphabet*

Roads

Suen, Anastasia. *Road work ahead*

Robbers *see* Crime

Robins *see* Birds – robins

Robots

Barnett, Mac. *Oh no!*
Lester, Helen. *Wodney Wat's wobot*
McNamara, Margaret. *The three little aliens and the big bad robot*
Reynolds, Aaron. *Snowbots*
Riddell, Chris. *Wendel's workshop*
Van Camp, Katie. *CookieBot!*

Rocks

McGuirk, Leslie. *If rocks could sing*

Roller skating *see* Sports – roller skating

Roosters *see* Birds – chickens

Rosh Hashanah *see* Holidays – Rosh Hashanah

Royalty

Hoffmann, E. T. A. *The nutcracker*
O'Malley, Kevin. *Once upon a royal superbaby*

Royalty – emperors

Andersen, Hans Christian. *The emperor's new clothes*
The nightingale

Royalty – kings

Barnett, Mac. *Mustache!*
Lewis, Jill. *Don't read this book!*
Manders, John. *The really awful musicians*
Perrault, Charles. *Puss in boots*
Rosenthal, Amy Krouse. *Al Pha's bet*
Van Dusen, Chris. *King Hugo's huge ego*

Royalty – pharaohs

Base, Graeme. *The Jewel Fish of Karnak*

Royalty – princes

Anderson, Brian. *The prince's new pet*
Gow, Nancy. *Ten big toes and a prince's nose*
Grimm, Jacob. *Rapunzel*
McLeod, Heather. *Kiss me!*
Manna, Anthony L. *The orphan*
Stampler, Ann Redisch. *The rooster prince of Breslov*

Royalty – princesses

Allen, Joy. *Princess Palooza*
Alley, Zoe. *There's a princess in the palace*
Andrews, Julie. *The very fairy princess*
Calvert, Pam. *Princess Peepers picks a pet*

Coyle, Carmela LaVigna. *Do princesses have best friends forever?*
Edwards, Pamela Duncan. *Princess Pigtoria and the pea*
Fleming, Candace. *Clever Jack takes the cake*
Gardner, Carol. *Princess Zelda and the frog*
Gow, Nancy. *Ten big toes and a prince's nose*
Grimm, Jacob. *Twelve dancing princesses*
Howland, Naomi. *Princess says goodnight*
Lee, YJ. *The little moon princess*
Lum, Kate. *Princesses are not perfect*
MacHale, D. J. *The monster princess*
Mortimer, Rachael. *Song for a princess*
Numeroff, Laura. *Ponyella*
Orr, Wendy. *The princess and her panther*
Ross, Tony. *I want a party!*
I want my light on!
I want to do it myself!
I want two birthdays!
Yolen, Jane. *Not all princesses dress in pink*

Royalty – queens

Wadham, Tim. *The queen of France*

Running away *see* Behavior – running away

Russia *see* Foreign lands – Russia

Sadness *see* Emotions – sadness

Safety

Jacobs, Paul Dubois. *Fire drill*
Miller, Edward. *Fireboy to the rescue!*
Murphy, Stuart J. *Freda is found*

Sailing *see* Sports – sailing

Saint Patrick's Day *see* Holidays – St. Patrick's Day

Salamanders *see* Reptiles – salamanders

Salesmen *see* Careers – salespeople

Sand

Nolan, Dennis. *Sea of dreams*

Sandcastles *see* Sand

Sanitation workers *see* Careers – sanitation workers

Santa Claus

Lester, Helen. *Tacky's Christmas*
McGinley, Phyllis. *The year without a Santa Claus*
Martin, Ruth. *Santa's on his way*
Milgrim, David. *Santa Duck and his merry helpers*
Moore, Clement Clarke. *'Twas the night before Christmas*
Pulver, Robin. *Christmas kitten, home at last*
Rawlinson, Julia. *Fletcher and the snowflake Christmas*
Rees, Douglas. *Jeannette Claus saves Christmas*

Scarecrows

Patten, Brian. *The big snuggle-up*

School

Al Abdullah, Rania. *The sandwich swap*
Alter, Anna. *Disappearing Desmond*
Bergman, Mara. *Lively Elizabeth!*
Bliss, Harry. *Bailey*
Bottner, Barbara. *Miss Brooks loves books! (and I don't)*
Bracken, Beth. *Too shy for show-and-tell*
Bromley, Anne C. *The lunch thief*
Brown, Marc. *Arthur turns green*
Button, Lana. *Willow's whispers*
Carlson, Nancy. *Henry and the bully*
Choldenko, Gennifer. *A giant crush*
Cocca-Leffler, Maryann. *Princess Kim and too much truth*
Conway, David. *Errol and his extraordinary nose*
Cook, Lisa Broadie. *Peanut butter and homework sandwiches*
Cox, Judy. *Carmen learns English*
Cuyler, Margery. *Guinea pigs add up*
  I repeat, don't cheat!
Danneberg, Julie. *The big test*
deGroat, Diane. *Ants in your pants, worms in your plants!*
Demas, Corinne. *Pirates go to school*
DeRubertis, Barbara. *Alexander Anteater's amazing act*
  Bobby Baboon's banana be-bop
  Dilly Dog's dizzy dancing
Elkin, Mark. *Samuel's baby*
Fine, Edith Hope. *Water, weed, and wait*
Formento, Alison. *This tree counts!*
  This tree, 1, 2, 3
Franco, Betsy. *Double play!*
Gall, Chris. *Substitute creacher*
The gingerbread boy. *The gingerbread man loose in the school*
Grigsby, Susan. *In the garden with Dr. Carver*
Hale, Sarah Josepha Buell. *Mary had a little lamb*
Hilton, Perez. *The boy with pink hair*
Holub, Joan. *Twinkle, star of the week*
Husband, Amy. *Dear teacher*
Jacobs, Paul Dubois. *Fire drill*
Kalz, Jill. *An a-maze-ing school adventure*
Kay, Verla. *Hornbooks and inkwells*
Knudsen, Michelle. *Argus*
Lehman, Barbara. *The secret box*
Lester, Helen. *Wodney Wat's wobot*

Lewis, J. Patrick. *Kindergarten cat*
Litwin, Eric. *Pete the cat*
Ljungkvist, Laura. *Follow the line to school*
Loewen, Nancy. *The last day of kindergarten*
Lyon, George Ella. *The pirate of kindergarten*
McGinty, Alice B. *Eliza's kindergarten pet*
Mackintosh, David. *Marshall Armstrong is new to our school*
Malaspina, Ann. *Yasmin's hammer*
Marx, Trish. *Kindergarten day USA and China*
Michelson, Richard. *Busing Brewster*
Milgrim, David. *Eddie gets ready for school*
Miller, Edward. *Fireboy to the rescue!*
Milord, Susan. *Happy 100th day!*
Morton, Carlene. *The library pages*
Moses, Will. *Mary and her little lamb*
Moss, Peggy. *One of us*
O'Connor, Jane. *Fancy Nancy*
Ohi, Ruth. *Chicken, pig, cow and the class pet*
Perl, Erica S. *Dotty*
Plourde, Lynn. *Dino pets go to school*
Polacco, Patricia. *The junkyard wonders*
Portis, Antoinette. *Kindergarten diary*
Poydar, Nancy. *No fair science fair*
Prelutsky, Jack. *There's no place like school*
Primavera, Elise. *Louise the big cheese and the back-to-school smarty-pants*
Pulver, Robin. *Happy endings*
  Thank you, Miss Doover
Reed, Lynn Rowe. *Basil's birds*
  Color chaos!
Reid, Barbara. *Perfect snow*
Rockwell, Anne. *St. Patrick's Day*
Rumford, James. *Rain school*
Russo, Marisabina. *A very big bunny*
Santoro, Scott. *Which way to witch school?*
Sauer, Tammi. *Mostly monsterly*
Schachner, Judy. *Skippyjon Jones class action*
Schmid, Paul. *Hugs from Pearl*
Shaw, Hannah. *School for bandits*
Smallcomb, Pam. *Earth to Clunk*
Spinelli, Eileen. *Miss Fox's class shapes up*
Stevens, Janet. *The little red pen*
Underwood, Deborah. *A balloon for Isabel*
Urdahl, Catherine. *Polka-dot fixes kindergarten*
Wallace, Nancy Elizabeth. *Ready, set, 100th day!*
Wells, Rosemary. *Hands off, Harry!*
  Yoko's show-and-tell
White, Kathryn. *Ruby's school walk*
Wortche, Allison. *Rosie Sprout's time to shine*
Yankovic, Al. *When I grow up*

School – field trips

Murphy, Stuart J. *Freda is found*
Parish, Herman. *Amelia Bedelia's first field trip*
Plourde, Lynn. *Field trip day*
Spinelli, Eileen. *Miss Fox's class earns a field trip*

School – first day

Amado, Elisa. *What are you doing?*
Buzzeo, Toni. *Adventure Annie goes to kindergarten*
Ferguson, Sarah. *Emily's first day of school*
George, Lucy M. *Back to school Tortoise*
Grandits, John. *Ten rules you absolutely must not break if you want to survive the school bus*
Lorenz, Albert. *The exceptionally, extraordinarily ordinary first day of school*

McCarty, Peter. *Henry in love*
Onyefulu, Ifeoma. *Deron goes to nursery school*
Preller, James. *A pirate's guide to first grade*
Quackenbush, Robert. *First grade jitters*
Rockwell, Anne. *First day of school*
Schaefer, Lola. *Frankie Stein starts school*
Sierra, Judy. *We love our school!*
Stewart, Amber. *Puddle's new school*
Vernick, Audrey. *Is your buffalo ready for kindergarten?*
Winters, Kay. *This school year will be the best!*
Yamashita, Haruo. *Seven little mice go to school*

School – nursery

Bottner, Barbara. *An annoying ABC*
Onyefulu, Ifeoma. *Deron goes to nursery school*

School principals see Careers – school principals

School teachers see Careers – teachers

Science

Barnett, Mac. *Oh no!*
Cole, Joanna. *The magic school bus and the climate challenge*
Drummond, Allan. *Energy island*
Greenstein, Elaine. *The goose man*
Hopkinson, Deborah. *The humblebee hunter*
Jenkins, Steve. *How to clean a hippopotamus*
Knudsen, Michelle. *Argus*
Lyon, George Ella. *All the water in the world*
Mayer, Lynne. *Newton and me*
Offill, Jenny. *11 experiments that failed*
Poydar, Nancy. *No fair science fair*
Verstraete, Larry. *S is for scientists*
Voake, Steve. *Insect detective*
Wallace, Nancy Elizabeth. *Pond walk*
Wells, Robert E. *Why do elephants need the sun?*

Scientists see Careers – scientists

Sea & seashore

Belton, Robyn. *Herbert*
Bouler, Olivia. *Olivia's birds*
Chin, Jason. *Coral reefs*
Cousins, Lucy. *Maisy goes on vacation*
Dunning, Joan. *Seabird in the forest*
Jackson, Ellen. *The seven seas*
Mason, Janeen. *Ocean commotion*
Neubecker, Robert. *Wow! Ocean!*
Nolan, Dennis. *Sea of dreams*
Perrin, Martine. *Look who's there!*
Roop, Peter. *Down east in the ocean*
Santoro, Lucio. *Wild oceans*
Sarcone-Roach, Julia. *Subway story*
Seven, John. *The ocean story*
Ziefert, Harriet. *Wiggle like an octopus*

Sea & seashore – beaches

Monroe, Chris. *Monkey with a tool belt and the seaside shenanigans*
Moore, Jodi. *When a dragon moves in*

Soman, David. *Ladybug Girl at the beach*
Williams, Karen Lynn. *A beach tail*
Willis, Jeanne. *I'm sure I saw a dinosaur*
Yoon, Salina. *At the beach*

Seagulls see Birds – seagulls

Seals see Animals – seals

Seasons

Berger, Carin. *Forever friends*
Blexbolex. *Seasons*
Cooper, Elisha. *Farm*
Fisher, Valorie. *Everything I need to know before I'm five*
Frisch, Aaron. *The lonely pine*
Gray, Luli. *Ant and Grasshopper*
Greene, Rhonda Gowler. *Daddy is a cozy hug Mommy is a soft, warm kiss*
Karas, G. Brian. *The village garage*
McGhee, Alison. *Making a friend*
Raczka, Bob. *Guyku*
Rose, Deborah Lee. *All the seasons of the year*
Saltzberg, Barney. *All around the seasons*
Willems, Mo. *City dog, country frog*

Seasons – fall

Freeman, Don. *One more acorn*
Maass, Robert. *A is for autumn*
Raczka, Bob. *Fall mixed up*
Spinelli, Eileen. *Now it is summer*
Watson, Wendy. *Bedtime bunnies*
Wright, Maureen. *Sneeze, Big Bear, sneeze*

Seasons – spring

Bauer, Marion Dane. *In like a lion out like a lamb*
Esbaum, Jill. *Everything spring*
Fernandes, Eugenie. *Kitten's spring*
Gershator, Phillis. *Who's awake in springtime?*
Hillenbrand, Will. *Spring is here*
Hulme, Joy N. *Easter babies*
Lamstein, Sarah Marwil. *Big night for salamanders*
Na, Il Sung. *Snow rabbit, spring rabbit*

Seasons – summer

Hayes, Karel. *The summer visitors*
Iwamura, Kazuo. *Hooray for summer!*
Korda, Lerryn. *It's vacation time*
McClure, Nikki. *Mama, is it summer yet?*
Spinelli, Eileen. *Now it is summer*

Seasons – winter

Baker, Keith. *No two alike*
Blackaby, Susan. *Brownie Groundhog and the February Fox*
Butler, M. Christina. *The smiley snowman*
Casanova, Mary. *Utterly otterly night*
Doodler, Todd H. *Bear in long underwear*
Fernandes, Eugenie. *Kitten's winter*
Ghigna, Charles. *I see winter*
Gibbons, Gail. *It's snowing!*
Glaser, Linda. *Not a buzz to be found*
Haas, Rick de. *Peter and the winter sleepers*

Harris, John. *Jingle bells*
Helquist, Brett. *Bedtime for Bear*
Judge, Lita. *Red sled*
McCue, Lisa. *Quiet Bunny and Noisy Puppy*
Messner, Kate. *Over and under the snow*
Na, Il Sung. *Snow rabbit, spring rabbit*
Norman, Kim. *Ten on the sled*
Rawlinson, Julia. *Fletcher and the snowflake Christmas*
Rylant, Cynthia. *Brownie and Pearl see the sights*
Yamashita, Haruo. *Seven little mice have fun on the ice*

Secrets *see* Behavior – secrets

Seeds

Galbraith, Kathryn O. *Planting the wild garden*
Kim, Sue. *How does a seed grow?*
Middleton, Charlotte. *Nibbles*
Pallotta, Jerry. *Who will plant a tree?*
Peterson, Cris. *Seed soil sun*
Wallace, Nancy Elizabeth. *Planting seeds*

Seeking better things *see* Behavior – seeking better things

Self-concept

Alexander, Claire. *Small Florence*
Andrews, Julie. *The very fairy princess*
Bansch, Helga. *Odd bird out*
Barnes, Brynne. *Colors of me*
Bonwill, Ann. *Naughty toes*
Brennan, Eileen. *Dirtball Pete*
Budnitz, Paul. *The hole in the middle*
Compestine, Ying Chang. *Crouching tiger*
Conway, David. *Errol and his extraordinary nose*
Cummings, Troy. *The Eensy Weensy Spider freaks out! (big-time!)*
De Sève, Randall. *Mathilda and the orange balloon*
Diggs, Taye. *Chocolate me!*
Evans, Kristina. *What's special about me, Mama?*
Gaiman, Neil. *Instructions*
Gow, Nancy. *Ten big toes and a prince's nose*
Hall, Michael. *Perfect square*
Harper, Charise Mericle. *Cupcake*
Hector, Julian. *The gentleman bug*
Hilton, Perez. *The boy with pink hair*
Hovland, Henrik. *John Jensen feels different*
Johnson, Dinah. *Black magic*
Kumin, Maxine. *What color is Caesar?*
Lee, Spike. *Giant steps to change the world*
Lichtenheld, Tom. *Bridget's beret*
Look at me!
Ludwig, Trudy. *Better than you*
Lum, Kate. *Princesses are not perfect*
McGhee, Alison. *So many days*
MacHale, D. J. *The monster princess*
Maclear, Kyo. *Spork*
Milgrim, David. *How you got so smart*
Newman, Lesléa. *Miss Tutu's star*
Obama, Barack. *Of thee I sing*
O'Connor, Jane. *Fancy Nancy*
Otoshi, Kathryn. *Zero*
Owen, Karen. *I could be, you could be*
Pelley, Kathleen T. *Raj the bookstore tiger*
Peters, Bernadette. *Stella is a star!*

Pett, Mark. *The girl who never made mistakes*
Polacco, Patricia. *The junkyard wonders*
Rosenthal, Amy Krouse. *One smart cookie*
Russo, Marisabina. *A very big bunny*
Scanlon, Liz Garton. *Noodle and Lou*
Schoonmaker, Elizabeth. *Square cat*
Shireen, Nadia. *Good little wolf*
Smallcomb, Pam. *I'm not*
Tillman, Nancy. *The crown on your head*
Timmers, Leo. *Crow*
Urdahl, Catherine. *Polka-dot fixes kindergarten*
Van Dusen, Chris. *King Hugo's huge ego*
Waldron, Kevin. *Mr. Peek and the misunderstanding at the zoo*
Wiesner, David. *Art and Max*

Self-esteem *see* Self-concept

Self-image *see* Self-concept

Self-reliance *see* Character traits – confidence

Senses

Wood, Douglas. *No one but you*

Senses – sight

Lyon, George Ella. *The pirate of kindergarten*

Sewing *see* Activities – sewing

White, Becky. *Betsy Ross*

Sex roles *see* Gender roles

Shadows

Lee, Suzy. *Shadow*

Shape *see* Concepts – shape

Sharing *see* Behavior – sharing

Sharks *see* Fish – sharks

Sheep *see* Animals – sheep

Shells

Slate, Jenny. *Marcel the shell with shoes on*

Shepherds *see* Careers – shepherds

Ships *see* Boats, ships

Shoemakers *see* Careers – shoemakers

Shopping

Baker, Jeannie. *Mirror*
Melvin, Alice. *The high street*
Rockwell, Anne. *At the supermarket*
Rylant, Cynthia. *Brownie and Pearl see the sights*
Stevens, April. *Edwin speaks up*
Verdick, Elizabeth. *On-the-go time*

Shops *see* Stores

Shoshone Indians *see* Indians of North America – Shoshone

Shows *see* Theater

Shrews *see* Animals – shrews

Shyness *see* Character traits – shyness

Sibling rivalry

Bradman, Tony. *The perfect baby*
Gay, Marie-Louise. *Caramba and Henry*
Manna, Anthony L. *The orphan*
Sullivan, Sarah. *Once upon a baby brother*

Sign language

Domney, Alexis. *Splish, splat!*

Signs & signboards

Ashman, Linda. *No dogs allowed*

Singers *see* Careers – singers

Singing *see* Activities – singing

Single-parent families *see* Family life – single-parent families

Size *see* Concepts – size

Skeletons *see* Anatomy – skeletons

Skiing *see* Sports – skiing

Skunks *see* Animals – skunks

Sky

Ray, Mary Lyn. *Stars*
Taylor, Jane. *Twinkle, twinkle, little star*
Wilson, Karma. *Mama, why?*

Slavery

Armand, Glenda. *Love twelve miles long*

Bauer, Marion Dane. *Harriet Tubman*
Evans, Shane W. *Underground*
Hill, Laban Carrick. *Dave the potter*
Walker, Sally M. *Freedom song*
Weatherford, Carole Boston. *The Beatitudes*

Sledding *see* Sports – sledding

Sleep

Braun, Sebastien. *Back to bed, Ed!*
Brown, Margaret Wise. *Sleepy ABC*
Dahl, Michael. *Nap time for Kitty*
Gorbachev, Valeri. *Shhh!*
Hill, Susanna Leonard. *Can't sleep without sheep*
Jenkins, Steve. *Time to sleep*
Long, Ethan. *One drowsy dragon*
McQuinn, Anna. *The sleep sheep*
Meadows, Michelle. *Hibernation station*
Mortimer, Anne. *Bunny's Easter egg*
Noullet, Georgette. *Bed hog*
Root, Phyllis. *Creak! said the bed*

Sleep – snoring

Ohora, Zachariah. *Stop snoring, Bernard!*

Sleepovers

Becker, Bonny. *A bedtime for Bear*
Joosse, Barbara. *Sleepover at Gramma's house*
Regan, Dian Curtis. *The Snow Blew Inn*

Sleight-of-hand *see* Magic

Slugs *see* Animals – slugs

Smallness *see* Character traits – smallness

Smiles, smiling *see* Anatomy – faces

Snails *see* Animals – snails

Snakes *see* Reptiles – snakes

Snoring *see* Sleep – snoring

Snow *see* Weather – blizzards; Weather – snow

Snow leopards *see* Animals – leopards

Snowmen

Buehner, Caralyn. *Snowmen all year*
Butler, M. Christina. *The smiley snowman*
Doodler, Todd H. *Bear in long underwear*
McGhee, Alison. *Making a friend*
Moser, Lisa. *Perfect soup*
Reid, Barbara. *Perfect snow*
Wright, Maureen. *Sneezy the snowman*

Soccer *see* Sports – soccer

Socks *see* Clothing – socks

Soldiers *see* Careers – military

Solitude *see* Behavior – solitude

Songs

Alexander, Cecil Frances. *All things bright and beautiful*
Allen, Nancy Kelly. *"Happy Birthday"*
Ashburn, Boni. *Over at the castle*
Cabrera, Jane. *Here we go round the mulberry bush*
    The wheels on the bus
Child, Lydia Maria. *Over the river and through the wood*
Comden, Betty. *What's new at the zoo?*
Downing, Johnette. *There was an old lady who swallowed some bugs*
Dylan, Bob. *Blowin' in the wind*
    Man gave names to all the animals
Emberley, Rebecca. *If you're a monster and you know it*
Goembel, Ponder. *Animal fair*
Harburg, E. Y. *Over the rainbow*
Harris, John. *Jingle bells*
House, Catherine. *A stork in a baobab tree*
Katz, Karen. *The babies on the bus*
Little old lady who swallowed a fly. *There was an old monkey who swallowed a frog*
Long, Ethan. *The croaky pokey!*
Marley, Cedella. *One love*
Norworth, Jack. *Take me out to the ball game*
Quattlebaum, Mary. *Jo MacDonald saw a pond*
Robinson, Fiona. *What animals really like*
Roslonek, Steve. *The shape song swingalong*
Sedaka, Neil. *Waking up is hard to do*
Taylor, Jane. *Twinkle, twinkle, little star*
Titcomb, Gordon. *The last train*
The twelve days of Christmas. English folk song. *Twelve days of Christmas*
    The twelve days of Christmas, ill. by Jane Ray
    The twelve days of Christmas, ill. by Laurel Long
Vasilovich, Guy. *The 13 nights of Halloween*
Washington, Ned. *When you wish upon a star*

Sorcerers *see* Wizards

Sounds *see* Noise, sounds

South Africa *see* Foreign lands – South Africa

South America *see* Foreign lands – South America

South Pole *see* Foreign lands – Antarctic

Space & space ships

Logan, Bob. *Rocket town*
McNamara, Margaret. *The three little aliens and the big bad robot*
Reidy, Jean. *Light up the night*
Smallcomb, Pam. *Earth to Clunk*

Spain *see* Foreign lands – Spain

Sparrows *see* Birds – sparrows

Spectacles *see* Glasses

Spelunking *see* Caves

Spiders

Cummings, Troy. *The Eensy Weensy Spider freaks out! (big-time!)*
Dodd, Emma. *I love bugs!*
Noble, Trinka Hakes. *A Christmas spider's miracle*

Sports – archery

San Souci, Robert D. *Robin Hood and the golden arrow*

Sports – baseball

Abrahams, Peter. *Quacky baseball*
Herzog, Brad. *I spy with my little eye*
Keane, Dave. *Daddy adventure day*
Krensky, Stephen. *Play ball, Jackie!*
Lies, Brian. *Bats at the ballgame*
Newman, Jeff. *The boys*
Norworth, Jack. *Take me out to the ball game*
Spradlin, Michael P. *Baseball from A to Z*
Tavares, Matt. *Henry Aaron's dream*
Vernick, Audrey. *She loved baseball*
Wheeler, Lisa. *Dino-baseball*
Yolen, Jane. *All star!*

Sports – basketball

Codell, Esmé Raji. *The basket ball*
Wheeler, Lisa. *Dino-basketball*

Sports – bicycling

Berry, Lynne. *Ducking for apples*
Edwards, Michelle. *The Hanukkah trike*
Ransome, James. *New red bike!*
Viva, Frank. *Along a long road*

Sports – boxing

Myers, Walter Dean. *Muhammad Ali*
Peña, Matt de la. *A nation's hope*

Sports – camping *see* Camps, camping

Sports – fishing

Yamashita, Haruo. *Seven little mice have fun on the ice*

Sports – football

Ransome, James. *Gunner, football hero*

Sports – hockey

Sylvester, Kevin. *Splinters*

Sports – ice skating

Child, Lauren. *I really, really need actual ice skates*
Yamaguchi, Kristi. *Dream big, little pig!*

Sports – Olympics

Herzog, Brad. *G is for gold medal*

Sports – racing

Blake, Robert J. *Painter and Ugly*
Dempsey, Kristy. *Mini racer*
Lord, Cynthia. *Hot rod Hamster*
McCarthy, Meghan. *The incredible life of Balto*
Morrison, Toni. *The tortoise or the hare*
O'Malley, Kevin. *The great race*

Sports – roller skating

Ashman, Linda. *Samantha on a roll*

Sports – sailing

van Lieshout, Maria. *Hopper and Wilson*

Sports – skiing

Van Dusen, Chris. *Learning to ski with Mr. Magee*

Sports – sledding

Blake, Robert J. *Painter and Ugly*
Judge, Lita. *Red sled*
McCarthy, Meghan. *The incredible life of Balto*
Norman, Kim. *Ten on the sled*

Sports – soccer

Capucilli, Alyssa Satin. *My first soccer game*
Javaherbin, Mina. *Goal!*
Nevius, Carol. *Soccer hour*
Pelé. *For the love of soccer!*
Sís, Peter. *Madlenka, soccer star*
Watson, Jesse Joshua. *Hope for Haiti*

Sports – surfing

Sattler, Jennifer. *Pig kahuna*

Sports – swimming

Rylant, Cynthia. *Brownie and Pearl take a dip*
Scotton, Rob. *Splish, splash, Splat!*

Spring *see* Seasons – spring

Squirrels *see* Animals – squirrels

Stage *see* Theater

Stars

Gerber, Carole. *Annie Jump Cannon, astronomer*
Grimm, Jacob. *The star child*
Holub, Joan. *Twinkle, star of the week*
Lee, YJ. *The little moon princess*
Ray, Mary Lyn. *Stars*
Taylor, Jane. *Twinkle, twinkle, little star*
Washington, Ned. *When you wish upon a star*

Stealing *see* Behavior – stealing

Steam shovels *see* Machines

Steamrollers *see* Machines

Stones *see* Rocks

Storekeepers *see* Careers – storekeepers

Stores

Fraser, Mary Ann. *Pet shop follies*
Juan, Ana. *The pet shop revolution*
Lewis, J. Patrick. *The fantastic 5 and 10¢ store*
Melvin, Alice. *The high street*
Pelley, Kathleen T. *Raj the bookstore tiger*
Rockwell, Anne. *At the supermarket*

Stories in rhyme *see* Rhyming text

Storms *see* Weather – storms

Storytelling *see* Activities – storytelling

Strangers *see* Behavior – talking to strangers

Streams *see* Rivers

Streets *see* Roads

String

Boyle, Bob. *Hugo and the really, really, really long
string*

Stubbornness *see* Character traits –
stubbornness

Submarines *see* Boats, ships

Sukkot *see* Holidays – Sukkot

Summer *see* Seasons – summer

Sun

Peterson, Cris. *Seed soil sun*
Wells, Robert E. *Why do elephants need the sun?*
Wood, Douglas. *Where the sunrise begins*

Surfing *see* Sports – surfing

Swamps

Jewell, Nancy. *Alligator wedding*
Root, Phyllis. *Big belching bog*

Swans *see* Birds – swans

Swimming *see* Sports – swimming

Swinging *see* Activities – swinging

Tails *see* Anatomy – tails

Talking to strangers *see* Behavior – talking to strangers

Talent shows *see* Theater

Tall tales

Bateman, Teresa. *Paul Bunyan vs. Hals Halson*
Holt, Kimberly Willis. *The adventures of Granny Clearwater and Little Critter*
Isaacs, Anne. *Dust Devil*
Johnston, Tony. *Levi Strauss gets a bright idea*
Smith, Cynthia Leitich. *Holler Loudly*

Tanzania *see* Foreign lands – Tanzania

Teachers *see* Careers – teachers

Teasing *see* Behavior – teasing

Teddy bears *see* Toys – bears

Teeth

Colato Laínez, René. *The Tooth Fairy meets El Ratón Pérez*
Graham, Bob. *April and Esme, tooth fairies*
Kann, Victoria. *Silverlicious*

Wilson, Karma. *Bear's loose tooth*

Television

Proimos, James. *Todd's TV*

Telling stories *see* Activities – storytelling

Temper tantrums *see* Emotions – anger

Texas

Burell, Sarah. *Diamond Jim Dandy and the sheriff*
King, M. G. *Librarian on the roof!*

Textless *see* Wordless

Thanksgiving *see* Holidays – Thanksgiving

Theater

Conway, David. *Errol and his extraordinary nose*
Crimi, Carolyn. *Rock 'n' roll Mole*
DeRubertis, Barbara. *Alexander Anteater's amazing act*
Hopkins, Lee Bennett. *Full moon and star*
Kontis, Alethea. *AlphaOops!*
LaChanze. *Little diva*
McLean, Dirk. *Curtain up!*
Sierra, Judy. *Zoozical*

Thieves *see* Crime

Thumb sucking

Primavera, Elise. *Thumb love*

Tibet *see* Foreign lands – Tibet

Tigers *see* Animals – tigers

Time

Adler, David A. *Time zones*
Bernhard, Durga. *While you are sleeping*
Jenkins, Steve. *Just a second*

Toilet training

Bolam, Emily. *I go potty*
O'Connell, Rebecca. *Danny is done with diapers*
Oud, Pauline. *Ian's new potty*
Patricelli, Leslie. *Potty*
Scheffler, Axel. *The little puddle*
Shea, Bob. *Dinosaur vs. the potty*
Vestergaard, Hope. *Potty animals*

Tongue twisters

Cleary, Brian P. *Six sheep sip thick shakes and other tricky tongue twisters*

Tools

Garcia, Emma. *Tap tap bang bang*
Garland, Sarah. *Eddie's toolbox and how to make and mend things*
Mandel, Peter. *Jackhammer Sam*
Meltzer, Lynn. *The construction crew*
Monroe, Chris. *Monkey with a tool belt and the seaside shenanigans*

Tornadoes *see* Weather – tornadoes

Tortoises *see* Reptiles – turtles, tortoises

Towns *see* Cities, towns

Toys

Beaumont, Karen. *Where's my t-r-u-c-k?*
Bianco, Margery Williams. *The velveteen rabbit*
Brown, Alan James. *Love-a-Duck*
Crews, Nina. *Sky-high Guy*
Crum, Shutta. *Mine!*
Denise, Anika. *Bella and Stella come home*
Gershator, Phillis. *Moo, moo, brown cow! Have you any milk?*
Hoffmann, E. T. A. *The nutcracker*
Holmes, Janet A. *Have you seen Duck?*
Hoppe, Paul. *The woods*
Ichikawa, Satomi. *My little train*
Kenney, Sean. *Cool city*
Kirk, Daniel. *Honk honk! Beep beep!*
Kirsch, Vincent X. *Two little boys from Toolittle Toys*
McDonnell, Patrick. *Me . . . Jane*
Nash, Sarah. *Purrfect!*
Ohi, Ruth. *Chicken, pig, cow and the class pet*
Chicken, pig, cow, horse around
Polacco, Patricia. *Bun Bun Button*
Rosenthal, Eileen. *I must have Bobo!*
Samuels, Barbara. *The trucker*
Schmid, Paul. *A pet for Petunia*
Taylor, Sean. *The world champion of staying awake*
Van Camp, Katie. *CookieBot!*
Wick, Walter. *Can you see what I see? toyland express*
Willems, Mo. *Knuffle Bunny free*
Ziefert, Harriet. *Bunny's lessons*

Toys – balloons

De Sève, Randall. *Mathilda and the orange balloon*
Johnson, Angela. *The day Ray got away*
Polacco, Patricia. *Bun Bun Button*
Sweet, Melissa. *Balloons over Broadway*

Toys – balls

George, Lindsay Barrett. *Maggie's ball*
Raschka, Chris. *A ball for Daisy*
Seeger, Laura Vaccaro. *What if?*

Toys – bears

Bart, Kathleen. *Town Teddy and Country Bear go global*
Crimi, Carolyn. *Principal Fred won't go to bed*
McGinness, Suzanne. *My bear Griz*
McGrath, Barbara Barbieri. *Teddy bear counting*

Meserve, Jessica. *Bedtime without Arthur*
Meyers, Susan. *Bear in the air*
Stead, Philip C. *Jonathan and the big blue boat*
Ungerer, Tomi. *Otto*

Toys – blocks

Banks, Kate. *Max's castle*

Toys – dolls

Parot, Annelore. *Kimonos*
Wells, Rosemary. *Yoko's show-and-tell*

Toys – pandas *see* Toys – bears

Toys – teddy bears *see* Toys – bears

Toys – wagons

Liwska, Renata. *Red wagon*

Tractors

Alborough, Jez. *The gobble gobble moooooo tractor book*
Garland, Michael. *Grandpa's tractor*
Long, Loren. *Otis and the tornado*

Trains

Barton, Chris. *Shark vs. train*
Caswell, Deanna. *Train trip*
De Roo, Elena. *The rain train*
Kulling, Monica. *All aboard!*
Maltbie, P. I. *Claude Monet*
Niemann, Christoph. *Subway*
Sarcone-Roach, Julia. *Subway story*
Steele, Philip. *Trains*
Titcomb, Gordon. *The last train*

Transportation

Cousins, Lucy. *Maisy's book of things that go*
Durango, Julia. *Go-go gorillas*
Kittinger, Jo S. *Rosa's bus*

Traveling *see* Activities – traveling

Trees

Brallier, Jess M. *Tess's tree*
Cole, Henry. *The littlest evergreen*
Devernay, Laetitia. *The conductor*
Dunrea, Olivier. *A Christmas tree for Pyn*
Florian, Douglas. *Poetrees*
Foggo, Cheryl. *Dear baobab*
Formento, Alison. *This tree counts!*
This tree, 1, 2, 3
Frisch, Aaron. *The lonely pine*
Galbraith, Kathryn O. *Arbor Day square*
Jeffers, Oliver. *Stuck*
Johnson, Jen Cullerton. *Seeds of change*
Light, Steve. *The Christmas giant*
Muldrow, Diane. *We planted a tree*
Napoli, Donna Jo. *Mama Miti*
Pallotta, Jerry. *Who will plant a tree?*

Smith, Linda. *The inside tree*
The tree house

Trickery *see* Behavior – trickery

Tricks *see* Magic

Trolls *see* Mythical creatures – trolls

Truck drivers *see* Careers – truck drivers

Trucks

Beaumont, Karen. *Where's my t-r-u-c-k?*
Crowther, Robert. *Amazing pop-up trucks*
Cyrus, Kurt. *Big rig bugs*
Dale, Penny. *Dinosaur dig!*
Hines, Anna Grossnickle. *I am a backhoe*
Houston, Gloria. *Miss Dorothy and her bookmobile*
My big book of trucks and diggers
Niemann, Christoph. *That's how!*
Rinker, Sherri Duskey. *Goodnight, goodnight, construction site*
Samuels, Barbara. *The trucker*

Turkey *see* Foreign lands – Turkey

Turkeys *see* Birds – turkeys

Turtles *see* Reptiles – turtles, tortoises

TV *see* Television

Twins *see* Multiple births – twins

U.S. history

Adler, David A. *A picture book of Cesar Chavez*
A picture book of John and Abigail Adams
Armand, Glenda. *Love twelve miles long*
Bandy, Michael S. *White water*
Bauer, Marion Dane. *Harriet Tubman*
Bildner, Phil. *The hallelujah flight*
Birtha, Becky. *Lucky beans*
Brown, Don. *A wizard from the start*
Brown, Monica. *Side by side / Lado a lado*
Brown, Tami Lewis. *Soar, Elinor!*
Evans, Shane W. *Underground*
Falken, Linda. *Can you find it?*
Glaser, Linda. *Emma's poem*
Gourley, Robbin. *First garden*

Griffin, Kitty. *The ride*
Grigsby, Susan. *In the garden with Dr. Carver*
Harvey, Jeanne Walker. *My hands sing the blues*
Hueston, M. P. *The all-American jump and jive jig*
Jurmain, Suzanne Tripp. *Worst of friends*
Kittinger, Jo S. *Rosa's bus*
Krull, Kathleen. *Lincoln tells a joke*
Lendroth, Susan. *Calico Dorsey*
Malaspina, Ann. *Phillis sings out freedom*
Marciano, John Bemelmans. *Madeline at the White House*
Marzollo, Jean. *The little plant doctor*
Michelson, Richard. *Busing Brewster*
Mitchell, Margaree King. *When Grandmama sings*
Moses, Will. *Mary and her little lamb*
Myers, Walter Dean. *Muhammad Ali*
Nolan, Janet. *The firehouse light*
Obama, Barack. *Of thee I sing*
Pinkney, Andrea Davis. *Sit-in*
Ramsey, Calvin Alexander. *Belle, the last mule at Gee's Bend*
Ruth and the Green Book
Rappaport, Doreen. *Jack's path of courage*
Reynolds, Aaron. *Back of the bus*
Slade, Suzanne. *Climbing Lincoln's steps*
Smith, Marie. *S is for Smithsonian*
Tavares, Matt. *Henry Aaron's dream*
Van Allsburg, Chris. *Queen of the falls*
Vernick, Audrey. *She loved baseball*
Walker, Sally M. *Freedom song*
Watkins, Angela Farris. *My Uncle Martin's big heart*
My Uncle Martin's words for America
Weatherford, Carole Boston. *The Beatitudes*
White, Becky. *Betsy Ross*
Yaccarino, Dan. *All the way to America*

U.S. history – frontier & pioneer life

Bateman, Teresa. *Paul Bunyan vs. Hals Halson*
Browning, Diane. *Signed, Abiah Rose*
Burell, Sarah. *Diamond Jim Dandy and the sheriff*
Casanova, Mary. *The day Dirk Yeller came to town*
Davis, David. *Fandango stew*
Galbraith, Kathryn O. *Arbor Day square*
Hallowell, George. *Wagons ho!*
Holt, Kimberly Willis. *The adventures of Granny Clearwater and Little Critter*
Isaacs, Anne. *Dust Devil*
Johnston, Tony. *Levi Strauss gets a bright idea*
Kay, Verla. *Hornbooks and inkwells*
Whatever happened to the Pony Express?
Napoli, Donna Jo. *The crossing*
Spradlin, Michael P. *Off like the wind!*
Yolen, Jane. *Elsie's bird*

Umbrellas

Na, Il Sung. *The thingamabob*
Schubert, Ingrid. *The umbrella*

Uncles *see* Family life – aunts, uncles

Unusual format *see* Format, unusual

Vacationing *see* Activities – vacationing

Valentine's Day *see* Holidays – Valentine's Day

Vampires *see* Monsters – vampires

Vanity *see* Character traits – vanity

Veterinarians *see* Careers – veterinarians

Vietnam *see* Foreign lands – Vietnam

Vikings

Smallman, Steve. *Dragon stew*

Violence, nonviolence

Brown, Monica. *Side by side / Lado a lado*
Dylan, Bob. *Blowin' in the wind*
Kittinger, Jo S. *Rosa's bus*
Ramsey, Calvin Alexander. *Belle, the last mule at Gee's Bend*
Watkins, Angela Farris. *My Uncle Martin's big heart My Uncle Martin's words for America*

Volcanoes

Peters, Lisa Westberg. *Volcano wakes up!*

Voles *see* Animals – voles

Wagons *see* Toys – wagons

Walking *see* Activities – walking

Walruses *see* Animals – walruses

War

Demi. *Joan of Arc*
Mckee, David. *Six men*
Nadel, Carolina. *Daddy's home*
Russo, Marisabina. *I will come back for you*
Ungerer, Tomi. *Otto*
Youme. *Mali under the night sky*

Washing machines *see* Machines

Watches *see* Clocks, watches

Water

Johnson, Neil. *The falling raindrop*
Lyon, George Ella. *All the water in the world*
McGhee, Alison. *Making a friend*
Seven, John. *The ocean story*

Weather

Cole, Joanna. *The magic school bus and the climate challenge*
Guiberson, Brenda Z. *Earth*

Weather – blizzards

Crummel, Susan Stevens. *Ten-Gallon Bart beats the heat*
Friedman, Laurie. *Ruby Valentine saves the day*
Haas, Rick de. *Peter and the winter sleepers*
Hill, Susanna Leonard. *April Fool, Phyllis!*
Regan, Dian Curtis. *The Snow Blew Inn*

Weather – clouds

Lichtenheld, Tom. *Cloudette*
Morrison, Toni. *Little Cloud and Lady Wind*

Weather – droughts

Faundez, Anne. *The day the rains fell*

Weather – floods

Krensky, Stephen. *Noah's bark*
Tebbs, Victoria. *Noah's Ark story*
Uhlberg, Myron. *A storm called Katrina*

Weather – hurricanes

Berne, Jennifer. *Calvin can't fly*
Uhlberg, Myron. *A storm called Katrina*
Watson, Renée. *A place where hurricanes happen*
Zelch, Patti R. *Ready, set . . . wait!*

Weather – rain

De Roo, Elena. *The rain train*
Feiffer, Kate. *My side of the car*
Gammell, Stephen. *Mudkin*
Herman, Charlotte. *First rain*
Johnson, Neil. *The falling raindrop*
Krensky, Stephen. *Noah's bark*
Lichtenheld, Tom. *Cloudette*
Macken, JoAnn Early. *Waiting out the storm*
Rumford, James. *Rain school*
Salzano, Tammi. *One rainy day*

Tebbs, Victoria. *Noah's Ark story*

Weather – snow *see also* Snowmen

Garland, Michael. *Super snow day seek and find*
Gibbons, Gail. *It's snowing!*
Helquist, Brett. *Bedtime for Bear*
Hubbell, Patricia. *Snow happy!*
Messner, Kate. *Over and under the snow*
Patten, Brian. *The big snuggle-up*
Petersen, David. *Snowy Valentine*
Pfister, Marcus. *Snow puppy*
Reid, Barbara. *Perfect snow*
Reynolds, Aaron. *Snowbots*
Roode, Daniel. *Little Bea and the snowy day*
Young, Ned. *Zoomer's summer snowstorm*

Weather – storms

Belton, Robyn. *Herbert*
Iwamura, Kazuo. *Hooray for summer!*
Macken, JoAnn Early. *Waiting out the storm*
Root, Phyllis. *Creak! said the bed*

Weather – tornadoes

Long, Loren. *Otis and the tornado*

Weather – wind

Birdsall, Jeanne. *Flora's very windy day*
Day, Nancy Raines. *On a windy night*
Drummond, Allan. *Energy island*
Morrison, Toni. *Little Cloud and Lady Wind*
Wright, Maureen. *Sneeze, Big Bear, sneeze*

Weaving *see* Activities – weaving

Weddings

Hartt-Sussman, Heather. *Nana's getting married*
Holabird, Katharine. *Angelina and the royal wedding*
Jewell, Nancy. *Alligator wedding*
Masini, Beatrice. *Here comes the bride*
Newman, Lesléa. *Donovan's big day*
Ziefert, Harriet. *Grandma's wedding album*

Weekdays *see* Days of the week, months of the year

Whales *see* Animals – whales

Wheelchairs *see* Handicaps – physical handicaps

Wind *see* Weather – wind

Winter *see* Seasons – winter

Wishing *see* Behavior – wishing

Witches

Baeten, Lieve. *The curious little witch*
    Happy birthday, Little Witch!

Brokamp, Elizabeth. *The picky little witch*
Brown, Lisa. *Vampire boy's good night*
Christian, Cheryl. *Witches*
Cohen, Caron Lee. *Broom, zoom!*
de Las Casas, Dianne. *The house that Witchy built*
dePaola, Tomie. *Strega Nona's gift*
Five little pumpkins
Grimm, Jacob. *Hansel and Gretel*
    Rapunzel
Santoro, Scott. *Which way to witch school?*
Sharratt, Nick. *What's in the witch's kitchen?*

Wizards

Morrissey, Dean. *The wizard mouse*
Seder, Rufus Butler. *The Wizard of Oz*

Wolves *see* Animals – wolves

Wombats *see* Animals – wombats

Woodchucks *see* Animals – groundhogs

Woods *see* Forest, woods

Word games *see* Language

Wordless

Baker, Jeannie. *Mirror*
Desrosiers, Sylvie. *Hocus pocus*
Devernay, Laetitia. *The conductor*
Frazier, Craig. *Bee and bird*
Geisert, Arthur. *Ice*
Lee, Suzy. *Mirror*
Lehman, Barbara. *The secret box*
Mayer, Mercer. *Octopus soup*
Newman, Jeff. *The boys*
Nolan, Dennis. *Sea of dreams*
Raschka, Chris. *A ball for Daisy*
Riphagen, Loes. *Animals home alone*
Rodriguez, Béatrice. *The chicken thief*
    Fox and hen together
Runton, Andy. *Owly and Wormy*
Savage, Stephen. *Where's Walrus?*
Schories, Pat. *When Jack goes out*
Schubert, Ingrid. *The umbrella*
Thomson, Bill. *Chalk*
The tree house

World

Ajmera, Maya et al. *Our grandparents*
Bart, Kathleen. *Town Teddy and Country Bear go global*
Laroche, Giles. *If you lived here*
Perlman, Willa. *Good night, world*
Schubert, Ingrid. *The umbrella*
Smith, David J. *This child, every child*

Worms *see* Animals – worms

Worrying *see* Behavior – worrying

Wrecking machines *see* Machines

Writing *see* Activities – writing

Writing letters *see* Letters, cards

Zebras *see* Animals – zebras

Zodiac

Chin, Oliver. *The year of the tiger*

Zookeepers *see* Careers – zookeepers

Zoos

Comden, Betty. *What's new at the zoo?*
Degman, Lori. *1 zany zoo*
Dyer, Sarah. *Batty*
Ellis, Andy. *When Lulu went to the zoo*
Feiffer, Kate. *My side of the car*
Hall, Michael. *My heart is like a zoo*
Kalz, Jill. *An a-maze-ing zoo adventure*
Kerr, Judith. *One night in the zoo*
Ketteman, Helen. *If Beaver had a fever*
Metzger, Steve. *The dancing clock*
Ohora, Zachariah. *Stop snoring, Bernard!*
Sendelbach, Brian. *The underpants zoo*
Sierra, Judy. *Zoozical*
Stead, Philip C. *A sick day for Amos McGee*
Waldron, Kevin. *Mr. Peek and the misunderstanding at the zoo*

Bibliographic Guide

Arranged alphabetically by author's name in boldface (or by title, if author is unknown), each entry includes title, illustrator, publisher, publication date, and subjects. Joint authors and their titles appear as short entries, with the main author name (in parentheses after the title) citing where the complete entry will be found. Where only an author and title are given, complete information is listed under the title as the main entry.

Abrahams, Peter. *Quacky baseball* ill. by Frank Morrison. HarperCollins, 2011. ISBN 978-0-06-122978-7 Subj: Birds – ducks. Sports – baseball.

Ada, Alma Flor. *¡Muu, moo! rimas de animales = animal nursery rhymes* by Alma Flor Ada and F. Isabel Campoy; ill. by Vivi Escriva. HarperCollins, 2010. ISBN 978-0-06-134613-2 Subj: Foreign languages. Nursery rhymes.

Adams, Sarah. *Dave and Violet* ill. by author. Frances Lincoln, 2011. ISBN 978-1-84780-052-7 Subj: Character traits – shyness. Dragons. Friendship.

Gary and Ray ill. by author. Frances Lincoln, 2010. ISBN 978-1-84507-955-0 Subj: Animals – gorillas. Birds. Friendship.

Addasi, Maha. *Time to pray* tr. by Nuha Albitar; ill. by Ned Gannon. Boyds Mills, 2010. ISBN 978-1-59078-611-6 Subj: Family life – grandmothers. Foreign lands – Middle East. Foreign languages. Religion.

Adler, David A. *A little at a time* ill. by Paul Tong. Holiday House, 2010. ISBN 978-0-8234-1739-1 Subj: Character traits – questioning. Family life – grandfathers.

A picture book of Cesar Chavez by David A. Adler and Michael S. Adler; ill. by Marie Olofsdotter. Holiday House, 2010. ISBN 978-0-8234-2202-9 Subj: Behavior – seeking better things. Farms. U.S. history.

A picture book of John and Abigail Adams by David A. Adler and Michael S. Adler; ill. by Ronald Him-

ler. Holiday House, 2010. ISBN 978-0-8234-2007-0 Subj: U.S. history.

The story of Hanukkah ill. by Jill Weber. Holiday House, 2011. ISBN 978-0-8234-2295-1 Subj: Holidays – Hanukkah. Jewish culture. Religion.

Time zones ill. by Edward Miller. Holiday House, 2010. ISBN 978-0-8234-2201-2 Subj: Time.

Adler, Michael S. *A picture book of Cesar Chavez* (Adler, David A.)

A picture book of John and Abigail Adams (Adler, David A.)

Adler, Victoria. *Baby, come away* ill. by David Walker. Farrar, 2011. ISBN 978-0-374-30480-5 Subj: Animals. Babies.

Aesop. *Aesop's fables* retold by Beverley Naidoo; ill. by Piet Grobler. Frances Lincoln, 2011. ISBN 978-1-84780-007-7 Subj: Folk & fairy tales. Foreign lands – Africa.

Aesop's fables retold by Fiona Waters; ill. by Fulvio Testa. Trafalgar Square, 2011. ISBN 978-1-84939-049-1 Subj: Folk & fairy tales.

Mouse and lion retold by Rand Burkert; ill. by Nancy Ekholm Burkert. Scholastic, 2011. ISBN 978-0-545-10147-9 Subj: Animals – lions. Animals – mice. Character traits – helpfulness. Character traits – kindness. Folk & fairy tales.

Agee, Jon. *Mr. Putney's quacking dog* ill. by author. Scholastic, 2010. ISBN 978-0-545-16203-6 Subj: Animals. Games. Riddles & jokes.

My rhinoceros ill. by author. Scholastic, 2011. ISBN 978-0-545-29441-6 Subj: Animals – rhinoceros. Crime. Pets.

Ainslie, Tamsin. *I can say please* ill. by author. Kane/Miller, 2011. ISBN 978-1-61067-037-1 Subj: Etiquette.

I can say thank you ill. by author. Kane/Miller, 2011. ISBN 978-1-61067-038-8 Subj: Etiquette.

Ainsworth, Kimberly. *Hootenanny! a festive counting book* ill. by Jo Brown. Simon & Schuster, 2011. ISBN 978-1-4424-2273-5 Subj: Birds – owls. Counting, numbers.

Ajmera, Maya, et al. *Our grandparents: a global album.* Charlesbridge, 2010. ISBN 978-1-57091-458-4 Subj: Family life – grandparents. World.

Akin, Sara Laux. *Three scoops and a fig* ill. by Susan Kathleen Hartung. Peachtree, 2010. ISBN 978-1-56145-522-5 Subj: Ethnic groups in the U.S. – Italian Americans. Family life. Food.

Al Abdullah, Rania. *The sandwich swap* by Rania Al Abdullah and Kelly DiPucchio; ill. by Tricia Tusa. Hyperion/Disney, 2010. ISBN 978-1-4231-2484-9 Subj: Character traits – being different. Food. Friendship. School.

Alborough, Jez. *The gobble gobble moooooo tractor book* ill. by author. Kane/Miller, 2010. ISBN 978-1-935279-66-2 Subj: Animals – sheep. Farms. Tractors.

Alda, Arlene. *Except the color grey.* Tundra, 2011. ISBN 978-1-77049-284-4 Subj: Concepts – color.

Lulu's piano lesson ill. by Lisa Desimini. Tundra, 2010. ISBN 978-0-88776-930-6 Subj: Activities – playing. Character traits – completing things. Musical instruments – pianos.

Alexander, Cecil Frances. *All things bright and beautiful* ill. by Ashley Bryan. Simon & Schuster, 2010. ISBN 978-1-4169-8939-4 Subj: Nature. Religion. Songs.

Alexander, Claire. *Small Florence: piggy pop star!* ill. by author. Whitman, 2010. ISBN 978-0-8075-7455-3 Subj: Animals – pigs. Behavior – teasing. Character traits – confidence. Family life – sisters. Self-concept.

Alexander, Kwame. *Acoustic Rooster and his barnyard band* ill. by Tim Bowers. Sleeping Bear, 2011. ISBN 978-1-58536-688-0 Subj: Birds – chickens. Careers – musicians. Contests. Musical instruments – bands. Rhyming text.

Aliki. *Push button* ill. by author. HarperCollins, 2010. ISBN 978-0-06-167308-5 Subj: Activities – playing. Rhyming text.

Alko, Selina. *Every-day dress-up* ill. by author. Random House, 2011. ISBN 978-0-375-86092-8 Subj: Activities – playing. Clothing. Imagination.

Allen, Elanna. *Itsy Mitsy runs away* ill. by author. Atheneum, 2011. ISBN 978-1-4424-0671-1 Subj: Bedtime. Behavior – running away. Family life – fathers.

Allen, Joy. *Princess Palooza* ill. by author. Penguin Group (USA), 2011. ISBN 978-0-399-25455-0 Subj: Activities – playing. Imagination. Parties. Rhyming text. Royalty – princesses.

Allen, Nancy Kelly. *"Happy Birthday": the story of the world's most popular song* ill. by Gary Undercuffler. Pelican, 2010. ISBN 978-1-58980-675-7 Subj: Birthdays. Songs.

Alley, Zoe. *There's a princess in the palace* ill. by R. W. Alley. Roaring Brook, 2010. ISBN 978-1-59643-471-4 Subj: Folk & fairy tales. Royalty – princesses.

Alter, Anna. *Disappearing Desmond* ill. by author. Random House, 2010. ISBN 978-0-375-86684-5 Subj: Animals. Behavior – hiding. Character traits – shyness. School.

A photo for Greta ill. by author. Random House, 2011. ISBN 978-0-375-85618-1 Subj: Careers – photographers. Family life – fathers.

Amado, Elisa. *What are you doing?* ill. by Manuel Monroy. Groundwood, 2011. ISBN 978-1-55498-070-3 Subj: Books, reading. Foreign lands – Mexico. School – first day.

Amenta, Charles A., III. *Russell's world: a story for kids about autism* ill. by Monika Pollak; photos by author. Magination, 2011. ISBN 978-1-4338-0975-0 Subj: Handicaps – autism.

American babies. Charlesbridge, 2010. ISBN 978-1-58089-280-3 Subj: Babies. Format, unusual – board books.

Andersen, Hans Christian. *The emperor's new clothes* retold by Louise John; ill. by Serena Curmi. Evans Brothers, 2011. ISBN 978-0-237-53895-8 Subj: Character traits – pride. Character traits – vanity. Clothing. Folk & fairy tales. Humorous stories. Imagination. Royalty – emperors.

The nightingale adapt. by Pirkko Vainio; ill. by Pirkko Vainio. NorthSouth, 2011. ISBN 978-0-7358-4029-4 Subj: Birds – nightingales. Character traits – freedom. Folk & fairy tales. Foreign lands – China. Royalty – emperors.

Sylvia Long's Thumbelina by Sylvia Long; ill. by author. Chronicle, 2010. ISBN 978-0-8118-5522-8 Subj: Character traits – smallness. Folk & fairy tales.

The ugly duckling adapt. by Sebastien Braun; ill. by adapter. Boxer, 2010. ISBN 978-1-907152-04-7 Subj: Birds – ducks. Birds – swans. Character traits – appearance. Character traits – being different. Folk & fairy tales.

The ugly duckling ill. by Roberta Wilson. Odyssey, 2010. ISBN 978-0-917665-86-8 Subj: Birds – ducks. Birds – swans. Character traits – appearance. Character traits – being different. Folk & fairy tales.

Anderson, Brian. *The prince's new pet* ill. by author. Roaring Brook, 2011. ISBN 978-1-59643-357-1 Subj: Concepts – color. Pets. Royalty – princes.

Anderson, Derek. *Story county: here we come!* ill. by author. Scholastic, 2011. ISBN 978-0-545-16844-1 Subj: Animals. Farms.

Andreae, Giles. *I love my mommy* ill. by Emma Dodd. Hyperion/Disney, 2011. ISBN 978-1-4231-4327-7 Subj: Family life – mothers. Rhyming text.

Andres, Kristina. *Elephant in the bathtub* ill. by author. NorthSouth, 2010. ISBN 978-0-7358-2291-7 Subj: Activities – bathing. Animals – elephants.

Andrews, Julie. *The very fairy princess* by Julie Andrews and Emma Walton Hamilton; ill. by Christine Davenier. Little, Brown, 2010. ISBN 978-0-316-04050-1 Subj: Royalty – princesses. Self-concept.

Animal I spy: what can you spot? ill. by Kate Sheppard. Kingfisher, 2010. ISBN 978-0-7534-6395-6 Subj: Animals. Format, unusual – board books. Picture puzzles.

Animal 123: one to ten and back again ill. by Kate Sheppard. Kingfisher, 2010. ISBN 978-0-7534-6394-9 Subj: Animals. Counting, numbers. Format, unusual – board books. Picture puzzles.

Annunziata, Jane. *Shy spaghetti and excited eggs: a kid's menu of feelings* (Nemiroff, Marc A.)

Appelt, Kathi. *Brand-new baby blues* ill. by Kelly Murphy. HarperCollins, 2010. ISBN 978-0-06-053233-8 Subj: Babies. Family life – new sibling. Rhyming text.

Archer, Peggy. *Name that dog! puppy poems from a to z* ill. by Stephanie Buscema. Penguin Group (USA), 2010. ISBN 978-0-8037-3322-0 Subj: ABC books. Animals – dogs. Poetry.

Argueta, Jorge. *Arroz con leche / Rice pudding: un poema para cocinar / a cooking poem* ill. by Fernando Vilela. Groundwood, 2010. ISBN 978-0-88899-981-8 Subj: Activities – baking, cooking. Food. Foreign languages. Poetry.

Armand, Glenda. *Love twelve miles long* ill. by Colin Bootman. Lee & Low, 2011. ISBN 978-1-60060-245-0 Subj: Ethnic groups in the U.S. – African Americans. Family life – mothers. Slavery. U.S. history.

Armstrong, Matthew S. *Jane and Mizmow* ill. by author. HarperCollins, 2011. ISBN 978-0061177194 Subj: Friendship. Monsters.

Arnosky, Jim. *At this very moment* ill. by author. Penguin Group (USA), 2011. ISBN 978-0-525-42252-5 Subj: Animals. Nature.

Slow down for manatees ill. by author. Penguin Group (USA), 2010. ISBN 978-0-399-24170-3 Subj: Animals – manatees. Character traits – kindness to animals.

Asch, Frank. *The Daily Comet: boy saves Earth from giant octopus!* ill. by Devin Asch. Kids Can, 2010. ISBN 978-1-55453-281-0 Subj: Activities – writing. Humorous stories.

Happy birthday, Big Bad Wolf ill. by author. Kids Can, 2011. ISBN 978-1-55337-368-1 Subj: Animals – pigs. Animals – wolves. Birthdays.

Ashburn, Boni. *I had a favorite dress* ill. by Julia Denos. Abrams, 2011. ISBN 978-1-4197-0016-3 Subj: Activities – sewing. Clothing – dresses.

Over at the castle ill. by Kelly Murphy. Abrams, 2010. ISBN 978-0-8109-8414-1 Subj: Castles. Counting, numbers. Dragons. Middle Ages. Rhyming text. Songs.

Ashman, Linda. *No dogs allowed* ill. by Kristin Sorra. Sterling, 2011. ISBN 978-1-4027-5837-9 Subj: Pets. Restaurants. Signs & signboards.

Samantha on a roll ill. by Christine Davenier. Farrar, 2011. ISBN 978-0-374-36399-4 Subj: Rhyming text. Sports – roller skating.

Aston, Dianna Hutts. *A butterfly is patient* ill. by Sylvia Long. Chronicle, 2011. ISBN 978-0-8118-6479-4 Subj: Insects – butterflies, caterpillars. Metamorphosis.

Averbeck, Jim. *Except if* ill. by author. Simon & Schuster, 2011. ISBN 978-1-4169-9544-9 Subj: Animals. Eggs.

Avraham, Kate Aver. *What will you be, Sara Mee?* ill. by Anne Sibley O'Brien. Charlesbridge, 2010. ISBN 978-1-58089-210-0 Subj: Birthdays. Ethnic groups in the U.S. – Korean Americans. Family life. Parties.

Badescu, Ramona. *Pomelo begins to grow* tr. by Claudia Bedrick; ill. by Benjamin Chaud. Enchanted Lion, 2011. ISBN 978-1-59270-111-7 Subj: Animals – elephants. Behavior – growing up.

Baehr, Patricia. *Boo Cow* ill. by Margot Apple. Charlesbridge, 2010. ISBN 978-1-58089-108-0 Subj: Animals – bulls, cows. Birds – chickens. Ghosts.

Baeten, Lieve. *The curious little witch.* NorthSouth, 2010. ISBN 978-0-7358-2305-1 Subj: Format, unusual. Witches.

Happy birthday, Little Witch! ill. by author. NorthSouth, 2011. ISBN 978-0-7358-4043-0 Subj: Animals – cats. Behavior – lost. Birthdays. Format, unusual – toy & movable books. Witches.

Bailey, Linda. *Stanley's little sister* ill. by Bill Slavin. Kids Can, 2010. ISBN 978-1-55453-487-6 Subj: Animals – cats. Animals – dogs. Friendship.

Baker, Jeannie. *Mirror* ill. by author. Candlewick, 2010. ISBN 978-0-7636-4848-0 Subj: Foreign lands – Australia. Foreign lands – Morocco. Format, unusual – toy & movable books. Mirrors. Shopping. Wordless.

Baker, Keith. *LMNO peas* ill. by author. Simon & Schuster, 2010. ISBN 978-1-4169-9141-0 Subj: ABC books. Careers. Food.

No two alike ill. by author. Simon & Schuster, 2011. ISBN 978-1-4424-1742-7 Subj: Birds. Character traits – individuality. Rhyming text. Seasons – winter.

Balouch, Kristen. *The little little girl with the big big voice* ill. by author. Simon & Schuster, 2011. ISBN 978-1-4424-0808-1 Subj: Character traits – smallness. Jungle. Noise, sounds.

Bandy, Michael S. *White water* by Michael S. Bandy and Eric Stein; ill. by Shadra Strickland. Candlewick, 2011. ISBN 978-0-7636-3678-4 Subj: Ethnic groups in the U.S. – African Americans. Prejudice. U.S. history.

Banks, Kate. *The eraserheads* ill. by Boris Kulikov. Farrar, 2010. ISBN 978-0-374-39920-7 Subj: Activities – drawing. Activities – writing. Imagination.

Max's castle ill. by Boris Kulikov. Farrar, 2011. ISBN 978-0-374-39919-1 Subj: Family life – brothers. Imagination. Knights. Language. Toys – blocks.

This baby ill. by Gabi Swiatkowska. Farrar, 2011. ISBN 978-0-374-37514-0 Subj: Babies. Family life – new sibling.

Bansch, Helga. *Brava, mimi!* ill. by author. NorthSouth, 2010. ISBN 978-0-7358-2322-8 Subj: Activities – dancing. Animals – mice. Ballet.

Odd bird out tr. by Monika Smith; ill. by author. Gecko, 2011. ISBN 978-1-8774-6708-0 Subj: Birds – ravens. Character traits – being different. Self-concept.

Bardhan-Quallen, Sudipta. *Chicks run wild* ill. by Ward Jenkins. Simon & Schuster, 2011. ISBN 978-1-4424-0673-5 Subj: Bedtime. Behavior – misbehavior. Birds – chickens. Family life – mothers. Rhyming text.

Hampire! ill. by Howard Fine. HarperCollins, 2011. ISBN 978-0-06-114239-0 Subj: Animals – pigs. Birds – ducks. Food. Humorous stories. Monsters – vampires.

Barner, Bob. *Animal baths* ill. by author. Chronicle, 2011. ISBN 978-1-4521-0056-2 Subj: Activities – bathing. Animals.

Bears! bears! bears! ill. by author. Chronicle, 2010. ISBN 978-0-8118-7057-3 Subj: Animals – bears. Rhyming text.

The Day of the Dead / El Día de los Muertos tr. by Teresa Mlawer; ill. by author. Holiday House, 2010. ISBN 978-0-8234-2214-2 Subj: Foreign languages. Holidays – Day of the Dead.

Barnes, Brynne. *Colors of me* ill. by Annika M. Nelson. Sleeping Bear, 2011. ISBN 978-1-58536-541-8 Subj: Concepts – color. Rhyming text. Self-concept.

Barnett, Mac. *Extra yarn* ill. by Jon Klassen. HarperCollins, 2012. ISBN 978-0-06-195338-5 Subj: Activities – knitting. Concepts – color. Humorous stories. Imagination.

Mustache! ill. by Kevin Cornell. Hyperion/Disney, 2011. ISBN 978-1-4231-1671-4 Subj: Anatomy. Character traits – appearance. Character traits – vanity. Royalty – kings.

Oh no! (or how my science project destroyed the world) ill. by Dan Santat. Hyperion/Disney, 2010. ISBN 978-1-4231-2312-5 Subj: Humorous stories. Robots. Science.

Barrett, Mary Brigid. *Shoebox Sam* ill. by Frank Morrison. Zonderkidz, 2011. ISBN 978-0-310-71549-8 Subj: Careers – shoemakers. Character traits – generosity. Character traits – kindness. Clothing – shoes. Ethnic groups in the U.S. – African Americans. Homeless.

Barry, Frances. *Let's look at dinosaurs: a flip-the-flap book* ill. by author. Candlewick, 2011. ISBN 978-0-7636-5354-5 Subj: Dinosaurs. Format, unusual – toy & movable books.

Let's save the animals: a flip-the-flap book ill. by author. Candlewick, 2010. ISBN 978-0-7636-4501-4 Subj: Animals – endangered animals. Format, unusual – toy & movable books.

Bart, Kathleen. *Town Teddy and Country Bear go global* ill. by author. Reverie, 2011. ISBN 978-1-932485-60-8 Subj: Activities – traveling. Toys – bears. World.

Bartoletti, Susan Campbell. *Naamah and the ark at night* ill. by Holly Meade. Candlewick, 2011. ISBN 978-0-7636-4242-6 Subj: Animals. Boats, ships. Night. Religion.

Barton, Chris. *Shark vs. train* ill. by Tom Lichtenheld. Little, Brown, 2010. ISBN 978-0-316-00762-7 Subj: Contests. Fish – sharks. Trains.

Base, Graeme. *The Jewel Fish of Karnak* ill. by author. Abrams, 2011. ISBN 978-1-4197-0086-6 Subj: Crime. Foreign lands – Egypt. Magic. Puzzles. Royalty – pharaohs.

The legend of the Golden Snail. Abrams, 2010. ISBN 978-0-8109-8965-8 Subj: Animals – snails. Boats, ships. Imagination.

Basher, Simon. *ABC kids* ill. by author. Kingfisher, 2011. ISBN 978-0-7534-6495-3 Subj: ABC books. Language.

Go! Go! Bobo: shapes ill. by author. Kingfisher, 2011. ISBN 978-0-7534-6494-6 Subj: Concepts – shape. Format, unusual – board books.

Bastianich, Lidia. *Nonna tell me a story: Lidia's Christmas kitchen* ill. by Laura Logan. Running Press, 2010. ISBN 978-0-7624-3692-7 Subj: Activities – baking, cooking. Ethnic groups in the U.S. – Italian Americans. Holidays – Christmas.

Bastin, Marjolein. *Christmas with Vera* ill. by author. NorthSouth, 2011. ISBN 978-0-7358-4044-7 Subj: Activities – making things. Animals – mice. Holidays – Christmas.

Bateman, Teresa. *Paul Bunyan vs. Hals Halson: the giant lumberjack challenge!* ill. by C. B. Canga. Whitman, 2011. ISBN 978-0-8075-6367-0 Subj: Careers – lumberjacks. Contests. Tall tales. U.S. history – frontier & pioneer life.

Battersby, Katherine. *Squish Rabbit* ill. by author. Penguin Group (USA), 2011. ISBN 978-0-670-01267-1 Subj: Animals – rabbits. Character traits – smallness. Emotions – loneliness. Friendship.

Battut, Eric. *The fox and the hen* ill. by author. Boxer, 2010. ISBN 978-1-907152-02-3 Subj: Animals. Animals – foxes. Birds – chickens. Eggs. Farms.

Little Mouse's big secret ill. by author. Sterling, 2011. ISBN 978-1-4027-7462-1 Subj: Animals. Animals – mice. Behavior – secrets. Behavior – sharing.

The little pea tr. by Sophie Pauze; ill. by author. Skyhorse/Sky Pony, 2011. ISBN 978-1-61608-482-0 Subj: Character traits – individuality.

Bauer, Marion Dane. *The cutest critter* ill. by Stan Tekiela. Adventure, 2010. ISBN 978-1-59193-253-6 Subj: Animals – babies.

Harriet Tubman ill. by Tammie Lyon. Scholastic, 2010. ISBN 978-0-545-23257-9 Subj: Ethnic groups in the U.S. – African Americans. Prejudice. Slavery. U.S. history.

In like a lion out like a lamb ill. by Emily Arnold McCully. Holiday House, 2011. ISBN 978-0-8234-2238-8 Subj: Rhyming text. Seasons – spring.

Thank you for me! ill. by Kristina Stephenson. Simon & Schuster, 2010. ISBN 978-0-689-85788-1 Subj: Anatomy. Rhyming text.

Beard, Alex. *Crocodile's tears* ill. by author. Abrams, 2012. ISBN 978-1-4197-0008-8 Subj: Animals – endangered animals. Ecology. Foreign lands – Africa. Reptiles – alligators, crocodiles.

Beaton, Clare. *Clare Beaton's action rhymes* ill. by author. Barefoot, 2010. ISBN 978-1-84686-473-5 Subj: Format, unusual – board books. Games.

Clare Beaton's nursery rhymes ill. by author. Barefoot, 2010. ISBN 978-1-84686-472-8 Subj: Format, unusual – board books. Nursery rhymes.

Beaty, Andrea. *Hide and sheep* ill. by Bill Mayer. Simon & Schuster, 2011. ISBN 978-1-4169-2544-6 Subj: Animals – sheep. Counting, numbers. Rhyming text.

Beaumont, Karen. *No sleep for the sheep!* ill. by Jackie Urbanovic. Houghton Harcourt, 2011. ISBN 978-0-15-204969-0 Subj: Animals. Animals – sheep. Bedtime. Farms. Noise, sounds. Rhyming text.

Shoe-la-la! ill. by LeUyen Pham. Scholastic, 2011. ISBN 978-0-545-06705-8 Subj: Character traits – appearance. Clothing – shoes. Rhyming text.

Where's my t-r-u-c-k? ill. by David Catrow. Penguin Group (USA), 2011. ISBN 978-0-8037-3222-3 Subj: Animals – dogs. Behavior – lost & found possessions. Toys. Trucks.

Becker, Bonny. *A bedtime for Bear* ill. by Kady MacDonald Denton. Candlewick, 2010. ISBN 978-0-7636-4101-6 Subj: Animals – bears. Animals – mice. Bedtime. Friendship. Sleepovers.

The sniffles for Bear ill. by Kady MacDonald Denton. Candlewick, 2011. ISBN 978-0-7636-4756-8 Subj: Animals – bears. Animals – mice. Friendship. Illness – cold (disease).

Belton, Robyn. *Herbert: the true story of a brave sea dog* ill. by author. Candlewick, 2010. ISBN 978-0-7636-4741-4 Subj: Animals – dogs. Sea & seashore. Weather – storms.

Bendall-Brunello, Tiziana. *I wish I could read! a story about making friends* ill. by John Bendall-Brunello. Amicus, 2011. ISBN 978-1-60992-109-5 Subj: Animals – pigs. Books, reading. Friendship.

Bennett, Artie. *The butt book* ill. by Mike Lester. Bloomsbury, 2010. ISBN 978-1-59990-311-8 Subj: Anatomy. Rhyming text.

Bennett, Kelly. *Dad and Pop: an ode to fathers and stepfathers* ill. by Paul Meisel. Candlewick, 2010. ISBN 978-0-7636-3379-0 Subj: Family life – fathers. Family life – stepfamilies.

Your daddy was just like you ill. by David Walker. Penguin Group (USA), 2010. ISBN 978-0-399-25258-7 Subj: Behavior. Family life – fathers.

Bently, Peter. *King Jack and the dragon* ill. by Helen Oxenbury. Penguin Group (USA), 2011. ISBN 978-0-8037-3698-6 Subj: Activities – playing. Emotions – fear. Imagination.

Benzwie, Teresa. *Numbers on the move: 1 2 3 dance and count with me* ill. by Mark Weber. Temple Univ., 2011. ISBN 978-1-4399-0342-1 Subj: Activities – dancing. Counting, numbers.

Berger, Carin. *Forever friends* ill. by author. HarperCollins, 2010. ISBN 978-0-06-191528-4 Subj: Animals – rabbits. Birds. Friendship. Seasons.

Berger, Samantha. *Martha doesn't share!* ill. by Bruce Whatley. Little, Brown, 2010. ISBN 978-0-316-07367-7 Subj: Animals – otters. Behavior – sharing.

Bergman, Mara. *Lively Elizabeth! what happens when you push* ill. by Cassia Thomas. Whitman, 2010. ISBN 978-0-8075-4702-1 Subj: Activities – playing. Behavior – carelessness. School.

Berkes, Marianne. *Animalogy: animal analogies* ill. by Cathy Morrison. Sylvan Dell, 2011. ISBN 978-1-60718-127-9 Subj: Animals. Language.

Going home: the mystery of animal migration ill. by Jennifer DiRubbio. Dawn, 2010. ISBN 978-1-58469-126-6 Subj: Animals. Migration.

Over in Australia: amazing animals down under ill. by Jill Dubin. Dawn, 2011. ISBN 978-1-58469-135-8 Subj: Counting, numbers. Foreign lands – Australia. Rhyming text.

Berne, Jennifer. *Calvin can't fly: the story of a bookworm birdie* ill. by Keith Bendis. Sterling, 2010. ISBN 978-1-4027-7323-5 Subj: Activities – flying. Birds. Books, reading. Migration. Weather – hurricanes.

Bernhard, Durga. *While you are sleeping: a lift-the-flap book of time around the world* ill. by author. Charlesbridge, 2011. ISBN 978-1-57091-473-7 Subj: Day. Format, unusual – toy & movable books. Night. Time.

Berry, Lynne. *Ducking for apples* ill. by Hiroe Nakata. Henry Holt, 2010. ISBN 978-0-8050-8935-6 Subj: Birds – ducks. Food. Rhyming text. Sports – bicycling.

Bertrand, Diane Gonzales. *The party for Papa Luis / La fiesta para Papa Luis* ill. by Alejandro Galindo. Arte Publico/Piñata, 2010. ISBN 978-1-55885-532-8 Subj: Birthdays. Cumulative tales. Ethnic groups in the U.S. – Mexican Americans. Language. Parties.

Best, Cari. *Easy as pie* ill. by Melissa Sweet. Farrar, 2010. ISBN 978-0-374-39929-0 Subj: Activities – baking, cooking. Food.

Bianco, Margery Williams. *The velveteen rabbit* ill. by Gennady Spirin. Marshall Cavendish, 2011. ISBN 978-0-7614-5848-7 Subj: Animals – rabbits. Emotions – love. Folk & fairy tales. Magic. Toys.

Bible. New Testament. Gospels. *The story of Christmas* ill. by Pamela Dalton. Chronicle, 2011. ISBN 978-1-4521-0470-6 Subj: Holidays – Christmas. Religion – Nativity.

Biedrzycki, David. *Ace Lacewing, bug detective: the big swat* ill. by author. Charlesbridge, 2010. ISBN 978-1-57091-747-9 Subj: Careers – detectives. Crime. Insects.

Me and my dragon ill. by author. Charlesbridge, 2011. ISBN 978-1-58089-278-0 Subj: Dragons. Pets.

Bildner, Phil. *The hallelujah flight* ill. by John Holyfield. Penguin Group (USA), 2010. ISBN 978-0-399-24789-7 Subj: Activities – flying. Careers – airplane pilots. Ethnic groups in the U.S. – African Americans. U.S. history.

Birdsall, Jeanne. *Flora's very windy day* ill. by Matt Phelan. Clarion, 2010. ISBN 978-0-618-98676-7 Subj: Family life – brothers & sisters. Weather – wind.

Birtha, Becky. *Lucky beans* ill. by Nicole Tadgell. Whitman, 2010. ISBN 978-0-8075-4782-3 Subj: Character traits – cleverness. Contests. Counting, numbers. Ethnic groups in the U.S. – African Americans. U.S. history.

Black, Michael Ian. *A pig parade is a terrible idea* ill. by Kevin Hawkes. Simon & Schuster, 2010. ISBN 978-1-4169-7922-7 Subj: Animals – pigs. Humorous stories. Parades.

The purple kangaroo ill. by Peter Brown. Simon & Schuster, 2010. ISBN 978-1-4169-5771-3 Subj: Animals – monkeys. Humorous stories. Imagination.

Blackaby, Susan. *Brownie Groundhog and the February Fox* ill. by Carmen Segovia. Sterling, 2011. ISBN 978-1-4027-4336-8 Subj: Animals – foxes. Animals – groundhogs. Behavior – trickery. Friendship. Holidays – Groundhog Day. Seasons – winter.

Blackall, Sophie. *Are you awake?* ill. by author. Henry Holt, 2011. ISBN 978-0-8050-7858-9 Subj: Bedtime. Character traits – questioning. Family life – mothers. Night.

Blackstone, Stella. *Bear's birthday* ill. by Debbie Harter. Barefoot, 2011. ISBN 978-1-84686-515-2 Subj: Animals – bears. Birthdays. Counting, numbers. Parties. Rhyming text.

Octopus opposites ill. by Stephanie Bauer. Barefoot, 2010. ISBN 978-1-84686-328-8 Subj: Animals. Concepts – opposites. Rhyming text.

Blackwood, Freya. *Ivy loves to give* ill. by author. Scholastic, 2010. ISBN 978-0-545-23467-2 Subj: Character traits – generosity. Gifts.

Blake, Robert J. *Painter and Ugly* ill. by author. Penguin Group (USA), 2011. ISBN 978-0-399-24323-3 Subj: Alaska. Animals – dogs. Friendship. Sports – racing. Sports – sledding.

Blexbolex. *Seasons* tr. by Claudia Bedrick; ill. by author. Enchanted Lion, 2010. ISBN 978-1-59270-095-0 Subj: Seasons.

Bliss, Harry. *Bailey* ill. by author. Scholastic, 2011. ISBN 978-0-545-23344-6 Subj: Animals – dogs. School.

Bloch, Serge. *You are what you eat: and other mealtime hazards* ill. by author. Sterling, 2010. ISBN 978-1-4027-7130-9 Subj: Food. Humorous stories. Language.

Bloom, Suzanne. *Feeding friendsies* ill. by author. Boyds Mills, 2011. ISBN 978-1-59078-529-4 Subj: Food. Imagination.

What about Bear? ill. by author. Boyds Mills, 2010. ISBN 978-1-59078-528-7 Subj: Activities – playing. Animals – bears. Animals – foxes. Birds – geese. Friendship.

Blumenthal, Deborah. *The blue house dog* ill. by Adam Gustavson. Peachtree, 2010. ISBN 978-1-

56145-537-9 Subj: Animals – dogs. Death. Emotions – grief.

Boelts, Maribeth. *Sweet dreams, little bunny!* ill. by Kathy Parkinson. Whitman, 2010. ISBN 978-0-8075-4589-8 Subj: Animals – rabbits. Bedtime. Format, unusual – board books.

Bolam, Emily. *Animals talk* ill. by author. ME Media/Tiger Tales, 2010. ISBN 978-1-58925-855-6 Subj: Animals. Format, unusual – board books. Noise, sounds.

I go potty ill. by author. Scholastic, 2010. ISBN 978-0-531-25233-8 Subj: Format, unusual – board books. Rhyming text. Toilet training.

Bond, Felicia. *Big hugs, little hugs* ill. by author. Penguin Group (USA), 2012. ISBN 978-0-399-25614-1 Subj: Animals. Hugging.

Bonwill, Ann. *Bug and Bear: a story of true friendship* ill. by Layn Marlow. Marshall Cavendish, 2011. ISBN 978-0-7614-5902-6 Subj: Animals – bears. Friendship. Insects.

Naughty toes ill. by Teresa Murfin. Tiger Tales, 2011. ISBN 978-1-58925-103-8 Subj: Activities – dancing. Ballet. Family life – sisters. Self-concept.

Borden, Louise. *Big brothers don't take naps* ill. by Emma Dodd. Simon & Schuster, 2011. ISBN 978-1-4169-5503-0 Subj: Family life – brothers. Family life – new sibling.

Bottner, Barbara. *An annoying ABC* ill. by Michael Emberley. Random House, 2011. ISBN 978-0-375-86708-8 Subj: ABC books. Behavior – misbehavior. School – nursery.

Miss Brooks loves books! (and I don't) ill. by Michael Emberley. Random House, 2010. ISBN 978-0-375-84682-3 Subj: Books, reading. Libraries. School.

Bouler, Olivia. *Olivia's birds: saving the Gulf* ill. by author. Sterling, 2011. ISBN 978-1-4027-8665-5 Subj: Birds. Character traits – generosity. Character traits – helpfulness. Behavior – resourcefulness. Sea & seashore.

Boyer, Cécile. *Woof meow tweet-tweet* ill. by author. Seven Footer, 2011. ISBN 978-1-934734-60-5 Subj: Animals – cats. Animals – dogs. Birds.

Boyle, Bob. *Hugo and the really, really, really long string* ill. by author. Random House, 2010. ISBN 978-0-375-83423-3 Subj: Animals. String.

Bracken, Beth. *Too shy for show-and-tell* ill. by Jennifer Bell. Picture Window, 2011. ISBN 978-1-4048-6654-6 Subj: Animals – giraffes. Character traits – shyness. School.

Bradford, Wade. *Why do I have to make my bed?* ill. by Johanna van der Sterre. Tricycle, 2011. ISBN 978-1-58246-327-8 Subj: Character traits – cleanliness. Family life – mothers.

Bradman, Tony. *The perfect baby* ill. by Holly Swain. Egmont USA, 2010. ISBN 978-1-4052-2755-1 Subj: Family life – new sibling. Sibling rivalry.

Brallier, Jess M. *Tess's tree* ill. by Peter H. Reynolds. HarperCollins, 2010. ISBN 978-0-06-168752-5 Subj: Trees.

Braun, Eric. *Trust me, Jack's beanstalk stinks: the story of Jack and the beanstalk as told by the giant* ill. by Cristian Bernardini. Picture Window, 2011. ISBN 978-1-4048-6675-1 Subj: Folk & fairy tales. Giants. Humorous stories. Plants.

Braun, Sebastien. *Back to bed, Ed!* ill. by author. Peachtree, 2010. ISBN 978-1-56145-518-8 Subj: Animals – mice. Bedtime. Sleep.

Brennan, Eileen. *Dirtball Pete* ill. by author. Random House, 2010. ISBN 978-0-375-83425-7 Subj: Behavior – messy. Character traits – cleanliness. Hygiene. Self-concept.

Brett, Jan. *The Easter egg* ill. by author. Penguin Group (USA), 2010. ISBN 978-0-399-25238-9 Subj: Animals – rabbits. Contests. Eggs. Holidays – Easter.

Home for Christmas ill. by author. Penguin Group (USA), 2011. ISBN 978-0-399-25653-0 Subj: Behavior – running away. Character traits – helpfulness. Holidays – Christmas. Mythical creatures – trolls.

The three little dassies ill. by author. Penguin Group (USA), 2010. ISBN 978-0-399-25499-4 Subj: Animals. Birds – eagles. Desert. Folk & fairy tales. Foreign lands – Africa. Homes, houses.

Brewer, Paul. *Lincoln tells a joke: how laughter saved the president (and the country)* (Krull, Kathleen)

Brimner, Larry Dane. *Trick or treat, Old Armadillo* ill. by Dominic Catalano. Boyds Mills, 2010. ISBN 978-1-59078-758-8 Subj: Animals – armadillos. Foreign languages. Holidays – Halloween.

Brisson, Pat. *Sometimes we were brave* ill. by France Brassard. Boyds Mills, 2010. ISBN 978-1-59078-586-7 Subj: Careers – military. Emotions. Family life. Family life – mothers.

Broach, Elise. *Gumption!* ill. by Richard Egielski. Simon & Schuster, 2010. ISBN 978-1-4169-1628-4 Subj: Animals. Family life – aunts, uncles. Jungle.

Brocket, Jane. *Ruby, violet, lime: looking for color* photos by author. Millbrook, 2011. ISBN 978-0-7613-4612-8 Subj: Concepts – color. Language.

Brokamp, Elizabeth. *The picky little witch* ill. by Marsha Riti. Pelican, 2011. ISBN 978-1-58980-882-9 Subj: Food. Holidays – Halloween. Witches.

Bromley, Anne C. *The lunch thief* ill. by Robert Casilla. Tilbury House, 2010. ISBN 978-0-88448-311-3 Subj: Behavior – stealing. Character traits – kindness. Homeless. School.

Brooks, Erik. *Polar opposites* ill. by author. Marshall Cavendish, 2010. ISBN 978-0-7614-5685-8 Subj: Animals – polar bears. Birds – penguins. Character traits – individuality. Concepts – opposites. Foreign lands – Antarctic. Foreign lands – Arctic.

Brown, Alan James. *Love-a-Duck* ill. by Francesca Chessa. Holiday House, 2010. ISBN 978-0-8234-2263-0 Subj: Activities – bathing. Behavior – lost & found possessions. Birds – ducks. Toys.

Brown, Calef. *Boy wonders* ill. by author. Simon & Schuster, 2011. ISBN 978-1-4169-7877-0 Subj: Character traits – questioning. Rhyming text.

Brown, Don. *A wizard from the start: the incredible boyhood and amazing inventions of Thomas Edison* ill. by author. Houghton Harcourt, 2010. ISBN 978-0-547-19487-5 Subj: Careers – inventors. U.S. history.

Brown, Lisa. *Vampire boy's good night* ill. by author. HarperCollins, 2010. ISBN 978-0-06-114011-2 Subj: Holidays – Halloween. Monsters – Vampires. Witches.

Brown, Marc. *Arthur turns green* ill. by author. Little, Brown, 2011. ISBN 978-0-316-12924-4 Subj: Animals – aardvarks. Ecology. Family life – brothers & sisters. School.

Brown, Margaret Wise. *The fathers are coming home* ill. by Stephen Savage. Simon & Schuster, 2010. ISBN 978-0-689-83345-8 Subj: Animals. Family life – fathers. Night.

Goodnight moon ABC: an alphabet book ill. by Clement Hurd. HarperCollins, 2010. ISBN 978-0-06-189484-8 Subj: ABC books. Animals – rabbits. Bedtime. Moon.

Sleepy ABC ill. by Karen Katz. HarperCollins, 2010. ISBN 978-0-06-128863-0 Subj: ABC books. Bedtime. Rhyming text. Sleep.

Brown, Monica. *Chavela and the magic bubble* ill. by Magaly Morales. Clarion, 2010. ISBN 978-0-547-24197-5 Subj: Ethnic groups in the U.S. – Mexican Americans. Family life – grandmothers. Magic.

Side by side / Lado a lado: the story of Dolores Huerta and Cesar Chavez / la historia de Dolores Huerta y Cesar Chavez ill. by Joe Cepeda. HarperCollins, 2010. ISBN 978-0-06-122781-3 Subj: Ethnic groups in the U.S. – Mexican Americans. Foreign languages. U.S. history. Violence, nonviolence.

Waiting for the Biblioburro ill. by John Parra. Tricycle, 2011. ISBN 978-1-58246-353-7 Subj: Animals – donkeys. Books, reading. Foreign lands – Colombia. Libraries.

Brown, Peter. *Children make terrible pets* ill. by author. Little, Brown, 2010. ISBN 978-0-316-01548-6 Subj: Animals – bears. Humorous stories. Pets.

You will be my friend! ill. by author. Little, Brown, 2011. ISBN 978-0-316-07030-0 Subj: Animals – bears. Friendship.

Brown, Ruth. *Gracie the lighthouse cat* ill. by author. Andersen, 2011. ISBN 978-0-7613-7454-1 Subj: Animals – cats. Behavior – lost. Lighthouses.

Brown, Tameka Fryer. *Around our way on Neighbors' Day* ill. by Charlotte Riley-Webb. Abrams, 2010. ISBN 978-0-8109-8971-9 Subj: Cities, towns. Communities, neighborhoods. Parties. Rhyming text.

Brown, Tami Lewis. *Soar, Elinor!* ill. by François Roca. Farrar, 2010. ISBN 978-0-374-37115-9 Subj: Activities – flying. Careers – airplane pilots. Gender roles. U.S. history.

Browne, Anthony. *Me and you* ill. by author. Farrar, 2010. ISBN 978-0-374-34908-0 Subj: Animals – bears. Behavior – lost. Cities, towns. Folk & fairy tales.

Browne, Eileen. *Handa's hen* ill. by author. Candlewick, 2011. ISBN 978-0-7636-5361-3 Subj: Animals. Birds – chickens. Counting, numbers. Foreign lands – Kenya.

Browning, Diane. *Signed, Abiah Rose* ill. by author. Tricycle, 2010. ISBN 978-1-58246-311-7 Subj: Careers – artists. Gender roles. U.S. history – frontier & pioneer life.

Browning, Kurt. *T is for tutu: a ballet alphabet* (Rodriguez, Sonia)

Bruchac, Joseph. *My father is taller than a tree* ill. by Wendy Anderson Halperin. Penguin Group (USA), 2010. ISBN 978-0-8037-3173-8 Subj: Family life – fathers. Rhyming text.

Bruel, Nick. *A Bad Kitty Christmas* ill. by author. Roaring Brook, 2011. ISBN 978-1-59643-668-8 Subj: Animals – cats. Behavior – misbehavior. Holidays – Christmas. Rhyming text.

Bruins, David. *The call of the cowboy* ill. by Hilary Leung. Kids Can, 2011. ISBN 978-1-55453-748-8 Subj: Animals – bears. Cowboys, cowgirls. Friendship. Noise, sounds.

Brun-Cosme, Nadine. *Big Wolf and Little Wolf, such a beautiful orange!* tr. by Claudia Bedrick; ill. by Olivier Tallec. Enchanted Lion, 2011. ISBN 978-1-59270-106-3 Subj: Animals – wolves. Behavior – worrying. Friendship.

Buck, Nola. *A Christmas goodnight* ill. by Sarah Jane Wright. HarperCollins, 2011. ISBN 978-0-06-166491-5 Subj: Holidays – Christmas. Religion. Rhyming text.

Budnitz, Paul. *The hole in the middle* ill. by Aya Kakeda. Hyperion/Disney, 2011. ISBN 978-1-4231-3761-0 Subj: Format, unusual. Friendship. Self-concept.

Buehner, Caralyn. *Snowmen all year* ill. by Mark Buehner. Penguin Group (USA), 2010. ISBN 978-0-8037-3383-1 Subj: Magic. Rhyming text. Snowmen.

Bunting, Eve. *Finn McCool and the great fish* ill. by Zachary Pullen. Sleeping Bear, 2010. ISBN 978-1-58536-366-7 Subj: Fish. Folk & fairy tales. Foreign lands – Ireland. Giants.

Hey diddle diddle ill. by Mary Ann Fraser. Boyds Mills, 2011. ISBN 978-1-59078-768-7 Subj: Animals. Musical instruments. Rhyming text.

My dog Jack is fat ill. by Michael Rex. Marshall Cavendish, 2011. ISBN 978-0-7614-5809-8 Subj: Animals – dogs. Health & fitness.

Pirate boy ill. by Julie Fortenberry. Holiday House, 2011. ISBN 978-0-8234-2321-7 Subj: Family life – mothers. Imagination. Pirates.

Tweak tweak ill. by Sergio Ruzzier. Clarion, 2011. ISBN 978-0-618-99851-7 Subj: Animals – elephants. Character traits – curiosity. Family life – mothers.

Will it be a baby brother? ill. by Beth Spiegel. Boyds Mills, 2010. ISBN 978-1-59078-439-6 Subj: Babies. Family life – new sibling.

Burell, Sarah. *Diamond Jim Dandy and the sheriff* ill. by Bryan Langdo. Sterling, 2010. ISBN 978-1-4027-5737-2 Subj: Babies. Reptiles – snakes. Texas. U.S. history – frontier & pioneer life.

Burg, Sarah Emmanuelle. *Do you still love me?* ill. by author. NorthSouth, 2010. ISBN 978-0-7358-2293-1 Subj: Behavior – fighting, arguing. Behavior – worrying. Family life – parents.

Burleigh, Robert. *Good-bye, Sheepie* ill. by Peter Catalanotto. Marshall Cavendish, 2010. ISBN 978-0-7614-5598-1 Subj: Animals – dogs. Death. Family life – fathers. Pets.

Burnell, Heather Ayris. *Bedtime monster / ¡A dormir, pequeño monstruo!* ill. by Bonnie Adamson. Raven Tree, 2010. ISBN 978-1-932748-80-2 Subj:

Bedtime. Emotions – anger. Foreign languages. Monsters.

Burningham, John. *There's going to be a baby* ill. by Helen Oxenbury. Candlewick, 2010. ISBN 978-0-7636-4907-4 Subj: Babies. Family life – new sibling.

Butler, M. Christina. *The smiley snowman* ill. by Tina Macnaughton. Good Books, 2010. ISBN 978-1-56148-696-0 Subj: Animals. Seasons – winter. Snowmen.

The special blankie ill. by Tina Macnaughton. Good Books, 2010. ISBN 978-1-56148-682-3 Subj: Activities – babysitting. Animals – hedgehogs. Behavior – lost & found possessions.

Butterworth, Chris. *How did that get in my lunchbox? the story of food* ill. by Lucia Gaggiotti. Candlewick, 2011. ISBN 978-0-7636-5005-6 Subj: Food. Health & fitness.

Button, Lana. *Willow's whispers* ill. by Tania Howells. Kids Can, 2010. ISBN 978-1-55453-280-3 Subj: Behavior – resourcefulness. Character traits – shyness. School.

Buzzeo, Toni. *Adventure Annie goes to kindergarten* ill. by Amy Wummer. Penguin Group (USA), 2010. ISBN 978-0-8037-3358-9 Subj: School – first day.

Lighthouse Christmas ill. by Nancy Carpenter. Penguin Group (USA), 2011. ISBN 978-0-8037-3053-3 Subj: Airplanes, airports. Family life – brothers & sisters. Holidays – Christmas. Lighthouses.

No T. Rex in the library ill. by Sachiko Yoshikawa. Simon & Schuster, 2010. ISBN 978-1-4169-3927-6 Subj: Behavior – misbehavior. Dinosaurs. Libraries.

Penelope Popper book doctor ill. by Jana Christy. Upstart, 2011. ISBN 978-1-60213-054-8 Subj: Books, reading. Libraries.

Cabrera, Jane. *Here we go round the mulberry bush* ill. by author. Holiday House, 2010. ISBN 978-0-8234-2288-3 Subj: Animals – dogs. Songs.

The wheels on the bus ill. by author. Holiday House, 2011. ISBN 978-0-8234-2350-7 Subj: Buses. Foreign lands – Africa. Music. Songs.

Cadow, Kenneth M. *Alfie runs away* ill. by Lauren Castillo. Farrar, 2010. ISBN 978-0-374-30202-3 Subj: Behavior – running away. Family life – mothers.

Callery, Sean. *Hide and seek in the jungle* ill. by Rebecca Robinson. Kingfisher, 2010. ISBN 978-0-7534-6392-5 Subj: Animals. Format, unusual – board books. Jungle.

Calvert, Pam. *Princess Peepers picks a pet* ill. by Tuesday Mourning. Marshall Cavendish, 2011. ISBN 978-0-7614-5815-9 Subj: Contests. Dragons. Glasses. Royalty – princesses.

Campoy, F. Isabel. *¡Muu, moo! rimas de animales = animal nursery rhymes* (Ada, Alma Flor)

Cantrell, Charlie. *A friend for Einstein: the smallest stallion* by Charlie Cantrell and Rachel Wagner. Hyperion/Disney, 2011. ISBN 978-1-4231-4563-9 Subj: Animals – horses, ponies. Character traits – smallness.

Capucilli, Alyssa Satin. *My first ballet class* photos by Leyah Jensen. Simon & Schuster, 2011. ISBN 978-1-4424-0895-1 Subj: Ballet. Format, unusual – toy & movable books.

My first soccer game: a book with foldout pages photos by Leyah Jensen. Simon & Schuster, 2011. ISBN 978-1-4424-2747-1 Subj: Format, unusual. Sports – soccer.

Carle, Eric. *The artist who painted a blue horse* ill. by author. Penguin Group (USA), 2011. ISBN 978-0-399-25713-1 Subj: Activities – painting. Animals. Art. Careers – artists. Concepts – color.

Carlson, Nancy. *Henry and the bully* ill. by author. Penguin Group (USA), 2010. ISBN 978-0-670-01148-3 Subj: Animals. Animals – mice. Behavior – bullying. School.

Carluccio, Maria. *I'm 3! Look what I can do* ill. by author. Henry Holt, 2010. ISBN 978-0-8050-8313-2 Subj: Behavior – growing up.

Carney, Mary Lou. *The yippy, yappy Yorkie in the green doggy sweater* (Macomber, Debbie)

Carrer, Chiara. *Otto Carrotto* ill. by author. Eerdmans, 2011. ISBN 978-0-8028-5393-6 Subj: Animals – rabbits. Character traits – individuality. Food.

Carroll, James Christopher. *The boy and the moon* ill. by author. Sleeping Bear, 2010. ISBN 978-1-58536-521-0 Subj: Moon. Night.

Cartaya, Pablo. *Tina Cocolina: queen of the cupcakes* by Pablo Cartaya and Martin Howard; ill. by Kirsten Richards. Random House, 2010. ISBN 978-0-375-85891-8 Subj: Activities – baking, cooking. Character traits – individuality. Contests. Food.

Casanova, Mary. *The day Dirk Yeller came to town* ill. by Ard Hoyt. Farrar, 2011. ISBN 978-0-374-31742-3 Subj: Books, reading. Crime. Libraries. U.S. history – frontier & pioneer life.

Utterly otterly night ill. by Ard Hoyt. Simon & Schuster, 2011. ISBN 978-1-4169-7562-5 Subj: Animals – otters. Night. Seasons – winter.

Castellucci, Cecil. *Grandma's gloves* ill. by Julia Denos. Candlewick, 2010. ISBN 978-0-7636-3168-0 Subj: Death. Family life – grandmothers. Gardens, gardening.

Castillo, Lauren. *Melvin and the boy* ill. by author. Henry Holt, 2011. ISBN 978-0-8050-8929-5 Subj: Pets. Reptiles – turtles, tortoises.

Caswell, Deanna. *Train trip* ill. by Dan Andreasen. Hyperion/Disney, 2011. ISBN 978-1-4231-1837-4 Subj: Rhyming text. Trains.

Celenza, Anna Harwell. *Duke Ellington's Nutcracker Suite* ill. by Don Tate. Charlesbridge, 2011. ISBN 978-1-57091-700-4 Subj: Careers – musicians. Ethnic groups in the U.S. – African Americans. Music.

Chaconas, Dori. *Don't slam the door!* ill. by Will Hillenbrand. Candlewick, 2010. ISBN 978-0-7636-3709-5 Subj: Animals. Cumulative tales. Humorous stories. Rhyming text.

Hurry down to Derry Fair ill. by Gillian Tyler. Candlewick, 2011. ISBN 978-0-7636-3208-3 Subj: Fairs, festivals. Family life. Rhyming text.

Chall, Marsha Wilson. *One pup's up* ill. by Henry Cole. Simon & Schuster, 2010. ISBN 978-1-4169-7960-9 Subj: Animals – dogs. Counting, numbers. Rhyming text.

Pick a pup ill. by Jed Henry. Simon & Schuster, 2011. ISBN 978-1-4169-7961-6 Subj: Animals – dogs. Character traits – kindness to animals. Pets.

Chapman, Susan Margaret. *Too much noise in the library* ill. by Abby Carter. Upstart, 2010. ISBN 978-1-60213-026-5 Subj: Libraries. Noise, sounds.

Charest, Emily MacLachlan. *Before you came* (MacLachlan, Patricia)

Chedru, Delphine. *Spot it again!* ill. by author. Abrams, 2011. ISBN 978-0-8109-9736-3 Subj: Format, unusual. Picture puzzles.

Chichester Clark, Emma. *Little Miss Muffet counts to ten* ill. by author. Andersen, 2010. ISBN 978-1-84270-955-9 Subj: Animals. Counting, numbers. Nursery rhymes. Rhyming text.

Child, Lauren. *I really, really need actual ice skates* ill. by author. Penguin Group (USA), 2010. ISBN 978-0-8037-3451-7 Subj: Family life – brothers & sisters. Money. Sports – ice skating.

My best, best friend ill. by author and Tiger Aspect Productions. Penguin Group (USA), 2011. ISBN 978-0-8037-3586-6 Subj: Family life – brothers & sisters. Friendship.

Child, Lydia Maria. *Over the river and through the wood: the New England boy's song about Thanksgiving Day* ill. by Matt Tavares. Candlewick, 2011. ISBN 978-0-7636-2790-4 Subj: Family life – grandparents. Farms. Holidays – Thanksgiving. Songs.

Chin, Jason. *Coral reefs* ill. by author. Roaring Brook, 2011. ISBN 978-1-59643-563-6 Subj: Books, reading. Ecology. Imagination. Sea & seashore.

Chin, Joel. *The falling raindrop* (Johnson, Neil)

Chin, Oliver. *The year of the tiger: tales from the Chinese zodiac* ill. by Justin Roth. Immedium, 2010. ISBN 978-1-59702-020-6 Subj: Animals. Animals – tigers. Zodiac.

Chivers, Natalie. *Rhino's great big itch!* ill. by author. Good Books, 2010. ISBN 978-1-56148-684-7 Subj: Animals. Animals – rhinoceros. Birds. Problem solving.

Choldenko, Gennifer. *A giant crush* ill. by Melissa Sweet. Penguin Group (USA), 2011. ISBN 978-0-399-24352-3 Subj: Character traits – shyness. Holidays – Valentine's Day. School.

Chou, Yih-Fen. *Mimi loves to mimic* ill. by Chih-Yuan Chen. Heryin, 2010. ISBN 978-0-9787550-8-9 Subj: Behavior – imitation. Character traits – curiosity.

Mimi says no ill. by Chih-Yuan Chen. Heryin, 2010. ISBN 978-0-9787550-7-2 Subj: Character traits – assertiveness. Character traits – stubbornness.

Christelow, Eileen. *The desperate dog writes again* ill. by author. Clarion, 2010. ISBN 978-0-547-24205-7 Subj: Activities – writing. Animals – dogs. Humorous stories. Letters, cards.

Five little monkeys reading in bed ill. by author. Clarion, 2011. ISBN 978-0-547-38610-2 Subj: Animals – monkeys. Bedtime. Books, reading. Rhyming text.

Christian, Cheryl. *Witches* ill. by Wish Williams. Star Bright, 2011. ISBN 978-1-59572-283-6 Subj: Holidays – Halloween. Rhyming text. Witches.

Church, Caroline Jayne. *One more hug for Madison* ill. by author. Scholastic, 2010. ISBN 978-

0-545-16179-4 Subj: Animals – mice. Bedtime. Family life – mothers. Hugging.

Clark, Julie Aigner. *You are the best medicine* ill. by Jana Christy. HarperCollins, 2010. ISBN 978-0-06-195644-7 Subj: Emotions – love. Family life – mothers. Illness – cancer.

Clark, Karen Henry. *Sweet moon baby: an adoption tale* ill. by Patrice Barton. Random House, 2010. ISBN 978-0-375-85709-6 Subj: Adoption. Foreign lands – China. Moon.

Clarke, Jane. *Gilbert the hero* ill. by Charles Fuge. Sterling, 2011. ISBN 978-1-4027-8040-0 Subj: Activities – playing. Family life – brothers. Fish – sharks.

Trumpet: the little elephant with a big temper ill. by Charles Fuge. Simon & Schuster, 2010. ISBN 978-1-4169-0482-3 Subj: Animals – elephants. Birthdays. Emotions – anger. Parties.

Cleary, Brian P. *Six sheep sip thick shakes and other tricky tongue twisters* ill. by Steve Mack. Millbrook, 2011. ISBN 978-1-58013-585-6 Subj: Tongue twisters.

Clement, Nathan. *Job site* ill. by author. Boyds Mills, 2011. ISBN 978-1-59078-769-4 Subj: Careers – construction workers. Machines.

Clements, Andrew. *The handiest things in the world* photos by Raquel Jaramillo. Simon & Schuster, 2010. ISBN 978-1-4169-6166-6 Subj: Anatomy – hands. Rhyming text.

Clifton-Brown, Holly. *Annie Hoot and the knitting extravaganza* ill. by author. Andersen, 2010. ISBN 978-0-7613-6444-3 Subj: Activities – knitting. Activities – traveling. Birds – owls.

Cocca-Leffler, Maryann. *Princess Kim and too much truth* ill. by author. Whitman, 2011. ISBN 978-0-8075-6618-3 Subj: Character traits – honesty. School.

Rain brings frogs: a little book of hope ill. by author. HarperCollins, 2011. ISBN 978-0-06-196106-9 Subj: Character traits – optimism. Hope.

Codell, Esmé Raji. *The basket ball* ill. by Jennifer Plecas. Abrams, 2011. ISBN 978-1-4197-0007-1 Subj: Gender roles. Sports – basketball.

Coerr, Eleanor. *Circus day in Japan* tr. by Yumi Matsunari; ill. by author. Tuttle, 2010. ISBN 978-4-8053-1059-5 Subj: Circus. Foreign lands – Japan. Foreign languages.

Coffelt, Nancy. *Catch that baby!* ill. by Scott Nash. Simon & Schuster, 2011. ISBN 978-1-4169-9148-9 Subj: Activities – bathing. Babies. Humorous stories.

Cohen, Caron Lee. *Broom, zoom!* ill. by Sergio Ruzzier. Simon & Schuster, 2010. ISBN 978-1-4169-9113-7 Subj: Behavior – cooperation. Character traits – cleanliness. Friendship. Monsters. Witches.

Colato Laínez, René. *My shoes and I* ill. by Fabricio Vanden Broeck. Boyds Mills, 2010. ISBN 978-1-59078-385-6 Subj: Clothing – shoes. Family life – fathers. Foreign lands – El Salvador. Immigrants.

The Tooth Fairy meets El Ratón Pérez ill. by Tom Lintern. Tricycle, 2010. ISBN 978-1-58246-296-7 Subj: Ethnic groups in the U.S. – Mexican Americans. Fairies. Teeth.

Cole, Brock. *The money we'll save* ill. by author. Farrar, 2011. ISBN 978-0-374-35011-6 Subj: Birds – turkeys. Family life. Holidays – Christmas.

Cole, Henry. *The littlest evergreen* ill. by author. HarperCollins, 2011. ISBN 978-0-06-114519-0 Subj: Ecology. Holidays – Christmas. Trees.

Cole, Joanna. *I'm a big sister* ill. by Rosalinda Kightley. HarperCollins, 2010. ISBN 978-0-06-190062-4 Subj: Family life – new sibling. Family life – sisters.

The magic school bus and the climate challenge ill. by Bruce Degen. Scholastic, 2010. ISBN 978-0-590-10826-3 Subj: Ecology. Science. Weather.

Collins, Ross. *Doodleday* ill. by author. Whitman, 2011. ISBN 978-0-8075-1683-6 Subj: Activities – drawing. Behavior – misbehavior. Family life – mothers.

Comden, Betty. *What's new at the zoo?* by Betty Comden and Adolph Green; ill. by Travis Foster. Blue Apple, 2011. ISBN 978-1-60905-088-7 Subj: Animals. Format, unusual – toy & movable books. Songs. Zoos.

Compestine, Ying Chang. *Crouching tiger* ill. by Yan Nascimbene. Candlewick, 2011. ISBN 978-0-7636-4642-4 Subj: Ethnic groups in the U.S. – Chinese Americans. Family life – grandfathers. Holidays – Chinese New Year. Self-concept.

The runaway wok: a Chinese New Year tale ill. by Sebastià Serra. Penguin Group (USA), 2011. ISBN 978-0-525-42068-2 Subj: Activities – baking, cooking. Foreign lands – China. Holidays – Chinese New Year. Magic.

Conahan, Carolyn. *The big wish* ill. by author. Chronicle, 2011. ISBN 978-0-8118-7040-5 Subj: Behavior – cooperation. Behavior – wishing. Contests.

Conway, David. *Errol and his extraordinary nose* ill. by Roberta Angaramo. Holiday House, 2010. ISBN 978-0-8234-2262-3 Subj: Anatomy – noses.

Animals – elephants. School. Self-concept. Theater.

Cook, Julia. *The "D" word: divorce* ill. by Phillip W. Rodgers. National Center for Youth Issues, 2011. ISBN 978-1-931636-76-6 Subj: Divorce.

Cook, Lisa Broadie. *Peanut butter and homework sandwiches* ill. by Jack E. Davis. Penguin Group (USA), 2011. ISBN 978-0-399-24533-6 Subj: Careers – teachers. Homework. School.

Cooper, Elisha. *Beaver is lost* ill. by author. Random House, 2010. ISBN 978-0-375-85765-2 Subj: Animals – beavers. Behavior – lost.

Farm ill. by author. Scholastic, 2010. ISBN 978-0-545-07075-1 Subj: Farms. Seasons.

Cora, Cat. *A suitcase surprise for Mommy* ill. by Joy Allen. Penguin Group (USA), 2011. ISBN 978-0-8037-3332-9 Subj: Activities – traveling. Emotions – sadness. Family life – mothers.

Corderoy, Tracey. *The little white owl* ill. by Jane Chapman. Good Books, 2010. ISBN 978-1-56148-693-9 Subj: Birds – owls. Character traits – being different. Friendship.

Corey, Dorothy. *You go away* ill. by Lisa Fox. Whitman, 2010. ISBN 978-0-8075-9440-7 Subj: Behavior – worrying. Family life.

Costello, David Hyde. *I can help* ill. by author. Farrar, 2010. ISBN 978-0-374-33526-7 Subj: Animals. Birds – ducks. Character traits – helpfulness.

Little Pig joins the band ill. by author. Charlesbridge, 2011. ISBN 978-1-58089-264-3 Subj: Animals – pigs. Careers – conductors (music). Character traits – smallness. Musical instruments – bands.

Côté, Geneviève. *Without you* ill. by author. Kids Can, 2011. ISBN 978-1-55453-620-7 Subj: Animals – pigs. Animals – rabbits. Behavior – fighting, arguing. Friendship.

Cousins, Lucy. *I'm the best* ill. by author. Candlewick, 2010. ISBN 978-0-7636-4684-4 Subj: Animals. Animals – dogs. Behavior – boasting. Character traits – pride. Character traits – vanity. Friendship.

Maisy goes on vacation ill. by author. Candlewick, 2010. ISBN 978-0-7636-4752-0 Subj: Activities – vacationing. Animals – mice. Sea & seashore.

Maisy's amazing big book of learning ill. by author. Candlewick, 2011. ISBN 978-0-7636-5481-8 Subj: Animals. Animals – mice. Concepts. Format, unusual – toy & movable books.

Maisy's book of things that go ill. by author. Candlewick, 2010. ISBN 978-0-7636-4614-1 Subj: Animals. Animals – mice. Format, unusual – toy & movable books. Transportation.

Cowcher, Helen. *Desert elephants* ill. by author. Farrar, 2011. ISBN 978-0-374-31774-4 Subj: Animals – elephants. Behavior – cooperation. Character traits – kindness to animals. Foreign lands – Mali. Migration.

Cowen-Fletcher, Jane. *Hello, puppy!* ill. by author. Candlewick, 2010. ISBN 978-0-7636-4303-4 Subj: Animals – babies. Animals – dogs. Pets.

Cox, Judy. *Carmen learns English* ill. by Angela Dominguez. Holiday House, 2010. ISBN 978-0-8234-2174-9 Subj: Ethnic groups in the U.S. – Mexican Americans. Family life – sisters. Foreign languages. School.

Cinco de Mouse-o! ill. by Jeffrey Ebbeler. Holiday House, 2010. ISBN 978-0-8234-2194-7 Subj: Animals – mice. Holidays – Cinco de Mayo.

Haunted house, haunted mouse ill. by Jeffrey Ebbeler. Holiday House, 2011. ISBN 978-0-8234-2315-6 Subj: Animals – mice. Holidays – Halloween.

Coyle, Carmela LaVigna. *Do princesses have best friends forever?* ill. by Mike Gordon and Carl Gordon. Taylor Trade, 2010. ISBN 978-1-58979-542-6 Subj: Friendship. Rhyming text. Royalty – princesses.

Craig, Lindsey. *Dancing feet!* ill. by Marc Brown. Random House, 2010. ISBN 978-0-375-86181-9 Subj: Activities – dancing. Animals. Rhyming text.

Farmyard beat ill. by Marc Brown. Random House, 2011. ISBN 978-0-375-86455-1 Subj: Animals. Bedtime. Farms. Noise, sounds. Rhyming text.

Crews, Nina. *Sky-high Guy* ill. by author. Henry Holt, 2010. ISBN 978-0-8050-8764-2 Subj: Activities – playing. Family life – brothers. Toys.

Crimi, Carolyn. *Dear Tabby* ill. by David Roberts. HarperCollins, 2011. ISBN 978-0-06-114245-1 Subj: Activities – writing. Animals. Animals – cats. Letters, cards.

Principal Fred won't go to bed ill. by Donald Wu. Marshall Cavendish, 2010. ISBN 978-0-7614-5709-1 Subj: Bedtime. Behavior – lost & found possessions. Careers – school principals. Rhyming text. Toys – bears.

Rock 'n' roll Mole ill. by Lynn Munsinger. Penguin Group (USA), 2011. ISBN 978-0-8037-3166-0 Subj: Animals – moles. Emotions – fear. Music. Theater.

Cronin, Doreen. *M.O.M. (Mom Operating Manual)* ill. by Laura Cornell. Simon & Schuster, 2011. ISBN 978-1-4169-6150-5 Subj: Family life – mothers. Humorous stories.

Rescue bunnies ill. by Scott Menchin. HarperCollins, 2010. ISBN 978-0-06-112871-4 Subj: Animals – giraffes. Animals – rabbits.

Crosby, Jeff. *Wiener Wolf* ill. by author. Hyperion/Disney, 2011. ISBN 978-1-4231-3983-6 Subj: Animals – dogs. Animals – wolves. Behavior – dissatisfaction.

Crowther, Robert. *Amazing pop-up trucks* ill. by author. Candlewick, 2011. ISBN 978-0-7636-5587-7 Subj: Format, unusual – toy & movable books. Trucks.

Crum, Shutta. *Mine!* ill. by Patrice Barton. Random House, 2011. ISBN 978-0-375-86711-8 Subj: Babies. Behavior – sharing. Toys.

Crummel, Susan Stevens. *The little red pen* (Stevens, Janet)

Ten-Gallon Bart beats the heat ill. by Dorothy Donohue. Marshall Cavendish, 2010. ISBN 978-0-7614-5634-6 Subj: Alaska. Animals – dogs. Weather – blizzards.

Cummings, Phil. *Boom bah!* ill. by Nina Rycroft. Kane/Miller, 2010. ISBN 978-1-935279-22-8 Subj: Animals. Music. Musical instruments. Noise, sounds.

Cummings, Troy. *The Eensy Weensy Spider freaks out! (big-time!)* ill. by author. Random House, 2010. ISBN 978-0-375-86582-4 Subj: Nursery rhymes. Self-concept. Spiders.

Cunnane, Kelly. *Chirchir is singing* ill. by Jude Daly. Random House, 2011. ISBN 978-0-375-86198-7 Subj: Activities – singing. Character traits – helpfulness. Family life. Foreign lands – Kenya.

Curtis, Jamie Lee. *My mommy hung the moon: a love story* ill. by Laura Cornell. HarperCollins, 2010. ISBN 978-0-06-029016-0 Subj: Family life – mothers. Rhyming text.

Cushman, Doug. *Christmas Eve good night* ill. by author. Henry Holt, 2011. ISBN 978-0-8050-6603-6 Subj: Bedtime. Holidays – Christmas. Rhyming text.

Halloween good night ill. by author. Henry Holt, 2010. ISBN 978-0-8050-8928-8 Subj: Bedtime. Holidays – Halloween. Monsters. Rhyming text.

Cusimano, Maryann K. *You are my wish* ill. by Satomi Ichikawa. Penguin Group (USA), 2010. ISBN 978-0-399-24752-1 Subj: Animals – bears. Family life – grandparents. Rhyming text.

Cuyler, Margery. *Guinea pigs add up* ill. by Tracey Campbell Pearson. Walker, 2010. ISBN 978-0-8027-9795-7 Subj: Animals – guinea pigs. Counting, numbers. Pets. Rhyming text. School.

I repeat, don't cheat! ill. by Arthur Howard. Simon & Schuster, 2010. ISBN 978-1-4169-7167-2 Subj: Behavior – cheating. Behavior – lying. Character traits – honesty. Friendship. School.

Cyrus, Kurt. *Big rig bugs* ill. by author. Walker, 2010. ISBN 978-0-8027-8674-6 Subj: Insects. Rhyming text. Trucks.

The voyage of turtle Rex ill. by author. Houghton Harcourt, 2011. ISBN 978-0-547-42924-3 Subj: Dinosaurs. Reptiles – turtles, tortoises. Rhyming text.

Czekaj, Jef. *A call for a new alphabet* ill. by author. Charlesbridge, 2011. ISBN 978-1-58089-228-5 Subj: ABC books. Humorous stories.

Cat secrets ill. by author. HarperCollins, 2011. ISBN 978-0-06-192088-2 Subj: Animals – cats. Humorous stories.

Hip and Hop, don't stop! ill. by author. Hyperion/Disney, 2010. ISBN 978-1-4231-1664-6 Subj: Animals – rabbits. Contests. Music. Reptiles – turtles, tortoises.

Dahl, Michael. *Nap time for Kitty* ill. by Oriol Vidal. Capstone, 2011. ISBN 978-1-4048-5216-7 Subj: Animals – cats. Format, unusual – board books. Sleep.

Dale, Penny. *Dinosaur dig!* ill. by author. Candlewick, 2011. ISBN 978-0-7636-5871-7 Subj: Careers – construction workers. Counting, numbers. Dinosaurs. Trucks.

Daly, Cathleen. *Prudence wants a pet* ill. by Stephen Michael King. Roaring Brook, 2011. ISBN 978-1-59643-468-4 Subj: Character traits – persistence. Imagination. Pets.

Daly, Niki. *A song for Jamela* ill. by author. Frances Lincoln, 2010. ISBN 978-1-84507-871-3 Subj: Beauty shops. Foreign lands – South Africa.

D'Amico, Carmela. *Suki the very loud bunny* by Carmela D'Amico and Steven D'Amico; ill. by Steven D'Amico. Penguin Group (USA), 2011. ISBN 978-0-525-42230-3 Subj: Animals – rabbits. Behavior – lost.

D'Amico, Steven. *Suki the very loud bunny* (D'Amico, Carmela)

Danneberg, Julie. *The big test* ill. by Judy Love. Charlesbridge, 2011. ISBN 978-1-58089-360-2 Subj: Emotions – fear. School.

Danticat, Edwidge. *Eight days: a story of Haiti* ill. by Alix Delinois. Scholastic, 2010. ISBN 978-0-545-27849-2 Subj: Character traits – bravery. Earthquakes. Foreign lands – Haiti.

Darrow, Sharon. *Yafi's family: an Ethiopian boy's journey of love, loss, and adoption* (Pettitt, Linda)

Davis, Anne. *No dogs allowed!* ill. by author. HarperCollins, 2011. ISBN 978-0-06-075353-5 Subj: Animals – cats. Animals – dogs. Character traits – kindness to animals. Friendship.

Davis, Aubrey. *Kishka for Koppel* ill. by Sheldon Cohen. Orca, 2011. ISBN 978-1-55469-299-6 Subj: Behavior – wishing. Character traits – foolishness. Folk & fairy tales. Jewish culture.

Davis, David. *Fandango stew* ill. by Ben Galbraith. Sterling, 2011. ISBN 978-1-4027-6527-8 Subj: Behavior – trickery. Character traits – cleverness. Folk & fairy tales. Food. U.S. history – frontier & pioneer life.

Davis, Jacky. *The amazing adventures of Bumblebee Boy* (Soman, David)

Ladybug Girl and the Bug Squad (Soman, David)

Ladybug Girl at the beach (Soman, David)

Davis, Jerry. *Little Chicken's big day* by Jerry Davis and Katie Davis; ill. by Katie Davis. Simon & Schuster, 2011. ISBN 978-1-4424-1401-3 Subj: Behavior – lost. Birds – chickens. Family life – mothers.

Davis, Jill. *Orangutans are ticklish: fun facts from an animal photographer* photos by Steve Grubman. Random House, 2010. ISBN 978-0-375-85886-4 Subj: Activities – photographing. Animals. Careers – photographers.

Davis, Katie. *Little Chicken's big day* (Davis, Jerry)

Day, Nancy Raines. *On a windy night* ill. by George Bates. Abrams, 2010. ISBN 978-0-8109-3900-4 Subj: Emotions – fear. Holidays – Halloween. Weather – wind.

De Beer, Hans. *Little Polar Bear and the submarine* tr. by Kristy Clark Koth; ill. by author. NorthSouth, 2011. ISBN 978-0-7358-4030-0 Subj: Animals – polar bears. Boats, ships.

de Las Casas, Dianne. *Blue frog: the legend of chocolate* ill. by Holly Stone-Barker. Pelican, 2011. ISBN 978-1-4556-1459-2 Subj: Folk & fairy tales. Food. Foreign lands – Mexico. Indians of North America – Aztec.

The house that Witchy built ill. by Holly Stone-Barker. Pelican, 2011. ISBN 978-1-58980-965-9 Subj: Cumulative tales. Holidays – Halloween. Witches.

Mama's bayou ill. by Holly Stone-Barker. Pelican, 2010. ISBN 978-1-58980-787-7 Subj: Family life – mothers. Lullabies. Rhyming text.

There's a dragon in the library ill. by Marita Gentry. Pelican, 2011. ISBN 978-1-58980-844-7 Subj: Books, reading. Dragons. Libraries.

de Lestrade, Agnès. *Phileas's fortune: a story about self-expression* tr. by Julia Frank McNeil; ill. by Valeria Docampo. Magination, 2010. ISBN 978-1-4338-0790-9 Subj: Communication. Language.

De Roo, Elena. *The rain train* ill. by Brian Lovelock. Candlewick, 2011. ISBN 978-0-7636-5313-2 Subj: Night. Trains. Weather – rain.

De Sève, Randall. *Mathilda and the orange balloon* ill. by Jen Corace. HarperCollins, 2010. ISBN 978-0-06-172685-9 Subj: Animals – sheep. Self-concept. Toys – balloons.

Deacon, Alexis. *A place to call home* ill. by Viviane Schwarz. Candlewick, 2011. ISBN 978-0-7636-5360-6 Subj: Activities – traveling. Animals – hamsters. Homes, houses.

Degman, Lori. *1 zany zoo* ill. by Colin Jack. Simon & Schuster, 2010. ISBN 978-1-4169-8990-5 Subj: Counting, numbers. Rhyming text. Zoos.

deGroat, Diane. *Ants in your pants, worms in your plants! (Gilbert goes green)* ill. by author. HarperCollins, 2011. ISBN 978-0-06-176511-7 Subj: Animals – possums. Ecology. Holidays – Earth Day. School.

Demas, Corinne. *Halloween surprise* ill. by R. W. Alley. Walker, 2011. ISBN 978-0-8027-8612-8 Subj: Clothing – costumes. Holidays – Halloween.

Pirates go to school ill. by John Manders. Scholastic, 2011. ISBN 978-0-545-20629-7 Subj: Pirates. Rhyming text. School.

Demi. *Joan of Arc* ill. by author. Marshall Cavendish, 2011. ISBN 978-0-7614-5953-8 Subj: Foreign lands – France. Religion. War.

Dempsey, Kristy. *Mini racer* ill. by Bridget Strevens-Marzo. Bloomsbury, 2010. ISBN 978-1-59990-170-1 Subj: Animals. Rhyming text. Sports – racing.

Denise, Anika. *Bella and Stella come home* ill. by Christopher Denise. Penguin Group (USA), 2010. ISBN 978-0-399-24243-4 Subj: Moving. Toys.

DePalma, Mary Newell. *The perfect gift* ill. by author. Scholastic, 2010. ISBN 978-0-545-15402-2 Subj: Animals. Birds – parakeets, parrots.

Books, reading. Family life – grandmothers. Gifts.

Uh-oh! ill. by author. Eerdmans, 2011. ISBN 978-0-8028-5372-1 Subj: Behavior – misbehavior. Dinosaurs.

dePaola, Tomie. *Let the whole earth sing praise* ill. by author. Penguin Group (USA), 2011. ISBN 978-0-399-25478-9 Subj: Creation. Religion.

My mother is so smart ill. by author. Penguin Group (USA), 2010. ISBN 978-0-399-25442-0 Subj: Family life – mothers.

Strega Nona's gift ill. by author. Penguin Group (USA), 2011. ISBN 978-0-399-25649-3 Subj: Holidays. Magic. Witches.

DeRubertis, Barbara. *Alexander Anteater's amazing act* ill. by R. W. Alley. Kane, 2010. ISBN 978-1-57565-304-4 Subj: ABC books. Animals – anteaters. School. Theater.

Bobby Baboon's banana be-bop ill. by R. W. Alley. Kane, 2010. ISBN 978-1-57565-305-1 Subj: ABC books. Animals – baboons. Counting, numbers. School.

Corky Cub's crazy caps ill. by R. W. Alley. Kane, 2010. ISBN 978-1-57565-306-8 Subj: Animals – bears. Clothing – hats. Friendship.

Dilly Dog's dizzy dancing ill. by R. W. Alley. Kane, 2010. ISBN 978-1-57565-307-5 Subj: ABC books. Activities – dancing. School.

Desrosiers, Sylvie. *Hocus pocus* by Sylvie Desrosiers and Rémy Simard. Kids Can, 2011. ISBN 978-1-55453-577-4 Subj: Animals – dogs. Animals – rabbits. Character traits – cleverness. Wordless.

Devernay, Laetitia. *The conductor* ill. by author. Chronicle, 2011. ISBN 978-1-4521-0491-1 Subj: Careers – conductors (music). Imagination. Trees. Wordless.

Devlin, Jane. *Hattie the bad* ill. by Joe Berger. Penguin Group (USA), 2010. ISBN 978-0-8037-3447-0 Subj: Behavior – misbehavior.

Dewdney, Anna. *Llama Llama home with Mama* ill. by author. Penguin Group (USA), 2011. ISBN 978-0-670-01232-9 Subj: Animals – llamas. Family life – mothers. Illness. Rhyming text.

Roly Poly pangolin ill. by author. Penguin Group (USA), 2010. ISBN 978-0-670-01160-5 Subj: Animals – anteaters. Animals – endangered animals. Emotions – fear. Friendship. Rhyming text.

Diesen, Deborah. *The barefooted, bad-tempered baby brigade* ill. by Tracy Dockray. Tricycle, 2010. ISBN 978-1-58246-274-5 Subj: Babies. Humor. Rhyming text.

The pout-pout fish in the big-big dark ill. by Dan Hanna. Farrar, 2010. ISBN 978-0-374-30798-1 Subj: Behavior – lost & found possessions. Emotions – fear. Fish. Rhyming text.

Diggs, Taye. *Chocolate me!* ill. by Shane W. Evans. Feiwel & Friends, 2011. ISBN 978-0-312-60326-7 Subj: Behavior – teasing. Character traits – individuality. Ethnic groups in the U.S. – African Americans. Family life – mothers. Self-concept.

DiPucchio, Kelly. *Alfred Zector, book collector* ill. by Macky Pamintuan. HarperCollins, 2010. ISBN 978-0-06-000581-8 Subj: Behavior – collecting things. Books, reading. Rhyming text.

Gilbert goldfish wants a pet ill. by Bob Shea. Penguin Group (USA), 2011. ISBN 978-0-8037-3394-7 Subj: Fish. Pets.

The sandwich swap (Al Abdullah, Rania)

Zombie in love ill. by Scott Campbell. Simon & Schuster, 2011. ISBN 978-1-4424-0270-6 Subj: Emotions – loneliness. Humorous stories. Monsters.

DiTerlizzi, Angela. *Say what?* ill. by Joey Chou. Simon & Schuster, 2011. ISBN 978-1-4169-8694-2 Subj: Animals. Noise, sounds. Rhyming text.

Docherty, Thomas. *Big scary monster* ill. by author. Candlewick, 2010. ISBN 978-0-7636-4787-2 Subj: Behavior – bullying. Concepts – size. Monsters.

Dockray, Tracy. *The lost and found pony* ill. by author. Feiwel & Friends, 2011. ISBN 978-0-312-59259-2 Subj: Animals – horses, ponies. Character traits – kindness to animals. Circus.

Dodd, Emma. *I am small* ill. by author. Scholastic, 2011. ISBN 978-0-545-35370-0 Subj: Birds – penguins. Character traits – smallness. Family life.

I don't want a cool cat! ill. by author. Little, Brown, 2010. ISBN 978-0-316-03674-0 Subj: Animals – cats. Rhyming text.

I love bugs! ill. by author. Holiday House, 2010. ISBN 978-0-8234-2280-7 Subj: Insects. Rhyming text. Spiders.

Meow said the cow ill. by author. Scholastic, 2011. ISBN 978-0-545-31861-7 Subj: Animals. Farms. Magic. Noise, sounds.

Doerrfeld, Cori. *Penny loves pink* ill. by author. Little, Brown, 2011. ISBN 978-0-316-05458-4 Subj: Babies. Concepts – color. Family life – brothers & sisters. Family life – new sibling.

Domney, Alexis. *Splish, splat!* ill. by Alice Crawford. Second Story, 2011. ISBN 978-1-897187-88-3 Subj: Careers – artists. Handicaps – deafness. Sign language.

Donaldson, Julia. *One mole digging a hole* ill. by Nick Sharratt. Macmillan UK, 2010. ISBN 978-0-230-70647-7 Subj: Counting, numbers. Gardens, gardening. Rhyming text.

What the ladybug heard ill. by Lydia Monks. Henry Holt, 2010. ISBN 978-0-8050-9028-4 Subj: Animals. Farms. Insects – ladybugs. Noise, sounds. Rhyming text.

Donovan, Sandy. *Bob the Alien discovers the Dewey Decimal System* ill. by Martin Haake. Picture Window, 2010. ISBN 978-1-4048-5757-5 Subj: Aliens. Books, reading.

Bored Bella learns about fiction and nonfiction ill. by Leeza Hernandez. Picture Window, 2010. ISBN 978-1-4048-5758-2 Subj: Behavior – boredom. Books, reading.

Karl and Carolina uncover the parts of a book ill. by Michael Mullan. Picture Window, 2010. ISBN 978-1-4048-5760-5 Subj: Books, reading.

Pingpong Perry experiences how a book is made ill. by James Christoph. Picture Window, 2010. ISBN 978-1-4048-5759-9 Subj: Books, reading.

Doodler, Todd H. *Bear in long underwear* ill. by author. Blue Apple, 2011. ISBN 978-1-60905-100-6 Subj: Animals – bears. Seasons – winter. Snowmen.

Dormer, Frank W. *Socksquatch* ill. by author. Henry Holt, 2010. ISBN 978-0-8050-8952-3 Subj: Clothing – socks. Monsters.

Dorros, Arthur. *Mama and me* ill. by Rudy Gutierrez. HarperCollins, 2011. ISBN 978-0-06-058160-2 Subj: Ethnic groups in the U.S. – Hispanic Americans. Family life – mothers. Foreign languages.

Downey, Lisa. *The pirates of plagiarism* (Fox, Kathleen)

Downing, Johnette. *Amazon alphabet* ill. by author. Pelican, 2011. ISBN 978-1-58980-879-9 Subj: ABC books. Foreign lands – South America. Jungle. Rivers.

There was an old lady who swallowed some bugs ill. by Johnette Downing. Pelican, 2010. ISBN 978-1-58980-858-4 Subj: Cumulative tales. Folk & fairy tales. Frogs & toads. Insects. Songs.

Doyle, Malachy. *Get happy* ill. by Caroline Uff. Walker, 2011. ISBN 978-0-8027-2271-3 Subj: Behavior. Emotions – happiness. Rhyming text.

Drehsen, Britta. *Flip-o-storic* tr. by Laura Lindgren; ill. by Sara Ball. Abbeville, 2011. ISBN 978-0-7892-1099-9 Subj: Dinosaurs. Format, unusual – toy & movable books.

Drummond, Allan. *Energy island: how one community harnessed the wind and changed their world* ill. by author. Farrar, 2011. ISBN 978-0-374-32184-0 Subj: Foreign lands – Denmark. Science. Weather – wind.

Drummond, Ree. *Charlie the ranch dog* ill. by Diane deGroat. HarperCollins, 2011. ISBN 978-0-06-199655-9 Subj: Animals – dogs. Careers – ranchers.

Duddle, Jonny. *The pirate cruncher* ill. by author. Candlewick, 2010. ISBN 978-0-7636-4876-3 Subj: Mythical creatures. Pirates. Rhyming text.

Dunklee, Annika. *My name is Elizabeth!* ill. by Matthew Forsythe. Kids Can, 2011. ISBN 978-1-55453-560-6 Subj: Character traits – assertiveness. Names.

Dunning, Joan. *Seabird in the forest: the mystery of the marbled murrelet.* Boyds Mills, 2011. ISBN 978-1-59078-715-1 Subj: Birds. Sea & seashore.

Dunrea, Olivier. *A Christmas tree for Pyn* ill. by author. Penguin Group (USA), 2011. ISBN 978-0-399-24506-0 Subj: Family life – fathers. Gifts. Holidays – Christmas. Trees.

Old Bear and his cub ill. by author. Penguin Group (USA), 2010. ISBN 978-0-399-24507-7 Subj: Animals – bears. Emotions – love. Family life – fathers.

Ollie's Easter eggs ill. by author. Houghton Mifflin, 2010. ISBN 978-0-618-53243-8 Subj: Birds – geese. Eggs. Holidays – Easter.

Ollie's Halloween ill. by author. Houghton Harcourt, 2010. ISBN 978-0-618-53241-4 Subj: Birds – geese. Holidays – Halloween.

Durand, Hallie. *Mitchell's license* ill. by Tony Fucile. Candlewick, 2011. ISBN 978-0-7636-4496-3 Subj: Activities – playing. Bedtime. Family life – fathers.

Durango, Julia. *Go-go gorillas* ill. by Eleanor Taylor. Simon & Schuster, 2010. ISBN 978-1-4169-3779-1 Subj: Animals – gorillas. Rhyming text. Transportation.

Dyer, Sarah. *Batty* ill. by author. Frances Lincoln, 2011. ISBN 978-1-84780-084-8 Subj: Animals – bats. Character traits – being different. Zoos.

Monster day at work ill. by author. Frances Lincoln, 2010. ISBN 978-1-84780-069-5 Subj: Family life – fathers. Monsters.

Dylan, Bob. *Blowin' in the wind* ill. by Jon J Muth. Sterling, 2011. ISBN 978-1-4027-8002-8 Subj: Music. Songs. Violence, nonviolence.

Man gave names to all the animals ill. by Jim Arnosky. Sterling, 2010. ISBN 978-1-4027-6858-3 Subj: Animals. Songs.

Eaton, Maxwell, III. *Two dumb ducks* ill. by author. Random House, 2010. ISBN 978-0-375-84576-5 Subj: Behavior – bullying. Behavior – name calling. Birds – ducks. Birds – seagulls.

Edwards, Michelle. *The Hanukkah trike* ill. by Kathryn Mitter. Whitman, 2010. ISBN 978-0-8075-3126-6 Subj: Holidays – Hanukkah. Jewish culture. Sports – bicycling.

Edwards, Pamela Duncan. *Princess Pigtoria and the pea* ill. by Henry Cole. Scholastic, 2010. ISBN 978-0-545-15625-7 Subj: Animals – pigs. Folk & fairy tales. Humorous stories. Royalty – princesses.

While the world is sleeping ill. by Daniel Kirk. Scholastic, 2010. ISBN 978-0-545-01756-5 Subj: Animals. Bedtime. Birds – owls. Night. Rhyming text.

Egan, Tim. *Dodsworth in Rome* ill. by author. Houghton Harcourt, 2011. ISBN 978-0-547-39006-2 Subj: Activities – traveling. Animals. Birds – ducks. Foreign lands – Italy.

Egielski, Richard. *The sleepless little vampire* ill. by author. Scholastic, 2011. ISBN 978-0-545-14597-8 Subj: Bedtime. Cumulative tales. Monsters – vampires.

Ehlert, Lois. *Lots of spots* ill. by author. Simon & Schuster, 2010. ISBN 978-1-4424-0289-8 Subj: Animals. Disguises. Rhyming text.

Rrralph ill. by author. Simon & Schuster, 2011. ISBN 978-1-4424-1305-4 Subj: Animals – dogs. Humorous stories.

Elissa, Barbara. *The remarkable journey of Josh's kippah* ill. by Farida Zaman. Lerner/Kar-Ben, 2010. ISBN 978-0-8225-9911-1 Subj: Activities – traveling. Jewish culture.

Elkin, Mark. *Samuel's baby* ill. by Amy Wummer. Tricycle, 2010. ISBN 978-1-58246-301-8 Subj: Babies. Family life – new sibling. School.

Elliot, Laura Malone. *A string of hearts* ill. by Lynn Munsinger. HarperCollins, 2010. ISBN 978-0-06-000085-1 Subj: Animals. Friendship. Holidays – Valentine's Day.

Elliott, David. *In the wild* ill. by Holly Meade. Candlewick, 2010. ISBN 978-0-7636-4497-0 Subj: Animals. Poetry.

Elliott, Rebecca. *Just because* ill. by author. Lion, 2011. ISBN 978-0-7459-6267-2 Subj: Family life – brothers & sisters. Handicaps – physical handicaps.

Ellis, Andy. *When Lulu went to the zoo* ill. by author. Andersen, 2010. ISBN 978-0-7613-5499-4 Subj: Zoos.

Elya, Susan Middleton. *No more, por favor* ill. by David Walker. Penguin Group (USA), 2010. ISBN 978-0-399-24766-8 Subj: Animals. Family life – parents. Food. Foreign languages. Jungle. Rhyming text.

Rubia and the three osos ill. by Melissa Sweet. Hyperion/Disney, 2010. ISBN 978-1-4231-1252-5 Subj: Animals – bears. Folk & fairy tales. Foreign languages. Rhyming text.

A year full of holidays ill. by Diana Cain Bluthenthal. Penguin Group (USA), 2010. ISBN 978-0-399-23733-1 Subj: Days of the week, months of the year. Holidays. Rhyming text.

Emberley, Ed. *If you're a monster and you know it* (Emberley, Rebecca)

The red hen by Ed Emberley and Rebecca Emberley; ill. by Ed Emberley. Roaring Brook, 2010. ISBN 978-1-59643-492-9 Subj: Activities – baking, cooking. Animals. Behavior – sharing. Birds – chickens. Character traits – helpfulness. Cumulative tales. Folk & fairy tales.

Ten little beasties (Emberley, Rebecca)

Where's my sweetie pie? ill. by author. Little, Brown, 2010. ISBN 978-0-316-01891-3 Subj: Animals. Format, unusual – board books. Format, unusual – toy & movable books.

Emberley, Rebecca. *If you're a monster and you know it* by Rebecca Emberley and Ed Emberley; ill. by Rebecca Emberley. Scholastic, 2010. ISBN 978-0-545-21829-0 Subj: Emotions – happiness. Monsters. Songs.

The red hen (Emberley, Ed)

Ten little beasties by Rebecca Emberley and Ed Emberley; ill. by authors. Roaring Brook, 2011. ISBN 978-1-59643-627-5 Subj: Counting, numbers. Monsters.

Engle, Margarita. *Summer birds: the butterflies of Maria Merian* ill. by Julie Paschkis. Henry Holt, 2010. ISBN 978-0-8050-8937-0 Subj: Activities – painting. Art. Insects – butterflies, caterpillars.

Ernst, Lisa Campbell. *The Gingerbread Girl goes animal crackers* ill. by author. Penguin Group (USA), 2011. ISBN 978-0-525-42259-4 Subj: Animals

– foxes. Behavior – running away. Cumulative tales. Food.

Sylvia Jean, scout supreme ill. by author. Penguin Group (USA), 2010. ISBN 978-0-525-47873-7 Subj: Animals – pigs. Character traits – helpfulness. Clubs, gangs. Disguises.

Esbaum, Jill. *Everything spring.* National Geographic, 2010. ISBN 978-1-4263-0607-5 Subj: Seasons – spring.

Tom's tweet ill. by Dan Santat. Random House, 2011. ISBN 978-0-375-85171-1 Subj: Animals – cats. Birds. Emotions – loneliness. Friendship.

Evans, Kristina. *What's special about me, Mama?* ill. by Javaka Steptoe. Hyperion/Disney, 2011. ISBN 978-0-7868-5274-1 Subj: Character traits – individuality. Emotions – love. Ethnic groups in the U.S. – African Americans. Family life – mothers. Self-concept.

Evans, Lezlie. *Who loves the little lamb?* ill. by David McPhail. Hyperion/Disney, 2010. ISBN 978-1-4231-1659-2 Subj: Animals – babies. Emotions – love. Family life – mothers. Rhyming text.

Evans, Nate. *The Jellybeans and the big book bonanza* (Numeroff, Laura)

The Jellybeans and the big camp kickoff (Numeroff, Laura)

Ponyella (Numeroff, Laura)

Evans, Shane W. *Underground: finding the light to freedom* ill. by author. Roaring Brook, 2011. ISBN 978-1-59643-538-4 Subj: Character traits – freedom. Ethnic groups in the U.S. – African Americans. Slavery. U.S. history.

Fagan, Cary. *Ella May and the wishing stone* ill. by Geneviève Côté. Tundra, 2011. ISBN 978-1-77049-225-7 Subj: Behavior – wishing. Friendship.

Falconer, Ian. *Olivia goes to Venice* ill. by author. Simon & Schuster, 2010. ISBN 978-1-4169-9674-3 Subj: Activities – vacationing. Animals – pigs. Foreign lands – Italy.

Falken, Linda. *Can you find it?* Abrams, 2010. ISBN 978-0-8109-8890-3 Subj: Art. Picture puzzles. U.S. history.

Falkenstern, Lisa. *A dragon moves in* ill. by author. Marshall Cavendish, 2011. ISBN 978-0-7614-5947-7 Subj: Animals – hedgehogs. Animals – rabbits. Dragons. Homes, houses.

Falwell, Cathryn. *Gobble gobble* ill. by author. Dawn, 2011. ISBN 978-158469-148-8; Subj: Birds – turkeys. Rhyming text.

Pond babies ill. by author. Down East, 2011. ISBN 978-0-89272-920-3 Subj: Animals – babies. Lakes, ponds.

Faundez, Anne. *The day the rains fell* ill. by Karin Littlewood. IPG/Tamarind, 2010. ISBN 978-1-84853-015-7 Subj: Foreign lands – Africa. Weather – droughts.

Fearnley, Jan. *Arthur and the meanies* ill. by author. Egmont UK, 2011. ISBN 978-1-4052-5380-2 Subj: Animals. Animals – elephants. Behavior – bullying. Friendship.

Feiffer, Kate. *But I wanted a baby brother!* ill. by Diane Goode. Simon & Schuster, 2010. ISBN 978-1-4169-3941-2 Subj: Babies. Family life – brothers & sisters.

My side of the car ill. by Jules Feiffer. Candlewick, 2011. ISBN 978-0-7636-4405-5 Subj: Family life – fathers. Weather – rain. Zoos.

Felix, Monique. *The rumor* ill. by author. Creative Education, 2011. ISBN 978-1-56846-219-6 Subj: Animals. Animals – wolves. Behavior – gossip. Communication.

Fenton, Joe. *Boo!* ill. by Jo Fenton. Simon & Schuster, 2010. ISBN 978-1-4169-7936-4 Subj: Disguises. Ghosts.

Ferguson, Sarah. *Emily's first day of school* ill. by Ian Cunliffe. Sterling, 2010. ISBN 978-1-4027-7392-1 Subj: School – first day.

Fernandes, Eugenie. *Kitten's spring* ill. by author. Kids Can, 2010. ISBN 978-1-55453-340-4 Subj: Animals – babies. Animals – cats. Farms. Rhyming text. Seasons – spring.

Kitten's winter ill. by author. Kids Can, 2011. ISBN 978-1-55453-343-5 Subj: Animals. Animals – cats. Seasons – winter.

Feutl, Rita. *Room enough for Daisy* (Waldman, Debby)

Fielding, Beth. *Animal eyes.* EarlyLight, 2011. ISBN 978-0-9797455-5-3 Subj: Anatomy – eyes. Animals.

Animal tails. EarlyLight, 2011. ISBN 978-0-9797455-8-4 Subj: Anatomy – tails. Animals.

Fine, Edith Hope. *Water, weed, and wait* by Edith Hope Fine and Angela Demos Halpin; ill. by Colleen M. Madden. Tricycle, 2010. ISBN 978-1-58246-320-9 Subj: Gardens, gardening. School.

Finlay, Lizzie. *Little Croc's purse* ill. by author. Eerdmans, 2011. ISBN 978-0-8028-5392-9 Subj: Behavior – bullying. Character traits – honesty. Clothing – handbags, purses. Money. Reptiles – alligators, crocodiles.

Fischer, Scott M. *Jump!* ill. by author. Simon & Schuster, 2010. ISBN 978-1-4169-7884-8 Subj: Activities – jumping. Animals. Rhyming text.

Fisher, Valorie. *Everything I need to know before I'm five* ill. by author. Random House, 2011. ISBN 978-0-375-86865-8 Subj: Concepts. Counting, numbers. Seasons.

Fishman, Anna Schnur. *Tashlich at Turtle Rock* (Schnur, Susan)

Fitzsimmons, David. *Curious critters* photos by author. Wild Iris, 2011. ISBN 978-1936607-69-3 Subj: Animals. Frogs & toads. Nature. Reptiles.

Five little pumpkins ill. by Ben Mantle. Tiger Tales, 2010. ISBN 978-1-58925-856-3 Subj: Counting, numbers. Format, unusual – board books. Holidays – Halloween. Plants. Rhyming text. Witches.

Fleischer-Camp, Dean. *Marcel the shell with shoes on: things about me* (Slate, Jenny)

Fleming, Candace. *Clever Jack takes the cake* ill. by G. Brian Karas. Random House, 2010. ISBN 978-0-375-84979-4 Subj: Activities – storytelling. Birthdays. Folk & fairy tales. Food. Royalty – princesses.

Seven hungry babies ill. by Eugene Yelchin. Simon & Schuster, 2010. ISBN 978-1-4169-5402-6 Subj: Babies. Birds. Counting, numbers. Rhyming text.

Fleming, Denise. *Shout! Shout it out!* ill. by author. Henry Holt, 2011. ISBN 978-0-8050-9237-0 Subj: ABC books. Animals – mice. Counting, numbers. Language.

Sleepy, oh so sleepy ill. by author. Henry Holt, 2010. ISBN 978-0-8050-8126-8 Subj: Animals. Bedtime. Family life – mothers.

Fletcher, Ashlee. *My dog, my cat* ill. by author. Tanglewood, 2011. ISBN 978-1-933718-22-4 Subj: Animals – cats. Animals – dogs.

Fliess, Sue. *Shoes for me!* ill. by Michael Laughead. Marshall Cavendish, 2011. ISBN 978-0-7614-5825-8 Subj: Animals – hippopotamuses. Clothing – shoes. Rhyming text.

Florian, Douglas. *Poetrees* ill. by author. Simon & Schuster, 2010. ISBN 978-1-4169-8672-0 Subj: Poetry. Trees.

Foggo, Cheryl. *Dear baobab* ill. by Qin Leng. Second Story, 2011. ISBN 978-1-897187-91-3 Subj: Adoption. Emotions – loneliness. Family life. Family life – aunts, uncles. Foreign lands – Africa. Trees.

Foley, Greg. *I miss you Mouse* ill. by author. Penguin Group (USA), 2010. ISBN 978-0-670-01238-1 Subj: Animals – bears. Animals – mice. Format, unusual – toy & movable books. Friendship.

Purple little bird ill. by author. HarperCollins, 2011. ISBN 978-0-06-200828-2 Subj: Animals. Birds. Concepts – color. Homes, houses.

Willoughby and the moon ill. by author. HarperCollins, 2010. ISBN 978-0-06-154753-9 Subj: Animals – snails. Emotions – fear. Moon.

Ford, Gilbert. *Flying lessons* ill. by author. Hyperion/Disney, 2010. ISBN 978-1-4231-1997-5 Subj: Airplanes, airports. Birds – doves. Character traits – being different.

Fore, S. J. *Read to tiger* ill. by R. W. Alley. Penguin Group (USA), 2010. ISBN 978-0-670-01140-7 Subj: Animals – tigers. Books, reading.

Foreman, Michael. *Fortunately, unfortunately* ill. by author. Andersen, 2011. ISBN 978-0-7613-7460-2 Subj: Activities – traveling. Behavior – resourcefulness.

Formento, Alison. *This tree counts!* ill. by Sarah Snow. Whitman, 2010. ISBN 978-0-8075-7890-2 Subj: Counting, numbers. Nature. School. Trees.

This tree, 1, 2, 3 ill. by Sarah Snow. Whitman, 2011. ISBN 978-0-8075-7891-9 Subj: Counting, numbers. Format, unusual – board books. Nature. School. Trees.

Fox, Kathleen. *The pirates of plagiarism* by Kathleen Fox and Lisa Downey; ill. by Lisa Downey. Upstart, 2010. ISBN 978-1-60213-053-1 Subj: Behavior – cheating. Books, reading. Libraries. Pirates.

Fox, Lee. *Ella Kazoo will not brush her hair* ill. by Jennifer Plecas. Walker, 2010. ISBN 978-0-8027-8836-8 Subj: Hair. Hygiene. Rhyming text.

Fox, Mem. *Let's count goats!* ill. by Jan Thomas. Simon & Schuster, 2010. ISBN 978-1-4424-0598-1 Subj: Animals – goats. Counting, numbers. Rhyming text.

Franceschelli, Christopher. *(Oliver)* ill. by Gaby Kooijman et al. Lemniscaat, 2011. ISBN 978-1-

9359-5401-9 Subj: Birds – chickens. Eggs. Format, unusual.

Franco, Betsy. *A dazzling display of dogs: concrete poems* ill. by Michael Wertz. Tricycle, 2011. ISBN 978-1-58246-343-8 Subj: Animals – dogs. Poetry.

Double play! monkeying around with addition ill. by Doug Cushman. Tricycle, 2011. ISBN 978-1-58246-384-1 Subj: Animals – monkeys. Counting, numbers. Rhyming text. School.

Fraser, Mary Ann. *Heebie-Jeebie Jamboree* ill. by author. Boyds Mills, 2011. ISBN 978-1-59078-857-8 Subj: Fairs, festivals. Family life – brothers & sisters. Holidays – Halloween.

Pet shop follies ill. by author. Boyds Mills, 2010. ISBN 978-1-59078-619-2 Subj: Behavior – cooperation. Pets. Stores.

Frasier, Debra. *A fabulous fair alphabet* ill. by author. Simon & Schuster, 2010. ISBN 978-1-4169-9817-4 Subj: ABC books. Fairs, festivals.

Frazee, Marla. *The boss baby* ill. by author. Simon & Schuster, 2010. ISBN 978-1-4424-0167-9 Subj: Babies. Behavior – bossy.

Frazier, Craig. *Bee and bird* ill. by author. Roaring Brook, 2011. ISBN 978-1-59643-660-2 Subj: Birds. Insects – bees. Wordless.

Lots of dots ill. by author. Chronicle, 2010. ISBN 978-0-8118-7715-2 Subj: Concepts – shape. Rhyming text.

Frederick, Heather Vogel. *Babyberry pie* ill. by Amy Schwartz. Harcourt, 2010. ISBN 978-0-15-205927-9 Subj: Babies. Bedtime. Rhyming text.

Hide and squeak. Simon & Schuster, 2011. ISBN 978-0-689-85570-2 Subj: Animals – mice. Bedtime. Family life – fathers. Rhyming text.

Freedman, Claire. *Dinosaurs love underpants* ill. by Ben Cort. Simon & Schuster, 2010. ISBN 978-1-4169-8938-7 Subj: Clothing – underwear. Dinosaurs. Rhyming text.

Freedman, Deborah. *Blue chicken* ill. by author. Penguin Group (USA), 2011. ISBN 978-0-670-01293-0 Subj: Activities – painting. Birds – chickens. Careers – artists. Character traits – helpfulness. Concepts – color.

Freeman, Don. *One more acorn* by Don Freeman and Roy Freeman; ill. by Don Freeman and Jody Wheeler. Penguin Group (USA), 2010. ISBN 978-0-670-01083-7 Subj: Animals – squirrels. Seasons – fall.

Freeman, Roy. *One more acorn* (Freeman, Don)

French, Jackie. *Diary of a baby wombat* ill. by Bruce Whatley. Clarion, 2010. ISBN 978-0-547-43005-8 Subj: Activities – writing. Animals – babies. Animals – wombats.

French, Vivian. *Yucky worms* ill. by Jessica Ahlberg. Candlewick, 2010. ISBN 978-0-7636-4446-8 Subj: Animals – worms. Family life – grandmothers. Gardens, gardening.

Friedland, Katy. *Art museum opposites* by Katy Friedland and Marla K. Shoemaker. Temple Univ., 2010. ISBN 978-1-4399-0523-4 Subj: Art. Concepts – opposites. Museums.

Friedman, Caitlin. *How do you feed a hungry giant? a munch-and-sip pop-up book* ill. by Shaw Nielsen. Workman, 2011. ISBN 978-0-7611-5752-6 Subj: Food. Format, unusual – toy & movable books. Giants.

Friedman, Laurie. *Ruby Valentine saves the day* ill. by Lynne Avril. Carolrhoda, 2010. ISBN 978-0-7613-4213-7 Subj: Holidays – Valentine's Day. Parties. Rhyming text. Weather – blizzards.

Frisch, Aaron. *The lonely pine* ill. by Etienne Delessert. Creative Editions, 2011. ISBN 978-1-56846-214-1 Subj: Nature. Seasons. Trees.

Fuge, Charles. *Astonishing animal ABC* ill. by author. Sterling, 2011. ISBN 978-1-4027-8645-7 Subj: ABC books. Animals. Rhyming text.

Fuller, Sandy F. *The Blues go birding across America* (Malnor, Carol L.)

My cat, coon cat ill. by Jeannie Brett. Islandport, 2011. ISBN 978-1-934031-32-2 Subj: Animals – cats.

Furstinger, Nancy. *Maggie's second chance: a gentle dog's rescue* ill. by Joe Hyatt. Gryphon, 2011. ISBN 978-0-940719-11-8 Subj: Animals – dogs. Character traits – kindness to animals.

Gadot, A. S. *Tower of Babel* ill. by Cecilia Rebora. Lerner/Kar-Ben, 2010. ISBN 978-0-8225-9917-3 Subj: Religion.

Gaiman, Neil. *Instructions* ill. by Charles Vess. HarperCollins, 2010. ISBN 978-0-06-196030-7 Subj: Activities – traveling. Self-concept.

Gainer, Cindy. *I'm like you, you're like me: a book about understanding and appreciating each other* ill. by Miki Sakamoto. Free Spirit, 2011. ISBN 978-1-57542-383-8 Subj: Behavior – cooperation. Character traits – individuality. Character traits – kindness.

Gal, Susan. *Please take me for a walk* ill. by author. Random House, 2010. ISBN 978-0-375-85863-5 Subj: Animals – dogs.

Galbraith, Kathryn O. *Arbor Day square* ill. by Cyd Moore. Peachtree, 2010. ISBN 978-1-56145-517-1 Subj: Family life – fathers. Holidays. Trees. U.S. history – frontier & pioneer life.

Planting the wild garden ill. by Wendy Anderson Halperin. Peachtree, 2011. ISBN 978-1-56145-563-8 Subj: Nature. Seeds.

Gall, Chris. *Substitute creacher* ill. by author. Little, Brown, 2011. ISBN 978-0-316-08915-9 Subj: Careers – teachers. Monsters. Rhyming text. School.

Gammell, Stephen. *Mudkin* ill. by author. Carolrhoda, 2011. ISBN 978-0-7613-5790-2 Subj: Activities – playing. Imagination. Weather – rain.

Garcia, Emma. *Tap tap bang bang* ill. by author. Boxer, 2010. ISBN 978-1-907152-00-9 Subj: Noise, sounds. Tools.

Gardner, Carol. *Princess Zelda and the frog* photos by Shane Young. Feiwel & Friends, 2011. ISBN 978-0-312-60325-0 Subj: Animals – dogs. Frogs & toads. Royalty – princesses.

Garland, Michael. *Grandpa's tractor* ill. by author. Boyds Mills, 2011. ISBN 978-1-59078-762-5 Subj: Family life – grandfathers. Farms. Memories, memory. Tractors.

Super snow day seek and find ill. by author. Penguin Group (USA), 2010. ISBN 978-0-525-42245-7 Subj: Family life – aunts, uncles. Picture puzzles. Weather – snow.

Garland, Sarah. *Eddie's toolbox and how to make and mend things* ill. by author. Frances Lincoln, 2011. ISBN 978-1-84780-053-4 Subj: Character traits – helpfulness. Communities, neighborhoods. Friendship. Tools.

Gassman, Julie. *Crabby pants* ill. by Richard Watson. Picture Window, 2010. ISBN 978-1-4048-6165-7 Subj: Behavior – misbehavior. Clothing – pants. Emotions – anger.

Gay, Marie-Louise. *Caramba and Henry* ill. by author. Groundwood, 2011. ISBN 978-1-55498-097-0 Subj: Animals – cats. Family life – brothers. Sibling rivalry.

Roslyn Rutabaga and the biggest hole on earth! ill. by author. Groundwood, 2010. ISBN 978-0-88899-994-8 Subj: Activities – digging. Animals – rabbits. Family life – fathers.

Geisert, Arthur. *Country road ABC: an illustrated journey through America's farmland* ill. by author. Houghton Harcourt, 2010. ISBN 978-0-547-19469-1 Subj: ABC books. Farms.

Ice ill. by author. Enchanted Lion, 2011. ISBN 978-1-59270-098-1 Subj: Animals – pigs. Behavior – cooperation. Character traits – cleverness. Wordless.

Genechten, Guido van. *Because you are my friend* ill. by author. Clavis, 2011. ISBN 978-1-60537-095-8 Subj: Animals – polar bears. Family life – mothers. Friendship.

Kai-Mook ill. by author. Clavis, 2011. ISBN 978-1-60537-096-5 Subj: Animals – babies. Animals – elephants.

No ghost under my bed ill. by author. Clavis, 2010. ISBN 978-1-60537-069-9 Subj: Bedtime. Birds – penguins. Emotions – fear.

Ricky and the squirrel ill. by author. Clavis, 2010. ISBN 978-1-60537-078-1 Subj: Animals – rabbits. Animals – squirrels. Death.

Ricky is brave ill. by author. Clavis, 2011. ISBN 978-1-60537-097-2 Subj: Animals – rabbits. Camps, camping. Character traits – bravery. Emotions – fear.

George, Jean Craighead. *The buffalo are back* ill. by Wendell Minor. Penguin Group (USA), 2010. ISBN 978-0-525-42215-0 Subj: Animals – buffaloes. Animals – endangered animals.

George, Kristine O'Connell. *Emma dilemma: big sister poems* ill. by Nancy Carpenter. Clarion, 2011. ISBN 978-0-618-42842-7 Subj: Family life – sisters. Poetry.

George, Lindsay Barrett. *Maggie's ball* ill. by author. HarperCollins, 2010. ISBN 978-0-06-172166-3 Subj: Animals – dogs. Behavior – lost & found possessions. Toys – balls.

That pup! ill. by author. HarperCollins, 2011. ISBN 978-0-06-200413-0 Subj: Animals – dogs. Animals – squirrels.

George, Lucy M. *Back to school Tortoise* ill. by Merel Eyckerman. Whitman, 2011. ISBN 978-0-8075-0510-6 Subj: Behavior – worrying. Careers – teachers. Reptiles – turtles, tortoises. School – first day.

Gerber, Carole. *Annie Jump Cannon, astronomer* ill. by Christina Wald. Pelican, 2011. ISBN 978-1-58980-911-6 Subj: Careers – astronomers. Gender roles. Stars.

Little red bat ill. by Christina Wald. Sylvan Dell, 2010. ISBN 978-1-60718-069-2 Subj: Animals – bats. Hibernation. Migration.

Geringer, Laura. *Boom boom go away!* ill. by Bagram Ibatoulline. Simon & Schuster, 2010. ISBN 978-0-689-85093-6 Subj: Bedtime. Musical instruments. Rhyming text.

Gershator, Phillis. *Moo, moo, brown cow! Have you any milk?* ill. by Giselle Potter. Random House, 2011. ISBN 978-0-375-86744-6 Subj: Animals. Bedtime. Farms. Rhyming text. Toys.

Who's awake in springtime? by Phillis Gershator and Mim Green; ill. by Emilie Chollat. Henry Holt, 2010. ISBN 978-0-8050-6390-5 Subj: Animals. Bedtime. Cumulative tales. Rhyming text. Seasons – spring.

Who's in the forest? ill. by Jill McDonald. Barefoot, 2010. ISBN 978-1-84686-476-6 Subj: Animals. Forest, woods. Rhyming text.

Gervais, Bernadette. *Out of sight* (Pittau, Francisco)

Ghigna, Charles. *I see winter* ill. by Ag Jatkowska. Picture Window, 2011. ISBN 978-1-4048-6588-4 Subj: Rhyming text. Seasons – winter.

Gibala-Broxholm, Scott. *Maddie's monster dad* ill. by author. Marshall Cavendish, 2011. ISBN 978-0-7614-5846-3 Subj: Activities – playing. Family life – fathers. Imagination. Monsters.

Gibbons, Gail. *Alligators and crocodiles* ill. by author. Holiday House, 2010. ISBN 978-0-8234-2234-0 Subj: Reptiles – alligators, crocodiles.

Gorillas ill. by author. Holiday House, 2011. ISBN 978-0-8234-2236-4 Subj: Animals – gorillas.

It's snowing! ill. by author. Holiday House, 2011. ISBN 978-0-8234-2237-1 Subj: Seasons – winter. Weather – snow.

Gibbs, Edward. *I spy with my little eye* ill. by author. Candlewick, 2011. ISBN 978-0-7636-5284-5 Subj: Animals. Concepts – color. Format, unusual.

Gilani-Williams, Fawzia. *Nabeel's new pants: an Eid tale* ill. by Proiti Roy. Marshall Cavendish, 2010. ISBN 978-0-7614-5629-2 Subj: Clothing – pants. Family life. Foreign lands – Turkey. Holidays – Ramadan. Religion.

The gingerbread boy. *The gingerbread man loose in the school* by Laura Murray; ill. by Mike Lowery. Penguin Group (USA), 2011. ISBN 978-0-399-25052-1 Subj: Behavior – running away. Cumulative tales. Folk & fairy tales. Food. Rhyming text. School.

The Library Gingerbread Man by Dotti Enderle; ill. by Colleen M. Madden. Upstart, 2010. ISBN 978-1-60213-048-7 Subj: Behavior – running away. Cumulative tales. Food. Libraries.

Glaser, Linda. *Emma's poem: the voice of the Statue of Liberty* ill. by Claire A. Nivola. Houghton Mifflin, 2010. ISBN 978-0-547-17184-5 Subj: Poetry. U.S. history.

Garbage helps our garden grow: a compost story ill. by Shelley Rotner. Millbrook, 2010. ISBN 978-0-7613-4911-2 Subj: Ecology. Gardens, gardening.

Hoppy Passover! ill. by Daniel Howarth. Whitman, 2011. ISBN 978-0-8075-3380-2 Subj: Animals – rabbits. Holidays – Passover. Jewish culture.

Not a buzz to be found: insects in winter ill. by Jaime Zollars. Millbrook, 2011. ISBN 978-0-7613-5644-8 Subj: Insects. Seasons – winter.

Glass, Beth Raisner. *Blue-ribbon dad* ill. by Margie Moore. Abrams, 2011. ISBN 978-0-8109-9727-1 Subj: Animals – squirrels. Family life – fathers. Rhyming text.

Gleeson, Libby. *Clancy and Millie and the very fine house* ill. by Freya Blackwood. Little Hare, 2010. ISBN 978-1-921541-19-3 Subj: Friendship. Homes, houses. Imagination. Moving.

Godwin, Laura. *One moon, two cats* ill. by Yoko Tanaka. Simon & Schuster, 2011. ISBN 978-1-4424-1202-6 Subj: Animals – cats. Cities, towns. Farms. Rhyming text.

Goembel, Ponder, adapt. *Animal fair* ill. by Ponder Goembel. Marshall Cavendish, 2010. ISBN 978-0-7614-5642-1 Subj: Animals. Fairs, festivals. Rhyming text. Songs.

Goldin, Barbara Diamond. *Cakes and miracles: a Purim tale* ill. by Jaime Zollars. Marshall Cavendish, 2010. ISBN 978-0-7614-5701-5 Subj: Activities – baking, cooking. Handicaps – blindness. Holidays – Purim. Jewish culture.

Gollub, Matthew. *Jazz Fly 2: the jungle pachanga* ill. by Karen Hanke. Tortuga, 2010. ISBN 978-1-889910-44-4 Subj: Foreign languages. Insects – flies. Jungle. Music. Rhyming text.

Gonyea, Mark. *A book about color* ill. by author. Henry Holt, 2010. ISBN 978-0-8050-9055-0 Subj: Concepts – color.

Goodings, Christina. *Creation story* ill. by Melanie Mitchell. Lion, 2010. ISBN 978-0-7459-6089-0 Subj: Creation. Religion.

Lost sheep story ill. by Melanie Mitchell. Lion, 2010. ISBN 978-0-7459-6087-6 Subj: Animals – sheep. Behavior – lost. Religion.

Goodrich, Carter. *Say hello to Zorro!* ill. by author. Simon & Schuster, 2011. ISBN 978-1-4169-3893-4 Subj: Animals – dogs.

Gorbachev, Valeri. *The best cat* ill. by author. Candlewick, 2010. ISBN 978-0-7636-3675-3 Subj: Animals – cats. Family life – brothers & sisters. Pets.

Shhh! ill. by author. Penguin Group (USA), 2011. ISBN 978-0-399-25429-1 Subj: Family life – brothers. Noise, sounds. Sleep.

What's the big idea, Molly? ill. by author. Penguin Group (USA), 2010. ISBN 978-0-399-25428-4 Subj: Activities – writing. Animals. Animals – mice. Birthdays. Gifts.

Gore, Leonid. *The wonderful book* ill. by author. Scholastic, 2010. ISBN 978-0-545-08598-4 Subj: Animals. Books, reading. Forest, woods.

Worms for lunch? ill. by author. Scholastic, 2011. ISBN 978-0-545-24338-4 Subj: Animals. Food. Format, unusual.

Gormley, Greg. *Dog in boots* ill. by Roberta Angaramo. Holiday House, 2011. ISBN 978-0-8234-2347-7 Subj: Animals – dogs. Clothing – shoes.

Gottfried, Maya. *Our farm: by the animals of Farm Sanctuary* ill. by Robert Rahway Zakanitch. Random House, 2010. ISBN 978-0-375-86118-5 Subj: Animals. Character traits – kindness to animals. Farms. Poetry.

Gourley, Robbin. *First garden: the White House garden and how it grew* ill. by author. Clarion, 2011. ISBN 978-0-547-48224-8 Subj: Food. Gardens, gardening. Plants. U.S. history.

Gow, Nancy. *Ten big toes and a prince's nose.* Sterling, 2010. ISBN 978-1-4027-6396-0 Subj: Anatomy – feet. Anatomy – noses. Rhyming text. Royalty – princes. Royalty – princesses. Self-concept.

Graham, Bob. *April and Esme, tooth fairies* ill. by author. Candlewick, 2010. ISBN 978-0-7636-4683-7 Subj: Fairies. Family life – sisters. Teeth.

Graham, Elspeth. *Cloud tea monkeys* (Peet, Mal)

Grandits, John. *Ten rules you absolutely must not break if you want to survive the school bus* ill. by Michael Allen Austin. Clarion, 2011. ISBN 978-0-618-78822-4 Subj: Buses. Emotions – fear. Family life – brothers. School – first day.

Graves, Keith. *Chicken Big* ill. by author. Chronicle, 2010. ISBN 978-0-8118-7237-9 Subj: Birds – chickens. Character traits – being different. Concepts – size.

Gravett, Emily. *Blue chameleon* ill. by author. Simon & Schuster, 2011. ISBN 978-1-4424-1958-

2 Subj: Concepts – color. Concepts – shape. Reptiles – chameleons.

Dogs ill. by author. Simon & Schuster, 2010. ISBN 978-1-4169-8703-1 Subj: Animals – dogs.

The rabbit problem ill. by author. Simon & Schuster, 2010. ISBN 978-1-4424-1255-2 Subj: Animals – rabbits. Counting, numbers. Days of the week, months of the year. Format, unusual – toy & movable books.

Gray, Luli. *Ant and Grasshopper* ill. by Giuliano Ferri. Simon & Schuster, 2011. ISBN 978-1-4169-5140-7 Subj: Activities – singing. Activities – working. Folk & fairy tales. Friendship. Insects – ants. Insects – grasshoppers. Seasons.

Green, Adolph. *What's new at the zoo?* (Comden, Betty)

Green, Alison. *The fox in the dark* ill. by Deborah Allwright. Tiger Tales, 2010. ISBN 978-1-58925-091-8 Subj: Animals. Emotions – fear.

Green, Dan. *Wild alphabet: an A to Zoo pop-up book* ill. by Mike Haines. Kingfisher, 2010. ISBN 978-0-7534-6472-4 Subj: ABC books. Animals. Format, unusual – toy & movable books.

Green, Mim. *Who's awake in springtime?* (Gershator, Phillis)

Greenberg, Jan. *Ballet for Martha: making Appalachian Spring* by Jan Greenberg and Sandra Jordan; ill. by Brian Floca. Roaring Brook, 2010. ISBN 978-1-59643-338-0 Subj: Activities – dancing. Ballet. Music.

Greene, Rhonda Gowler. *Daddy is a cozy hug* ill. by Maggie Smith. Walker, 2010. ISBN 978-0-8027-9728-5 Subj: Family life – fathers. Rhyming text. Seasons.

Mommy is a soft, warm kiss ill. by Maggie Smith. Walker, 2010. ISBN 978-0-8027-9729-2 Subj: Family life – mothers. Rhyming text. Seasons.

Greenfield, Howard. *Waking up is hard to do* (Sedaka, Neil)

Greenstein, Elaine. *The goose man: the story of Konrad Lorenz* ill. by author. Clarion, 2010. ISBN 978-0-547-08459-6 Subj: Birds – geese. Careers – scientists. Foreign lands – Austria. Science.

Grey, Mini. *Three by the sea* ill. by author. Random House, 2011. ISBN 978-0-375-86784-2 Subj: Animals. Behavior – cooperation. Friendship.

Griffin, Kitty. *The ride: the legend of Betsy Dowdy* ill. by Marjorie Priceman. Simon & Schuster, 2010. ISBN 978-1-4169-2816-4 Subj: Character traits – bravery. U.S. history.

Griffin, Molly Beth. *Loon baby* ill. by Anne Hunter. Houghton Mifflin, 2011. ISBN 978-0-547-25487-6 Subj: Behavior – worrying. Birds – loons.

Grigsby, Susan. *In the garden with Dr. Carver* ill. by Nicole Tadgell. Whitman, 2010. ISBN 978-0-8075-3630-8 Subj: Ethnic groups in the U.S. – African Americans. Gardens, gardening. Plants. School. U.S. history.

Grimm, Jacob. *Hansel and Gretel* by Jacob Grimm and Wilhelm Grimm; retold by Amy Ehrlich; ill. by Susan Jeffers. Penguin Group (USA), 2011. ISBN 978-0-525-4221-1 Subj: Behavior – lost. Folk & fairy tales. Forest, woods. Witches.

Little Red Riding Hood by Jacob Grimm and Wilhelm Grimm; adapt. and ill. by Gennady Spirin. Marshall Cavendish, 2010. ISBN 978-0-7614-5704-6 Subj: Animals – wolves. Behavior – talking to strangers. Folk & fairy tales.

Rapunzel by Jacob Grimm and Wilhelm Grimm; adapt. by Allison Sage; ill. by Sarah Gibb. Whitman, 2011. ISBN 978-0-8075-6804-0 Subj: Folk & fairy tales. Hair. Royalty – princes. Witches.

Snow White by Jacob Grimm and Wilhelm Grimm; ill. by Charles Santore. Sterling, 2010. ISBN 978-1-4027-7157-6 Subj: Dwarfs, midgets. Emotions – envy, jealousy. Folk & fairy tales. Magic.

The star child by Jacob Grimm and Wilhelm Grimm; tr. and adapt. by J. Alison James; ill. by Bernadette Watts. NorthSouth, 2010. ISBN 978-0-7358-2330-3 Subj: Behavior – sharing. Character traits – generosity. Folk & fairy tales. Stars.

The story of Little Red Riding Hood by Jacob Grimm and Wilhelm Grimm; ill. by Christopher Bing. Chronicle, 2010. ISBN 978-0-8118-6886-7 Subj: Animals – wolves. Behavior – talking to strangers. Folk & fairy tales.

Twelve dancing princesses by Jacob Grimm and Wilhelm Grimm; retold and ill. by Brigette Barrager. Chronicle, 2011. ISBN 978-0-8118-7696-4 Subj: Activities – dancing. Folk & fairy tales. Royalty – princesses.

Grimm, Wilhelm. *Hansel and Gretel* (Grimm, Jacob)

Little Red Riding Hood (Grimm, Jacob)

Rapunzel (Grimm, Jacob)

Snow White (Grimm, Jacob)

The star child (Grimm, Jacob)

The story of Little Red Riding Hood (Grimm, Jacob)

Twelve dancing princesses (Grimm, Jacob)

Grogan, John. *Trick or treat, Marley!* ill. by Richard Cowdrey. HarperCollins, 2011. ISBN 978-0-06-185755-3 Subj: Animals – dogs. Holidays – Halloween.

Guarnaccia, Steven. *The three little pigs: an architectural tale* ill. by author. Abrams, 2010. ISBN 978-0-8109-8941-2 Subj: Animals – pigs. Animals – wolves. Careers – architects. Character traits – cleverness. Folk & fairy tales.

Gudeon, Adam. *Me and Meow* ill. by author. HarperCollins, 2011. ISBN 978-0-06-199821-8 Subj: Activities – playing. Animals – cats.

Guiberson, Brenda Z. *Earth: feeling the heat* ill. by Chad Wallace. Henry Holt, 2010. ISBN 978-0-8050-7719-3 Subj: Earth. Ecology. Weather.

Moon bear ill. by Ed Young. Henry Holt, 2010. ISBN 978-0-8050-8977-6 Subj: Animals – bears. Animals – endangered animals.

Guidone, Thea. *Drum city* ill. by Vanessa Newton. Tricycle, 2010. ISBN 978-1-58246-308-7 Subj: Musical instruments – drums. Parades. Rhyming text.

Guthrie, James. *Last song* ill. by Eric Rohmann. Roaring Brook, 2010. ISBN 978-1-59643-508-7 Subj: Animals – squirrels. Bedtime. Lullabies. Poetry.

Guy, Ginger Foglesong. *¡Bravo!* ill. by Rene King Moreno. HarperCollins, 2010. ISBN 978-0-06-173180-8 Subj: Activities – playing. Foreign languages. Language.

Haas, Rick de. *Peter and the winter sleepers* ill. by author. NorthSouth, 2011. ISBN 978-0-7358-4033-1 Subj: Animals. Lighthouses. Seasons – winter. Weather – blizzards.

Hacohen, Dean. *Tuck me in!* by Dean Hacohen and Sherry Scharschmidt; ill. by Dean Hacohen. Candlewick, 2010. ISBN 978-0-7636-4728-5 Subj: Animals. Bedtime. Format, unusual – toy & movable books.

Hale, Dean. *Scapegoat: the story of a goat named Oat and a chewed-up coat.* Bloomsbury, 2011. ISBN 978-1-59990-468-9 Subj: Animals – goats. Behavior – lying.

Hale, Sarah Josepha Buell. *Mary had a little lamb* ill. by Laura Huliska-Beith. Marshall Cavendish, 2011. ISBN 978-0-7614-5824-1 Subj: Animals – sheep. Music. Nursery rhymes. School.

Hall, Michael. *My heart is like a zoo* ill. by author. HarperCollins, 2010. ISBN 978-0-06-191510-9 Subj: Animals. Concepts – shape. Emotions. Rhyming text. Zoos.

Perfect square ill. by author. HarperCollins, 2011. ISBN 978-0-06-191513-0 Subj: Character traits – individuality. Concepts – shape. Emotions – happiness. Self-concept.

Hallowell, George. *Wagons ho!* by George Hallowell and Joan Holub; ill. by Lynne Avril. Whitman, 2011. ISBN 978-0-8075-8612-9 Subj: Moving. U.S. history – frontier & pioneer life.

Halpin, Angela Demos. *Water, weed, and wait* (Fine, Edith Hope)

Hamilton, Emma Walton. *The very fairy princess* (Andrews, Julie)

Hamilton, Libby. *The monstrous book of monsters* ill. by Jonny Duddle and Aleksei Bitskoff. Candlewick, 2011. ISBN 978-0-7636-5756-7 Subj: Format, unusual – toy & movable books. Monsters.

Harburg, E. Y. *Over the rainbow* ill. by Eric Puybaret. Imagine, 2010. ISBN 978-1-936140-00-8 Subj: Songs.

Hardin, Melinda. *Hero dad* ill. by Bryan Langdo. Marshall Cavendish, 2010. ISBN 978-0-7614-5713-8 Subj: Careers – military. Family life – fathers.

Harline, Leigh. *When you wish upon a star* (Washington, Ned)

Harper, Charise Mericle. *The best birthday ever! by me (Lana Kittie)* ill. by author. Hyperion/Disney, 2011. ISBN 978-1-4231-3776-4 Subj: Animals – cats. Birthdays. Etiquette. Imagination.

Cupcake: a journey to special ill. by author. Hyperion/Disney, 2010. ISBN 978-1-4231-1897-8 Subj: Character traits – appearance. Food. Friendship. Self-concept.

Henry's heart ill. by author. Henry Holt, 2011. ISBN 978-0-8050-8989-9 Subj: Anatomy. Animals – dogs. Emotions. Health & fitness. Pets.

Pink me up ill. by author. Random House, 2010. ISBN 978-0-375-85607-5 Subj: Activities – picnicking. Animals – rabbits. Concepts – color. Family life – fathers.

Harper, Jamie. *Miles to go* ill. by author. Candlewick, 2010. ISBN 978-0-7636-3598-5 Subj: Automobiles. Imagination.

Harper, Lee. *The Emperor's cool clothes* ill. by author. Marshall Cavendish, 2011. ISBN 978-0-7614-

5948-4 Subj: Birds – penguins. Character traits – appearance. Character traits – vanity. Clothing. Folk & fairy tales. Humorous stories.

Harris, John. *A giraffe goes to Paris* (Holmes, Mary Tavener)

Jingle bells: how the holiday classic came to be ill. by Adam Gustavson. Peachtree, 2011. ISBN 978-1-56145-590-4 Subj: Music. Seasons – winter. Songs.

Harris, Robie H. *Who has what? all about girls' bodies and boys' bodies* ill. by Nadine Bernard Westcott. Candlewick, 2011. ISBN 978-0-7636-2931-1 Subj: Anatomy.

Harris, Teresa E. *Summer Jackson: grown up* ill. by A. G. Ford. HarperCollins, 2011. ISBN 978-0-06-185757-7 Subj: Behavior – growing up. Ethnic groups in the U.S. – African Americans. Family life.

Harris, Trudy. *Say something, Perico* ill. by Cecilia Rébora. Lerner, 2011. ISBN 978-0-7613-5231-0 Subj: Birds – parakeets, parrots. Foreign languages.

Tally cat keeps track ill. by Andrew N. Harris. Millbrook, 2010. ISBN 978-0-7613-4451-3 Subj: Animals – cats. Counting, numbers. Friendship.

Hartland, Jessie. *How the dinosaur got to the museum* ill. by author. Blue Apple, 2011. ISBN 978-1-60905-090-0 Subj: Careers – paleontologists. Dinosaurs. Museums.

How the sphinx got to the museum ill. by author. Blue Apple, 2010. ISBN 978-1-60905-032-0 Subj: Art. Foreign lands – Egypt. Museums.

Hartt-Sussman, Heather. *Nana's getting married* ill. by Georgia Graham. Tundra, 2010. ISBN 978-0-88776-911-5 Subj: Family life – grandmothers. Weddings.

Harvey, Jeanne Walker. *My hands sing the blues: Romare Bearden's childhood journey* ill. by Elizabeth Zunon. Marshall Cavendish, 2011. ISBN 978-0-7614-5810-4 Subj: Art. Careers – artists. Ethnic groups in the U.S. – African Americans. U.S. history.

Hassett, Ann. *Too many frogs!* by Ann Hassett and John Hassett; ill. by John Hassett. Houghton Harcourt, 2011. ISBN 978-0-547-36299-1 Subj: Activities – baking, cooking. Family life – grandmothers. Frogs & toads.

Hassett, John. *Too many frogs!* (Hassett, Ann)

Hatkoff, Craig, et al. *Leo the snow leopard: the true story of an amazing rescue.* Scholastic, 2010. ISBN 978-0-545-22927-2 Subj: Animals – endangered animals. Animals – leopards.

Haughton, Chris. *Little Owl lost* ill. by author. Candlewick, 2010. ISBN 978-0-7636-5022-3 Subj: Behavior – lost. Birds – owls.

Havill, Juanita. *Call the horse lucky* ill. by Nancy Lane. Gryphon, 2010. ISBN 978-0-940719-10-1 Subj: Animals – horses, ponies. Character traits – kindness to animals.

Hawkes, Kevin. *The wicked big toddlah goes to New York* ill. by author. Random House, 2011. ISBN 978-0-375-86188-8 Subj: Activities – traveling. Babies. Behavior – lost. Giants. Humorous stories.

Hayes, Geoffrey. *The bunny's night-light: a glow-in-the-dark search* ill. by author. Random House, 2012. ISBN 978-0-375-86926-6 Subj: Animals – rabbits. Bedtime. Light, lights.

Hayes, Karel. *The summer visitors* ill. by author. Down East, 2011. ISBN 978-0-89272-918-0 Subj: Animals – bears. Seasons – summer.

Hector, Julian. *The gentleman bug* ill. by author. Simon & Schuster, 2010. ISBN 978-1-4169-9467-1 Subj: Books, reading. Insects. Self-concept.

Heide, Florence Parry. *Always listen to your mother* by Florence Parry Heide and Roxanne Heide Pierce; ill. by Kyle M. Stone. Hyperion/Disney, 2010. ISBN 978-1-4231-1395-9 Subj: Behavior – cooperation. Behavior – misbehavior. Humorous stories.

Helakoski, Leslie. *Big chickens go to town* ill. by Henry Cole. Penguin Group (USA), 2010. ISBN 978-0-525-42162-7 Subj: Birds – chickens. Cities, towns. Emotions – fear.

Fair cow ill. by author. Marshall Cavendish, 2010. ISBN 978-0-7614-5684-1 Subj: Animals – bulls, cows. Character traits – individuality. Fairs, festivals.

Heller, Linda. *How Dalia put a big yellow comforter inside a tiny blue box: and other wonders of tzedakah* ill. by Stacey Dressen McQueen. Tricycle, 2011. ISBN 978-1-58246-378-0 Subj: Character traits – generosity. Family life – brothers & sisters. Jewish culture.

Helmore, Jim. *Oh no, monster tomato!* ill. by Karen Wall. Egmont UK, 2011. ISBN 978-1-4052-4741-2 Subj: Contests. Gardens, gardening. Plants.

Helquist, Brett. *Bedtime for Bear* ill. by author. HarperCollins, 2010. ISBN 978-0-06-050205-8 Subj: Animals – bears. Hibernation. Seasons – winter. Weather – snow.

Henderson, Kathy. *Hush, baby, hush! lullabies from around the world* ill. by Pam Smy. Frances Lincoln, 2011. ISBN 978-1-84507-967-3 Subj: Foreign languages. Lullabies.

Hendra, Sue. *Barry, the fish with fingers* ill. by author. Random House, 2010. ISBN 978-0-375-85894-9 Subj: Anatomy – fingers. Fish.

Henkes, Kevin. *Little white rabbit* ill. by author. HarperCollins, 2011. ISBN 978-0-06-200642-4 Subj: Animals – rabbits. Character traits – curiosity. Imagination.

My garden ill. by author. HarperCollins, 2010. ISBN 978-0-06-171517-4 Subj: Gardens, gardening. Imagination.

Henrichs, Wendy. *I am Tama, lucky cat: a Japanese legend* ill. by Yoshiko Jaeggi. Peachtree, 2011. ISBN 978-1-56145-589-8 Subj: Animals – cats. Folk & fairy tales. Foreign lands – Japan.

When Anju loved being an elephant ill. by John Butler. Sleeping Bear, 2011. ISBN 978-1-58536-533-3 Subj: Animals – elephants. Character traits – kindness to animals. Circus. Foreign lands – Indonesia.

Heos, Bridget. *What to expect when you're expecting joeys: a guide for marsupial parents (and curious kids)* ill. by Stéphane Jorisch. Millbrook, 2011. ISBN 978-0-7613-5859-6 Subj: Animals – babies. Animals – marsupials.

Herman, Charlotte. *First rain* ill. by Kathryn Mitter. Whitman, 2010. ISBN 978-0-8075-2453-4 Subj: Foreign lands – Israel. Jewish culture. Weather – rain.

Herzog, Brad. *G is for gold medal: an Olympics alphabet* ill. by Doug Bowles. Sleeping Bear, 2011. ISBN 978-1-58536-462-6 Subj: ABC books. Sports – Olympics.

I spy with my little eye: baseball ill. by David Milne. Sleeping Bear, 2011. ISBN 978-1-58536-496-1 Subj: Picture puzzles. Sports – baseball.

Hill, Isabel. *Building stories* photos by author. Star Bright, 2011. ISBN 978-1-59572-279-9 Subj: Buildings. Rhyming text.

Hill, Laban Carrick. *Dave the potter: artist, poet, slave* ill. by Bryan Collier. Little, Brown, 2010. ISBN 978-0-316-10731-0 Subj: Art. Caldecott award honor books. Ethnic groups in the U.S. – African Americans. Slavery.

Hill, Meggan. *Nico and Lola: kindness shared between a boy and a dog* photos by Susan M. Graunke. HarperCollins, 2010. ISBN 978-0-06-199043-4 Subj: Animals – dogs. Character traits – kindness to animals.

Hill, Susanna Leonard. *April Fool, Phyllis!* ill. by Jeffrey Ebbeler. Holiday House, 2011. ISBN 978-0-

8234-2270-8 Subj: Animals – groundhogs. Holidays – April Fools' Day. Weather – blizzards.

Can't sleep without sheep ill. by Mike Wohnoutka. Walker, 2010. ISBN 978-0-8027-2066-5 Subj: Animals. Animals – sheep. Bedtime. Counting, numbers. Sleep.

Hillenbrand, Will. *Mother Goose picture puzzles* ill. by author. Marshall Cavendish, 2011. ISBN 978-0-7614-5808-1 Subj: Nursery rhymes. Picture puzzles.

Spring is here ill. by author. Holiday House, 2011. ISBN 978-0-8234-1602-8 Subj: Animals – bears. Animals – moles. Seasons – spring.

Hills, Tad. *How Rocket learned to read* ill. by author. Random House, 2010. ISBN 978-0-375-85899-4 Subj: Animals – dogs. Birds. Books, reading.

Hilton, Perez. *The boy with pink hair* ill. by Jen Hill. Penguin Group (USA), 2011. ISBN 978-0-451-23420-9 Subj: Behavior – teasing. Character traits – being different. Hair. School. Self-concept.

Himmelman, John. *Cows to the rescue* ill. by author. Henry Holt, 2011. ISBN 978-0-8050-9249-3 Subj: Animals – bulls, cows. Fairs, festivals. Farms. Humorous stories.

Pigs to the rescue ill. by author. Henry Holt, 2010. ISBN 978-0-8050-8683-6 Subj: Animals – pigs. Character traits – helpfulness. Farms.

10 little hot dogs ill. by author. Marshall Cavendish, 2010. ISBN 978-0-7614-5797-8 Subj: Animals – dogs. Counting, numbers.

Hines, Anna Grossnickle. *I am a backhoe* ill. by author. Tricycle, 2010. ISBN 978-1-58246-306-3 Subj: Activities – playing. Imagination. Machines. Trucks.

I am a Tyrannosaurus ill. by author. Tricycle, 2011. ISBN 978-1-58246-413-8 Subj: Dinosaurs. Imagination.

Hobbie, Holly. *Everything but the horse* ill. by author. Little, Brown, 2010. ISBN 978-0-316-07019-5 Subj: Animals – horses, ponies. Birthdays. Farms. Moving.

Hodge, Deborah. *Watch me grow! a down-to-earth look at growing food in the city* photos by Brian Harris. Kids Can, 2011. ISBN 978-1-55453-618-4 Subj: Cities, towns. Gardens, gardening.

Hodgkinson, Leigh. *Limelight Larry* ill. by author. Tiger Tales, 2011. ISBN 978-1-58925-102-1 Subj: Animals. Behavior – boasting. Birds – peacocks, peahens.

Smile! ill. by author. HarperCollins, 2010. ISBN 978-0-06-185269-5 Subj: Anatomy – faces. Behavior – bad day. Behavior – lost & found possessions. Emotions. Family life.

Hoffman, Mary. *Grace at Christmas* ill. by Cornelius Van Wright and Ying-Hwa Hu. Penguin Group (USA), 2011. ISBN 978-0-8037-3577-4 Subj: Ethnic groups in the U.S. – African Americans. Family life. Holidays – Christmas.

Hoffmann, E. T. A. *The nutcracker* by Alison Jay; ill. by author. Penguin Group (USA), 2010. ISBN 978-0-8037-3285-8 Subj: Activities – dancing. Animals – mice. Ballet. Folk & fairy tales. Holidays – Christmas. Imagination. Royalty. Toys.

Holabird, Katharine. *Angelina and the royal wedding* ill. by Helen Craig. Penguin Group (USA), 2010. ISBN 978-0-670-01213-8 Subj: Animals – mice. Weddings.

Holmes, Janet A. *Have you seen Duck?* ill. by Jonathan Bentley. Scholastic, 2011. ISBN 978-0-545-22488-8 Subj: Behavior – lost & found possessions. Birds – ducks. Toys.

Holmes, Mary Tavener. *A giraffe goes to Paris* by Mary Tavener Holmes and John Harris; ill. by Jon Cannell. Marshall Cavendish, 2010. ISBN 978-0-7614-5595-0 Subj: Activities – traveling. Animals – giraffes. Foreign lands – France.

Holt, Kimberly Willis. *The adventures of Granny Clearwater and Little Critter* ill. by Laura Huliska-Beith. Henry Holt, 2010. ISBN 978-0-8050-7899-2 Subj: Behavior – lost. Family life – grandmothers. Tall tales. U.S. history – frontier & pioneer life.

Holt, Sharon. *Did my mother do that?* ill. by Brian Lovelock. Candlewick, 2010. ISBN 978-0-7636-4685-1 Subj: Animals – babies. Bedtime. Birth.

Holub, Joan. *Twinkle, star of the week* ill. by Paul Nicholls. Whitman, 2010. ISBN 978-0-8075-8131-5 Subj: Behavior – wishing. School. Stars.

Wagons ho! (Hallowell, George)

Hop a little, jump a little! ill. by Annie Kubler. Child's Play, 2010. ISBN 978-1-84643-341-2 Subj: Activities. Babies. Format, unusual – board books. Rhyming text.

Hopkins, Lee Bennett. *Full moon and star* ill. by Marcellus Hall. Abrams, 2011. ISBN 978-1-4197-0013-2 Subj: Activities – writing. Behavior – cooperation. Friendship. Theater.

Hopkinson, Deborah. *The humblebee hunter: inspired by the life and experiments of Charles Darwin and his children* ill. by Jen Corace. Hyperion, 2010. ISBN 978-1-4231-1356-0 Subj: Foreign lands – England. Insects – bees. Science.

Hoppe, Paul. *The woods* ill. by author. Chronicle, 2011. ISBN 978-0-8118-7547-9 Subj: Bedtime. Behavior – lost & found possessions. Character traits – bravery. Emotions – fear. Toys.

Horowitz, Dave. *Buy my hats!* ill. by author. Penguin Group (USA), 2010. ISBN 978-0-399-25275-4 Subj: Animals. Careers – salespeople. Clothing – hats. Friendship.

Horrocks, Anita. *Silas' seven grandparents* ill. by Helen Flook. Orca, 2010. ISBN 978-1-55143-561-9 Subj: Family life – grandparents. Family life – stepfamilies.

Hosford, Kate. *Big bouffant* ill. by Holly Clifton-Brown. Carolrhoda, 2011. ISBN 978-0-7613-5409-3 Subj: Character traits – appearance. Character traits – individuality. Hair. Rhyming text.

House, Catherine. *A stork in a baobab tree: an African twelve days of Christmas* ill. by Polly Alakija. Frances Lincoln, 2011. ISBN 978-1-84780-116-6 Subj: Cumulative tales. Foreign lands – Africa. Holidays – Christmas. Music. Songs.

Houston, Gloria. *Miss Dorothy and her bookmobile* ill. by Susan Condie Lamb. HarperCollins, 2011. ISBN 978-0-06-029155-6 Subj: Books, reading. Libraries. Trucks.

Hovland, Henrik. *John Jensen feels different* tr. by Don Bartlett; ill. by Torill Kove. Eerdmans, 2011. ISBN 978-0-8028-5399-8 Subj: Character traits – being different. Character traits – individuality. Reptiles – alligators, crocodiles. Self-concept.

Howard, Martin. *Tina Cocolina: queen of the cupcakes* (Cartaya, Pablo)

Howe, James. *Brontorina* ill. by Randy Cecil. Candlewick, 2010. ISBN 978-0-7636-4437-6 Subj: Ballet. Concepts – size. Dinosaurs.

Howland, Naomi. *Princess says goodnight* ill. by David Small. HarperCollins, 2010. ISBN 978-0-06-145525-4 Subj: Bedtime. Rhyming text. Royalty – princesses.

Hruby, Emily. *Counting in the garden* ill. by Patrick Hruby. AMMO, 2011. ISBN 978-1-934429-70-9 Subj: Animals. Counting, numbers. Gardens, gardening.

Hubbell, Patricia. *Check it out! reading, finding, helping* ill. by Nancy Speir. Marshall Cavendish, 2011. ISBN 978-0-7614-5803-6 Subj: Books, reading. Libraries. Rhyming text.

Horses: trotting! prancing! racing! ill. by Joe Mathieu. Marshall Cavendish, 2011. ISBN 978-0-7614-5949-1 Subj: Animals – horses, ponies. Rhyming text.

Shaggy dogs, waggy dogs ill. by Donald Wu. Marshall Cavendish, 2011. ISBN 978-0-7614-5957-6 Subj: Animals – dogs. Rhyming text.

Snow happy! ill. by Hiroe Nakata. Tricycle, 2010. ISBN 978-1-58246-329-2 Subj: Activities – playing. Rhyming text. Weather – snow.

Hudes, Quiara Alegría. *Welcome to my neighborhood! a barrio ABC* ill. by Shino Arihara. Scholastic, 2010. ISBN 978-0-545-09424-5 Subj: ABC books. Communities, neighborhoods. Ethnic groups in the U.S. – Hispanic Americans. Foreign languages. Rhyming text.

Hudson, Cheryl Willis. *My friend Maya loves to dance* ill. by Eric Velasquez. Abrams, 2010. ISBN 978-0-8109-8328-1 Subj: Activities – dancing. Ethnic groups in the U.S. – African Americans. Handicaps – physical handicaps. Rhyming text.

Hueston, M. P. *The all-American jump and jive jig* ill. by Amanda Haley. Sterling, 2010. ISBN 978-1-4027-5143-1 Subj: Activities – dancing. Rhyming text. U.S. history.

Huget, Jennifer LaRue. *The best birthday party ever* ill. by LeUyen Pham. Random House, 2011. ISBN 978-0-375-84763-9 Subj: Birthdays. Parties.

How to clean your room in 10 easy steps ill. by Edward Koren. Random House, 2010. ISBN 978-0-375-84410-2 Subj: Character traits – cleanliness. Humorous stories.

Hughes, Shirley. *The Christmas Eve ghost* ill. by author. Candlewick, 2010. ISBN 978-0-7636-4472-7 Subj: Holidays – Christmas. Prejudice. Religion.

Don't want to go! ill. by author. Candlewick, 2010. ISBN 978-0-7636-5091-9 Subj: Activities – babysitting. Emotions – anger. Emotions – fear.

Hulbert, Laura. *Who has these feet?* ill. by Erik Brooks. Henry Holt, 2011. ISBN 978-0-8050-8907-3 Subj: Anatomy – feet. Animals.

Huling, Jan. *Ol' Bloo's boogie-woogie band and blues ensemble* ill. by Henri Sørensen. Peachtree, 2010. ISBN 978-1-56145-436-5 Subj: Animals. Careers – musicians. Crime. Folk & fairy tales. Old age.

Hulme, Joy N. *Easter babies: a springtime counting book* ill. by Dan Andreasen. Sterling, 2010. ISBN 978-1-4027-6352-6 Subj: Animals – babies. Counting, numbers. Farms. Holidays – Easter. Rhyming text. Seasons – spring.

Huneck, Stephen. *Sally's great balloon adventure* ill. by author. Abrams, 2010. ISBN 978-0-8109-8331-1 Subj: Activities – ballooning. Animals – dogs.

Hurd, Thacher. *The weaver* ill. by Elisa Kleven. Farrar, 2010. ISBN 978-0-374-38254-4 Subj: Activities – weaving. Dreams.

Husband, Amy. *Dear teacher* ill. by author. Sourcebooks, 2010. ISBN 978-1-4022-4268-7 Subj: Imagination. Letters, cards. School.

Ichikawa, Satomi. *My little train* ill. by author. Penguin Group (USA), 2010. ISBN 978-0-399-25453-6 Subj: Animals. Imagination. Toys.

Ingalls, Ann. *The little piano girl: the story of Mary Lou Williams, jazz legend* by Ann Ingalls and Maryann Macdonald; ill. by Giselle Potter. Houghton Mifflin, 2010. ISBN 978-0-618-95974-7 Subj: Careers – musicians. Ethnic groups in the U.S. – African Americans. Music. Musical instruments – pianos.

Intriago, Patricia. *Dot* ill. by author. Farrar, 2011. ISBN 978-0-374-31835-2 Subj: Concepts – opposites.

Isaacs, Anne. *Dust Devil* ill. by Paul O. Zelinsky. Random House, 2010. ISBN 978-0-375-86722-4 Subj: Animals – horses, ponies. Tall tales. U.S. history – frontier & pioneer life.

Isadora, Rachel. *Say hello!* ill. by author. Penguin Group (USA), 2010. ISBN 978-0-399-25230-3 Subj: Cities, towns. Communities, neighborhoods. Foreign languages.

Isol. *Petit, the monster* tr. by Elisa Amado; ill. by author. Groundwood, 2010. ISBN 978-0-88899-947-4 Subj: Behavior – misbehavior.

Isop, Laurie. *How do you hug a porcupine?* ill. by Gwen Millward. Simon & Schuster, 2011. ISBN 978-1-4424-1291-0 Subj: Animals. Hugging. Rhyming text.

Iwai, Melissa. *Soup day* ill. by author. Henry Holt, 2010. ISBN 978-0-8050-9004-8 Subj: Activities – baking, cooking. Family life – mothers. Food.

Iwamura, Kazuo. *Bedtime in the forest* ill. by author. NorthSouth, 2010. ISBN 978-0-7358-2310-5 Subj: Animals – squirrels. Bedtime. Birds – owls.

Hooray for summer! ill. by author. NorthSouth, 2010. ISBN 978-0-7358-2285-6 Subj: Animals – squirrels. Seasons – summer. Weather – storms.

Jack and the beanstalk. *Jack and the beanstalk* retold by Nina Crews; ill. by reteller. Henry Holt, 2011. ISBN 978-0-8050-8765-9 Subj: Cities, towns. Folk & fairy tales. Giants. Plants.

Jacques and de beanstalk by Mike Artell; ill. by Jim Harris. Penguin Group (USA), 2010. ISBN 978-0-8037-2816-5 Subj: Folk & fairy tales. Giants. Plants. Rhyming text.

Jackson, Ellen. *The seven seas* ill. by Bill Slavin and Esperança Melo. Eerdmans, 2011. ISBN 978-0-8028-5341-7 Subj: Animals – rabbits. Concepts – color. Geography. Imagination. Rhyming text. Sea & seashore.

Jackson, Kathryn. *Pantaloon* ill. by Steven Salerno. Random House, 2010. ISBN 978-0-375-85624-2 Subj: Activities – baking, cooking. Animals – dogs. Careers – bakers. Character traits – helpfulness.

Jackson, Shelley. *Mimi's Dada Catifesto* ill. by author. Clarion, 2010. ISBN 978-0-547-12681-4 Subj: Animals – cats. Art.

Jacobs, Paul Dubois. *Fire drill* by Paul Dubois Jacobs and Jennifer Swender; ill. by Huy Voun Lee. Henry Holt, 2010. ISBN 978-0-8050-8953-0 Subj: Fire. Rhyming text. Safety. School.

Jadoul, Émile. *Good night, Chickie* ill. by author. Eerdmans, 2011. ISBN 978-0-8028-5378-3 Subj: Bedtime. Behavior – worrying. Birds – chickens. Family life – mothers.

Jahn-Clough, Lisa. *Felicity and Cordelia: a tale of two bunnies* ill. by author. Farrar, 2011. ISBN 978-0-374-32300-4 Subj: Activities – ballooning. Activities – traveling. Animals – rabbits. Friendship.

Jalali, Reza. *Moon watchers: Shirin's Ramadan miracle* ill. by Anne Sibley O'Brien. Tilbury House, 2010. ISBN 978-0-88448-321-2 Subj: Family life – brothers & sisters. Holidays – Ramadan. Religion.

James, Simon. *George flies south* ill. by author. Candlewick, 2011. ISBN 978-0-7636-5724-6 Subj: Activities – flying. Behavior – growing up. Birds.

Jane, Pamela. *Little goblins ten* ill. by Jane Manning. HarperCollins, 2011. ISBN 978-0-06-176798-

2 Subj: Counting, numbers. Holidays – Halloween. Monsters. Mythical creatures.

Janni, Rebecca. *Every cowgirl needs a horse* ill. by Lynne Avril. Penguin Group (USA), 2010. ISBN 978-0-525-42164-1 Subj: Birthdays. Cowboys, cowgirls. Imagination.

Every cowgirl needs dancing boots ill. by Lynne Avril. Penguin Group (USA), 2011. ISBN 978-0-525-42341-6 Subj: Activities – dancing. Character traits – compromising. Cowboys, cowgirls. Emotions – loneliness. Friendship.

Janovitz, Marilyn. *Baby, baby, baby!* ill. by author. Sourcebooks, 2010. ISBN 978-1-4022-4414-8 Subj: Babies. Format, unusual – board books.

Jarka, Jeff. *Love that kitty! the story of a boy who wanted to be a cat* ill. by author. Henry Holt, 2010. ISBN 978-0-8050-9053-6 Subj: Animals – cats. Family life. Imagination. Pets.

Javaherbin, Mina. *Goal!* ill. by A. G. Ford. Candlewick, 2010. ISBN 978-0-7636-4571-7 Subj: Behavior – bullying. Foreign lands – South Africa. Friendship. Sports – soccer.

The secret message ill. by Bruce Whatley. Hyperion/Disney, 2010. ISBN 978-1-4231-1044-6 Subj: Birds – parakeets, parrots. Folk & fairy tales. Foreign lands – Iran.

Javernick, Ellen. *What if everybody did that?* ill. by Colleen M. Madden. Marshall Cavendish, 2010. ISBN 978-0-7614-5686-5 Subj: Behavior. Character traits.

Jay, Alison. *Red green blue: a first book of colors* ill. by author. Penguin Group (USA), 2010. ISBN 978-0-525-42303-4 Subj: Concepts – color. Nursery rhymes. Picture puzzles. Rhyming text.

Jeffers, Oliver. *The heart and the bottle* ill. by author. Penguin Group (USA), 2010. ISBN 978-0-399-25452-9 Subj: Death. Emotions – grief. Emotions – loneliness.

Stuck ill. by author. Penguin Group (USA), 2011. ISBN 978-0-399-25737-7 Subj: Humorous stories. Kites. Trees.

Up and down. Penguin Group (USA), 2010. ISBN 978-0-399-25545-8 Subj: Activities – flying. Birds – penguins. Friendship.

Jenkins, Emily. *Small medium large* ill. by Tomek Bogacki. Star Bright, 2011. ISBN 978-1-59572-278-2 Subj: Concepts – size. Language.

Jenkins, Martin. *Can we save the tiger?* ill. by Vicky White. Candlewick, 2011. ISBN 978-0-7636-4909-8 Subj: Animals – endangered animals. Nature.

Jenkins, Steve. *How to clean a hippopotamus: a look at unusual animal partnerships* by Steve Jenkins and Robin Page; ill. by Steve Jenkins. Houghton Mifflin, 2010. ISBN 978-0-547-24515-7 Subj: Animals. Nature. Science.

Just a second: a different way to look at time ill. by author. Houghton Mifflin, 2011. ISBN 978-0-618-70896-3 Subj: Nature. Time.

Time for a bath by Steve Jenkins and Robin Page; ill. by Steve Jenkins. Houghton Mifflin, 2011. ISBN 978-0-547-25037-3 Subj: Activities – bathing. Animals.

Time to eat by Steve Jenkins and Robin Page; ill. by Steve Jenkins. Houghton Mifflin, 2011. ISBN 978-0-547-25032-8 Subj: Animals. Food.

Time to sleep by Steve Jenkins and Robin Page; ill. by Steve Jenkins. Houghton Mifflin, 2011. ISBN 978-0-547-25040-3 Subj: Animals. Sleep.

Jennings, Sharon. *C'mere, boy!* ill. by Ashley Spires. Kids Can, 2010. ISBN 978-1-55453-440-1 Subj: Animals – dogs. Humorous stories.

Jewell, Nancy. *Alligator wedding* ill. by J. Rutland. Henry Holt, 2010. ISBN 978-0-8050-6819-1 Subj: Reptiles – alligators, crocodiles. Rhyming text. Swamps. Weddings.

Jocelyn, Marthe. *Ones and twos* by Marthe Jocelyn and Nell Jocelyn; ill. by Marthe Jocelyn. Tundra, 2011. ISBN 978-1-77049-220-2 Subj: Counting, numbers. Friendship. Rhyming text.

Jocelyn, Nell. *Ones and twos* (Jocelyn, Marthe)

Johnson, Angela. *The day Ray got away* ill. by Luke LaMarca. Simon & Schuster, 2010. ISBN 978-0-689-87375-1 Subj: Behavior – running away. Parades. Toys – balloons.

Lottie Paris lives here ill. by Scott M Fischer. Simon & Schuster, 2011. ISBN 978-0-689-87377-5 Subj: Activities. Behavior. Day. Ethnic groups in the U.S. – African Americans. Family life – fathers. Imagination.

Johnson, D. B. *Palazzo inverso* ill. by author. Houghton Harcourt, 2010. ISBN 978-0-15-23999-6 Subj: Art. Buildings. Careers – artists. Format, unusual.

Johnson, Dinah. *Black magic* ill. by R. Gregory Christie. Henry Holt, 2010. ISBN 978-0-8050-7833-6 Subj: Ethnic groups in the U.S. – African Americans. Self-concept.

Johnson, Jen Cullerton. *Seeds of change: planting a path to peace* ill. by Sonia Lynn Sadler. Lee & Low, 2010. ISBN 978-1-60060-367-9 Subj: Character traits – responsibility. Ecology. Foreign lands – Kenya. Trees.

Johnson, Neil. *The falling raindrop* by Neil Johnson and Joel Chin; ill. by authors. Tricycle, 2010. ISBN 978-1-58246-312-4 Subj: Behavior – worrying. Water. Weather – rain.

Johnston, Tony. *Levi Strauss gets a bright idea: a fairly fabricated story of a pair of pants* ill. by Stacy Innerst. Houghton Harcourt, 2011. ISBN 978-0-15-206145-6 Subj: Activities – sewing. Clothing – pants. Tall tales. U.S. history – frontier & pioneer life.

Joosse, Barbara. *Dog parade* ill. by Eugene Yelchin. Houghton Harcourt, 2011. ISBN 978-0-15-206690-1 Subj: Animals – dogs. Clothing – costumes. Parades.

Friends (mostly) ill. by Tomaso Milian. HarperCollins, 2010. ISBN 978-0-06-088221-1 Subj: Friendship.

Higgledy-piggledy chicks ill. by Rick Chrustowski. HarperCollins, 2010. ISBN 978-0-06-075042-8 Subj: Animals – babies. Birds – chickens. Farms.

Sleepover at Gramma's house ill. by Jan Jutte. Penguin Group (USA), 2010. ISBN 978-0-399-25261-7 Subj: Activities – playing. Animals – elephants. Family life – grandmothers. Sleepovers.

Jordan, Deloris. *Baby blessings: a prayer for the day you are born* ill. by James Ransome. Simon & Schuster, 2010. ISBN 978-1-4169-5362-3 Subj: Emotions – love. Ethnic groups in the U.S. – African Americans. Family life – parents. Religion.

Jordan, Sandra. *Ballet for Martha: making Appalachian Spring* (Greenberg, Jan)

Joubert, Beverly. *African animal alphabet* by Beverly Joubert and Dereck Joubert; photos by author. National Geographic, 2011. ISBN 978-1-4263-0781-2 Subj: ABC books. Animals. Foreign lands – Africa.

Joubert, Dereck. *African animal alphabet* (Joubert, Beverly)

Joyce, William. *The Man in the Moon* ill. by author. Simon & Schuster, 2011. ISBN 978-1-4424-3041-9 Subj: Imagination. Moon.

Juan, Ana. *The pet shop revolution* ill. by author. Scholastic, 2011. ISBN 978-0-545-12810-0 Subj: Animals. Character traits – kindness to animals. Pets. Stores.

Judge, Lita. *Red sled* ill. by author. Simon & Schuster, 2011. ISBN 978-1-4424-2007-6 Subj: Animals. Seasons – winter. Sports – sledding.

Jules, Jacqueline. *Picnic at Camp Shalom* ill. by Deborah Melmon. Lerner/Kar-Ben, 2011. ISBN 978-0-7613-6661-4 Subj: Camps, camping. Friendship. Jewish culture.

Jurmain, Suzanne Tripp. *Worst of friends: Thomas Jefferson, John Adams, and the true story of an American feud* ill. by Larry Day. Penguin Group (USA), 2011. ISBN 978-0-525-47903-1 Subj: Friendship. U.S. history.

Juster, Norton. *Neville* ill. by G. Brian Karas. Random House, 2011. ISBN 978-0-375-86765-1 Subj: Behavior – resourcefulness. Emotions – loneliness. Moving.

The odious ogre ill. by Jules Feiffer. Scholastic, 2010. ISBN 978-0-545-16202-9 Subj: Character traits – kindness. Mythical creatures – ogres.

Kabakov, Vladimir. *R is for Russia* photos by Prodeepta Das. Frances Lincoln, 2011. ISBN 978-1-84780-102-9 Subj: ABC books. Foreign lands – Russia.

Kalz, Jill. *An a-maze-ing amusement park adventure* ill. by Mattia Cerato. Capstone, 2010. ISBN 978-1-4048-6023-0 Subj: Mazes. Parks – amusement.

An a-maze-ing farm adventure ill. by Mattia Cerato. Picture Window, 2010. ISBN 978-1-4048-6038-4 Subj: Farms. Mazes.

An a-maze-ing school adventure ill. by Mattia Cerato. Picture Window, 2010. ISBN 978-1-4048-6039-1 Subj: Mazes. School.

An a-maze-ing zoo adventure ill. by Mattia Cerato. Picture Window, 2010. ISBN 978-1-4048-6024-7 Subj: Mazes. Zoos.

Kann, Victoria. *Silverlicious* ill. by author. HarperCollins, 2011. ISBN 978-0-06-178123-0 Subj: Fairies. Family life – brothers & sisters. Teeth.

Kaplan, Bruce Eric. *Monsters eat whiny children* ill. by author. Simon & Schuster, 2010. ISBN 978-1-4169-8689-8 Subj: Behavior – misbehavior. Family life – brothers & sisters. Monsters.

Kaplan, Michael B. *Betty Bunny loves chocolate cake* ill. by Stéphane Jorisch. Penguin Group (USA), 2011. ISBN 978-0-8037-3407-4 Subj: Animals – rabbits. Character traits – patience. Food.

Karas, G. Brian. *The village garage* ill. by author. Henry Holt, 2010. ISBN 978-0-8050-8716-1 Subj: Careers. Cities, towns. Seasons.

Kasbarian, Lucine, reteller. *The greedy sparrow: an Armenian tale* ill. by Maria Zaikina. Marshall Cavendish, 2011. ISBN 978-0-7614-5821-2 Subj: Behavior – greed. Behavior – trickery. Birds – sparrows. Folk & fairy tales.

Kato, Yukiko. *In the meadow* tr. by Yuki Kaneko; ill. by Komako Sakai. Enchanted Lion, 2011. ISBN 978-1-59270-108-7 Subj: Behavior – lost. Nature.

Katz, Bobbi. *Nothing but a dog* ill. by Jane Manning. Penguin Group (USA), 2010. ISBN 978-0-525-47858-4 Subj: Animals – dogs. Pets.

Katz, Jon. *Meet the dogs of Bedlam Farm* photos by author. Henry Holt, 2011. ISBN 978-0-8050-9219-6 Subj: Animals – dogs. Farms.

Katz, Karen. *The babies on the bus* ill. by author. Henry Holt, 2011. ISBN 978-0-8050-9011-6 Subj: Babies. Buses. Music. Songs.

Katz, Susan B. *ABC, baby me!* ill. by Alicia Padrón. Random House, 2010. ISBN 978-0-375-86679-1 Subj: ABC books. Babies. Format, unusual – board books.

Katzman, Nicole. *Nathan blows out the Hanukkah candles* (Lehman-Wilzig, Tami)

Kaufman, Jeanne. *Young Henry and the dragon* ill. by Daria Tessler. Shenanigan, 2011. ISBN 978-1-934860-11-3 Subj: Dragons. Fire. Middle Ages. Rhyming text.

Kay, Verla. *Hornbooks and inkwells* ill. by S. D. Schindler. Penguin Group (USA), 2011. ISBN 978-0-399-23870-3 Subj: Rhyming text. School. U.S. history – frontier & pioneer life.

Whatever happened to the Pony Express? ill. by Kimberly Bulcken Root and Barry Root. Penguin Group (USA), 2010. ISBN 978-0-399-24483-4 Subj: Animals – horses, ponies. Careers – postal workers. Rhyming text. U.S. history – frontier & pioneer life.

Keane, Dave. *Daddy adventure day* ill. by Sue Ramá. Penguin Group (USA), 2011. ISBN 978-0-399-24627-2 Subj: Family life – fathers. Sports – baseball.

Kelly, Irene. *Even an octopus needs a home* ill. by author. Holiday House, 2011. ISBN 978-0-8234-2235-7 Subj: Animals. Homes, houses.

Kelly, Mij. *A bed of your own!* ill. by Mary McQuillan. Barron's, 2011. ISBN 978-0-7641-4768-5 Subj: Animals. Bedtime. Farms. Rhyming text.

Kelly, Sheila M. *I'm adopted!* (Rotner, Shelley)

Kempter, Christa. *When Mama can't sleep* ill. by Natascha Rosenberg. NorthSouth, 2011. ISBN 978-0-7358-4015-7 Subj: Bedtime. Behavior – worrying. Family life.

Kenney, Sean. *Cool city* photos by John E. Barrett. Henry Holt, 2011. ISBN 978-0-8050-8762-8 Subj: Cities, towns. Toys.

Kerby, Johanna. *Little pink pup* photos by author. Penguin Group (USA), 2010. ISBN 978-0-399-25435-2 Subj: Animals – dogs. Animals – pigs. Pets.

Kerr, Judith. *One night in the zoo* ill. by author. Kane/Miller, 2010. ISBN 978-1-935279-37-2 Subj: Counting, numbers. Rhyming text. Zoos.

Ketteman, Helen. *Goodnight, Little Monster* ill. by Bonnie Leick. Marshall Cavendish, 2010. ISBN 978-0-7614-5683-4 Subj: Bedtime. Monsters. Rhyming text.

If Beaver had a fever ill. by Kevin O'Malley. Marshall Cavendish, 2011. ISBN 978-0-7614-5951-4 Subj: Animals – bears. Careers – doctors. Family life – mothers. Illness. Rhyming text. Zoos.

Khan, Rukhsana. *Big red lollipop* ill. by Sophie Blackall. Penguin Group (USA), 2010. ISBN 978-0-670-06287-4 Subj: Birthdays. Ethnic groups in the U.S. – Pakistani Americans. Family life – sisters. Parties.

Killen, Nicola. *Not me!* ill. by author. Egmont USA, 2010. ISBN 978-1-4052-4829-7 Subj: Behavior – messy. Character traits – responsibility.

Kilodavis, Cheryl. *My princess boy* ill. by Suzanne DeSimone. Simon & Schuster, 2010. ISBN 978-1-4424-2988-8 Subj: Behavior – bullying. Character traits – being different. Character traits – individuality. Gender roles.

Kim, Sue. *How does a seed grow?* ill. by Tilde. Simon & Schuster, 2010. ISBN 978-1-4169-9435-0 Subj: Format, unusual – board books. Plants. Seeds.

Kimmel, Eric A., adapt. *Joha makes a wish: a Middle Eastern tale* ill. by Omar Rayyan. Marshall Cavendish, 2010. ISBN 978-0-7614-5599-8 Subj: Behavior – wishing. Foreign lands – Middle East. Magic.

Joseph and the Sabbath fish ill. by Martina Peluso. Lerner/Kar-Ben, 2011. ISBN 978-0-7613-5908-1 Subj: Folk & fairy tales. Jewish culture. Religion.

Medio Pollito: a Spanish tale ill. by Valeria Docampo. Marshall Cavendish, 2010. ISBN 978-0-7614-5705-3 Subj: Birds – chickens. Folk & fairy tales. Foreign lands – Spain.

Kimmelman, Leslie. *The three bully goats* ill. by Will Terry. Whitman, 2011. ISBN 978-0-8075-7900-8 Subj: Animals – babies. Animals – goats. Behavior – bullying. Mythical creatures – ogres.

Kimura, Ken. *999 tadpoles* ill. by Yasunari Murakami. NorthSouth, 2011. ISBN 978-0-7358-4013-3 Subj: Birds – hawks. Frogs & toads.

King, Dedie. *I see the sun in Afghanistan* tr. by Mohd Vahidi; ill. by Judith Inglese. Satya House, 2011. ISBN 978-0-9818720-8-7 Subj: Family life. Foreign lands – Afghanistan. Foreign languages.

King, M. G. *Librarian on the roof! a true story* ill. by Stephen Gilpin. Whitman, 2010. ISBN 978-0-8075-4512-6 Subj: Careers – librarians. Libraries. Texas.

King, Stephen Michael. *You: a story of love and friendship* ill. by author. HarperCollins, 2011. ISBN 978-0-06-206014-3 Subj: Animals – dogs. Birds. Friendship.

Kinney, Jessica. *The pig scramble* ill. by Sarah S. Brannen. Islandport, 2011. ISBN 978-1-934031-61-2 Subj: Animals – pigs. Contests. Fairs, festivals.

Kirk, Daniel. *Honk honk! Beep beep!* ill. by author. Hyperion/Disney, 2010. ISBN 978-1-4231-2486-3 Subj: Activities – traveling. Automobiles. Imagination. Rhyming text. Toys.

Library mouse: a world to explore ill. by author. Abrams, 2010. ISBN 978-0-8109-8968-9 Subj: Animals – mice. Careers – explorers. Character traits – bravery. Emotions – fear. Friendship. Libraries.

Kirk, Katie. *Eli, no!* ill. by author. Abrams, 2011. ISBN 978-0-8109-8964-1 Subj: Animals – dogs. Behavior – misbehavior.

Kirsch, Vincent X. *Forsythia and me* ill. by author. Farrar, 2011. ISBN 978-0-374-32438-4 Subj: Behavior – sharing. Character traits – helpfulness. Friendship.

Two little boys from Toolittle Toys ill. by author. Bloomsbury, 2010. ISBN 978-1-59990-428-3 Subj: Family life – brothers. Toys.

Kittinger, Jo S. *Rosa's bus: the ride to civil rights* ill. by Steven Walker. Calkins Creek, 2010. ISBN 978-1-59078-722-9 Subj: Ethnic groups in the U.S. – African Americans. Prejudice. Transportation. U.S. history. Violence, nonviolence.

Klassen, Jon. *I want my hat back* ill. by author. Candlewick, 2011. ISBN 978-0-7636-5598-3 Subj: Animals – bears. Behavior – lost & found possessions. Clothing – hats.

Kleven, Elisa. *The friendship wish* ill. by author. Penguin Group (USA), 2011. ISBN 978-0-525-42374-4 Subj: Angels. Animals – dogs. Emotions – loneliness. Friendship. Moving.

Welcome home, Mouse ill. by author. Tricycle, 2010. ISBN 978-1-58246-277-6 Subj: Animals – elephants. Animals – mice. Character traits – clumsiness. Friendship. Homes, houses.

Kling, Kevin. *Big little brother* ill. by Chris Monroe. Borealis, 2011. ISBN 978-0-87351-844-4 Subj: Behavior – bullying. Family life – brothers.

Klise, Kate. *Little Rabbit and the Meanest Mother on Earth* ill. by M. Sarah Klise. Harcourt, 2010. ISBN 978-0-15-206201-9 Subj: Animals – rabbits. Behavior – messy. Circus. Family life – mothers.

Stand straight, Ella Kate: the true story of a real giant ill. by M. Sarah Klise. Penguin Group (USA), 2010. ISBN 978-0-8037-3404-3 Subj: Character traits – being different. Concepts – size. Giants.

Knapp, Ruthie. *Who stole Mona Lisa?* ill. by Jill McElmurry. Bloomsbury, 2010. ISBN 978-1-59990-058-2 Subj: Activities – painting. Art. Crime.

Kneen, Maggie. *Chocolate moose* ill. by author. Penguin Group (USA), 2011. ISBN 978-0-525-42202-0 Subj: Activities – baking, cooking. Animals – mice. Animals – moose. Careers – bakers.

Knudsen, Michelle. *Argus* ill. by Andréa Wesson. Candlewick, 2011. ISBN 978-0-7636-3790-3 Subj: Birds – chickens. Dragons. School. Science.

Kochan, Vera. *What if your best friend were blue?* ill. by Viviana Garofoli. Marshall Cavendish, 2011. ISBN 978-0-7614-5897-5 Subj: Character traits – appearance. Character traits – being different. Friendship. Prejudice.

Kolanovic, Dubravka. *Everyone needs a friend* ill. by author. Price Stern Sloan, 2010. ISBN 978-0-8431-9918-5 Subj: Animals – mice. Animals – wolves. Emotions – loneliness. Friendship.

Könnecke, Ole. *Anton can do magic* ill. by author. Gecko, 2011. ISBN 978-1-8774-6737-0 Subj: Clothing – hats. Humorous stories. Magic.

Kontis, Alethea. *AlphaOops! H is for Halloween* ill. by Bob Kolar. Candlewick, 2010. ISBN 978-0-7636-3966-2 Subj: ABC books. Holidays – Halloween. Theater.

Korda, Lerryn. *Into the wild* ill. by author. Candlewick, 2010. ISBN 978-0-7636-4812-1 Subj: Animals. Camps, camping. Friendship.

It's vacation time ill. by author. Candlewick, 2010. ISBN 978-0-7636-4813-8 Subj: Activities – vacationing. Animals. Friendship. Seasons – summer.

Kornell, Max. *Bear with me* ill. by author. Penguin Group (USA), 2011. ISBN 978-0-399-25257-0 Subj: Animals – bears. Behavior – dissatisfaction. Family life.

Korngold, Jamie S. *Sadie's sukkah breakfast* ill. by Julie Fortenberry. Lerner/Kar-Ben, 2011. ISBN 978-0-7613-5647-9 Subj: Holidays – Sukkot. Jewish culture.

Kostecki-Shaw, Jenny Sue. *Same, same but different* ill. by author. Henry Holt, 2011. ISBN 978-0-8050-8946-2 Subj: Foreign lands – India. Friendship. Pen pals.

Kramer, Andrew. *Pajama pirates* ill. by Leslie Lammle. HarperCollins, 2010. ISBN 978-0-06-125194-8 Subj: Bedtime. Pirates. Rhyming text.

Krasnesky, Thad. *That cat can't stay* ill. by David Parkins. Flashlight, 2010. ISBN 978-0-9799746-5-6 Subj: Animals – cats. Rhyming text.

Krause, Ute. *Oscar and the very hungry dragon* ill. by author. NorthSouth, 2010. ISBN 978-0-7358-2306-8 Subj: Activities – baking, cooking. Behavior – trickery. Character traits – cleverness. Dragons. Restaurants.

Krauss, Ruth. *And I love you* ill. by Steven Kellogg. Scholastic, 2010. ISBN 978-0-439-02459-4 Subj: Animals – cats. Emotions – love. Family life.

Krebs, Laurie. *We're roaming in the rainforest: an Amazon adventure* ill. by Anne Wilson. Barefoot, 2010. ISBN 978-1-84686-331-8 Subj: Animals. Jungle. Rhyming text.

Krensky, Stephen. *Mother's Day surprise* ill. by Kathi Ember. Marshall Cavendish, 2010. ISBN 978-0-7614-5633-9 Subj: Animals. Gifts. Holidays – Mother's Day. Reptiles – snakes.

Noah's bark ill. by Roge. Carolrhoda, 2010. ISBN 978-0-8225-7645-7 Subj: Animals. Boats, ships. Noise, sounds. Religion – Noah. Weather – floods. Weather – rain.

Play ball, Jackie! ill. by Joe Morse. Millbrook, 2011. ISBN 978-0-8225-9030-9 Subj: Ethnic groups in the U.S. – African Americans. Prejudice. Sports – baseball.

Krilanovich, Nadia. *Chicken, chicken, duck!* ill. by author. Tricycle, 2011. ISBN 978-1-58246-385-8 Subj: Animals. Birds. Farms. Games. Noise, sounds.

Moon child ill. by Elizabeth Sayles. Tricycle, 2010. ISBN 978-1-58246-325-4 Subj: Animals. Bedtime. Moon.

Kroll, Steven. *Super-dragon* ill. by Douglas Holgate. Marshall Cavendish, 2011. ISBN 978-0-7614-5819-7 Subj: Activities – flying. Contests. Dragons.

The Tyrannosaurus game ill. by S. D. Schindler. Marshall Cavendish, 2010. ISBN 978-0-7614-5603-2 Subj: Activities – storytelling. Dinosaurs. Games. Imagination.

Krosoczka, Jarrett J. *Ollie the purple elephant* ill. by author. Random House, 2011. ISBN 978-0-375-86654-8 Subj: Activities – dancing. Animals – cats. Animals – elephants. Circus. Family life.

Krull, Kathleen. *Big wig* ill. by Peter Malone. Scholastic, 2011. ISBN 978-0-439-67640-3 Subj: Hair.

Lincoln tells a joke: how laughter saved the president (and the country) by Kathleen Krull and Paul Brewer; ill. by Stacy Innerst. Harcourt, 2010. ISBN 978-0-15-206639-0 Subj: Riddles & jokes. U.S. history.

Kulling, Monica. *All aboard! Elijah McCoy's steam engine* ill. by Bill Slavin. Tundra, 2010. ISBN 978-0-88776-945-0 Subj: Careers – inventors. Ethnic groups in the U.S. – African Americans. Inventions. Trains.

Kumin, Maxine. *Oh, Harry!* ill. by Barry Moser. Roaring Brook, 2011. ISBN 978-1-59643-439-4 Subj: Animals – horses, ponies. Behavior – misbehavior. Rhyming text.

What color is Caesar? ill. by Alison Friend. Candlewick, 2010. ISBN 978-0-7636-3432-2 Subj: Animals – dogs. Concepts – color. Self-concept.

Kuskin, Karla. *A boy had a mother who bought him a hat* ill. by Kevin Hawkes. HarperCollins, 2010. ISBN 978-0-06-075330-6 Subj: Family life – mothers. Rhyming text.

LaChanze. *Little diva* ill. by Brian Pinkney. Feiwel & Friends, 2010. ISBN 978-0-312-37010-7 Subj: Careers – actors. Family life – mothers. Theater.

Lamb, Albert. *The abandoned lighthouse* ill. by David McPhail. Roaring Brook, 2011. ISBN 978-1-59643-525-4 Subj: Animals – bears. Boats, ships. Lighthouses.

Tell me the day backwards ill. by David McPhail. Candlewick, 2011. ISBN 978-0-7636-5055-1 Subj: Animals – bears. Bedtime. Day. Family life – mothers.

Laminack, Lester L. *Three hens and a peacock* ill. by Henry Cole. Peachtree, 2011. ISBN 978-1-56145-

564-5 Subj: Behavior – dissatisfaction. Birds – chickens. Birds – peacocks, peahens. Farms.

Lamstein, Sarah Marwil. *Big night for salamanders* ill. by Carol Benioff. Boyds Mills, 2010. ISBN 978-1-932425-98-7 Subj: Character traits – kindness to animals. Ecology. Migration. Nature. Reptiles – salamanders. Seasons – spring.

Landa, Norbert. *The great monster hunt* ill. by Tim Warnes. Good Books, 2010. ISBN 978-1-56148-681-6 Subj: Animals. Emotions – fear. Imagination.

Landman, Tanya. *Mary's penny* ill. by Richard Holland. Candlewick, 2010. ISBN 978-0-7636-4768-1 Subj: Farms. Gender roles.

Langdo, Bryan. *Tornado Slim and the magic cowboy hat* ill. by author. Marshall Cavendish, 2011. ISBN 978-0-7614-5962-0 Subj: Clothing – hats. Cowboys, cowgirls. Magic.

Langen, Annette. *I won't comb my hair!* ill. by Frauke Bahr. NorthSouth, 2010. ISBN 978-0-7358-2315-0 Subj: Character traits – appearance. Character traits – stubbornness. Hair.

LaReau, Kara. *Mr. Prickles: a quill-fated love story* ill. by Scott Magoon. Roaring Brook, 2011. ISBN 978-1-59643-483-7 Subj: Animals – porcupines. Emotions – loneliness. Friendship.

Otto: the boy who loved cars ill. by Scott Magoon. Roaring Brook, 2011. ISBN 978-1-59643-484-4 Subj: Automobiles. Humorous stories.

Laroche, Giles. *If you lived here: houses of the world* ill. by author. Houghton Harcourt, 2011. ISBN 978-0-547-23892-0 Subj: Homes, houses. World.

LaRochelle, David. *The haunted hamburger and other ghostly stories* ill. by Paul Meisel. Penguin Group (USA), 2011. ISBN 978-0-525-42272-3 Subj: Activities – storytelling. Bedtime. Family life – brothers & sisters. Ghosts.

1+1=5: and other unlikely additions ill. by Brenda Sexton. Sterling, 2010. ISBN 978-1-4027-5995-6 Subj: Counting, numbers. Imagination.

Latimer, Alex. *The boy who cried ninja* ill. by author. Peachtree, 2011. ISBN 978-0-56145-579-9 Subj: Behavior – lying. Character traits – honesty.

Lawler, Janet. *A mother's song* ill. by Kathleen Kemly. Sterling, 2010. ISBN 978-1-4027-6968-9 Subj: Family life – mothers. Nature. Rhyming text.

Lawlor, Laurie. *Muddy as a duck puddle and other American similes* ill. by Ethan Long. Holiday House, 2010. ISBN 978-0-8234-2229-6 Subj: ABC books. Language.

Lawson, Dorie McCullough. *Tex* photos by author. Trafalgar Square, 2011. ISBN 978-1-57076-501-8 Subj: Careers – ranchers. Cowboys, cowgirls. Dreams. Imagination.

Lee, Spike. *Giant steps to change the world* by Spike Lee and Tonya Lewis Lee; ill. by Sean Qualls. Simon & Schuster, 2011. ISBN 978-0-689-86815-3 Subj: Character traits. Character traits – perseverance. Self-concept.

Lee, Suzy. *Mirror* ill. by author. Seven Footer, 2010. ISBN 978-1-934734-39-1 Subj: Mirrors. Wordless.

Shadow ill. by author. Chronicle, 2010. ISBN 978-0-8118-7280-5 Subj: Imagination. Shadows.

Lee, Tonya Lewis. *Giant steps to change the world* (Lee, Spike)

Lee, Y. J. *The little moon princess* ill. by author. HarperCollins, 2010. ISBN 978-0-06-154736-2 Subj: Birds – sparrows. Royalty – princesses. Stars.

Lehman, Barbara. *The secret box* ill. by author. Houghton Mifflin, 2011. ISBN 978-0-547-23868-5 Subj: Behavior – secrets. Imagination. School. Wordless.

Lehman-Wilzig, Tami. *Nathan blows out the Hanukkah candles* by Tami Lehman-Wilzig and Nicole Katzman; ill. by Jeremy Tugeau. Lerner/Kar-Ben, 2011. ISBN 978-0-7613-6657-7 Subj: Family life – brothers. Handicaps – autism. Holidays – Hanukkah. Jewish culture.

Lendroth, Susan. *Calico Dorsey: mail dog of the mining camps* ill. by Adam Gustavson. Tricycle, 2010. ISBN 978-1-58246-318-6 Subj: Animals – dogs. Careers – postal workers. Post office. U.S. history.

Lerch. *Swim! swim!* ill. by author. Scholastic, 2010. ISBN 978-0-545-09419-1 Subj: Emotions – loneliness. Fish. Friendship.

Lester, Alison. *Running with the horses* ill. by author. NorthSouth, 2011. ISBN 978-0-7358-4002-7 Subj: Animals – horses, ponies. Character traits – bravery. Character traits – loyalty. Foreign lands – Austria.

Lester, Helen. *Tacky's Christmas* ill. by Lynn Munsinger. Houghton Mifflin, 2010. ISBN 978-0-547-17208-8 Subj: Birds – penguins. Holidays – Christmas. Santa Claus.

Wodney Wat's wobot ill. by Lynn Munsinger. Houghton Harcourt, 2011. ISBN 978-0-547-36756-9 Subj: Animals. Animals – rats. Behavior – bullying. Handicaps. Robots. School.

Levine, Arthur A. *Monday is one day* ill. by Julian Hector. Scholastic, 2011. ISBN 978-0-439-78924-

0 Subj: Activities – working. Counting, numbers. Days of the week, months of the year. Family life. Rhyming text.

Levine, Gail Carson. *Betsy Red Hoodie* ill. by Scott Nash. HarperCollins, 2010. ISBN 978-0-06-146870-4 Subj: Animals – sheep. Animals – wolves. Birthdays. Careers – shepherds. Family life – grandmothers. Parties.

Lewin, Betsy. *Where is Tippy Toes?* ill. by author. Simon & Schuster, 2010. ISBN 978-1-4169-3808-8 Subj: Animals – cats. Format, unusual – toy & movable books. Rhyming text.

Lewis, Anne Margaret. *What am I? Christmas* ill. by Tom Mills. Whitman, 2011. ISBN 978-0-8075-8958-8 Subj: Format, unusual – toy & movable books. Holidays – Christmas.

Lewis, J. Patrick. *The fantastic 5 and 10¢ store: a rebus adventure* ill. by Valorie Fisher. Random House, 2010. ISBN 978-0-375-85878-9 Subj: Rebuses. Rhyming text. Stores.

Kindergarten cat ill. by Ailie Busby. Random House, 2010. ISBN 978-0-375-84475-1 Subj: Animals – cats. Rhyming text. School.

Lewis, Jill. *Don't read this book!* ill. by Deborah Allwright. Tiger Tales, 2010. ISBN 978-1-58925-094-9 Subj: Folk & fairy tales. Royalty – kings.

Lewis, Kevin. *Not inside this house!* ill. by David Ercolini. Scholastic, 2011. ISBN 978-0-439-43981-7 Subj: Animals. Character traits – curiosity. Humorous stories. Nature. Rhyming text.

Lewis, Rose. *Orange Peel's pocket* ill. by Grace Zong. Abrams, 2010. ISBN 978-0-8109-8394-6 Subj: Adoption. Clothing. Ethnic groups in the U.S. – Chinese Americans.

Lichtenheld, Tom. *Bridget's beret* ill. by author. Henry Holt, 2010. ISBN 978-0-8050-8775-8 Subj: Activities – drawing. Careers – artists. Clothing – hats. Self-concept.

Cloudette ill. by author. Henry Holt, 2011. ISBN 978-0-8050-8776-5 Subj: Character traits – smallness. Concepts – size. Weather – clouds. Weather – rain.

E-mergency! by Tom Lichtenheld and Ezra Fields Meyer; ill. by Tom Lichtenheld. Chronicle, 2011. ISBN 978-0-8118-7898-2 Subj: ABC books. Humorous stories.

Lies, Brian. *Bats at the ballgame* ill. by author. Houghton Harcourt, 2010. ISBN 978-0-547-24970-4 Subj: Animals – bats. Rhyming text. Sports – baseball.

Light, Steve. *The Christmas giant* ill. by author. Candlewick, 2010. ISBN 978-0-7636-4692-9 Subj:

Friendship. Giants. Holidays – Christmas. Mythical creatures – elves. Trees.

Lin, Grace. *Thanking the moon: celebrating the Mid-Autumn Moon Festival* ill. by author. Random House, 2010. ISBN 978-0-375-86101-7 Subj: Ethnic groups in the U.S. – Chinese Americans. Fairs, festivals. Family life. Food. Holidays. Moon.

Lindbergh, Reeve. *Homer the library cat* ill. by Anne Wilsdorf. Candlewick, 2011. ISBN 978-0-7636-3448-3 Subj: Animals – cats. Libraries. Rhyming text.

Little old lady who swallowed a fly. *There was an old monkey who swallowed a frog* by Jennifer Ward; ill. by Steve Gray. Marshall Cavendish, 2010. ISBN 978-0-7614-5580-6 Subj: Animals. Cumulative tales. Folk & fairy tales. Frogs & toads. Rhyming text. Songs.

The little red hen. *The Little Red Hen and the Passover matzah* by Leslie Kimmelman; ill. by Paul Meisel. Holiday House, 2010. ISBN 978-0-8234-1952-4 Subj: Activities – baking, cooking. Animals. Behavior – sharing. Birds – chickens. Character traits – laziness. Folk & fairy tales. Holidays – Passover. Jewish culture.

Litwin, Eric. *Pete the cat: I love my white shoes* ill. by James Dean. HarperCollins, 2010. ISBN 978-0-06-190622-0 Subj: Animals – cats. Clothing – shoes. Concepts – color.

Pete the cat: rocking in my school shoes ill. by James Dean. HarperCollins, 2011. ISBN 978-0-06-191024-1 Subj: Activities – singing. Animals – cats. Clothing – shoes. Rhyming text. School.

Liwska, Renata. *Red wagon* ill. by author. Penguin Group (USA), 2011. ISBN 978-0-399-25237-2 Subj: Activities – playing. Animals. Animals – foxes. Imagination. Toys – wagons.

Ljungkvist, Laura. *Follow the line to school* ill. by author. Penguin Group (USA), 2011. ISBN 978-0-670-01226-8 Subj: Picture puzzles. School.

Pepi sings a new song ill. by author. Simon & Schuster, 2010. ISBN 978-1-4169-9138-0 Subj: Activities – singing. Birds – parakeets, parrots. Foreign languages.

Lloyd-Jones, Sally. *How to get a job—by me, the boss* ill. by Sue Heap. Random House, 2011. ISBN 978-0-375-86664-7 Subj: Careers.

Song of the stars: a Christmas story ill. by Alison Jay. Zonderkidz, 2011. ISBN 978-0-310-72291-5 Subj: Holidays – Christmas. Religion – Nativity.

Lobel, Anita. *Nini lost and found* ill. by author. Random House, 2010. ISBN 978-0-375-85880-

2 Subj: Animals – cats. Behavior – lost & found possessions.

Loewen, Nancy. *The last day of kindergarten* ill. by Sachiko Yoshikawa. Marshall Cavendish, 2011. ISBN 978-0-7614-5807-7 Subj: School.

Logan, Bob. *Rocket town* ill. by author. Sourcebooks, 2011. ISBN 978-1-4022-4186-4 Subj: Format, unusual – board books. Space & space ships.

London, Jonathan. *Froggy goes to Hawaii* ill. by Frank Remkiewicz. Penguin Group (USA), 2011. ISBN 978-0-670-01221-3 Subj: Activities – traveling. Frogs & toads. Hawaii.

I'm a truck driver ill. by David Parkins. Henry Holt, 2010. ISBN 978-0-8050-7989-0 Subj: Careers – truck drivers. Rhyming text.

Little penguin: the Emperor of Antarctica ill. by Julie Olson. Marshall Cavendish, 2011. ISBN 978-0-7614-5954-5 Subj: Animals – babies. Birds – penguins. Foreign lands – Antarctic.

A plane goes ka-zoom! ill. by Denis Roche. Henry Holt, 2010. ISBN 978-0-8050-8970-7 Subj: Airplanes, airports. Rhyming text.

Long, Ethan. *Bird and Birdie in a fine day* ill. by author. Tricycle, 2010. ISBN 978-1-58246-321-6 Subj: Birds. Friendship.

The book that Zack wrote ill. by author. Blue Apple, 2011. ISBN 978-1-60905-060-3 Subj: Activities – writing. Books, reading. Cumulative tales. Format, unusual.

Chamelia ill. by author. Little, Brown, 2011. ISBN 978-0-316-08612-7 Subj: Character traits – appearance. Character traits – individuality. Clothing. Reptiles – chameleons.

The croaky pokey! ill. by author. Holiday House, 2011. ISBN 978-0-8234-2291-3 Subj: Frogs & toads. Songs.

My dad, my hero ill. by author. Sourcebooks, 2011. ISBN 978-1-4022-4239-7 Subj: Family life – fathers.

One drowsy dragon ill. by author. Scholastic, 2010. ISBN 978-0-545-16557-0 Subj: Counting, numbers. Dragons. Sleep.

Long, Loren. *Otis and the tornado* ill. by author. Penguin Group (USA), 2011. ISBN 978-0-399-25477-2 Subj: Farms. Tractors. Weather – tornadoes.

Look at me! ill. by Rachel Fuller. Child's Play, 2010. ISBN 978-1-84643-278-1 Subj: Format, unusual – board books. Self-concept.

Look, Lenore. *Polka Dot Penguin Pottery* ill. by Yumi Heo. Random House, 2011. ISBN 978-0-

375-86332-5 Subj: Activities – writing. Ethnic groups in the U.S. – Chinese Americans. Family life – grandparents.

López, Susana. *The best family in the world* ill. by Ulises Wensell. Kane/Miller, 2010. ISBN 978-1-935279-47-1 Subj: Adoption. Family life.

Lord, Cynthia. *Happy birthday, Hamster* ill. by Derek Anderson. Scholastic, 2011. ISBN 978-0-545-25522-6 Subj: Animals – hamsters. Birthdays. Parties.

Hot rod Hamster ill. by Derek Anderson. Scholastic, 2010. ISBN 978-0-545-03530-9 Subj: Animals – dogs. Animals – hamsters. Animals – mice. Automobiles. Sports – racing.

Lord, Janet. *Where is Catkin?* ill. by Julie Paschkis. Peachtree, 2010. ISBN 978-1-56145-523-2 Subj: Animals – cats.

Lorenz, Albert. *The exceptionally, extraordinarily ordinary first day of school* ill. by author. Abrams, 2010. ISBN 978-0-8109-8960-3 Subj: Moving. School – first day.

Loth, Sebastian. *Clementine* ill. by author. NorthSouth, 2011. ISBN 978-0-7358-4009-6 Subj: Activities – traveling. Animals – snails. Concepts – shape. Format, unusual. Moon.

Remembering Crystal ill. by author. NorthSouth, 2010. ISBN 978-0-7358-2300-6 Subj: Birds – geese. Death. Reptiles – turtles, tortoises.

Lucke, Deb. *Sneezenesia* ill. by author. Clarion, 2010. ISBN 978-0-547-33006-8 Subj: Anatomy – noses. Humorous stories. Memories, memory. Noise, sounds.

Ludwig, Trudy. *Better than you* ill. by Adam Gustavson. Random House, 2011. ISBN 978-1-58246-380-3 Subj: Behavior – boasting. Friendship. Self-concept.

Lum, Kate. *Princesses are not perfect* ill. by Sue Hellard. Bloomsbury, 2010. ISBN 978-1-59990-432-0 Subj: Royalty – princesses. Self-concept.

Lunde, Darrin. *Hello, baby beluga* ill. by Patricia J. Wynne. Charlesbridge, 2011. ISBN 978-1-57091-739-4 Subj: Animals – whales.

Luxbacher, Irene. *Mattoo, let's play!* ill. by author. Kids Can, 2010. ISBN 978-1-55453-424-1 Subj: Animals – cats.

Lynn, Sarah. *Tip-tap pop* ill. by Valeria Docampo. Marshall Cavendish, 2010. ISBN 978-0-7614-5712-1 Subj: Activities – dancing. Family life – grandfathers. Memories, memory.

Lyon, George Ella. *All the water in the world* ill. by Katherine Tillotson. Atheneum, 2011. ISBN 978-1-4169-7130-6 Subj: Science. Water.

The pirate of kindergarten ill. by Lynne Avril. Simon & Schuster, 2010. ISBN 978-1-4169-5024-0 Subj: Anatomy – eyes. School. Senses – sight.

Lyon, Tammie. *Olive and Snowflake* ill. by author. Marshall Cavendish, 2011. ISBN 978-0-7614-5955-2 Subj: Animals – dogs. Behavior – worrying. Pets.

Maass, Robert. *A is for autumn* photos by author. Henry Holt, 2011. ISBN 978-0-8050-9093-2 Subj: ABC books. Seasons – fall.

McAllister, Angela. *Little Mist* ill. by Sarah Fox-Davies. Random House, 2011. ISBN 978-0-375-86788-0 Subj: Animals – babies. Animals – leopards.

My mom has x-ray vision ill. by Alex T. Smith. Tiger Tales, 2011. ISBN 978-1-58925-097-0 Subj: Family life – mothers. Humorous stories.

Yuck! That's not a monster ill. by Alison Edgson. Good Books, 2010. ISBN 978-1-56148-683-0 Subj: Character traits – being different. Character traits – individuality. Family life. Monsters.

McArthur, Meher. *An ABC of what art can be* ill. by Esther Pearl Watson. Getty Museum, 2010. ISBN 978-0-89236-999-7 Subj: ABC books. Art. Rhyming text.

Maccarone, Grace. *Miss Lina's ballerinas* ill. by Christine Davenier. Feiwel & Friends, 2010. ISBN 978-0-312-38243-8 Subj: Ballet. Counting, numbers. Problem solving. Rhyming text.

Miss Lina's ballerinas and the prince ill. by Christine Davenier. Feiwel & Friends, 2011. ISBN 978-0-312-64963-0 Subj: Activities – dancing. Ballet. Character traits – shyness. Rhyming text.

McCarthy, Meghan. *The incredible life of Balto* ill. by author. Random House, 2011. ISBN 978-0-375-84460-7 Subj: Alaska. Animals – dogs. Sports – racing. Sports – sledding.

McCarty, Peter. *Henry in love* ill. by author. HarperCollins, 2010. ISBN 978-0-06-114288-8 Subj: Animals – cats. Animals – rabbits. Emotions – love. School – first day.

McClatchy, Lisa. *Dear Tyrannosaurus Rex* ill. by John Manders. Random House, 2010. ISBN 978-0-375-85608-2 Subj: Birthdays. Dinosaurs. Letters, cards. Parties.

McClure, Nikki. *Mama, is it summer yet?* ill. by author. Abrams, 2010. ISBN 978-0-8109-8468-4 Subj: Character traits – questioning. Seasons – summer.

McCue, Lisa. *Quiet Bunny and Noisy Puppy* ill. by author. Sterling, 2011. ISBN 978-1-4027-8559-7 Subj: Animals – dogs. Animals – rabbits. Friendship. Seasons – winter.

McCully, Emily Arnold. *The secret cave: discovering Lascaux* ill. by author. Farrar, 2010. ISBN 978-0-374-36694-0 Subj: Art. Caves. Prehistory.

Wonder horse: the true story of the world's smartest horse ill. by author. Henry Holt, 2010. ISBN 978-0-8050-8793-2 Subj: Animals – horses, ponies. Careers – veterinarians. Ethnic groups in the U.S. – African Americans. Prejudice.

McDermott, Gerald. *Monkey: a trickster tale from India* ill. by author. Houghton Harcourt, 2011. ISBN 978-0-15-216596-3 Subj: Animals – monkeys. Behavior – trickery. Character traits – cleverness. Folk & fairy tales. Foreign lands – India.

MacDonald, Margaret Read, reteller. *Too many fairies: a Celtic tale* ill. by Susan Mitchell. Marshall Cavendish, 2010. ISBN 978-0-7614-5604-9 Subj: Fairies. Folk & fairy tales.

Macdonald, Maryann. *How to hug* ill. by Jana Christy. Marshall Cavendish, 2011. ISBN 978-0-7614-5804-3 Subj: Hugging.

The little piano girl: the story of Mary Lou Williams, jazz legend (Ingalls, Ann)

The pink party ill. by Judy Stead. Marshall Cavendish, 2011. ISBN 978-0-7614-5814-2 Subj: Concepts – color. Emotions – envy, jealousy. Friendship.

MacDonald, Suse. *Circus opposites: an interactive extravaganza!* ill. by author. Simon & Schuster, 2010. ISBN 978-1-4169-7154-2 Subj: Circus. Concepts – opposites. Format, unusual – toy & movable books.

McDonnell, Christine. *Goyangi means cat* ill. by Steve Johnson and Lou Fancher. Penguin Group (USA), 2011. ISBN 978-0-670-01179-7 Subj: Adoption. Animals – cats. Behavior – lost & found possessions. Emotions – loneliness. Ethnic groups in the U.S. – Korean Americans.

McDonnell, Patrick. *Me . . . Jane* ill. by author. Little, Brown, 2011. ISBN 978-0-316-04546-9 Subj: Animals. Animals – chimpanzees. Caldecott

Award honor books. Careers – scientists. Nature. Toys.

McElligott, Matthew. *Even monsters need haircuts* ill. by author. Walker, 2010. ISBN 978-0-8027-8819-1 Subj: Careers – barbers. Monsters.

McGhee, Alison. *Making a friend* ill. by Marc Rosenthal. Simon & Schuster, 2011. ISBN 978-1-4169-8998-1 Subj: Friendship. Seasons. Snowmen. Water.

So many days ill. by Taeeun Yoo. Simon & Schuster, 2010. ISBN 978-1-4169-5857-4 Subj: Self-concept.

McGinley, Phyllis. *The year without a Santa Claus* ill. by John Manders. Marshall Cavendish, 2010. ISBN 978-0-7614-5799-2 Subj: Character traits – generosity. Gifts. Holidays – Christmas. Rhyming text. Santa Claus.

McGinness, Suzanne. *My bear Griz* ill. by author. Frances Lincoln, 2011. ISBN 978-1-84780-113-5 Subj: Animals – bears. Toys – bears.

McGinty, Alice B. *Eliza's kindergarten pet* ill. by Nancy Speir. Marshall Cavendish, 2010. ISBN 978-0-7614-5702-2 Subj: Animals – guinea pigs. Behavior – lost & found possessions. Behavior – worrying. School.

McGowan, Michael. *Sunday is for God* ill. by Steve Johnson and Lou Fancher. Random House, 2010. ISBN 978-0-375-84188-0 Subj: Days of the week, months of the year. Ethnic groups in the U.S. – African Americans. Family life. Religion.

McGrath, Barbara Barbieri. *Teddy bear counting* ill. by Tim Nihoff. Charlesbridge, 2010. ISBN 978-1-58089-215-5 Subj: Concepts – color. Concepts – shape. Counting, numbers. Rhyming text. Toys – bears.

McGuirk, Leslie. *If rocks could sing: a discovered alphabet* ill. by author. Tricycle, 2011. ISBN 978-1-58246-370-4 Subj: ABC books. Rocks.

Machado, Ana Maria. *Wolf wanted* tr. by Elisa Amado; ill. by Laurent Cardon. Groundwood, 2010. ISBN 978-0-88899-880-4 Subj: Animals – wolves. Folk & fairy tales.

MacHale, D. J. *The monster princess* ill. by Alexandra Boiger. Simon & Schuster, 2010. ISBN 978-1-4169-4809-4 Subj: Monsters. Royalty – princesses. Self-concept.

Mackall, Dandi Daley. *The story of the Easter robin* ill. by Anna Vojtech. Zonderkidz, 2010. ISBN 978-0-310-71331-9 Subj: Birds – robins. Family life – grandmothers. Holidays – Easter. Religion.

McKee, David. *Elmer and Rose* ill. by author. Andersen, 2010. ISBN 978-0-7613-5493-2 Subj: Animals – elephants. Character traits – being different. Character traits – individuality.

Elmer and the hippos ill. by author. Andersen, 2010. ISBN 978-0-7613-6442-9 Subj: Animals – elephants. Animals – hippopotamuses. Behavior – cooperation. Problem solving.

Elmer's Christmas ill. by author. Lerner, 2011. ISBN 978-0-7613-8088-7 Subj: Animals – elephants. Holidays – Christmas.

Six men ill. by author. NorthSouth, 2011. ISBN 978-0-7358-4050-8 Subj: War.

Macken, JoAnn Early. *Baby says "moo!"* ill. by David Walker. Hyperion/Disney, 2011. ISBN 978-1-4231-3400-8 Subj: Babies. Noise, sounds. Rhyming text.

Waiting out the storm ill. by Susan Gaber. Candlewick, 2010. ISBN 978-0-7636-3378-3 Subj: Family life – mothers. Rhyming text. Weather – rain. Weather – storms.

Mackintosh, David. *Marshall Armstrong is new to our school* ill. by author. Abrams, 2011. ISBN 978-1-4197-0036-1 Subj: Birthdays. Character traits – individuality. Parties. School.

MacLachlan, Patricia. *Before you came* by Patricia MacLachlan and Emily MacLachlan Charest; ill. by David Diaz. HarperCollins, 2011. ISBN 978-0-06-051234-7 Subj: Babies. Family life – mothers.

Lala salama: a Tanzanian lullaby ill. by Elizabeth Zunon. Candlewick, 2011. ISBN 978-0-7636-4747-6 Subj: Family life – mothers. Foreign lands – Tanzania. Lullabies.

Your moon, my moon: a grandmother's words to a faraway child ill. by Bryan Collier. Simon & Schuster, 2011. ISBN 978-1-4169-7950-0 Subj: Family life – grandmothers. Foreign lands – Africa.

McLean, Dirk. *Curtain up!* ill. by France Brassard. Tundra, 2010. ISBN 978-0-88776-899-6 Subj: Careers – actors. Theater.

Maclear, Kyo. *Spork* ill. by Isabelle Arsenault. Kids Can, 2010. ISBN 978-1-55337-736-8 Subj: Character traits – being different. Character traits – individuality. Self-concept.

McLeod, Heather. *Kiss me! (I'm a prince!)* ill. by Brooke Kerrigan. Fitzhenry & Whiteside, 2011. ISBN 978-1-55455-161-3 Subj: Folk & fairy tales. Frogs & toads. Kissing. Royalty – princes.

McMullan, Kate. *Bulldog's big day* ill. by Pascal Lemaitre. Scholastic, 2011. ISBN 978-0-545-17155-7 Subj: Activities – baking, cooking. Animals – dogs. Careers. Careers – bakers.

I'm big! ill. by Jim McMullan. HarperCollins, 2010. ISBN 978-0-06-122974-9 Subj: Behavior – lost. Dinosaurs.

McNamara, Margaret. *The three little aliens and the big bad robot* ill. by Mark Fearing. Random House, 2011. ISBN 978-0-375-86689-0 Subj: Aliens. Humorous stories. Planets. Robots. Space & space ships.

Macomber, Debbie. *The yippy, yappy Yorkie in the green doggy sweater* by Debbie Macomber and Mary Lou Carney; ill. by Sally Anne Lambert. HarperCollins, 2012. ISBN 978-0-06-165096-3 Subj: Animals – dogs. Behavior – running away. Moving.

McPhail, David. *Pig Pig returns* ill. by author. Charlesbridge, 2011. ISBN 978-1-58089-356-5 Subj: Activities – traveling. Animals – pigs. Behavior – worrying.

Waddles ill. by author. Abrams, 2011. ISBN 978-0-8109-8415-8 Subj: Animals – raccoons. Birds – ducks. Friendship.

McQuinn, Anna. *Lola loves stories* ill. by Rosalind Beardshaw. Charlesbridge, 2010. ISBN 978-1-58089-258-2 Subj: Activities – playing. Activities – storytelling. Books, reading. Ethnic groups in the U.S. – African Americans. Imagination.

The sleep sheep ill. by Hannah Shaw. Scholastic, 2010. ISBN 978-0-545-23145-9 Subj: Animals – sheep. Bedtime. Counting, numbers. Sleep.

Mair, Samia J. *The perfect gift* ill. by Craig Howarth. Kube, 2010. ISBN 978-0-86037-438-1 Subj: Family life – brothers & sisters. Gifts. Holidays. Plants. Religion – Islam.

Malaspina, Ann. *Phillis sings out freedom: the story of George Washington and Phillis Wheatley* ill. by Susan Keeter. Whitman, 2010. ISBN 978-0-8075-6545-2 Subj: Careers – poets. Ethnic groups in the U.S. – African Americans. U.S. history.

Yasmin's hammer ill. by Doug Chayka. Lee & Low, 2010. ISBN 978-1-60060-359-4 Subj: Foreign lands – Bangladesh. School.

Malnor, Carol L. *The Blues go birding across America* by Carol L. Malnor and Sandy F. Fuller; ill. by Louise Schroeder. Dawn, 2010. ISBN 978-1-58469-124-2 Subj: Birds. Holidays – Fourth of July.

Maloney, Peter. *One foot two feet: an exceptional counting book* by Peter Maloney and Felicia Zekauskas; ill. by authors. Penguin Group (USA), 2011. ISBN 978-0-399-25446-8 Subj: Concepts. Counting, numbers.

Maltbie, P. I. *Claude Monet: the painter who stopped the trains* ill. by Joseph A. Smith. Abrams, 2010.

ISBN 978-0-8109-8961-0 Subj: Art. Careers – artists. Trains.

Mandel, Peter. *Jackhammer Sam* ill. by David Catrow. Roaring Brook, 2011. ISBN 978-1-59643-034-1 Subj: Careers – construction workers. Rhyming text. Tools.

Mandell, Muriel, adapt. *A donkey reads: adapted from a Turkish folktale* ill. by André Letria. Star Bright, 2011. ISBN 978-1-59572-256-0 Subj: Animals – donkeys. Character traits – cleverness. Folk & fairy tales. Foreign lands – Turkey.

Manders, John. *The really awful musicians* ill. by author. Clarion, 2011. ISBN 978-0-547-32820-1 Subj: Careers – musicians. Music. Royalty – kings.

Manna, Anthony L. *The orphan: a Cinderella story from Greece* by Anthony L. Manna and Soula Mitakidou; ill. by Giselle Potter. Random House, 2011. ISBN 978-0-375-86691-3 Subj: Family life – stepfamilies. Folk & fairy tales. Foreign lands – Greece. Orphans. Royalty – princes. Sibling rivalry.

Manners mash-up: a goofy guide to good behavior ill. by Tedd Arnold et al. Penguin Group (USA), 2011. ISBN 978-0-8037-3480-7 Subj: Etiquette.

Marciano, John Bemelmans. *Madeline at the White House* ill. by author. Penguin Group (USA), 2011. ISBN 978-0-670-01228-2 Subj: Holidays – Easter. Orphans. U.S. history.

Marcus, Kimberly. *Scritch-scratch a perfect match* ill. by Mike Lester. Penguin Group (USA), 2011. ISBN 978-0-399-25004-0 Subj: Animals – dogs. Insects – fleas. Rhyming text.

Marino, Gianna. *One too many: a seek and find counting book* ill. by author. Chronicle, 2010. ISBN 978-0-8118-6908-9 Subj: Animals. Counting, numbers. Picture puzzles.

Markle, Sandra. *Butterfly tree* ill. by Leslie Wu. Peachtree, 2011. ISBN 978-1-56145-539-3 Subj: Insects – butterflies, caterpillars. Migration.

Family pack ill. by Alan Marks. Charlesbridge, 2011. ISBN 978-1-58089-217-9 Subj: Animals – endangered animals. Animals – wolves.

Hip-pocket papa ill. by Alan Marks. Charlesbridge, 2010. ISBN 978-1-57091-708-0 Subj: Foreign lands – Australia. Frogs & toads.

Marley, Cedella, adapt. *One love: based on the song by Bob Marley* ill. by Vanessa Newton. Chronicle, 2011. ISBN 978-1-4521-0224-5 Subj: Emotions – love. Songs.

Marshall, Linda Elovitz. *Talia and the rude vegetables* ill. by Francesca Assirelli. Lerner/Kar-Ben,

2011. ISBN 978-0-7613-5217-4 Subj: Food. Gardens, gardening. Holidays – Rosh Hashanah.

Martin, Bill, Jr. *Kitty Cat, Kitty Cat, are you going to sleep?* by Bill Martin, Jr. and Michael Sampson; ill. by Laura J. Bryant. Marshall Cavendish, 2011. ISBN 978-0-7614-5946-0 Subj: Animals – cats. Bedtime. Rhyming text.

Ten little caterpillars ill. by Lois Ehlert. Simon & Schuster, 2011. ISBN 978-1-4424-3385-4 Subj: Counting, numbers. Insects – butterflies, caterpillars. Metamorphosis. Rhyming text.

Martin, David. *Little Bunny and the magic Christmas tree* ill. by Valeri Gorbachev. Candlewick, 2011. ISBN 978-0-7636-3693-7 Subj: Animals – rabbits. Character traits – smallness. Holidays – Christmas.

Martin, Jacqueline Briggs. *The chiru of High Tibet: a true story* ill. by Linda Wingerter. Houghton Harcourt, 2010. ISBN 978-0-618-58130-6 Subj: Animals – endangered animals. Foreign lands – Tibet.

Martin, Ruth. *Moon dreams* ill. by Olivier Latyk. Candlewick, 2010. ISBN 978-0-7636-5012-4 Subj: Day. Dreams. Moon. Night.

Santa's on his way ill. by Sophy Williams. Candlewick, 2011. ISBN 978-0-7636-5555-6 Subj: Format, unusual – toy & movable books. Holidays – Christmas. Santa Claus.

Marx, Trish. *Kindergarten day USA and China: a flip-me-over book* photos by Ellen B. Senisi. Charlesbridge, 2010. ISBN 978-1-58089-219-3 Subj: Foreign lands – China. Format, unusual. School.

Marzollo, Jean. *Help me learn numbers 0-20* photos by Chad Phillips. Holiday House, 2011. ISBN 978-0-8234-2334-7 Subj: Counting, numbers.

The little plant doctor: a story about George Washington Carver ill. by Ken Wilson-Max. Holiday House, 2011. ISBN 978-0-8234-2325-5 Subj: Careers – scientists. Ethnic groups in the U.S. – African Americans. U.S. history.

Pierre the penguin: a true story ill. by Laura Regan. Sleeping Bear, 2010. ISBN 978-1-58536-485-5 Subj: Birds – penguins. Character traits – kindness to animals. Rhyming text.

Masini, Beatrice. *Here comes the bride* ill. by Anna Laura Cantone. Tundra, 2010. ISBN 978-0-88776-898-9 Subj: Activities – sewing. Clothing – dresses. Weddings.

Mason, Janeen. *Ocean commotion: life on the reef* ill. by author. Pelican, 2010. ISBN 978-1-58980-783-9 Subj: Crustaceans – crabs. Sea & seashore.

Mason, Margaret H. *These hands* ill. by Floyd Cooper. Houghton Harcourt, 2011. ISBN 978-0-547-21566-2 Subj: Anatomy – hands. Ethnic groups in the U.S. – African Americans. Family life – grandfathers. Prejudice.

Matthies, Janna. *The goodbye cancer garden* ill. by Kristi Valiant. Whitman, 2011. ISBN 978-0-8075-2994-2 Subj: Family life – mothers. Gardens, gardening. Illness – cancer.

Mayer, Lynne. *Newton and me* ill. by Sherry Rogers. Sylvan Dell, 2010. ISBN 978-1-60718-067-8 Subj: Rhyming text. Science.

Mayer, Mercer. *Octopus soup* ill. by author. Marshall Cavendish, 2011. ISBN 978-0-7614-5812-8 Subj: Octopuses. Wordless.

Too many dinosaurs ill. by author. Holiday House, 2011. ISBN 978-0-8234-2316-3 Subj: Dinosaurs. Pets.

Mayhew, James. *Ella Bella ballerina and Swan Lake* ill. by author. Barron's, 2011. ISBN 978-0-7641-6407-1 Subj: Ballet. Music.

Mayo, Margaret. *Stomp, dinosaur, stomp!* ill. by Alex Ayliffe. Walker, 2010. ISBN 978-0-8027-2195-2 Subj: Activities. Dinosaurs. Rhyming text.

Meade, Holly. *If I never forever endeavor* ill. by author. Candlewick, 2011. ISBN 978-0-7636-4071-2 Subj: Activities – flying. Birds. Character traits – assertiveness. Character traits – bravery. Rhyming text.

Meadows, Michelle. *Hibernation station* ill. by Kurt Cyrus. Simon & Schuster, 2010. ISBN 978-1-4169-3788-3 Subj: Animals. Hibernation. Rhyming text. Sleep.

Piggies in the kitchen ill. by Ard Hoyt. Simon & Schuster, 2011. ISBN 978-1-4169-3787-6 Subj: Activities – baking, cooking. Animals – pigs. Rhyming text.

Traffic pups ill. by Dan Andreasen. Simon & Schuster, 2011. ISBN 978-1-4169-2485-2 Subj: Animals – dogs. Careers – police officers. Motorcycles.

Meddaugh, Susan. *Martha says it with flowers* ill. by author. Houghton Mifflin, 2010. ISBN 978-0-547-21058-2 Subj: Animals – dogs. Birthdays. Family life – grandmothers. Gifts.

Medina, Meg. *Tía Isa wants a car* ill. by Claudio Muñoz. Candlewick, 2011. ISBN 978-0-7636-4156-6 Subj: Automobiles. Behavior – resourcefulness. Ethnic groups in the U.S. – Hispanic Americans. Family life – aunts, uncles. Money.

Melanson, Luc. *Topsy-Turvy Town* ill. by author. Tundra, 2010. ISBN 978-0-88776-920-7 Subj: Imagination.

Melling, David. *Don't worry, Douglas!* ill. by author. Tiger Tales, 2011. ISBN 978-1-58925-106-9 Subj: Animals – bears. Character traits – helpfulness. Clothing – hats.

Hugless Douglas ill. by author. Tiger Tales, 2010. ISBN 978-1-58925-098-7 Subj: Animals – bears. Hugging.

Melmed, Laura Krauss. *Eight winter nights: a family Hanukkah book* ill. by Elisabeth Schlossberg. Chronicle, 2010. ISBN 978-0-8118-5552-5 Subj: Holidays – Hanukkah. Jewish culture. Rhyming text.

Meltzer, Amy. *The Shabbat Princess* ill. by Martha Avilés. Lerner/Kar-Ben, 2011. ISBN 978-0-7613-5142-9 Subj: Family life. Jewish culture.

Meltzer, Lynn. *The construction crew* ill. by Carrie Eko-Burgess. Henry Holt, 2011. ISBN 978-0-8050-8884-7 Subj: Careers – construction workers. Machines. Rhyming text. Tools.

Melvin, Alice. *Counting birds* ill. by author. Abrams, 2010. ISBN 978-1-85437-855-2 Subj: Birds. Counting, numbers. Rhyming text.

The high street ill. by author. Abrams, 2011. ISBN 978-1-85437-943-6 Subj: Cumulative tales. Shopping. Stores.

Menchin, Scott. *What if everything had legs?* ill. by author. Candlewick, 2011. ISBN 978-0-7636-4220-4 Subj: Anatomy. Character traits – questioning. Imagination.

Meng, Cece. *I will not read this book* ill. by Joy Ang. Clarion, 2011. ISBN 978-0-547-04971-7 Subj: Bedtime. Books, reading. Family life.

Merlin, Christophe. *Under the hood* ill. by author. Candlewick, 2011. ISBN 978-0-7636-5535-8 Subj: Animals – bears. Automobiles. Careers – mechanics. Format, unusual – toy & movable books.

Meserve, Jessica. *Bedtime without Arthur* ill. by author. Andersen, 2010. ISBN 978-0-7613-5497-0 Subj: Bedtime. Behavior – lost & found possessions. Emotions – fear. Family life – brothers & sisters. Toys – bears.

Messner, Kate. *Over and under the snow* ill. by Christopher Silas Neal. Chronicle, 2011. ISBN 978-0-8118-6784-9 Subj: Animals. Hibernation. Nature. Seasons – winter. Weather – snow.

Metzger, Steve. *The dancing clock* ill. by John Abbott Nez. Tiger Tales, 2011. ISBN 978-1-58925-

100-7 Subj: Animals – monkeys. Clocks, watches. Zoos.

Detective Blue ill. by Tedd Arnold. Scholastic, 2011. ISBN 978-0-545-17286-8 Subj: Careers – detectives. Humorous stories. Nursery rhymes.

Meyer, Ezra Fields. *E-mergency!* (Lichtenheld, Tom)

Meyers, Susan. *Bear in the air* ill. by Amy Bates. Abrams, 2010. ISBN 978-0-8109-8398-4 Subj: Behavior – lost & found possessions. Rhyming text. Toys – bears.

Michelson, Richard. *Busing Brewster* ill. by R. G. Roth. Random House, 2010. ISBN 978-0-375-83334-2 Subj: Ethnic groups in the U.S. – African Americans. Prejudice. School. U.S. history.

Micklethwait, Lucy. *In the picture.* Frances Lincoln, 2010. ISBN 978-1-84507-636-8 Subj: Art. Picture puzzles.

Middleton, Charlotte. *Nibbles: a green tale* ill. by author. Marshall Cavendish, 2010. ISBN 978-0-7614-5791-6 Subj: Animals – guinea pigs. Ecology. Gardens, gardening. Libraries. Seeds.

Milgrim, David. *Eddie gets ready for school* ill. by author. Scholastic, 2011. ISBN 978-0-545-27329-9 Subj: Character traits – assertiveness. Character traits – confidence. Humorous stories. School.

How you got so smart ill. by author. Penguin Group (USA), 2010. ISBN 978-0-399-25260-0 Subj: Behavior – growing up. Rhyming text. Self-concept.

Santa Duck and his merry helpers ill. by author. Penguin Group (USA), 2010. ISBN 978-0-399-25473-4 Subj: Birds – ducks. Family life – brothers & sisters. Holidays – Christmas. Santa Claus.

Miller, Edward. *Fireboy to the rescue! a fire safety book* ill. by author. Holiday House, 2010. ISBN 978-0-8234-2222-7 Subj: Careers – firefighters. Safety. School.

Miller, Pat. *Squirrel's New Year's resolution* ill. by Kathi Ember. Whitman, 2010. ISBN 978-0-8075-7591-8 Subj: Animals. Animals – squirrels. Character traits – helpfulness. Holidays – New Year's.

Milord, Susan. *Happy 100th day!* ill. by Mary Newell DePalma. Scholastic, 2011. ISBN 978-0-439-88281-1 Subj: Birthdays. Books, reading. Counting, numbers. School.

Milway, Katie Smith. *The good garden: how one family went from hunger to having enough* ill. by Sylvie Daigneault. Kids Can, 2010. ISBN 978-1-55453-488-3 Subj: Food. Foreign lands – Honduras. Gardens, gardening.

Minor, Wendell. *My farm friends* ill. by author. Penguin Group (USA), 2011. ISBN 978-0-399-24477-3 Subj: Animals. Farms. Rhyming text.

Mitakidou, Soula. *The orphan: a Cinderella story from Greece* (Manna, Anthony L.)

Mitchell, Margaree King. *When Grandmama sings* ill. by James Ransome. HarperCollins, 2012. ISBN 978-0-688-17563-4 Subj: Activities – singing. Ethnic groups in the U.S. – African Americans. Family life – grandmothers. Prejudice. U.S. history.

Mitton, Tony. *Rumble, roar, dinosaur! more prehistoric poems with lift-the-flap surprises!* ill. by Lynne Chapman. Kingfisher, 2010. ISBN 978-0-7534-1932-8 Subj: Dinosaurs. Format, unusual – toy & movable books.

Modarressi, Mitra. *Taking care of Mama* ill. by author. Penguin Group (USA), 2010. ISBN 978-0-399-25216-7 Subj: Animals – raccoons. Family life – mothers. Illness.

Monari, Manuela. *Zero kisses for me!* ill. by Virginie Soumagnac. Tundra, 2010. ISBN 978-1-77049-208-0 Subj: Animals – bears. Bedtime. Kissing.

Monroe, Chris. *Monkey with a tool belt and the seaside shenanigans* ill. by author. Carolrhoda, 2011. ISBN 978-0-7613-5616-5 Subj: Animals – elephants. Animals – monkeys. Sea & seashore – beaches. Tools.

Sneaky sheep ill. by author. Carolrhoda, 2010. ISBN 978-0-7613-5615-8 Subj: Animals – dogs. Animals – sheep. Behavior – misbehavior.

Montijo, Rhode. *The Halloween Kid* ill. by author. Simon & Schuster, 2010. ISBN 978-1-4169-3575-9 Subj: Cowboys, cowgirls. Holidays – Halloween.

Moore, Clement Clarke. *'Twas the night before Christmas* ill. by Christopher Wormell. Running Press, 2010. ISBN 978-0-7624-2717-8 Subj: Holidays – Christmas. Poetry. Santa Claus.

Moore, Genevieve. *Catherine's story* ill. by Karin Littlewood. Frances Lincoln, 2010. ISBN 978-1-84507-655-9 Subj: Family life – fathers. Family life – single-parent families. Handicaps – physical handicaps.

Moore, Inga. *A house in the woods* ill. by author. Candlewick, 2011. ISBN 978-0-7636-5277-7 Subj: Animals. Homes, houses.

Moore, Jodi. *When a dragon moves in* ill. by Howard McWilliam. Flashlight, 2011. ISBN 978-0-979974-67-0 Subj: Dragons. Imagination. Sea & seashore – beaches.

Morales, Melita. *Jam and honey* ill. by Laura J. Bryant. Tricycle, 2011. ISBN 978-1-58246-299-8 Subj: Insects – bees. Rhyming text.

Morris, Jackie, comp. *The cat and the fiddle: a treasury of nursery rhymes* ill. by Jackie Morris. Frances Lincoln, 2011. ISBN 978-1-84507-987-4-1 Subj: Nursery rhymes.

Morrison, Slade. *Little Cloud and Lady Wind* (Morrison, Toni)

The tortoise or the hare (Morrison, Toni)

Morrison, Toni. *Little Cloud and Lady Wind* by Toni Morrison and Slade Morrison; ill. by Sean Qualls. Simon & Schuster, 2010. ISBN 978-1-4169-8523-5 Subj: Character traits – individuality. Weather – clouds. Weather – wind.

The tortoise or the hare by Toni Morrison and Slade Morrison; ill. by Joe Cepeda. Simon & Schuster, 2010. ISBN 978-1-4169-8334-7 Subj: Animals – rabbits. Folk & fairy tales. Reptiles – turtles, tortoises. Sports – racing.

Morrissey, Dean. *The wizard mouse* ill. by author. HarperCollins, 2011. ISBN 978-0-06-008066-2 Subj: Animals – mice. Magic. Wizards.

Mortimer, Anne. *Bunny's Easter egg* ill. by author. HarperCollins, 2010. ISBN 978-0-06-126664-2 Subj: Animals – rabbits. Eggs. Holidays – Easter. Sleep.

Pumpkin cat ill. by author. HarperCollins, 2011. ISBN 978-0-06-187485-7 Subj: Animals – cats. Animals – mice. Gardens, gardening. Holidays – Halloween.

Mortimer, Rachael. *Song for a princess* ill. by Maddy McClellan. Scholastic, 2010. ISBN 978-0-545-24835-8 Subj: Activities – storytelling. Birds. Communication. Emotions – loneliness. Language. Royalty – princesses.

The three Billy Goats Fluff ill. by Liz Pichon. Tiger Tales, 2011. ISBN 978-1-58925-101-4 Subj: Activities – knitting. Animals – goats. Mythical creatures – trolls.

Morton, Carlene. *The library pages* ill. by Valeria Docampo. Upstart, 2010. ISBN 978-1-60213-045-6 Subj: Holidays – April Fools' Day. Libraries. School.

Moser, Lisa. *Perfect soup* ill. by Ben Mantle. Random House, 2010. ISBN 978-0-375-86014-0 Subj: Animals – mice. Cumulative tales. Food. Snowmen.

Moses, Will. *Mary and her little lamb: the true story of the famous nursery rhyme* ill. by author. Penguin Group (USA), 2011. ISBN 978-0-399-25154-

2 Subj: Animals – sheep. Farms. School. U.S. history.

Moss, Miriam. *Matty in a mess!* ill. by Jane Simmons. Andersen, 2010. ISBN 978-1-84270-812-5 Subj: Animals – bears. Animals – cats. Behavior – messy. Character traits – cleanliness.

Matty takes off! ill. by Jane Simmons. Andersen, 2010. ISBN 978-1-84270-758-6 Subj: Activities – traveling. Animals – bears. Animals – cats. Behavior – lost & found possessions.

This is the mountain ill. by Adrienne Kennaway. Frances Lincoln, 2011. ISBN 978-1-84507-984-0 Subj: Foreign lands – Africa. Mountains.

Moss, Peggy. *One of us* ill. by Penny Weber. Tilbury House, 2010. ISBN 978-0-88448-322-9 Subj: Character traits – individuality. Friendship. Moving. School.

Mother Goose. *Humpty Dumpty* ill. by Annie Kubler. Child's Play, 2010. ISBN 978-1-84643-339-9 Subj: Eggs. Format, unusual – board books. Nursery rhymes. Rhyming text.

Pat-a-cake ill. by Annie Kubler. Child's Play, 2010. ISBN 978-1-84643-338-2 Subj: Activities – baking, cooking. Format, unusual – board books. Nursery rhymes. Rhyming text.

Moulton, Mark Kimball. *The very best pumpkin* ill. by Karen Hillard Good. Simon & Schuster, 2010. ISBN 978-1-4169-8288-3 Subj: Farms. Friendship. Gardens, gardening.

Moundlic, Charlotte. *The scar* ill. by Olivier Tallec. Candlewick, 2011. ISBN 978-0-7636-5341-5 Subj: Death. Emotions – grief. Family life – mothers.

Muir, Leslie. *The little bitty bakery* ill. by Betsy Lewin. Hyperion/Disney, 2011. ISBN 978-1-4231-1640-0 Subj: Activities – baking, cooking. Animals – elephants. Animals – mice. Birthdays. Rhyming text.

Muldrow, Diane. *We planted a tree* ill. by Bob Staake. Random House, 2010. ISBN 978-0-375-86432-2 Subj: Ecology. Trees.

Munro, Roxie. *Desert days, desert nights* ill. by author. Bright Sky, 2010. ISBN 978-1-933979-77-9 Subj: Day. Desert. Ecology. Night.

Ecomazes: twelve Earth adventures ill. by author. Sterling, 2010. ISBN 978-1-4027-6393-9 Subj: Earth. Ecology. Picture puzzles.

Hatch! ill. by author. Marshall Cavendish, 2011. ISBN 978-0-7614-5882-1 Subj: Birds. Character traits – questioning. Eggs.

Murphy, Sally. *Pearl verses the world* ill. by Heather Potter. Candlewick, 2011. ISBN 978-0-7636-4821-

3 Subj: Death. Emotions – grief. Emotions – loneliness. Family life – grandmothers. Poetry.

Murphy, Stuart J. *Freda is found* ill. by Tim Jones. Charlesbridge, 2011. ISBN 978-1-58089-462-3 Subj: Animals. Behavior – lost. Safety. School – field trips.

Write on, Carlos! ill. by Tim Jones Illustration. Charlesbridge, 2011. ISBN 978-1-58089-464-7 Subj: Activities – writing. Animals. Names.

Murray, Alison. *Apple pie ABC* ill. by author. Hyperion/Disney, 2011. ISBN 978-1-4231-3694-1 Subj: ABC books. Activities – baking, cooking. Animals – dogs.

Muth, Jon J. *Zen ghosts* ill. by author. Scholastic, 2010. ISBN 978-0-439-63430-4 Subj: Activities – storytelling. Animals – pandas. Family life – brothers & sisters. Ghosts. Holidays – Halloween.

My big book of trucks and diggers. Chronicle, 2011. ISBN 978-0-8118-7892-0 Subj: Format, unusual – board books. Machines. Trucks.

My new baby ill. by Rachel Fuller. Child's Play, 2010. ISBN 978-1-84643-276-7 Subj: Family life – new sibling. Format, unusual – board books.

Myers, Walter Dean. *Looking for the easy life* ill. by Lee Harper. HarperCollins, 2011. ISBN 978-0-06-054375-4 Subj: Animals – monkeys. Behavior – seeking better things.

Muhammad Ali: the people's champion ill. by Alix Delinois. HarperCollins, 2010. ISBN 978-0-06-029131-0 Subj: Ethnic groups in the U.S. – African Americans. Prejudice. Sports – boxing. U.S. history.

Na, Il Sung. *Snow rabbit, spring rabbit: a book of changing seasons* ill. by author. Random House, 2011. ISBN 978-0-375-86786-6 Subj: Animals. Animals – rabbits. Seasons – spring. Seasons – winter.

The thingamabob ill. by author. Random House, 2010. ISBN 978-0-375-86106-2 Subj: Animals – elephants. Imagination. Umbrellas.

Nadel, Carolina. *Daddy's home* ill. by author. Mookind, 2011. ISBN 978-0-9792761-4-9 Subj: Careers – military. Emotions – anger. Family life – fathers. War.

Napoli, Donna Jo. *The crossing* ill. by Jim Madsen. Simon & Schuster, 2011. ISBN 978-1-4169-9474-9 Subj: Indians of North America – Shoshone. U.S. history – frontier & pioneer life.

Mama Miti: Wangari Maathai and the trees of Kenya ill. by Kadir Nelson. Simon & Schuster, 2010. ISBN 978-1-4169-3505-6 Subj: Character traits – responsibility. Ecology. Foreign lands – Kenya. Trees.

Nargi, Lela. *The honeybee man* ill. by Krysten Brooker. Random House, 2011. ISBN 978-0-375-84980-0 Subj: Careers – beekeepers. Insects – bees.

Nash, Sarah. *Purrfect!* ill. by Pamela Venus. Tamarind, 2010. ISBN 978-1-870516-86-0 Subj: Ethnic groups in the U.S. – African Americans. Toys.

Nelson, Marilyn. *Snook alone* ill. by Timothy Basil Ering. Candlewick, 2010. ISBN 978-0-7636-2667-9 Subj: Animals – dogs. Character traits – loyalty. Friendship. Religion.

Nelson-Schmidt, Michelle. *Cats, cats!* ill. by author. Kane/Miller, 2011. ISBN 978-1-61067-042-5 Subj: Animals – cats. Format, unusual. Pets.

Dogs, dogs! ill. by author. Kane/Miller, 2011. ISBN 978-1-61067-041-8 Subj: Animals – dogs. Format, unusual. Pets.

Nemiroff, Marc A. *Shy spaghetti and excited eggs: a kid's menu of feelings* by Marc A. Nemiroff and Jane Annunziata; ill. by Christine Battuz. Magination, 2011. ISBN 978-1-4338-0956-9 Subj: Emotions.

Nesbitt, Kenn. *More bears!* ill. by Troy Cummings. Sourcebooks, 2010. ISBN 978-1-4022-3835-2 Subj: Animals – bears. Careers – authors. Humorous stories.

Neubecker, Robert. *Wow! Ocean!* ill. by author. Hyperion/Disney, 2011. ISBN 978-1-4231-3113-7 Subj: Sea & seashore.

Nevius, Carol. *Soccer hour* ill. by Bill Thomson. Marshall Cavendish, 2011. ISBN 978-0-7614-5689-6 Subj: Rhyming text. Sports – soccer.

Newman, Jeff. *The boys* ill. by author. Simon & Schuster, 2010. ISBN 978-1-4169-5012-7 Subj: Character traits – shyness. Days of the week, months of the year. Old age. Sports – baseball. Wordless.

Newman, Lesléa. *Donovan's big day* ill. by Mike Dutton. Tricycle, 2011. ISBN 978-1-58246-332-2 Subj: Family life – mothers. Homosexuality. Weddings.

Just like Mama ill. by Julia Gorton. Abrams, 2010. ISBN 978-0-8109-8393-9 Subj: Family life – mothers. Rhyming text.

Miss Tutu's star ill. by Carey Armstrong-Ellis. Abrams, 2010. ISBN 978-0-8109-8396-0 Subj: Ballet. Emotions – fear. Self-concept.

Newton, Jill. *Crash bang donkey!* ill. by author. Whitman, 2010. ISBN 978-0-8075-1330-9 Subj: Animals – donkeys. Farms. Musical instruments. Noise, sounds.

Niemann, Christoph. *Subway* ill. by author. HarperCollins, 2010. ISBN 978-0-06-157779-6 Subj: Cities, towns. Family life – fathers. Rhyming text. Trains.

That's how! ill. by author. HarperCollins, 2011. ISBN 978-0-06-201963-9 Subj: Imagination. Machines. Trucks.

Nijssen, Elfi. *Laurie* ill. by Eline van Lindenhuizen. Clavis, 2010. ISBN 978-1-60537-072-9 Subj: Handicaps – deafness.

Nivola, Claire A. *Orani: my father's village* ill. by author. Farrar, 2011. ISBN 978-0-374-35657-6 Subj: Foreign lands – Italy. Memories, memory.

Noble, Trinka Hakes. *A Christmas spider's miracle* ill. by Stephen Costanza. Sleeping Bear, 2011. ISBN 978-1-58536-602-6 Subj: Folk & fairy tales. Holidays – Christmas. Spiders.

Nolan, Dennis. *Sea of dreams* ill. by author. Roaring Brook, 2011. ISBN 978-1-59643-470-7 Subj: Sand. Sea & seashore. Wordless.

Nolan, Janet. *The firehouse light* ill. by Marie Lafrance. Tricycle, 2010. ISBN 978-1-58246-298-1 Subj: Careers – firefighters. Fire. U.S. history.

Norman, Kim. *Ten on the sled* ill. by Liza Woodruff. Sterling, 2010. ISBN 978-1-4027-7076-0 Subj: Animals. Counting, numbers. Rhyming text. Seasons – winter. Sports – sledding.

North, Sherry. *Because I am your daddy* ill. by Marcellus Hall. Abrams, 2010. ISBN 978-0-8109-8392-2 Subj: Family life – fathers. Rhyming text.

Champ's story: dogs get cancer too! ill. by Kathleen Rietz. Sylvan Dell, 2010. ISBN 978-1-60718-077-7 Subj: Animals – dogs. Illness – cancer.

Norworth, Jack. *Take me out to the ball game* ill. by Amiko Hirao. Imagine, 2011. ISBN 978-1-936140-26-8 Subj: Songs. Sports – baseball.

Noullet, Georgette. *Bed hog* ill. by David Slonim. Marshall Cavendish, 2011. ISBN 978-0-7614-5823-4 Subj: Animals – dogs. Sleep.

Novak, Matt. *A wish for you* ill. by author. HarperCollins, 2010. ISBN 978-0-06-155202-1 Subj: Babies. Family life. Rhyming text.

Numeroff, Laura. *If you give a dog a donut* ill. by Felicia Bond. HarperCollins, 2011. ISBN 978-0-06-026683-7 Subj: Animals – dogs. Character traits – kindness to animals. Circular tales.

The Jellybeans and the big book bonanza by Laura Numeroff and Nate Evans; ill. by Lynn Munsinger. Abrams, 2010. ISBN 978-0-8109-8412-7 Subj: Animals. Books, reading. Friendship. Libraries.

The Jellybeans and the big camp kickoff by Laura Numeroff and Nate Evans; ill. by Lynn Munsinger. Abrams, 2011. ISBN 978-0-8109-9765-3 Subj: Animals. Camps, camping. Character traits – cooperation. Friendship.

Otis and Sydney and the best birthday ever ill. by Dan Andreasen. Abrams, 2010. ISBN 978-0-8109-8959-7 Subj: Animals – bears. Birthdays. Friendship. Parties.

Ponyella by Laura Numeroff and Nate Evans; ill. by Lynn Munsinger. Hyperion/Disney, 2011. ISBN 978-1-4231-0259-5 Subj: Animals – horses, ponies. Fairies. Folk & fairy tales. Royalty – princesses.

What puppies do best ill. by Lynn Munsinger. Chronicle, 2011. ISBN 978-0-8118-6601-9 Subj: Activities. Animals – babies. Animals – dogs.

Nyeu, Tao. *Bunny days* ill. by author. Penguin Group (USA), 2010. ISBN 978-0-8037-3330-5 Subj: Animals – babies. Animals – bears. Animals – rabbits.

Obama, Barack. *Of thee I sing: a letter to my daughters* ill. by Loren Long. Random House, 2010. ISBN 978-0-375-83527-8 Subj: Character traits. Self-concept. U.S. history.

O'Connell, Rebecca. *Danny is done with diapers: a potty ABC* ill. by Amanda Gulliver. Whitman, 2010. ISBN 978-0-8075-1466-5 Subj: ABC books. Toilet training.

O'Connor, Jane. *Fancy Nancy: aspiring artist* ill. by Robin Preiss Glasser. HarperCollins, 2011. ISBN 978-0-06-191526-0 Subj: Activities – drawing. Art. Language.

Fancy Nancy: ooh la la! it's beauty day ill. by Robin Preiss Glasser. HarperCollins, 2010. ISBN 978-0-06-191525-3 Subj: Beauty shops. Birthdays. Language. Self-concept.

Fancy Nancy: poet extraordinaire! ill. by Robin Preiss Glasser. HarperCollins, 2010. ISBN 978-0-06-189643-9 Subj: Activities – writing. Poetry. School.

Fancy Nancy and the fabulous fashion boutique ill. by Robin Preiss Glasser. HarperCollins, 2010. ISBN 978-0-06-123592-4 Subj: Character traits – generosity. Family life – sisters. Language. Money.

Oelschlager, Vanita. *Bonyo Bonyo: the true story of a brave boy from Kenya* ill. by Kristin Blackwood. Vanita, 2010. ISBN 978-0-9819714-3-8 Subj: Careers – doctors. Foreign lands – Kenya.

A tale of two daddies ill. by Kristin Blackwood. Vanita, 2010. ISBN 978-0-9819714-5-2 Subj: Family life – fathers. Homosexuality.

A tale of two mommies ill. by Mike Blanc. Vanita, 2011. ISBN 978-0-9826366-6-4 Subj: Family life – mothers. Homosexuality.

Offill, Jenny. *11 experiments that failed* ill. by Nancy Carpenter. Random House, 2011. ISBN 978-0-375-84762-2 Subj: Careers – scientists. Character traits – questioning. Science.

O'Hair, Margaret. *My kitten* ill. by Tammie Lyon. Marshall Cavendish, 2011. ISBN 978-0-7614-5811-1 Subj: Animals – babies. Animals – cats. Rhyming text.

Ohi, Ruth. *Chicken, pig, cow and the class pet* ill. by author. Annick, 2011. ISBN 978-1-55451-347-5 Subj: Animals – bulls, cows. Animals – hamsters. Animals – pigs. Birds – chickens. School. Toys.

Chicken, pig, cow, horse around ill. by author. Annick, 2010. ISBN 978-1-55451-245-4 Subj: Animals – bulls, cows. Animals – horses, ponies. Animals – pigs. Birds – chickens. Toys.

Ohora, Zachariah. *Stop snoring, Bernard!* ill. by author. Henry Holt, 2011. ISBN 978-0-8050-9002-4 Subj: Animals – otters. Sleep – snoring. Zoos.

Oldland, Nicholas. *The busy beaver* ill. by author. Kids Can, 2011. ISBN 978-1-55453-749-5 Subj: Animals – beavers. Behavior – carelessness.

Making the moose out of life ill. by author. Kids Can, 2010. ISBN 978-1-55453-580-4 Subj: Animals – moose. Friendship. Reptiles – turtles, tortoises.

Olson, Julie. *Tickle, tickle! itch, twitch!* ill. by author. Marshall Cavendish, 2010. ISBN 978-0-7614-5714-5 Subj: Animals – groundhogs. Animals – mice.

Olson-Brown, Ellen. *Ooh la la polka-dot boots* ill. by Christiane Engel. Tricycle, 2010. ISBN 978-1-58246-287-5 Subj: Clothing – boots. Format, unusual. Rhyming text.

O'Malley, Kevin. *Animal crackers fly the coop* ill. by author. Walker, 2010. ISBN 978-0-8027-9837-4 Subj: Animals. Humorous stories. Language.

The great race ill. by author. Walker, 2011. ISBN 978-0-8027-2158-7 Subj: Animals – rabbits. Folk & fairy tales. Reptiles – turtles, tortoises. Sports – racing.

Once upon a royal superbaby ill. by author et al. Walker, 2010. ISBN 978-0-8027-2164-8 Subj: Activities – writing. Babies. Royalty.

Onyefulu, Ifeoma. *Deron goes to nursery school* photos by author. Frances Lincoln, 2010. ISBN 978-1-84507-864-5 Subj: Foreign lands – Ghana. School – first day. School – nursery.

Grandma comes to stay photos by author. Frances Lincoln, 2010. ISBN 978-1-84507-865-7 Subj: Family life – grandmothers. Foreign lands – Ghana.

Omer's favorite place photos by author. Frances Lincoln, 2011. ISBN 978-1-84780-241-5 Subj: Activities – playing. Family life. Foreign lands – Ethiopia.

Orgill, Roxane. *Skit-scat raggedy cat: Ella Fitzgerald* ill. by Sean Qualls. Candlewick, 2010. ISBN 978-0-7636-1733-2 Subj: Careers – singers. Ethnic groups in the U.S. – African Americans. Music.

Orloff, Karen Kaufman. *I wanna new room* ill. by David Catrow. Penguin Group (USA), 2010. ISBN 978-0-399-25405-5 Subj: Behavior – sharing. Family life. Homes, houses. Letters, cards.

Orr, Wendy. *The princess and her panther* ill. by Lauren Stringer. Simon & Schuster, 2010. ISBN 978-1-4169-9780-1 Subj: Animals – leopards. Camps, camping. Family life – sisters. Imagination. Royalty – princesses.

Otoshi, Kathryn. *Zero* ill. by author. KO Kids, 2010. ISBN 978-0-9723946-3-5 Subj: Behavior – cooperation. Counting, numbers. Self-concept.

Oud, Pauline. *Ian's new potty* ill. by author. Clavis, 2011. ISBN 978-1-60537-103-0 Subj: Behavior – growing up. Toilet training.

Owen, Karen. *I could be, you could be* ill. by Barroux. Barefoot, 2011. ISBN 978-1-84686-405-6 Subj: Rhyming text. Self-concept.

Page, Robin. *How to clean a hippopotamus: a look at unusual animal partnerships* (Jenkins, Steve)

Time for a bath (Jenkins, Steve)

Time to eat (Jenkins, Steve)

Time to sleep (Jenkins, Steve)

Palatini, Margie. *Goldie and the three hares* ill. by Jack E. Davis. HarperCollins, 2011. ISBN 978-0-06-125314-0 Subj: Animals – rabbits. Behavior – misbehavior.

Hogg, Hogg, and Hog ill. by author. Simon & Schuster, 2011. ISBN 978-1-4424-0322-2 Subj: Animals – pigs. Character traits – ambition. Cities, towns.

Stuff ill. by Noah Jones. HarperCollins, 2011. ISBN 978-0-06-171921-9 Subj: Animals – rabbits. Behavior – collecting things. Friendship.

Pallotta, Jerry. *Who will plant a tree?* ill. by Tom Leonard. Sleeping Bear, 2010. ISBN 978-1-58536-502-9 Subj: Seeds. Trees.

Pamintuan, Macky. *Twelve haunted rooms of Halloween* ill. by author. Sterling, 2011. ISBN 978-1-4027-7935-0 Subj: Animals – bears. Counting, numbers. Holidays – Halloween. Picture puzzles. Rhyming text.

Parish, Herman. *Amelia Bedelia's first apple pie* ill. by Lynne Avril. HarperCollins, 2010. ISBN 978-0-06-196409-1 Subj: Activities – baking, cooking. Family life – grandparents. Humorous stories.

Amelia Bedelia's first field trip ill. by Lynne Avril. HarperCollins, 2011. ISBN 978-0-06-196413-8 Subj: Farms. Humorous stories. School – field trips.

Go west, Amelia Bedelia! ill. by Lynn Sweat. HarperCollins, 2011. ISBN 978-0060843618 Subj: Careers – ranchers. Family life – aunts, uncles. Humorous stories.

Park, Linda Sue. *The third gift* ill. by Bagram Ibatoulline. Clarion, 2011. ISBN 978-0-547-20195-5 Subj: Family life – fathers. Holidays – Christmas. Religion.

Parker, Marjorie Blain. *A paddling of ducks: animals in groups from A to Z* ill. by Joseph Kelly. Kids Can, 2010. ISBN 978-1-55337-682-8 Subj: ABC books. Animals. Language.

Parkhurst, Carolyn. *Cooking with Henry and Elliebelly* ill. by Dan Yaccarino. Feiwel & Friends, 2010. ISBN 978-0-312-54848-3 Subj: Activities – baking, cooking. Family life – brothers & sisters. Imagination.

Parnell, Peter. *Christian, the hugging lion* (Richardson, Justin)

Parot, Annelore. *Kimonos* ill. by author. Chronicle, 2011. ISBN 978-1-4521-0493-5 Subj: Foreign lands – Japan. Format, unusual – toy & movable books. Toys – dolls.

Parr, Todd. *The earth book* ill. by author. Little, Brown, 2010. ISBN 978-0-316-04265-9 Subj: Earth. Ecology.

Paterson, Katherine, reteller. *Brother Sun, Sister Moon: Saint Francis of Assisi's canticle of the creatures* ill. by Pamela Dalton. Chronicle, 2011. ISBN 978-0-8118-7734-3 Subj: Nature. Religion.

Patricelli, Leslie. *Be quiet, Mike!* ill. by author. Candlewick, 2011. ISBN 978-0-7636-4477-2 Subj: Animals – monkeys. Musical instruments – drums. Noise, sounds.

The Patterson puppies and the midnight monster party ill. by author. Candlewick, 2010. ISBN 978-0-7636-3243-4 Subj: Animals – dogs. Bedtime. Emotions – fear. Monsters.

Potty ill. by author. Candlewick, 2010. ISBN 978-0-7636-4476-5 Subj: Toilet training.

Tubby ill. by author. Candlewick, 2010. ISBN 978-0-7636-4567-0 Subj: Activities – bathing. Activities – playing.

Patten, Brian. *The big snuggle-up* ill. by Nicola Bayley. Kane/Miller, 2011. ISBN 978-1-61067-036-4 Subj: Animals. Behavior – sharing. Character traits – generosity. Rhyming text. Scarecrows. Weather – snow.

Pearce, Clemency. *Frangoline and the midnight dream* ill. by Rebecca Elliott. Scholastic, 2011. ISBN 978-0-545-31426-8 Subj: Behavior – misbehavior. Moon. Night. Rhyming text.

Pearson, Susan. *How to teach a slug to read* ill. by David Slonim. Marshall Cavendish, 2011. ISBN 978-0-7614-5805-0 Subj: Animals – slugs. Books, reading.

Peet, Mal. *Cloud tea monkeys* by Mal Peet and Elspeth Graham; ill. by Juan Wijngaard. Candlewick, 2010. ISBN 978-0-7636-4453-6 Subj: Animals – monkeys. Character traits – kindness to animals. Family life – mothers. Foreign lands – Himalayas. Illness.

Peete, Holly Robinson. *My brother Charlie* by Holly Robinson Peete and Ryan Elizabeth Peete; ill. by Shane W. Evans. Scholastic, 2010. ISBN 978-0-545-09466-5 Subj: Ethnic groups in the U.S. – African Americans. Family life – brothers & sisters. Handicaps – autism. Multiple births – twins.

Peete, Ryan Elizabeth. *My brother Charlie* (Peete, Holly Robinson)

Pelé. *For the love of soccer!* ill. by Frank Morrison. Hyperion/Disney, 2010. ISBN 978-1-4231-1538-0 Subj: Sports – soccer.

Pelley, Kathleen T. *Magnus Maximus, a marvelous measurer* ill. by S. D. Schindler. Farrar, 2010. ISBN 978-0-374-34725-3 Subj: Concepts – measurement. Counting, numbers.

Raj the bookstore tiger ill. by Paige Keiser. Charlesbridge, 2011. ISBN 978-1-58089-230-8 Subj: Animals – cats. Self-concept. Stores.

Peña, Matt de la. *A nation's hope: the story of boxing legend Joe Louis* ill. by Kadir Nelson. Penguin Group (USA), 2011. ISBN 978-0-8037-3167-7 Subj: Ethnic groups in the U.S. – African Americans. Sports – boxing.

Penn, Audrey. *A bedtime kiss for Chester Raccoon* ill. by Barbara L. Gibson. Tanglewood, 2011. ISBN 978-1-933718-52-1 Subj: Animals – raccoons. Bedtime. Emotions – fear. Format, unusual – board books. Rhyming text.

Perl, Erica S. *Chicken Butt's back!* ill. by Henry Cole. Abrams, 2011. ISBN 978-0-8109-9729-5 Subj: Birds – chickens. Humorous stories. Language.

Dotty ill. by Julia Denos. Abrams, 2010. ISBN 978-0-8109-8962-7 Subj: Emotions – anger. Imagination – imaginary friends. School.

Perlman, Willa. *Good night, world* ill. by Carolyn Fisher. Simon & Schuster, 2011. ISBN 978-1-4424-0197-4 Subj: Bedtime. Rhyming text. World.

Perrault, Charles. *Puss in boots* retold by John Cech; ill. by Bernhard Oberdieck. Sterling, 2010. ISBN 978-1-4027-4436-5 Subj: Animals – cats. Character traits – cleverness. Folk & fairy tales. Royalty – kings.

Perrin, Martine. *Look who's there!* tr. by Marianne Martens; ill. by author. Whitman, 2011. ISBN 978-0-8075-7676-2 Subj: Animals. Format, unusual – toy & movable books. Sea & seashore.

Perrow, Angeli. *Many hands: a Penobscot Indian story* ill. by Heather Austin. Down East, 2010. ISBN 978-0-89272-782-7 Subj: Activities – weaving. Family life – grandmothers. Indians of North America.

Perry, Andrea. *The Bicklebys' birdbath* ill. by Roberta Angaramo. Simon & Schuster, 2010. ISBN 978-1-4169-0624-7 Subj: Birds. Cumulative tales. Rhyming text.

Perry, Phyllis J. *Pandas' earthquake escape* ill. by Susan Detwiler. Sylvan Dell, 2010. ISBN 978-1-60718-071-5 Subj: Animals – pandas. Earthquakes. Foreign lands – China.

Peters, Bernadette. *Stella is a star!* ill. by Liz Murphy. Blue Apple, 2010. ISBN 978-1-60905-008-5 Subj: Animals – dogs. Ballet. Disguises. Self-concept.

Peters, Lisa Westberg. *Frankie works the night shift* ill. by Jennifer Taylor. HarperCollins, 2010. ISBN 978-0-06-009095-1 Subj: Animals – cats. Counting, numbers. Night.

Volcano wakes up! ill. by Steve Jenkins. Henry Holt, 2010. ISBN 978-0-8050-8287-6 Subj: Poetry. Volcanoes.

Petersen, David. *Snowy Valentine* ill. by author. HarperCollins, 2011. ISBN 978-0-06-146378-5 Subj: Animals. Animals – rabbits. Holidays – Valentine's Day. Weather – snow.

Peterson, Cris. *Seed soil sun: Earth's recipe for food* photos by David R. Lundquist. Boyds Mills, 2010. ISBN 978-1-59078-713-7 Subj: Gardens, gardening. Plants. Seeds. Sun.

Peterson, Mary. *Piggies in the pumpkin patch* by Mary Peterson and Jennifer Rofé; ill. by Mary Peterson. Charlesbridge, 2010. ISBN 978-1-57091-460-7 Subj: Animals – pigs. Farms.

Pett, Mark. *The girl who never made mistakes* by Mark Pett and Gary Rubinstein; ill. by Mark Pett. Sourcebooks, 2011. ISBN 978-1-4022-5544-1 Subj: Behavior – worrying. Character traits – perfectionism. Self-concept.

Pettitt, Linda. *Yafi's family: an Ethiopian boy's journey of love, loss, and adoption* by Linda Pettitt and Sharon Darrow; ill. by Jan Spivey Gilchrist. Amharic Kids, 2010. ISBN 978-0-9797481-4-1 Subj: Adoption. Foreign lands – Australia. Foreign lands – Ethiopia.

Pfister, Marcus. *Happy birthday, Bertie!* ill. by author. NorthSouth, 2010. ISBN 978-0-7358-2280-1 Subj: Animals – hippopotamuses. Birthdays. Parties.

Questions, questions ill. by author. NorthSouth, 2011. ISBN 978-0-7358-4000-3 Subj: Animals – hippopotamuses. Character traits – questioning. Nature. Rhyming text.

Snow puppy ill. by author. NorthSouth, 2011. ISBN 978-0-7358-4031-7 Subj: Animals – dogs. Behavior – lost. Weather – snow.

Pham, LeUyen. *All the things I love about you* ill. by author. HarperCollins, 2010. ISBN 978-0-06-199029-8 Subj: Emotions – love. Family life – mothers.

Pierce, Roxanne Heide. *Always listen to your mother* (Heide, Florence Parry)

Pinfold, Levi. *The Django* ill. by author. Candlewick, 2010. ISBN 978-0-7636-4788-9 Subj: Behavior – misbehavior. Gypsies. Imagination – imaginary friends. Musical instruments – banjos.

Pinkney, Andrea Davis. *Sit-in: how four friends stood up by sitting down* ill. by Brian Pinkney. Little, Brown, 2010. ISBN 978-0-316-07016-4 Subj: Ethnic groups in the U.S. – African Americans. Prejudice. U.S. history.

Pinkney, Jerry. *Three little kittens* ill. by author. Penguin Group (USA), 2010. ISBN 978-0-8037-3533-0 Subj: Animals – cats. Behavior – lost & found possessions. Clothing – gloves, mittens. Nursery rhymes.

Pinkwater, Daniel. *Beautiful Yetta: the Yiddish chicken* Yiddish tr. by Edward Weiss; Spanish tr. by Guillermo Casallo; ill. by Jill Pinkwater. Feiwel & Friends, 2010. ISBN 978-0-312-55824-6 Subj: Behavior – lost. Birds – chickens. Birds – parakeets, parrots. Cities, towns. Foreign languages.

I am the dog ill. by Jack E. Davis. HarperCollins, 2010. ISBN 978-0-06-055505-4 Subj: Animals – dogs. Humorous stories.

Piper, Sophie. *I can say a prayer* ill. by Emily Bolam. IPG/Lion, 2011. ISBN 978-0-7459-6233-7 Subj: Religion.

Pittau, Francisco. *Out of sight* by Francisco Pittau and Bernadette Gervais; ill. by authors. Chronicle, 2010. ISBN 978-0-8118-7712-1 Subj: Animals. Format, unusual – toy & movable books.

Platt, Cynthia. *A little bit of love* ill. by Hannah Whitty. Tiger Tales, 2011. ISBN 978-1-58925-095-6 Subj: Activities – baking, cooking. Animals – mice. Family life – mothers.

Plecas, Jennifer. *Pretend* ill. by author. Penguin Group (USA), 2011. ISBN 978-0-399-23430-9 Subj: Family life – fathers. Imagination.

Plourde, Lynn. *Dino pets go to school* ill. by Gideon Kendall. Penguin Group (USA), 2011. ISBN 978-0-525-42232-7 Subj: Dinosaurs. Pets. Rhyming text. School.

Field trip day ill. by Thor Wickstrom. Penguin Group (USA), 2010. ISBN 978-0-525-47994-9 Subj: Farms. School – field trips.

Only cows allowed! ill. by Rebecca Harrison Reed. Down East, 2011. ISBN 978-0-89272-790-2 Subj: Animals. Animals – bulls, cows. Farms. Humorous stories.

Polacco, Patricia. *Bun Bun Button* ill. by author. Penguin Group (USA), 2011. ISBN 978-0-399-25472-7 Subj: Behavior – lost & found possessions. Character traits – luck. Family life – grandmothers. Toys. Toys – balloons.

The junkyard wonders ill. by author. Penguin Group (USA), 2010. ISBN 978-0-399-25078-1 Subj: Careers – teachers. Handicaps. Inventions. School. Self-concept.

Portis, Antoinette. *Kindergarten diary* ill. by author. HarperCollins, 2010. ISBN 978-0-06-145691-6 Subj: School.

Princess Super Kitty ill. by author. HarperCollins, 2011. ISBN 978-0-06-182725-9 Subj: Activities – playing. Imagination.

Portnoy, Mindy Avra. *A tale of two seders* ill. by Valeria Cis. Lerner/Kar-Ben, 2010. ISBN 978-0-8225-9907-4 Subj: Divorce. Family life. Holidays – Passover.

Postgate, Daniel. *Smelly Bill: love stinks* ill. by author. Whitman, 2010. ISBN 978-0-8075-7464-5 Subj: Activities – bathing. Animals – dogs. Rhyming text.

Poydar, Nancy. *No fair science fair* ill. by author. Holiday House, 2011. ISBN 978-0-8234-2269-2 Subj: Character traits – persistence. School. Science.

Prap, Lila. *Dinosaurs?!* ill. by author. NorthSouth, 2010. ISBN 978-0-7358-2284-9 Subj: Dinosaurs.

Doggy whys ill. by author. NorthSouth, 2011. ISBN 978-0-7358-4014-0 Subj: Animals – cats. Animals – dogs. Pets.

Preller, James. *A pirate's guide to first grade* ill. by Greg Ruth. Feiwel & Friends, 2010. ISBN 978-0-312-36928-6 Subj: Pirates. School – first day.

Prelutsky, Jack. *There's no place like school* ill. by Jane Manning. HarperCollins, 2010. ISBN 978-0-06-082338-2 Subj: Poetry. School.

Price, Mara. *Grandma's chocolate / El chocolate de Abuelita* ill. by Lisa Fields. Arte Publico/Piñata, 2010. ISBN 978-1-55885-587-8 Subj: Ethnic groups in the U.S. – Mexican Americans. Family life – grandmothers. Foreign languages. Gifts. Indians of Central America – Maya.

Primavera, Elise. *Louise the big cheese and the back-to-school smarty-pants* ill. by Diane Goode. Simon & Schuster, 2011. ISBN 978-1-4424-0600-1 Subj: Careers – teachers. Character traits – ambition. School.

Louise the big cheese and the la-di-da shoes ill. by Diane Goode. Simon & Schuster, 2010. ISBN 978-1-4169-7181-8 Subj: Character traits – appearance. Character traits – vanity. Clothing – shoes.

Thumb love ill. by author. Random House, 2010. ISBN 978-0-375-84481-2 Subj: Humorous stories. Thumb sucking.

Proimos, James. *Todd's TV* ill. by author. HarperCollins, 2010. ISBN 978-0-06-170985-2 Subj: Family life – parents. Television.

Protopopescu, Orel. *Thelonious Mouse* ill. by Anne Wilsdorf. Farrar, 2011. ISBN 978-0-374-37447-1 Subj: Animals – cats. Animals – mice. Music.

Pulver, Robin. *Christmas kitten, home at last* ill. by Layne Johnson. Whitman, 2010. ISBN 978-0-8075-1157-2 Subj: Animals – cats. Holidays – Christmas. Illness – allergies. Santa Claus.

Happy endings: a story about suffixes ill. by Lynn Rowe Reed. Holiday House, 2011. ISBN 978-0-8234-2296-8 Subj: Language. School.

Thank you, Miss Doover ill. by Stephanie Roth Sisson. Holiday House, 2010. ISBN 978-0-8234-2046-9 Subj: Activities – writing. Letters, cards. School.

Puttock, Simon. *Little lost cowboy* ill. by Caroline Jayne Church. Egmont USA, 2011. ISBN 978-1-60684-259-1 Subj: Animals – coyotes. Behavior – lost.

Quackenbush, Robert. *First grade jitters* ill. by Yan Nascimbene. HarperCollins, 2010. ISBN 978-0-06-077632-9 Subj: Behavior – worrying. School – first day.

Quattlebaum, Mary. *Jo MacDonald saw a pond* ill. by Laura J. Bryant. Dawn, 2011. ISBN 978-1-58469-150-1 Subj: Lakes, ponds. Songs.

Pirate vs. pirate: the terrific tale of a big, blustery maritime match ill. by Alexandra Boiger. Hyperion/Disney, 2011. ISBN 978-1-4231-2201-2 Subj: Contests. Emotions – love. Pirates.

Raczka, Bob. *Fall mixed up* ill. by Chad Cameron. Carolrhoda, 2011. ISBN 978-0-7613-4606-7 Subj: Picture puzzles. Rhyming text. Seasons – fall.

Guyku: a year of haiku for boys ill. by Peter H. Reynolds. Houghton Harcourt, 2010. ISBN 978-0-547-24003-9 Subj: Poetry. Seasons.

Ramos, Mario. *I am so strong* tr. by Jean Anderson; ill. by author. Gecko, 2011. ISBN 978-0-9582-7877-5 Subj: Animals – wolves. Behavior – bullying. Dragons.

Ramsden, Ashley, reteller. *Seven fathers* ill. by Ed Young. Roaring Brook, 2011. ISBN 978-1-59643-544-5 Subj: Behavior – lost. Character traits – persistence. Folk & fairy tales. Old age.

Ramsey, Calvin Alexander. *Belle, the last mule at Gee's Bend: a civil rights story* by Calvin Alexander Ramsey and Bettye Stroud; ill. by John Holyfield. Candlewick, 2011. ISBN 978-0-7636-4058-3 Subj: Animals – mules. Ethnic groups in the U.S. – African Americans. U.S. history. Violence, nonviolence.

Ruth and the Green Book ill. by Floyd Cooper. Carolrhoda, 2010. ISBN 978-0-7613-5255-6 Subj: Activities – traveling. Ethnic groups in the U.S. – African Americans. Prejudice. U.S. history.

Rand, Betseygail. *Big Bunny* by Betseygail Rand and Colleen Rand; ill. by C. S. W. Rand. Tricycle, 2011. ISBN 978-1-58246-376-6 Subj: Animals – rabbits. Behavior – running away. Concepts – size. Eggs. Holidays – Easter.

Rand, Colleen. *Big Bunny* (Rand, Betseygail)

Randall, Angel. *Snow angels* by Angel Randall and Chris Schoebinger; ill. by Brandon Dorman. Shadow Mountain, 2011. ISBN 978-1-60641-046-2 Subj: Angels. Character traits – helpfulness.

Ransome, James. *Gunner, football hero* ill. by author. Holiday House, 2010. ISBN 978-0-8234-2053-7 Subj: Sports – football.

New red bike! ill. by author. Holiday House, 2011. ISBN 978-0-8234-2226-5 Subj: Behavior – sharing. Sports – bicycling.

Rappaport, Doreen. *Jack's path of courage: the life of John F. Kennedy* ill. by Matt Tavares. Hyperion/Disney, 2010. ISBN 978-1-4231-2272-2 Subj: Character traits – bravery. U.S. history.

Raschka, Chris. *A ball for Daisy* ill. by author. Random House, 2011. ISBN 978-0-375-85861-1 Subj: Animals – dogs. Caldecott award books. Toys – balls. Wordless.

Hip Hop Dog ill. by Vladimir Radunsky. HarperCollins, 2010. ISBN 978-0-06-123963-2 Subj: Animals – dogs. Music. Rhyming text.

Little black crow ill. by author. Simon & Schuster, 2010. ISBN 978-0-689-84601-4 Subj: Birds – crows. Character traits – questioning. Imagination. Rhyming text.

Rausch, Molly. *My cold went on vacation* ill. by Nora Krug. Penguin Group (USA), 2011. ISBN 978-0-399-25474-1 Subj: Humorous stories. Illness – cold (disease).

Rave, Friederike. *Outfoxing the fox* ill. by author. NorthSouth, 2010. ISBN 978-0-7358-2295-5 Subj: Animals – foxes. Birds – chickens.

Rawlinson, Julia. *Fletcher and the snowflake Christmas* ill. by Tiphanie Beeke. HarperCollins, 2010. ISBN 978-0-06-199033-5 Subj: Animals – foxes. Friendship. Holidays – Christmas. Santa Claus. Seasons – winter.

Ray, Jane. *The dollhouse fairy* ill. by author. Candlewick, 2010. ISBN 978-0-7636-4411-6 Subj: Behavior – worrying. Fairies. Family life – fathers. Illness.

Ray, Mary Lyn. *Stars* ill. by Marla Frazee. Simon & Schuster, 2011. ISBN 978-1-4424-2249-1 Subj: Concepts – shape. Night. Sky. Stars.

Rayner, Catherine. *The bear who shared* ill. by author. Penguin Group (USA), 2011. ISBN 978-0-8037-3576-7 Subj: Animals – bears. Animals – mice. Animals – raccoons. Behavior – sharing. Friendship.

Ernest, the moose who doesn't fit ill. by author. Farrar, 2010. ISBN 978-0-374-32217-5 Subj: Animals – moose. Behavior – resourcefulness. Concepts – size. Format, unusual – toy & movable books.

Solomon Crocodile ill. by author. Farrar, 2011. ISBN 978-0-374-38064-9 Subj: Activities – playing. Friendship. Reptiles – alligators, crocodiles.

Reasoner, Charles. *Animal babies!* ill. by author. Rourke, 2011. ISBN 978-1-61236-054-6 Subj: Animals – babies.

One blue fish: a colorful counting book ill. by author. Simon & Schuster, 2010. ISBN 978-1-4169-9672-9 Subj: Concepts – color. Counting, numbers. Format, unusual – toy & movable books.

Reed, Lynn Rowe. *Basil's birds* ill. by author. Marshall Cavendish, 2010. ISBN 978-0-7614-5627-8 Subj: Birds. Careers – custodians, janitors. School.

Color chaos! ill. by author. Holiday House, 2010. ISBN 978-0-8234-2257-9 Subj: Concepts – color. School.

Roscoe and the pelican rescue ill. by author. Holiday House, 2011. ISBN 978-0-8234-2352-1 Subj: Birds – pelicans. Character traits – kindness to animals. Ecology.

Rees, Douglas. *Jeannette Claus saves Christmas* ill. by Olivier Latyk. Simon & Schuster, 2010. ISBN 978-1-4169-2686-3 Subj: Behavior – resourcefulness. Holidays – Christmas. Illness. Santa Claus.

Regan, Dian Curtis. *The Snow Blew Inn* ill. by Doug Cushman. Holiday House, 2011. ISBN 978-0-8234-2351-4 Subj: Animals. Animals – cats. Sleepovers. Weather – blizzards.

Reid, Barbara. *Perfect snow* ill. by author. Whitman, 2011. ISBN 978-0-8075-6492-9 Subj: Behavior – cooperation. School. Snowmen. Weather – snow.

Reid, Margarette S. *Lots and lots of coins* ill. by True Kelley. Penguin Group (USA), 2011. ISBN 978-0-525-47879-9 Subj: Behavior – collecting things. Counting, numbers. Money.

Reidy, Jean. *Light up the night* ill. by Margaret Chodos-Irvine. Hyperion/Disney, 2011. ISBN 978-1-4231-2024-7 Subj: Bedtime. Cumulative tales. Imagination. Rhyming text. Space & space ships.

Too pickley! ill. by Geneviève Leloup. Bloomsbury, 2010. ISBN 978-1-59990-309-5 Subj: Behavior. Food. Rhyming text.

Too purpley! ill. by Geneviève Leloup. Bloomsbury, 2010. ISBN 978-1-59990-307-1 Subj: Behavior – indecision. Character traits – appearance. Clothing. Rhyming text.

Reinhart, Matthew. *Gods and heroes* by Matthew Reinhart and Robert Sabuda; ill. by authors. Candlewick, 2010. ISBN 978-0-7636-3171-0 Subj: Format, unusual – toy & movable books. Mythical creatures.

Rex, Michael. *Furious George goes bananas: a primate parody* ill. by author. Penguin Group (USA),

2010. ISBN 978-0-399-25433-8 Subj: Animals – gorillas. Humorous stories.

Reynolds, Aaron. *Back of the bus* ill. by Floyd Cooper. Penguin Group (USA), 2010. ISBN 978-0-399-25091-0 Subj: Character traits – bravery. Ethnic groups in the U.S. – African Americans. Prejudice. U.S. history.

Snowbots ill. by David Barneda. Random House, 2010. ISBN 978-0-375-85873-4 Subj: Rhyming text. Robots. Weather – snow.

Reynolds, Peter H. *I'm here* ill. by author. Simon & Schuster, 2011. ISBN 978-1-4169-9649-4 Subj: Airplanes, airports. Character traits – being different. Friendship. Handicaps – autism. Paper.

Richardson, Justin. *Christian, the hugging lion* by Justin Richardson and Peter Parnell; ill. by Amy Bates. Simon & Schuster, 2010. ISBN 978-1-4169-8662-1 Subj: Animals – lions. Foreign lands – England. Foreign lands – Kenya.

Rickards, Lynne. *Jacob O'Reilly wants a pet* ill. by Lee Wildish. Barron's, 2010. ISBN 978-0-7641-6311-1 Subj: Pets. Rhyming text.

Riddell, Chris. *Wendel's workshop* ill. by author. HarperCollins, 2010. ISBN 978-0-06-144930-7 Subj: Animals – mice. Character traits – cleanliness. Inventions. Robots.

Rim, Sujean. *Birdie's big-girl dress* ill. by author. Little, Brown, 2011. ISBN 978-0-316-13287-9 Subj: Birthdays. Clothing – dresses. Parties.

Rinker, Sherri Duskey. *Goodnight, goodnight, construction site* ill. by Tom Lichtenheld. Chronicle, 2011. ISBN 978-0-8118-7782-4 Subj: Bedtime. Trucks.

Riphagen, Loes. *Animals home alone.* Seven Footer, 2011. ISBN 978-1-934734-55-1 Subj: Animals. Wordless.

Ritz, Karen. *Windows with birds* ill. by author. Boyds Mills, 2010. ISBN 978-1-59078-656-7 Subj: Animals – cats. Friendship. Homes, houses. Moving.

Roberton, Fiona. *Wanted: the perfect pet* ill. by author. Penguin Group (USA), 2010. ISBN 978-0-399-25461-1 Subj: Birds – ducks. Disguises. Pets.

Roberts, Victoria. *The best pet ever* ill. by Deborah Allwright. Tiger Tales, 2010. ISBN 978-1-58925-089-5 Subj: Imagination. Pets.

Robey, Katharine Crawford. *Where's the party?* ill. by Kate Endle. Charlesbridge, 2011. ISBN 978-1-58089-268-1 Subj: Birds. Nature.

Robinson, Fiona. *What animals really like: a new song composed & conducted by Mr. Herbert Timberteeth* ill. by author. Abrams, 2011. ISBN 978-0-8109-8976-4 Subj: Animals. Careers – composers. Careers – conductors (music). Humorous stories. Songs.

Rocco, John. *Blackout* ill. by author. Hyperion/Disney, 2011. ISBN 978-1-4231-2190-9 Subj: Caldecott award honor books. Family life. Light, lights. Night.

Rockwell, Anne. *Apples and pumpkins* ill. by Lizzy Rockwell. Simon & Schuster, 2011. ISBN 978-1-4424-0350-5 Subj: Food. Holidays – Halloween.

At the supermarket ill. by author. Henry Holt, 2010. ISBN 978-0-8050-7662-2 Subj: Shopping. Stores.

First day of school ill. by Lizzy Rockwell. HarperCollins, 2011. ISBN 978-0-06-050191-4 Subj: School – first day.

St. Patrick's Day ill. by Lizzy Rockwell. HarperCollins, 2010. ISBN 978-0-06-050197-6 Subj: Holidays – St. Patrick's Day. School.

Rodriguez, Béatrice. *The chicken thief* ill. by author. Enchanted Lion, 2010. ISBN 978-1-59270-092-9 Subj: Animals – foxes. Birds – chickens. Wordless.

Fox and hen together ill. by author. Enchanted Lion, 2011. ISBN 978-1-59270-109-4 Subj: Animals – foxes. Birds – chickens. Friendship. Wordless.

Rodriguez, Sonia. *T is for tutu: a ballet alphabet* by Sonia Rodriguez and Kurt Browning; ill. by Wilson Ong. Sleeping Bear, 2011. ISBN 978-1-58536-312-4 Subj: ABC books. Ballet.

Rofé, Jennifer. *Piggies in the pumpkin patch* (Peterson, Mary)

Rohmann, Eric. *Bone dog* ill. by author. Roaring Brook, 2011. ISBN 978-1-59643-150-8 Subj: Anatomy – skeletons. Animals – dogs. Death. Holidays – Halloween.

Roode, Daniel. *Little Bea and the snowy day* ill. by author. HarperCollins, 2011. ISBN 978-0-06-199395-4 Subj: Activities – playing. Insects – bees. Rhyming text. Weather – snow.

Roop, Connie. *Down east in the ocean: a Maine counting book* (Roop, Peter)

Roop, Peter. *Down east in the ocean: a Maine counting book* by Peter Roop and Connie Roop; ill. by Nicole Fazio. Down East, 2011. ISBN 978-0-89272-709-4 Subj: Counting, numbers. Sea & seashore.

Root, Phyllis. *Big belching bog* ill. by Betsy Bowen. Univ. of Minnesota, 2010. ISBN 978-0-8166-3359-3 Subj: Ecology. Swamps.

Creak! said the bed ill. by Regan Dunnick. Candlewick, 2010. ISBN 978-0-7636-2004-2 Subj: Cumulative tales. Family life. Furniture – beds. Rhyming text. Sleep. Weather – storms.

Scrawny cat ill. by Alison Friend. Candlewick, 2011. ISBN 978-0-7636-4164-1 Subj: Animals – cats. Behavior – lost. Emotions – loneliness.

Rose, Deborah Lee. *All the seasons of the year* ill. by Kay Chorao. Abrams, 2010. ISBN 978-0-8109-8395-3 Subj: Animals – cats. Emotions – love. Family life – mothers. Rhyming text. Seasons.

Rose, Naomi C. *Tashi and the Tibetan flower cure* ill. by author. Lee & Low, 2011. ISBN 978-1-60060-425-6 Subj: Communities, neighborhoods. Ethnic groups in the U.S. – Tibetan Americans. Family life – grandfathers. Illness.

Rosen, Michael. *Tiny little fly* ill. by Kevin Waldron. Candlewick, 2010. ISBN 978-0-7636-4681-3 Subj: Animals. Insects – flies. Jungle.

Rosen, Michael J. *Chanukah lights* ill. by Robert Sabuda. Candlewick, 2011. ISBN 978-0-7636-5533-4 Subj: Format, unusual – toy & movable books. Holidays – Hanukkah.

Night of the pumpkinheads ill. by Hugh McMahon. Penguin Group (USA), 2011. ISBN 978-0-8037-3452-4 Subj: Contests. Holidays – Halloween.

Rosenberg, Liz. *Nobody* ill. by Julie Downing. Roaring Brook, 2010. ISBN 978-1-59643-120-1 Subj: Family life – parents. Imagination – imaginary friends. Morning.

Tyrannosaurus dad ill. by Matthew Myers. Roaring Brook, 2011. ISBN 978-1-59643-531-5 Subj: Dinosaurs. Family life – fathers.

Rosenthal, Amy Krouse. *Al Pha's bet* ill. by Delphine Durand. Penguin Group (USA), 2011. ISBN 978-0-399-24601-2 Subj: ABC books. Language. Royalty – kings.

Bedtime for Mommy ill. by LeUyen Pham. Bloomsbury, 2010. ISBN 978-1-59990-341-5 Subj: Bedtime. Family life – mothers.

One smart cookie: bite-size lessons for the school years and beyond ill. by Jane Dyer and Brooke Dyer. HarperCollins, 2010. ISBN 978-0-06-142970-5 Subj: Activities – baking, cooking. Behavior. Character traits. Food. Self-concept.

Plant a kiss ill. by Peter H. Reynolds. HarperCollins, 2011. ISBN 978-0-06-198675-8 Subj: Behavior – sharing. Emotions – love. Kissing.

This plus that: life's little equations ill. by Jen Corace. HarperCollins, 2011. ISBN 978-0-06-172655-2 Subj: Behavior. Concepts. Counting, numbers.

Rosenthal, Betsy R. *Which shoes would you choose?* ill. by Nancy Cote. Penguin Group (USA), 2010. ISBN 978-0-399-25013-2 Subj: Clothing – shoes. Rhyming text.

Rosenthal, Eileen. *I must have Bobo!* ill. by Marc Rosenthal. Simon & Schuster, 2011. ISBN 978-1-4424-0377-2 Subj: Animals – cats. Behavior – lost & found possessions. Toys.

Roslonek, Steve. *The shape song swingalong* ill. by David Sim. Barefoot, 2011. ISBN 978-1-84686-671-5 Subj: Activities – drawing. Concepts – shape. Songs.

Ross, Fiona. *Chilly Milly Moo* ill. by author. Candlewick, 2011. ISBN 978-0-7636-5693-5 Subj: Animals – bulls, cows. Character traits – being different.

Ross, Tony. *I want a party!* ill. by author. Andersen, 2011. ISBN 978-0-7613-8089-4 Subj: Parties. Royalty – princesses.

I want my light on! a Little Princess story ill. by author. Andersen, 2010. ISBN 978-0-7613-6443-6 Subj: Bedtime. Emotions – fear. Ghosts. Royalty – princesses.

I want to do it myself! a Little Princess story ill. by author. Andersen, 2011. ISBN 978-0-7613-7412-1 Subj: Camps, camping. Royalty – princesses.

I want two birthdays! ill. by author. Andersen, 2010. ISBN 978-0-7613-5495-6 Subj: Birthdays. Royalty – princesses.

Rossell, Judith. *Ruby and Leonard and the great big surprise* ill. by author. IPG/Little Hare, 2010. ISBN 978-1-921272-96-7 Subj: Activities – baking, cooking. Animals – mice. Birthdays. Family life – brothers & sisters.

Rostoker-Gruber, Karen. *Bandit's surprise* ill. by Vincent Nguyen. Marshall Cavendish, 2010. ISBN 978-0-7614-5623-0 Subj: Animals – babies. Animals – cats. Behavior – sharing.

Ferret fun ill. by Paul Rátz de Tagyos. Marshall Cavendish, 2011. ISBN 978-0-7614-5817-3 Subj: Animals – cats. Animals – ferrets. Pets.

Roth, Carol. *Will you still love me?* ill. by Daniel Howarth. Whitman, 2010. ISBN 978-0-8075-9114-7 Subj: Animals. Emotions – love. Family life – mothers. Family life – new sibling. Rhyming text.

Rotner, Shelley. *The buzz on bees: why are they disappearing?* by Shelley Rotner and Anne Woodhull; photos by author. Holiday House, 2010. ISBN 978-0-8234-2247-0 Subj: Ecology. Insects – bees.

I'm adopted! by Shelley Rotner and Sheila M. Kelly; photos by author. Holiday House, 2011. ISBN 978-0-8234-2294-4 Subj: Adoption.

Rubin, Adam. *Those darn squirrels and the cat next door* ill. by Daniel Salmieri. Clarion, 2011. ISBN 978-0-547-42922-9 Subj: Animals – cats. Animals – squirrels. Birds. Old age.

Rubinger, Ami. *Dog number 1 dog number 10* tr. by Ray Baitner; ill. by author. Abbeville, 2011. ISBN 978-0-7892-1066-1 Subj: Animals – dogs. Counting, numbers. Rhyming text.

I dream of an elephant ill. by author. Abbeville, 2010. ISBN 978-0-7892-1058-6 Subj: Animals – elephants. Concepts – color. Rhyming text.

Rubinstein, Gary. *The girl who never made mistakes* (Pett, Mark)

Ruddell, Deborah. *Who said coo?* ill. by Robin Luebs. Simon & Schuster, 2010. ISBN 978-1-4169-8510-5 Subj: Animals – pigs. Bedtime. Behavior – cooperation. Birds – owls. Birds – pigeons.

Rueda, Claudia. *No* tr. by Elisa Amado; ill. by author. Groundwood, 2010. ISBN 978-0-88899-991-7 Subj: Animals – bears. Bedtime. Hibernation.

Rumford, James. *Rain school* ill. by author. Houghton Harcourt, 2010. ISBN 978-0-547-24307-8 Subj: Foreign lands – Chad. School. Weather – rain.

Tiger and turtle ill. by author. Roaring Brook, 2010. ISBN 978-1-59643-416-5 Subj: Animals – tigers. Behavior – fighting, arguing. Friendship. Reptiles – turtles, tortoises.

Runton, Andy. *Owly and Wormy: friends all aflutter!* ill. by author. Simon & Schuster, 2011. ISBN 978-1-4169-5774-4 Subj: Animals – worms. Birds. Friendship. Insects – butterflies, caterpillars. Metamorphosis. Wordless.

Russell, Natalie. *Brown Rabbit in the city* ill. by author. Penguin Group (USA), 2010. ISBN 978-0-670-01234-3 Subj: Animals – rabbits. Cities, towns. Friendship.

Russo, Marisabina. *I will come back for you: a family in hiding during World War II* ill. by author. Random House, 2011. ISBN 978-0-375-86695-1 Subj: Family life – grandmothers. Foreign lands – Italy. Holocaust. Jewish culture. War.

A very big bunny ill. by author. Random House, 2010. ISBN 978-0-375-84463-8 Subj: Animals – rabbits. Character traits – being different. Concepts – size. Friendship. School. Self-concept.

Ruzzier, Sergio. *Hey, rabbit!* ill. by author. Roaring Brook, 2010. ISBN 978-1-59643-502-5 Subj: Animals – rabbits. Friendship. Imagination.

Ryan, Candace. *Ribbit rabbit* ill. by Mike Lowery. Walker, 2011. ISBN 978-0-8027-2180-8 Subj: Animals – rabbits. Friendship. Frogs & toads.

Ryan, Pam Muñoz. *Tony Baloney* ill. by Edwin Fotheringham. Scholastic, 2011. ISBN 978-0-545-23135-0 Subj: Birds – penguins. Family life – brothers & sisters.

Rylant, Cynthia. *Brownie and Pearl get dolled up* ill. by Brian Biggs. Simon & Schuster, 2010. ISBN 978-1-4169-8631-7 Subj: Activities – playing. Animals – cats. Character traits – appearance.

Brownie and Pearl grab a bite ill. by Brian Biggs. Simon & Schuster, 2011. ISBN 978-1-4169-8634-8 Subj: Animals – cats. Food.

Brownie and Pearl hit the hay ill. by Brian Biggs. Simon & Schuster, 2011. ISBN 978-1-4169-8635-5 Subj: Animals – cats. Bedtime.

Brownie and Pearl see the sights ill. by Brian Biggs. Simon & Schuster, 2010. ISBN 978-1-4169-8637-9 Subj: Animals – cats. Seasons – winter. Shopping.

Brownie and Pearl take a dip ill. by Brian Biggs. Simon & Schuster, 2011. ISBN 978-1-4169-8638-6 Subj: Animals – cats. Sports – swimming.

Sabuda, Robert. *Beauty and the beast: a pop-up book of the classic fairy tale* ill. by author. Simon & Schuster, 2010. ISBN 978-1-4169-6079-9 Subj: Animals. Character traits – appearance. Character traits – loyalty. Emotions – love. Folk & fairy tales. Format, unusual – toy & movable books. Magic.

Gods and heroes (Reinhart, Matthew)

Sacre, Antonio. *La Noche Buena: a Christmas story* ill. by Angela Dominguez. Abrams, 2010. ISBN 978-0-8109-8967-2 Subj: Ethnic groups in the U.S. – Cuban Americans. Family life – grandmothers. Holidays – Christmas.

A mango in the hand: a story told through proverbs ill. by Sebastià Serra. Abrams, 2011. ISBN 978-0-8109-9734-9 Subj: Character traits – generosity. Family life. Foreign lands – Cuba. Foreign languages.

Safran, Sheri. *All kinds of families: a lift-the-flap book* ill. by Rachel Fuller. IPG/Trafalgar Square, 2011. ISBN 978-1-85707-756-8 Subj: Family life. Format, unusual – toy & movable books.

Sakai, Komako. *Mad at Mommy* ill. by author. Scholastic, 2010. ISBN 978-0-545-21209-0 Subj: Animals – rabbits. Emotions – anger. Family life – mothers.

Saltzberg, Barney. *All around the seasons* ill. by author. Candlewick, 2010. ISBN 978-0-7636-3694-4 Subj: Rhyming text. Seasons.

Kisses: a pull, touch, lift, squeak, and smooch book! ill. by author. Houghton Harcourt, 2010. ISBN 978-0-15-206534-8 Subj: Emotions – love. Format, unusual – toy & movable books. Kissing. Rhyming text.

Salzano, Tammi. *One little blueberry* ill. by Kat Whelan. Tiger Tales, 2011. ISBN 978-1-58925-859-4 Subj: Counting, numbers. Food. Insects.

One rainy day ill. by Hannah Wood. ME Media/Tiger Tales, 2011. ISBN 978-1-58925-860-0 Subj: Birds – ducks. Concepts – color. Format, unusual – board books. Weather – rain.

Sampson, Michael. *Kitty Cat, Kitty Cat, are you going to sleep?* (Martin, Bill, Jr.)

Samuels, Barbara. *The trucker* ill. by author. Farrar, 2010. ISBN 978-0-374-37804-2 Subj: Animals – cats. Toys. Trucks.

San Souci, Robert D., reteller. *Robin Hood and the golden arrow* ill. by E. B. Lewis. Scholastic, 2010. ISBN 978-0-439-62538-8 Subj: Folk & fairy tales. Foreign lands – England. Sports – archery.

Santoro, Lucio. *Wild oceans: a pop-up book with revolutionary technology* by Lucio Santoro and Meera Santoro; ill. by Lucio Santoro. Simon & Schuster, 2010. ISBN 978-1-4169-8467-2 Subj: Format, unusual – toy & movable books. Sea & seashore.

Santoro, Meera. *Wild oceans: a pop-up book with revolutionary technology* (Santoro, Lucio)

Santoro, Scott. *Which way to witch school?* ill. by author. HarperCollins, 2010. ISBN 978-0-06-078181-1 Subj: Rhyming text. School. Witches.

Sarcone-Roach, Julia. *Subway story* ill. by author. Random House, 2011. ISBN 978-0-375-85859-8 Subj: Sea & seashore. Trains.

Sartell, Debra. *Time for bed, Baby Ted* ill. by Kay Chorao. Holiday House, 2010. ISBN 978-0-8234-1968-5 Subj: Babies. Bedtime. Rhyming text.

Sattler, Jennifer. *Chick 'n' Pug.* Bloomsbury, 2010. ISBN 978-1-59990-534-1 Subj: Animals – dogs. Birds – chickens.

Pig kahuna ill. by author. Bloomsbury, 2011. ISBN 978-1-59990-635-5 Subj: Animals – pigs. Emotions – fear. Sports – surfing.

Sauer, Tammi. *Mostly monsterly* ill. by Scott Magoon. Simon & Schuster, 2010. ISBN 978-1-4169-

6110-9 Subj: Character traits – being different. Character traits – individuality. Monsters. School.

Mr. Duck means business ill. by Jeff Mack. Simon & Schuster, 2011. ISBN 978-1-4169-8522-8 Subj: Animals. Birds – ducks. Character traits – compromising.

Saunders, Karen. *Baby Badger's wonderful night* ill. by Dubravka Kolanovic. Egmont USA, 2011. ISBN 978-1-60684-172-3 Subj: Animals – badgers. Emotions – fear. Family life – fathers. Night.

Savage, Stephen. *Where's Walrus?* ill. by author. Scholastic, 2011. ISBN 978-0-439-70049-8 Subj: Animals – walruses. Behavior – running away. Careers – zookeepers. Clothing – hats. Disguises. Wordless.

Say, Allen. *The boy in the garden* ill. by author. Houghton Harcourt, 2010. ISBN 978-0-547-21410-8 Subj: Birds – cranes. Character traits – kindness. Foreign lands – Japan. Gardens, gardening.

Sayre, April Pulley. *If you're hoppy* ill. by Jackie Urbanovic. HarperCollins, 2011. ISBN 978-0-06-156634-9 Subj: Animals. Rhyming text.

Meet the howlers! ill. by Woody Miller. Charlesbridge, 2010. ISBN 978-1-57091-733-2 Subj: Animals – monkeys.

Rah, rah, radishes! a vegetable chant photos by author. Simon & Schuster, 2011. ISBN 978-1-4424-2141-7 Subj: Food. Rhyming text.

Turtle, turtle, watch out! ill. by Annie Patterson. Charlesbridge, 2010. ISBN 978-1-58089-148-6 Subj: Character traits – kindness to animals. Migration. Reptiles – turtles, tortoises.

Scanlon, Liz Garton. *Noodle and Lou* ill. by Arthur Howard. Simon & Schuster, 2011. ISBN 978-1-4424-0288-1 Subj: Animals – worms. Birds. Friendship. Self-concept.

Schachner, Judy. *Skippyjon Jones class action* ill. by author. Penguin Group (USA), 2011. ISBN 978-0-525-42228-0 Subj: Animals – cats. Animals – dogs. School.

Schaefer, Carole Lexa. *Who's there?* ill. by Pierr Morgan. Penguin Group (USA), 2011. ISBN 978-0-670-01241-1 Subj: Bedtime. Emotions – fear.

Schaefer, Lola. *Frankie Stein starts school* ill. by Kevan Atteberry. Marshall Cavendish, 2010. ISBN 978-0-7614-5656-8 Subj: Behavior – teasing. Character traits – being different. Friendship. Monsters. School – first day.

Just one bite: 11 animals and their bites at life size! ill. by Geoff Waring. Chronicle, 2010. ISBN 978-0-8118-6473-2 Subj: Animals. Food.

Scharschmidt, Sherry. *Tuck me in!* (Hacohen, Dean)

Scheffler, Axel. *The little puddle* ill. by author. Candlewick, 2011. ISBN 978-0-7636-5878-6 Subj: Animals – mice. Animals – rabbits. Behavior – mistakes. Toilet training.

The super scooter ill. by author. Candlewick, 2011. ISBN 978-0-7636-5877-9 Subj: Activities – playing. Animals – mice. Animals – rabbits. Friendship.

Schmid, Paul. *Hugs from Pearl* ill. by author. HarperCollins, 2011. ISBN 978-0-06-180434-2 Subj: Animals – porcupines. Hugging. Problem solving. School.

A pet for Petunia ill. by author. HarperCollins, 2011. ISBN 978-0-06-196331-5 Subj: Animals – skunks. Pets. Toys.

Schnur, Susan. *Tashlich at Turtle Rock* by Susan Schnur and Anna Schnur Fishman; ill. by Alex Steele-Morgan. Lerner/Kar-Ben, 2010. ISBN 978-0-7613-4509-1 Subj: Holidays – Rosh Hashanah. Jewish culture.

Schoebinger, Chris. *Snow angels* (Randall, Angel)

Schoenherr, Ian. *Don't spill the beans!* ill. by author. HarperCollins, 2010. ISBN 978-0-06-172457-2 Subj: Animals – bears. Behavior – secrets. Birthdays. Rhyming text.

Schoonmaker, Elizabeth. *Square cat* ill. by author. Simon & Schuster, 2011. ISBN 978-1-4424-0619-3 Subj: Animals – cats. Character traits – individuality. Concepts – shape. Self-concept.

Schories, Pat. *When Jack goes out* ill. by author. Boyds Mills, 2010. ISBN 978-1-59078-652-9 Subj: Aliens. Animals – dogs. Wordless.

Schubert, Dieter. *The umbrella* (Schubert, Ingrid)

Schubert, Ingrid. *The umbrella* by Ingrid Schubert and Dieter Schubert; ill. by Ingrid Schubert. Lemniscaat, 2011. ISBN 978-1-9359-5400-2 Subj: Animals – dogs. Umbrellas. Wordless. World.

Schubert, Leda. *Feeding the sheep* ill. by Andrea U'Ren. Farrar, 2010. ISBN 978-0-374-32296-0 Subj: Activities – weaving. Animals – sheep. Family life – mothers. Farms. Rhyming text.

The Princess of Borscht ill. by Bonnie Christensen. Roaring Brook, 2011. ISBN 978-1-59643-515-5 Subj: Activities – baking, cooking. Family life – grandmothers. Illness. Jewish culture.

Reading to Peanut ill. by Amanda Haley. Holiday House, 2011. ISBN 978-0-8234-2339-2 Subj: Activities – writing. Animals – dogs. Books, reading. Character traits – perseverance.

Schulman, Janet. *10 Easter egg hunters: a holiday counting book* ill. by Linda Davick. Random House, 2011. ISBN 978-0-375-86787-3 Subj: Counting, numbers. Eggs. Holidays – Easter. Rhyming text.

10 Valentine friends: a holiday counting book ill. by Linda Davick. Random House, 2011. ISBN 978-0-375-86967-9 Subj: Counting, numbers. Holidays – Valentine's Day. Rhyming text.

Schwartz, Howard. *Gathering sparks* ill. by Kristina Swarner. Roaring Brook, 2010. ISBN 978-1-59643-280-2 Subj: Character traits – kindness. Character traits – responsibility. Family life – grandfathers. Jewish culture. Religion.

Schwartz, Roslyn. *The Vole brothers* ill. by author. OwlKids, 2011. ISBN 978-1-926818-83-2 Subj: Animals – voles. Family life – brothers. Food.

Schwarz, Viviane. *There are no cats in this book* ill. by author. Candlewick, 2010. ISBN 978-0-7636-4954-8 Subj: Animals – cats. Format, unusual – toy & movable books.

Scotton, Rob. *Splish, splash, Splat!* ill. by author. HarperCollins, 2011. ISBN 978-0-06-197868-5 Subj: Animals – cats. Emotions – fear. Friendship. Sports – swimming.

Sebe, Masayuki. *Let's count to 100!* ill. by author. Kids Can, 2011. ISBN 978-1-55453-661-0 Subj: Counting, numbers.

Sedaka, Neil. *Waking up is hard to do* by Neil Sedaka and Howard Greenfield; ill. by Daniel Miyares. Imagine, 2010. ISBN 978-1-936140-13-8 Subj: Morning. Reptiles – alligators, crocodiles. Songs.

Seder, Rufus Butler. *The Wizard of Oz: a Scanimation book* ill. by author. Workman, 2011. ISBN 978-0-7611-6373-2 Subj: Format, unusual – toy & movable books. Wizards.

Seeger, Laura Vaccaro. *What if?* ill. by author. Roaring Brook, 2010. ISBN 978-1-59643-398-4 Subj: Animals – seals. Behavior – sharing. Friendship. Toys – balls.

Segal, John. *Pirates don't take baths* ill. by author. Penguin Group (USA), 2011. ISBN 978-0-399-25425-3 Subj: Activities – bathing. Animals – pigs. Imagination.

Sendak, Maurice. *Bumble-ardy* ill. by author. HarperCollins, 2011. ISBN 978-0-06-205198-1 Subj: Animals – pigs. Birthdays. Parties. Rhyming text.

Sendelbach, Brian. *The underpants zoo* ill. by author. Scholastic, 2011. ISBN 978-0-545-24935-

5 Subj: Clothing – underwear. Rhyming text. Zoos.

Seven, John. *The ocean story* ill. by Jana Christy. Picture Window, 2011. ISBN 978-1-4048-6785-7 Subj: Ecology. Sea & seashore. Water.

Shannon, Molly. *Tilly the trickster* ill. by Ard Hoyt. Abrams, 2011. ISBN 978-1-4197-0030-9 Subj: Behavior – misbehavior.

Shapiro, J. H. *Magic trash: a story of Tyree Guyton and his art* ill. by Vanessa Brantley-Newton. Charlesbridge, 2011. ISBN 978-1-58089-385-5 Subj: Art. Careers – artists. Cities, towns. Ethnic groups in the U.S. – African Americans.

Sharratt, Nick. *What's in the witch's kitchen?* ill. by author. Candlewick, 2011. ISBN 978-0-7636-5224-1 Subj: Format, unusual – toy & movable books. Rhyming text. Witches.

Shaskan, Stephen. *A dog is a dog* ill. by author. Chronicle, 2011. ISBN 978-0-8118-7896-8 Subj: Animals. Animals – dogs. Circular tales. Disguises. Rhyming text.

Shaskan, Trisha Speed. *Seriously, Cinderella is so annoying! the story of Cinderella as told by the wicked stepmother* ill. by Gerald Guerlais. Picture Window, 2011. ISBN 978-1-4048-6674-4 Subj: Family life – stepfamilies. Folk & fairy tales. Humorous stories.

Shaw, Hannah. *School for bandits* ill. by author. Random House, 2011. ISBN 978-0-375-86768-2 Subj: Animals – raccoons. Behavior – misbehavior. Character traits – helpfulness. Etiquette. School.

Shaw, Natalie, adapt. *Olivia plans a tea party* ill. by Patrick Spaziante. Simon & Schuster, 2011. ISBN 978-1-4423-3962-0 Subj: Animals – pigs. Parties.

Shea, Bob. *Dinosaur vs. the library* ill. by author. Hyperion/Disney, 2011. ISBN 978-1-4231-3338-4 Subj: Dinosaurs. Libraries.

Dinosaur vs. the potty ill. by author. Hyperion/Disney, 2010. ISBN 978-1-4231-3339-1 Subj: Dinosaurs. Toilet training.

I'm a shark ill. by author. HarperCollins, 2011. ISBN 978-0-06-199846-1 Subj: Emotions – fear. Fish – sharks.

Oh, Daddy! ill. by author. HarperCollins, 2010. ISBN 978-0-06-173080-1 Subj: Animals – hippopotamuses. Family life – fathers.

Race you to bed ill. by author. HarperCollins, 2010. ISBN 978-0-06-170417-8 Subj: Bedtime. Rhyming text.

Shea, Susan A. *Do you know which one will grow?* ill. by Tom Slaughter. Blue Apple, 2011. ISBN 978-1-60905-062-7 Subj: Behavior – growing up. Concepts – change. Format, unusual – toy & movable books. Rhyming text.

Sheridan, Sara. *I'm me!* ill. by Margaret Chamberlain. Scholastic, 2011. ISBN 978-0-545-28222-2 Subj: Activities – playing. Family life – aunts, uncles. Imagination.

Shields, Gillian. *Library Lily* ill. by Francesca Chessa. Eerdmans, 2011. ISBN 978-0-8028-5401-8 Subj: Activities – playing. Books, reading. Friendship. Libraries.

When the world was waiting for you ill. by Anna Currey. Bloomsbury, 2011. ISBN 978-1-59990-531-0 Subj: Animals – rabbits. Family life – new sibling. Rhyming text.

Shireen, Nadia. *Good little wolf* ill. by author. Random House, 2011. ISBN 978-0-375-86904-4 Subj: Animals – wolves. Character traits – individuality. Self-concept.

Shoemaker, Marla K. *Art museum opposites* (Friedland, Katy)

Shoulders, Michael. *Goodnight Baby Bear* ill. by Teri Weidner. Sleeping Bear, 2010. ISBN 978-1-58536-471-8 Subj: Animals – bears. Bedtime. Books, reading. Family life.

Siddals, Mary McKenna. *Compost stew: an A to Z recipe for the earth* ill. by Ashley Wolff. Tricycle, 2010. ISBN 978-1-58246-316-2 Subj: ABC books. Ecology. Rhyming text.

Sidman, Joyce. *Swirl by swirl: spirals in nature* ill. by Beth Krommes. Houghton Harcourt, 2011. ISBN 978-0-547-31583-6 Subj: Concepts – shape.

Ubiquitous: celebrating nature's survivors ill. by Beckie Prange. Houghton Mifflin, 2010. ISBN 978-0-618-71719-4 Subj: Nature. Poetry.

Siegel, Mark. *Moving house* ill. by author. Roaring Brook, 2011. ISBN 978-1-59643-635-0 Subj: Homes, houses. Moving.

Siegel, Randy. *Grandma's smile* ill. by DyAnne DiSalvo. Roaring Brook, 2010. ISBN 978-1-59643-438-7 Subj: Activities – traveling. Anatomy – faces. Behavior – lost & found possessions. Family life – grandmothers.

Sierra, Judy. *Tell the truth, B.B. Wolf* ill. by J. Otto Seibold. Random House, 2010. ISBN 978-0-375-85620-4 Subj: Activities – storytelling. Animals – wolves. Character traits – honesty. Folk & fairy tales. Humorous stories.

We love our school! a read-together rebus story. Random House, 2011. ISBN 978-0-375-86728-6 Subj: Animals. Rebuses. Rhyming text. School – first day.

Zoozical ill. by Marc Brown. Random House, 2011. ISBN 978-0-375-86847-4 Subj: Animals. Rhyming text. Theater. Zoos.

Sill, Cathryn. *About hummingbirds: a guide for children* ill. by John Sill. Peachtree, 2011. ISBN 978-1-56145-588-1 Subj: Birds – hummingbirds.

Silverman, Erica. *The Hanukkah hop!* ill. by Steven D'Amico. Simon & Schuster, 2011. ISBN 978-1-4424-0604-9 Subj: Activities – dancing. Holidays – Hanukkah. Jewish culture. Rhyming text.

Simard, Rémy. *Hocus pocus* (Desrosiers, Sylvie)

Simhaee, Rebeka. *Sara finds a mitzva* ill. by Michael Weber. Hachai, 2010. ISBN 978-1-929628-46-9 Subj: Behavior – lost & found possessions. Family life – grandmothers. Jewish culture.

Siminovich, Lorena. *I like bugs* ill. by author. Candlewick, 2010. ISBN 978-0-7636-4802-2 Subj: Counting, numbers. Format, unusual – board books. Insects.

I like vegetables ill. by author. Candlewick, 2011. ISBN 978-0-7636-5283-8 Subj: Concepts – opposites. Food. Format, unusual. Gardens, gardening.

Singer, Marilyn. *Caterpillars.* EarlyLight, 2011. ISBN 978-0-9797455-7-7 Subj: Insects – butterflies, caterpillars.

Tallulah's tutu ill. by Alexandra Boiger. Clarion, 2011. ISBN 978-0-547-17353-5 Subj: Ballet. Character traits – perseverance.

What is your dog doing? ill. by Kathleen Habbley. Simon & Schuster, 2011. ISBN 978-1-4169-7931-9 Subj: Animals – dogs. Rhyming text.

Sís, Peter. *Madlenka, soccer star* ill. by author. Farrar, 2010. ISBN 978-0-374-34702-4 Subj: Communities, neighborhoods. Imagination. Sports – soccer.

Skeers, Linda. *Tutus aren't my style* ill. by Anne Wilsdorf. Penguin Group (USA), 2010. ISBN 978-0-8037-3212-4 Subj: Ballet. Character traits – appearance. Character traits – individuality.

Slack, Michael. *Monkey truck* ill. by author. Henry Holt, 2011. ISBN 978-0-8050-8878-6 Subj: Animals. Animals – monkeys. Character traits – helpfulness. Jungle. Rhyming text.

Slade, Suzanne. *Climbing Lincoln's steps: the African American journey* ill. by Colin Bootman. Whitman, 2010. ISBN 978-0-8075-1204-3 Subj: Ethnic groups in the U.S. – African Americans. Prejudice. U.S. history.

What's the difference? an endangered animal subtraction story ill. by Joan Waites. Sylvan Dell, 2010. ISBN 978-1-60718-070-8 Subj: Animals – endangered animals. Counting, numbers.

Slate, Jenny. *Marcel the shell with shoes on: things about me* by Jenny Slate and Dean Fleischer-Camp; ill. by Amy Lind. Penguin Group (USA), 2011. ISBN 978-1-59514-455-3 Subj: Imagination. Shells.

Slater, Teddy. *Smooch your pooch* ill. by Arthur Howard. Scholastic, 2010. ISBN 978-0-545-16736-9 Subj: Animals – dogs. Rhyming text.

Slegers, Liesbet. *The child in the manger* ill. by author. Clavis, 2010. ISBN 978-1-60537-084-2 Subj: Holidays – Christmas. Religion.

Funny ears ill. by author. Clavis, 2011. ISBN 978-1-60537-088-0 Subj: Anatomy – ears. Animals. Format, unusual – board books.

Funny feet ill. by author. Clavis, 2011. ISBN 978-1-60537-089-7 Subj: Anatomy – feet. Animals. Format, unusual – board books.

Funny tails ill. by author. Clavis, 2011. ISBN 978-1-60537-090-3 Subj: Anatomy – tails. Animals. Format, unusual – board books.

Katie goes to the doctor ill. by author. Clavis, 2011. ISBN 978-1-60537-076-7 Subj: Careers – doctors.

Kevin goes to the library ill. by author. Clavis, 2011. ISBN 978-1-60537-075-0 Subj: Libraries.

Playing ill. by author. Clavis, 2011. ISBN 978-1-60537-091-0 Subj: Activities – playing. Format, unusual – board books.

Smallcomb, Pam. *Earth to Clunk* ill. by Joe Berger. Penguin Group (USA), 2011. ISBN 978-0-8037-3439-5 Subj: Aliens. Family life – brothers & sisters. Pen pals. School. Space & space ships.

I'm not ill. by Robert Weinstock. Random House, 2011. ISBN 978-0-375-86115-4 Subj: Character traits – individuality. Friendship. Self-concept.

Smallman, Steve. *Dragon stew* ill. by Lee Wildish. Good Books, 2010. ISBN 978-1-56148-695-3 Subj: Dragons. Rhyming text. Vikings.

Smee, Nicola. *What's the matter, Bunny Blue?* ill. by author. Boxer, 2010. ISBN 978-1-906250-91-1 Subj: Animals – rabbits. Behavior – lost. Family life – grandmothers. Rhyming text.

Smith, Alex T. *Foxy and Egg* ill. by author. Holiday House, 2011. ISBN 978-0-8234-2330-9 Subj: Animals – foxes. Behavior – trickery. Eggs. Humorous stories.

Smith, Cynthia Leitich. *Holler Loudly* ill. by Barry Gott. Penguin Group (USA), 2010. ISBN 978-0-525-42256-3 Subj: Character traits – being different. Tall tales.

Smith, Danna. *Pirate nap: a book of colors* ill. by Valeria Petrone. Clarion, 2011. ISBN 978-0-574-57531-5 Subj: Concepts – color. Pirates. Rhyming text.

Smith, David J. *This child, every child: a book about the world's children* ill. by Shelagh Armstrong. Kids Can, 2011. ISBN 978-1-55453-466-1 Subj: World.

Smith, Lane. *Grandpa Green* ill. by author. Roaring Brook, 2011. ISBN 978-1-59643-607-7 Subj: Caldecott award honor books. Family life – great-grandparents. Gardens, gardening. Memories, memory. Old age.

It's a book ill. by author. Roaring Brook, 2010. ISBN 978-1-59643-606-0 Subj: Animals. Books, reading. Humorous stories.

Smith, Linda. *The inside tree* ill. by David Parkins. HarperCollins, 2010. ISBN 978-0-06-028241-7 Subj: Animals – dogs. Homes, houses. Humorous stories. Trees.

Smith, Marie. *S is for Smithsonian: America's museum alphabet* by Marie Smith and Roland Smith; ill. by Gijsbert van Frankenhuyzen. Sleeping Bear, 2010. ISBN 978-1-58536-314-8 Subj: ABC books. Museums. U.S. history.

Smith, Roland. *S is for Smithsonian: America's museum alphabet* (Smith, Marie)

Snicket, Lemony. *13 words* ill. by Maira Kalman. HarperCollins, 2010. ISBN 978-0-06-166465-6 Subj: Animals – dogs. Birds. Language.

Snyder, Betsy. *Sweet dreams lullaby* ill. by author. Random House, 2010. ISBN 978-0-375-85852-9 Subj: Bedtime. Lullabies. Nature. Rhyming text.

Snyder, Laurel. *Baxter, the pig who wanted to be kosher* ill. by David Goldin. Tricycle, 2010. ISBN 978-1-58246-315-5 Subj: Animals – pigs. Jewish culture.

Solheim, James. *Born yesterday: the diary of a young journalist* ill. by Simon James. Penguin Group (USA), 2010. ISBN 978-0-399-25155-9 Subj: Activities – writing. Babies. Humorous stories.

Soltis, Sue. *Nothing like a puffin* ill. by Bob Kolar. Candlewick, 2011. ISBN 978-0-7636-3617-3 Subj: Birds – puffins.

Soman, David. *The amazing adventures of Bumblebee Boy* by David Soman and Jacky Davis; ill. by David Soman. Penguin Group (USA), 2011. ISBN 978-0-8037-3418-0 Subj: Activities – playing. Family life – brothers. Imagination.

Ladybug Girl and the Bug Squad by David Soman and Jacky Davis; ill. by David Soman. Penguin

Group (USA), 2011. ISBN 978-0-8037-3419-7 Subj: Activities – playing. Behavior – cooperation. Friendship. Imagination.

Ladybug Girl at the beach by David Soman and Jacky Davis; ill. by David Soman. Penguin Group (USA), 2010. ISBN 978-0-8037-3416-6 Subj: Emotions – fear. Sea & seashore – beaches.

Souders, Taryn. *Whole-y cow! fractions are fun* ill. by Tatjana Mai-Wyss. Sleeping Bear, 2010. ISBN 978-1-58536-460-2 Subj: Animals – bulls, cows. Counting, numbers. Rhyming text.

Sperring, Mark. *The sunflower sword* ill. by Miriam Latimer. Andersen, 2011. ISBN 978-0-7613-7486-2 Subj: Dragons. Friendship. Knights.

Spinelli, Eileen. *Buzz* ill. by Vincent Nguyen. Simon & Schuster, 2010. ISBN 978-1-4169-4925-1 Subj: Activities – flying. Insects – bees.

Do you have a cat? ill. by Geraldo Valério. Eerdmans, 2010. ISBN 978-0-8028-5351-6 Subj: Animals – cats. Rhyming text.

Do you have a dog? ill. by Geraldo Valério. Eerdmans, 2011. ISBN 978-0-8028-5387-5 Subj: Animals – dogs. Rhyming text.

Miss Fox's class earns a field trip ill. by Anne Kennedy. Whitman, 2010. ISBN 978-0-8075-5169-1 Subj: Animals – foxes. Counting, numbers. School – field trips.

Miss Fox's class shapes up ill. by Anne Kennedy. Whitman, 2011. ISBN 978-0-8075-5171-4 Subj: Animals – foxes. Careers – teachers. Health & fitness – exercise. School.

Now it is summer ill. by Mary Newell DePalma. Eerdmans, 2011. ISBN 978-0-8028-5340-0 Subj: Animals – mice. Family life. Seasons – fall. Seasons – summer.

The perfect Christmas ill. by JoAnn Adinolfi. Henry Holt, 2011. ISBN 978-0-8050-9702-4 Subj: Family life. Holidays – Christmas. Rhyming text.

Spinelli, Jerry. *I can be anything!* ill. by Jimmy Liao. Little, Brown, 2010. ISBN 978-0-316-16226-5 Subj: Careers. Rhyming text.

Spires, Ashley. *Small Saul* ill. by author. Kids Can, 2011. ISBN 978-1-55453-503-3 Subj: Character traits – being different. Character traits – smallness. Pirates.

Spradlin, Michael P. *Baseball from A to Z* ill. by Macky Pamintuan. HarperCollins, 2010. ISBN 978-0-06-124081-2 Subj: ABC books. Sports – baseball.

Off like the wind! the first ride of the Pony Express ill. by Layne Johnson. Walker, 2010. ISBN 978-0-8027-9652-3 Subj: Careers – postal workers. U.S. history – frontier & pioneer life.

Srinivasan, Divya. *Little Owl's night* ill. by author. Penguin Group (USA), 2011. ISBN 978-0-670-01295-4 Subj: Animals. Birds – owls. Night.

Staake, Bob. *The first pup: the real story of how Bo got to the White House* ill. by author. Feiwel & Friends, 2010. ISBN 978-0-312-61346-4 Subj: Animals – dogs. Pets.

Look! A book! ill. by author. Little, Brown, 2011. ISBN 978-0-316-11862-0 Subj: Books, reading. Picture puzzles. Rhyming text.

Stalder, Päivi. *Ernest's first Easter* ill. by Frauke Weldin. NorthSouth, 2010. ISBN 978-0-7358-2241-2 Subj: Animals – rabbits. Eggs. Holidays – Easter.

Stampler, Ann Redisch, reteller. *The rooster prince of Breslov* ill. by Eugene Yelchin. Clarion, 2010. ISBN 978-0-618-98974-4 Subj: Birds – chickens. Folk & fairy tales. Jewish culture. Royalty – princes.

Stanley, Malaika Rose. *Baby Ruby bawled* ill. by Ken Wilson-Max. Tamarind, 2011. ISBN 978-1-84-853017-1 Subj: Babies. Bedtime. Emotions. Family life.

Stead, Philip C. *Jonathan and the big blue boat* ill. by author. Roaring Brook, 2011. ISBN 978-1-59643-562-9 Subj: Activities – traveling. Behavior – lost. Boats, ships. Toys – bears.

A sick day for Amos McGee ill. by Erin E. Stead. Roaring Brook, 2010. ISBN 978-1-59643-402-8 Subj: Animals. Caldecott award books. Illness. Old age. Zoos.

Steele, Philip. *Trains: the slide-out, see-through story of world-famous trains and railroads* ill. by Sebastian Quigley and Nicholas Forder. Kingfisher, 2010. ISBN 978-0-7534-6465-6 Subj: Format, unusual – toy & movable books. Trains.

Steggall, Susan. *Busy boats* ill. by author. Frances Lincoln, 2011. ISBN 978-1-84780-074-9 Subj: Boats, ships.

Stein, David Ezra. *Interrupting chicken* ill. by author. Candlewick, 2010. ISBN 978-0-7636-4168-9 Subj: Bedtime. Birds – chickens. Caldecott award honor books. Humorous stories.

Love, Mouserella ill. by author. Penguin Group (USA), 2011. ISBN 978-0-399-25410-9 Subj: Activities – writing. Animals – mice. Family life – grandmothers. Letters, cards.

Stein, Eric. *White water* (Bandy, Michael S.)

Stein, Peter. *Cars galore* ill. by Bob Staake. Candlewick, 2011. ISBN 978-0-7636-4743-8 Subj: Automobiles. Rhyming text.

Stemple, Heidi E. Y. *Not all princesses dress in pink* (Yolen, Jane)

Stephens, Helen. *Fleabag* ill. by author. Henry Holt, 2010. ISBN 978-0-8050-7975-2 Subj: Animals – dogs. Moving.

Steven, Kenneth. *The biggest thing in the world* ill. by Melanie Mitchell. IPG/Lion, 2010. ISBN 978-0-7459-6204-7 Subj: Animals – polar bears. Character traits – questioning. Emotions – love. Family life – mothers.

Stevens, April. *Edwin speaks up* ill. by Sophie Blackall. Random House, 2011. ISBN 978-0-375-85337-1 Subj: Babies. Birthdays. Shopping.

Stevens, Janet. *The little red pen* by Janet Stevens and Susan Stevens Crummel; ill. by Janet Stevens. Houghton Harcourt, 2011. ISBN 978-0-15-206432-7 Subj: Behavior – cooperation. Humorous stories. School.

Stewart, Amber. *Puddle's new school* ill. by Layn Marlow. Barron's, 2011. ISBN 978-0-7641-4683-1 Subj: Birds – ducks. School – first day.

Stewart, Melissa. *A place for frogs* ill. by Higgins Bond. Peachtree, 2010. ISBN 978-1-56145-521-8 Subj: Ecology. Frogs & toads.

Stickland, Henrietta. *A number of dinosaurs: a pop-up counting book* (Stickland, Paul)

Stickland, Paul. *A number of dinosaurs: a pop-up counting book* by Paul Stickland and Henrietta Stickland. Sterling, 2010. ISBN 978-1-4027-6479-0 Subj: Counting, numbers. Dinosaurs. Format, unusual – toy & movable books.

Stiegemeyer, Julie. *Seven little bunnies* ill. by Laura J. Bryant. Marshall Cavendish, 2010. ISBN 978-0-7614-5600-1 Subj: Animals – rabbits. Bedtime. Counting, numbers. Rhyming text.

Stileman, Kali. *Roly-poly egg* ill. by author. ME Media/Tiger Tales, 2011. ISBN 978-1-58925-852-5 Subj: Birds. Eggs. Format, unusual – toy & movable books.

Stockdale, Susan. *Bring on the birds* ill. by author. Peachtree, 2011. ISBN 978-1-56145-560-7 Subj: Birds. Rhyming text.

Stoeke, Janet Morgan. *The Loopy Coop hens* ill. by author. Penguin Group (USA), 2011. ISBN 978-0-525-42190-0 Subj: Birds – chickens. Farms.

Stott, Ann. *I'll be there* ill. by Matt Phelan. Candlewick, 2010. ISBN 978-0-7636-4711-7 Subj: Behavior – growing up. Emotions – love. Family life – mothers.

Stroud, Bettye. *Belle, the last mule at Gee's Bend: a civil rights story* (Ramsey, Calvin Alexander)

Stuchner, Joan Betty. *Can hens give milk?* ill. by Joe Weissmann. Orca, 2011. ISBN 978-1-55469-319-1 Subj: Birds – chickens. Farms. Humorous stories. Jewish culture.

Sturgis, Brenda Reeves. *10 turkeys in the road* ill. by David Slonim. Marshall Cavendish, 2011. ISBN 978-0-7614-5847-0 Subj: Birds – turkeys. Careers – farmers. Circus. Counting, numbers. Rhyming text.

Stutson, Caroline. *Cats' night out* ill. by J. Klassen. Simon & Schuster, 2010. ISBN 978-1-4169-4005-0 Subj: Activities – dancing. Animals – cats. Cities, towns. Night. Rhyming text.

Stuve-Bodeen, Stephanie. *A small brown dog with a wet pink nose* ill. by Linzie Hunter. Little, Brown, 2010. ISBN 978-0-316-05830-8 Subj: Animals – dogs. Behavior – resourcefulness. Pets.

Suen, Anastasia. *Road work ahead* ill. by Jannie Ho. Penguin Group (USA), 2011. ISBN 978-0-670-01288-6 Subj: Activities – traveling. Rhyming text. Roads.

Sullivan, Sarah. *Once upon a baby brother* ill. by Tricia Tusa. Farrar, 2010. ISBN 978-0-374-34635-5 Subj: Activities – storytelling. Activities – writing. Family life – new sibling. Sibling rivalry.

Sutton, Benn. *Hedgehug: a sharp lesson in love.* HarperCollins, 2011. ISBN 978-0-06-196101-4 Subj: Animals – hedgehogs. Holidays – Valentine's Day. Hugging.

Sutton, Jane. *Don't call me Sidney* ill. by Renata Gallio. Penguin Group (USA), 2010. ISBN 978-0-8037-2753-3 Subj: Activities – writing. Animals. Animals – pigs. Names.

Sweet, Melissa. *Balloons over Broadway: the true story of the puppeteer of Macy's Parade* ill. by author. Houghton Harcourt, 2011. ISBN 978-0-547-19945-0 Subj: Parades. Puppets. Toys – balloons.

Swender, Jennifer. *Fire drill* (Jacobs, Paul Dubois)

Swinburne, Stephen R. *Whose shoes? a shoe for every job* ill. by Stephen R. Swinburne. Boyds Mills, 2010. ISBN 978-1-59078-569-0 Subj: Careers. Clothing – shoes.

Sylver, Adrienne. *Hot diggity dog: the history of the hot dog* ill. by Elwood H. Smith. Penguin Group (USA), 2010. ISBN 978-0-525-47897-3 Subj: Activities – baking, cooking. Food.

Sylvester, Kevin. *Splinters* ill. by author. Tundra, 2010. ISBN 978-0-88776-944-3 Subj: Folk & fairy tales. Sports – hockey.

Symes, Ruth. *Little Rex, big brother* ill. by Sean Julian. Whitman, 2010. ISBN 978-0-8075-4636-9 Subj: Character traits – smallness. Dinosaurs. Family life – brothers.

Symes, Sally. *Yawn* ill. by Nick Sharratt. Candlewick, 2011. ISBN 978-0-7636-5725-3 Subj: Animals. Bedtime.

Taback, Simms. *Postcards from camp* ill. by author. Penguin Group (USA), 2011. ISBN 978-0-399-23973-3 Subj: Activities – writing. Camps, camping. Format, unusual. Letters, cards.

Simms Taback's farm animals ill. by author. Blue Apple, 2011. ISBN 978-1-60905-078-8 Subj: Animals. Farms. Format, unusual – toy & movable books.

Tafolla, Carmen. *Fiesta babies* ill. by Amy Córdova. Tricycle, 2010. ISBN 978-1-58246-319-3 Subj: Babies. Ethnic groups in the U.S. – Mexican Americans. Fairs, festivals. Rhyming text.

Tafuri, Nancy. *All kinds of kisses* ill. by author. Little, Brown, 2012. ISBN 978-0-316-12235-1 Subj: Animals. Family life – mothers. Kissing.

Tarpley, Todd. *How about a kiss for me?* ill. by Liza Woodruff. Penguin Group (USA), 2010. ISBN 978-0-525-42235-8 Subj: Kissing. Rhyming text.

Tavares, Matt. *Henry Aaron's dream* ill. by author. Candlewick, 2010. ISBN 978-0-7636-3224-3 Subj: Ethnic groups in the U.S. – African Americans. Prejudice. Sports – baseball. U.S. history.

Taxali, Gary. *This is silly!* ill. by author. Scholastic, 2010. ISBN 978-0-439-71836-3 Subj: Humorous stories. Rhyming text.

Taylor, Jane. *Twinkle, twinkle, little star* ill. by Jerry Pinkney. Little, Brown, 2011. ISBN 978-0-316-05696-0 Subj: Animals – chipmunks. Nursery rhymes. Sky. Songs. Stars.

Taylor, Sean. *The grizzly bear with the frizzly hair* ill. by Hannah Shaw. Frances Lincoln, 2011. ISBN 978-1-84780-085-5 Subj: Animals – bears. Animals – rabbits. Behavior – trickery. Character traits – cleverness.

Huck runs amuck! ill. by Peter H. Reynolds. Penguin Group (USA), 2011. ISBN 978-0-8037-3261-2 Subj: Animals – goats. Flowers.

The ring went zing! a story that ends with a kiss ill. by Jill Barton. Penguin Group (USA), 2010. ISBN 978-0-8037-3311-4 Subj: Cumulative tales. Humorous stories.

The world champion of staying awake ill. by Jimmy Liao. Candlewick, 2011. ISBN 978-0-7636-4957-9 Subj: Bedtime. Toys.

Taylor, Thomas. *Little Mouse and the big cupcake* ill. by Jill Barton. Boxer, 2010. ISBN 978-1-907152-47-4 Subj: Animals – mice. Behavior – sharing. Food.

Teague, David. *Franklin's big dreams* ill. by Boris Kulikov. Hyperion/Disney, 2010. ISBN 978-1-4231-1919-7 Subj: Bedtime. Dreams. Night.

Teague, Mark. *Firehouse!* ill. by author. Scholastic, 2010. ISBN 978-0-439-91500-7 Subj: Animals – dogs. Careers – firefighters.

LaRue across America: postcards from the vacation ill. by author. Scholastic, 2011. ISBN 978-0-439-91502-1 Subj: Activities – vacationing. Activities – writing. Animals – cats. Animals – dogs. Letters, cards.

Tebbs, Victoria. *Noah's Ark story* ill. by Melanie Mitchell. Lion, 2010. ISBN 978-0-7459-4901-7 Subj: Animals. Boats, ships. Religion. Weather – floods. Weather – rain.

Teckentrup, Britta. *Little Wolf's song* ill. by author. Boxer, 2010. ISBN 978-1-907152-33-7 Subj: Animals – wolves. Behavior – growing up. Behavior – teasing. Noise, sounds.

Tegen, Katherine. *The story of the leprechaun* ill. by Sally Anne Lambert. HarperCollins, 2011. ISBN 978-0-06-143086-2 Subj: Careers – shoemakers. Mythical creatures – leprechauns.

Thimmesh, Catherine. *Friends: true stories of extraordinary animal friendships.* Houghton Harcourt, 2011. ISBN 978-0-547-39010-9 Subj: Animals. Friendship.

Thisdale, François. *Nini* ill. by author. Tundra, 2011. ISBN 978-1-77049-270-7 Subj: Adoption. Foreign lands – China.

Thomas, Jan. *Is everyone ready for fun?* ill. by author. Simon & Schuster, 2011. ISBN 978-1-4424-2364-1 Subj: Animals – bulls, cows. Birds – chickens. Humorous stories.

Pumpkin trouble ill. by author. HarperCollins, 2011. ISBN 978-0-06-169284-0 Subj: Animals – mice. Animals – pigs. Birds – ducks. Holidays – Halloween.

Thomas, Shelley Moore. *A Good Knight's rest* ill. by Jennifer Plecas. Penguin Group (USA), 2011.

ISBN 978-0-525-42195-5 Subj: Activities – vacationing. Dragons. Friendship. Knights.

Thompson, Lauren. *Chew, chew, gulp!* ill. by Jarrett J. Krosoczka. Simon & Schuster, 2011. ISBN 978-1-4169-9744-3 Subj: Food. Rhyming text.

Leap back home to me ill. by Matthew Cordell. Simon & Schuster, 2011. ISBN 978-1-4169-0664-3 Subj: Family life – mothers. Frogs & toads. Rhyming text.

One starry night ill. by Jonathan Bean. Simon & Schuster, 2011. ISBN 978-0-689-82851-5 Subj: Animals. Holidays – Christmas. Religion – Nativity.

Wee little bunny ill. by John Butler. Simon & Schuster, 2010. ISBN 978-1-4169-7937-1 Subj: Animals – babies. Animals – rabbits.

Thomson, Bill. *Chalk* ill. by author. Marshall Cavendish, 2010. ISBN 978-0-7614-5526-4 Subj: Activities – drawing. Magic. Wordless.

Thomson, Sarah L. *Where do polar bears live?* ill. by Jason Chin. HarperCollins, 2010. ISBN 978-0-06-157518-1 Subj: Animals – polar bears. Foreign lands – Arctic.

Thong, Roseanne. *Fly free!* ill. by Enjin Kim Neilan. Boyds Mills, 2010. ISBN 978-1-59078-550-8 Subj: Birds. Character traits – kindness. Foreign lands – Vietnam. Religion.

The three bears. *Goldilocks and the three bears* by Emma Chichester Clark; ill. by author. Candlewick, 2010. ISBN 978-0-7636-4680-6 Subj: Animals – bears. Folk & fairy tales.

Goldilocks and the three bears retold by Gerda Muller; ill. by reteller. Floris, 2011. ISBN 978-0-86315-795-0 Subj: Animals – bears. Folk & fairy tales.

Thurlby, Paul. *Paul Thurlby's alphabet* ill. by author. Candlewick, 2011. ISBN 978-0-7636-5565-5 Subj: ABC books.

Thurman, Kathryn K. *A garden for Pig* ill. by Lindsay Ward. Kane/Miller, 2010. ISBN 978-1-935279-24-2 Subj: Animals – pigs. Food. Gardens, gardening.

Tierney, Fiona. *Lion's lunch?* ill. by Margaret Chamberlain. Scholastic, 2010. ISBN 978-0-545-17691-0 Subj: Activities – drawing. Animals – lions. Behavior – bullying. Jungle.

Tillman, Nancy. *The crown on your head* ill. by author. Feiwel & Friends, 2011. ISBN 978-0-312-64521-2 Subj: Animals. Character traits – individuality. Rhyming text. Self-concept.

Tumford the terrible ill. by author. Feiwel & Friends, 2011. ISBN 978-0-312-36840-1 Subj: Animals – cats. Behavior – misbehavior. Rhyming text.

Wherever you are: my love will find you ill. by author. Feiwel & Friends, 2010. ISBN 978-0-312-54966-4 Subj: Emotions – love. Rhyming text.

Timmers, Leo. *Crow* ill. by author. Clavis, 2010. ISBN 978-1-60537-071-2 Subj: Birds. Birds – crows. Character traits – being different. Self-concept.

Titcomb, Gordon. *The last train* ill. by Wendell Minor. Roaring Brook, 2010. ISBN 978-1-59643-164-5 Subj: Music. Songs. Trains.

Tompert, Ann. *Little Fox goes to the end of the world* ill. by Laura J. Bryant. Marshall Cavendish, 2010. ISBN 978-0-7614-5703-9 Subj: Animals – foxes. Family life – mothers. Imagination.

Tonatiuh, Duncan. *Dear Primo: a letter to my cousin* ill. by author. Abrams, 2010. ISBN 978-0-8109-3872-4 Subj: Activities – writing. Ethnic groups in the U.S. – Mexican Americans. Family life – cousins. Foreign lands – Mexico. Letters, cards.

Diego Rivera: his world and ours ill. by author. Abrams, 2011. ISBN 978-0-8109-9731-8 Subj: Art. Careers – artists. Foreign lands – Mexico.

Torrey, Richard. *Because* ill. by author. HarperCollins, 2011. ISBN 978-0-06-156173-3 Subj: Behavior.

Why? ill. by author. HarperCollins, 2010. ISBN 978-0-06-156170-2 Subj: Character traits – curiosity. Character traits – questioning.

Toscano, Charles. *Papa's pastries* ill. by Sonja Lamut. Zonderkidz, 2010. ISBN 978-0-310-71602-0 Subj: Behavior – sharing. Character traits – generosity. Character traits – kindness. Food. Poverty.

Trapani, Iza. *Rufus and friends: school days* ill. by author. Charlesbridge, 2010. ISBN 978-1-58089-248-3 Subj: Nursery rhymes. Picture puzzles.

The tree house ill. by Marije Tolman and Ronald Tolman. Boyds Mills, 2010. ISBN 978-1-59078-806-6 Subj: Animals. Homes, houses. Trees. Wordless.

Tuck, Justin. *Home-field advantage* ill. by Leonardo Rodriguez. Simon & Schuster, 2011. ISBN 978-1-4424-0369-7 Subj: Family life – sisters. Hair. Multiple births – twins.

Tucker, Lindy. *Porkelia: a pig's tale* ill. by author. Charlesbridge, 2011. ISBN 978-1-934133-28-6 Subj: Activities – dancing. Animals – pigs. Character traits – ambition. Rhyming text.

Tullet, Hervé. *The book with a hole.* Abrams, 2011. ISBN 978-1-85437-946-7 Subj: Format, unusual. Imagination. Participation.

Press here tr. by Christopher Franceschelli; ill. by author. Chronicle, 2011. ISBN 978-0-8118-7954-5 Subj: Format, unusual. Imagination. Participation.

Tusa, Tricia. *Follow me* ill. by author. Harcourt, 2011. ISBN 978-0-547-27201-6 Subj: Activities – swinging. Concepts – color. Imagination.

The twelve days of Christmas. English folk song. *Twelve days of Christmas* by Rachel Isadora; ill. by author. Penguin Group (USA), 2010. ISBN 978-0-399-25073-6 Subj: Cumulative tales. Holidays – Christmas. Music. Songs.

The twelve days of Christmas ill. by Laurel Long. Penguin Group (USA), 2011. ISBN 978-0-8037-3357-2 Subj: Cumulative tales. Holidays – Christmas. Music. Songs.

The twelve days of Christmas ill. by Jane Ray. Candlewick, 2011. ISBN 978-0-7636-5735-2 Subj: Cumulative tales. Holidays – Christmas. Music. Songs.

Twohy, Mike. *Poindexter makes a friend* ill. by author. Simon & Schuster, 2011. ISBN 978-1-4424-0965-1 Subj: Animals – pigs. Books, reading. Character traits – shyness. Friendship. Libraries.

Uhlberg, Myron. *A storm called Katrina* ill. by Colin Bootman. Peachtree, 2011. ISBN 978-1-56145-591-1 Subj: Behavior – lost. Ethnic groups in the U.S. – African Americans. Musical instruments. Weather – floods. Weather – hurricanes.

Underwood, Deborah. *A balloon for Isabel.* HarperCollins, 2010. ISBN 978-0-06-177987-9 Subj: Animals – porcupines. Character traits – being different. School.

The loud book! ill. by Renata Liwska. Houghton Mifflin, 2011. ISBN 978-0-547-39008-6 Subj: Day. Noise, sounds.

The quiet book ill. by Renata Liwska. Houghton Mifflin, 2010. ISBN 978-0-547-21567-9 Subj: Animals. Behavior – solitude. Noise, sounds.

Ungerer, Tomi. *Otto: the autobiography of a teddy bear* ill. by author. Phaidon, 2010. ISBN 978-0-

7148-5766-4 Subj: Foreign lands – Germany. Holocaust. Jewish culture. Toys – bears. War.

Urbanovic, Jackie. *Sitting duck* ill. by author. HarperCollins, 2010. ISBN 978-0-06-176583-4 Subj: Activities – babysitting. Animals – dogs. Birds – ducks.

Urdahl, Catherine. *Polka-dot fixes kindergarten* ill. by Mai S. Kemble. Charlesbridge, 2011. ISBN 978-1-57091-737-0 Subj: Behavior – misbehavior. Character traits – assertiveness. Friendship. School. Self-concept.

Vainio, Pirkko. *Who hid the Easter eggs?* ill. by author. NorthSouth, 2011. ISBN 978-0-7358-2304-4 Subj: Animals – squirrels. Behavior – hiding things. Eggs. Holidays – Easter.

Vamos, Samantha R. *The cazuela that the farm maiden stirred* ill. by Rafael López. Charlesbridge, 2011. ISBN 978-1-58089-242-1 Subj: Activities – baking, cooking. Animals. Cumulative tales. Farms. Food. Foreign languages.

Van Allsburg, Chris. *Queen of the falls* ill. by author. Houghton Harcourt, 2011. ISBN 978-0-547-31581-2 Subj: Character traits – bravery. Character traits – persistence. U.S. history.

Van Camp, Katie. *CookieBot! a Harry and Horsie adventure* ill. by Lincoln Agnew. HarperCollins, 2011. ISBN 978-0-06-197445-8 Subj: Food. Imagination. Robots. Toys.

Van Dusen, Chris. *King Hugo's huge ego* ill. by author. Candlewick, 2011. ISBN 978-0-7636-5004-9 Subj: Behavior – boasting. Magic. Rhyming text. Royalty – kings. Self-concept.

Learning to ski with Mr. Magee ill. by author. Chronicle, 2010. ISBN 978-0-8118-7495-3 Subj: Animals – dogs. Rhyming text. Sports – skiing.

Van Fleet, Matthew. *Heads* ill. by author. Simon & Schuster, 2010. ISBN 978-1-4424-0379-6 Subj: Animals. Format, unusual – toy & movable books.

Moo photos by Brian Stanton. Simon & Schuster, 2011. ISBN 978-1-4424-3503-2 Subj: Animals. Farms. Format, unusual – toy & movable books.

van Lieshout, Maria. *Hopper and Wilson* ill. by author. Penguin Group (USA), 2011. ISBN 978-0-

399-25184-9 Subj: Animals – elephants. Animals – mice. Friendship. Sports – sailing.

Tumble! a little book about having it all ill. by author. Feiwel & Friends, 2010. ISBN 978-0-312-54859-9 Subj: Animals – bears. Behavior – sharing.

Vande Griek, Susan. *Loon* ill. by Karen Reczuch. Groundwood, 2011. ISBN 978-1-55498-077-2 Subj: Behavior – growing up. Birds – loons.

Vasilovich, Guy. *The 13 nights of Halloween* ill. by author. HarperCollins, 2011. ISBN 978-0-06-180445-8 Subj: Cumulative tales. Holidays – Halloween. Rhyming text. Songs.

Velasquez, Eric. *Grandma's gift* ill. by author. Walker, 2010. ISBN 978-0-8027-2082-5 Subj: Art. Ethnic groups in the U.S. – Puerto Rican Americans. Family life – grandmothers. Foreign languages. Gifts. Holidays – Christmas.

Verburg, Bonnie. *The kiss box* ill. by Henry Cole. Orchard, 2011. ISBN 978-0-545-11284-0 Subj: Activities – traveling. Animals – bears. Emotions – love. Family life – mothers. Kissing.

Verdick, Elizabeth. *On-the-go time* ill. by Marieka Heinlen. Free Spirit, 2011. ISBN 978-1-57542-379-1 Subj: Character traits – helpfulness. Format, unusual – board books. Shopping.

Vere, Ed. *Banana!* ill. by author. Henry Holt, 2010. ISBN 978-0-8050-9214-1 Subj: Animals – monkeys. Behavior – sharing.

Chick ill. by author. Henry Holt, 2010. ISBN 978-0-8050-9168-7 Subj: Birds – chickens.

Vernick, Audrey. *Is your buffalo ready for kindergarten?* ill. by Daniel Jennewein. HarperCollins, 2010. ISBN 978-0-06-176275-8 Subj: Animals – buffaloes. School – first day.

She loved baseball: the Effa Manley story ill. by Don Tate. HarperCollins, 2010. ISBN 978-0-06-134920-1 Subj: Ethnic groups in the U.S. – African Americans. Gender roles. Prejudice. Sports – baseball. U.S. history.

Teach your buffalo to play drums ill. by Daniel Jennewein. HarperCollins, 2011. ISBN 978-0-06-176253-6 Subj: Animals – buffaloes. Musical instruments – drums. Noise, sounds.

Verstraete, Larry. *S is for scientists: a discovery alphabet* ill. by David Geister. Sleeping Bear, 2010. ISBN 978-1-58536-470-1 Subj: ABC books. Careers – scientists. Science.

Vestergaard, Hope. *Potty animals: what to know when you've gotta go!* ill. by Valeria Petrone. Sterling, 2010. ISBN 978-1-4027-5996-3 Subj: Animals. Etiquette. Hygiene. Rhyming text. Toilet training.

Villeneuve, Anne. *The red scarf* ill. by author. Tundra, 2010. ISBN 978-0-88776-989-4 Subj: Animals – moles. Behavior – lost & found possessions. Careers – magicians. Circus. Clothing – scarves.

Villnave, Erica Pelton. *Sophie's lovely locks* ill. by author. Marshall Cavendish, 2011. ISBN 978-0-7614-5820-3 Subj: Character traits – generosity. Hair.

Vischer, Frans. *Fuddles* ill. by author. Simon & Schuster, 2011. ISBN 978-1-4169-9155-7 Subj: Animals – cats. Behavior – lost.

Viva, Frank. *Along a long road* ill. by author. Little, Brown, 2011. ISBN 978-0-316-12925-1 Subj: Sports – bicycling.

Voake, Charlotte. *Ginger and the mystery visitor* ill. by author. Candlewick, 2010. ISBN 978-0-7636-4865-7 Subj: Animals – cats.

Voake, Steve. *Insect detective* ill. by Charlotte Voake. Candlewick, 2010. ISBN 978-0-7636-4447-5 Subj: Gardens, gardening. Insects. Science.

Von Konigslow, Andrea Wayne. *How do you read to a rabbit?* ill. by author. Annick, 2010. ISBN 978-1-55451-232-4 Subj: Animals. Books, reading.

Waber, Bernard. *Lyle walks the dogs: a counting book* ill. by Paulis Waber. Houghton Harcourt, 2010. ISBN 978-0-547-22323-0 Subj: Activities – walking. Animals – dogs. Counting, numbers. Reptiles – alligators, crocodiles.

Waddell, Martin. *Captain Small Pig* ill. by Susan Varley. Peachtree, 2010. ISBN 978-1-56145-519-5 Subj: Animals – goats. Animals – pigs. Birds – turkeys. Boats, ships.

Wadham, Tim. *The queen of France* ill. by Kady MacDonald Denton. Candlewick, 2011. ISBN 978-0-7636-4102-3 Subj: Family life – parents. Imagination. Royalty – queens.

Wagner, Rachel. *A friend for Einstein: the smallest stallion* (Cantrell, Charlie)

Wahl, Jan. *The art collector* ill. by Rosalinde Bonnet. Charlesbridge, 2011. ISBN 978-1-58089-270-4 Subj: Art. Behavior – collecting things.

Wahman, Wendy. *A cat like that* ill. by author. Henry Holt, 2011. ISBN 978-0-8050-8942-4 Subj: Animals – cats.

Waiting for baby ill. by Rachel Fuller. Child's Play, 2010. ISBN 978-1-84643-275-0 Subj: Babies. Birth. Format, unusual – board books.

Waldman, Debby. *Room enough for Daisy* by Debby Waldman and Rita Feutl; ill. by Cindy Revell. Orca, 2011. ISBN 978-1-55469-255-2 Subj: Behavior – messy. Behavior – sharing. Jewish culture.

Waldron, Kevin. *Mr. Peek and the misunderstanding at the zoo* ill. by author. Candlewick, 2010. ISBN 978-0-7636-4549-6 Subj: Animals. Behavior – misunderstanding. Behavior – worrying. Self-concept. Zoos.

Walker, Anna. *I love birthdays* ill. by author. Simon & Schuster, 2010. ISBN 978-1-4169-8320-0 Subj: Animals – zebras. Birthdays. Parties. Rhyming text.

I love my dad ill. by author. Simon & Schuster, 2010. ISBN 978-1-4169-8319-4 Subj: Animals – zebras. Family life – fathers. Rhyming text.

I love my mom ill. by author. Simon & Schuster, 2010. ISBN 978-1-4169-8318-7 Subj: Animals – zebras. Family life – mothers. Rhyming text.

Walker, Sally M. *Freedom song: the story of Henry "Box" Brown* ill. by Sean Qualls. HarperCollins, 2012. ISBN 978-0-06-058310-1 Subj: Character traits – freedom. Ethnic groups in the U.S. – African Americans. Slavery. U.S. history.

Wallace, Nancy Elizabeth. *Planting seeds* ill. by author. Marshall Cavendish, 2010. ISBN 978-0-7614-5643-8 Subj: Animals – rabbits. Counting, numbers. Gardens, gardening. Seeds.

Pond walk ill. by author. Marshall Cavendish, 2011. ISBN 978-0-7614-5816-6 Subj: Animals – bears. Lakes, ponds. Science.

Ready, set, 100th day! ill. by author. Marshall Cavendish, 2011. ISBN 978-0-7614-5956-9 Subj: Animals – rabbits. Behavior – cooperation. Counting, numbers. Family life. School.

Walsh, Ellen Stoll. *Balancing act* ill. by author. Simon & Schuster, 2010. ISBN 978-1-4424-0757-2 Subj: Animals – mice. Concepts.

Walsh, Joanna. *The biggest kiss* ill. by Judi Abbot. Simon & Schuster, 2011. ISBN 978-1-4424-2769-3 Subj: Kissing. Rhyming text.

Walton, Rick. *Baby's first year!* ill. by Caroline Jayne Church. Penguin Group (USA), 2011. ISBN 978-0-399-25025-5 Subj: Babies. Rhyming text.

Wardlaw, Lee. *Won Ton: a cat tale told in haiku* ill. by Eugene Yelchin. Henry Holt, 2011. ISBN 978-0-8050-8995-0 Subj: Animals – cats. Character traits – kindness to animals. Poetry.

Wargin, Kathy-jo. *Scare a bear* ill. by John Bendall-Brunello. Sleeping Bear, 2010. ISBN 978-1-58536-430-5 Subj: Animals – bears. Rhyming text.

Warren, Rick, commentary. *The Lord's prayer* ill. by Richard Jesse Watson. Zonderkidz, 2011. ISBN 978-0-310-71086-8 Subj: Religion.

Warwick, Dionne. *Little Man* by Dionne Warwick and David Freeman Wooley; ill. by Fred Willingham. Charlesbridge, 2011. ISBN 978-1-57091-731-8 Subj: Activities – working. Character traits – perseverance. Ethnic groups in the U.S. – African Americans. Money. Musical instruments – drums.

Washington, Donna L. *Li'l Rabbit's Kwanzaa* ill. by Shane W. Evans. HarperCollins, 2010. ISBN 978-0-06-072816-8 Subj: Animals – rabbits. Holidays – Kwanzaa.

Washington, Kathy Gates. *Three colors of Katie* ill. by Kathy Farina. College of Dupage, 2010. ISBN 978-1-932514-18-6 Subj: Ethnic groups in the U.S. – racially mixed. Family life.

Washington, Ned. *When you wish upon a star* by Ned Washington and Leigh Harline; ill. by Eric Puybaret. Imagine, 2011. ISBN 978-1-936140-35-0 Subj: Behavior – wishing. Dreams. Songs. Stars.

Watkins, Angela Farris. *My Uncle Martin's big heart* ill. by Eric Velasquez. Abrams, 2010. ISBN 978-0-8109-8975-7 Subj: Ethnic groups in the U.S. – African Americans. Family life – aunts, uncles. U.S. history. Violence, nonviolence.

My Uncle Martin's words for America: Martin Luther King Jr.'s niece tells how he made a difference ill. by Eric Velasquez. Abrams, 2011. ISBN 978-1-4197-0022-4 Subj: Ethnic groups in the U.S. – African Americans. Prejudice. U.S. history. Violence, nonviolence.

Watson, Jesse Joshua. *Hope for Haiti* ill. by author. Penguin Group (USA), 2010. ISBN 978-0-399-25547-2 Subj: Earthquakes. Foreign lands – Haiti. Hope. Sports – soccer.

Watson, Renée. *A place where hurricanes happen* ill. by Shadra Strickland. Random House, 2010. ISBN 978-0-375-85609-9 Subj: Cities, towns. Communities, neighborhoods. Weather – hurricanes.

Watson, Wendy. *Bedtime bunnies* ill. by author. Clarion, 2010. ISBN 978-0-547-22312-4 Subj: Animals – rabbits. Bedtime. Seasons – fall.

Watt, Mélanie. *Chester's masterpiece* ill. by author. Kids Can, 2010. ISBN 978-1-55453-566-8 Subj: Activities – drawing. Activities – writing. Animals – cats.

Scaredy Squirrel has a birthday party ill. by author. Kids Can, 2011. ISBN 978-1-55453-468-5 Subj: Animals – squirrels. Birthdays. Emotions – fear. Parties.

You're finally here! ill. by author. Hyperion/Disney, 2011. ISBN 978-1-4231-3486-2 Subj: Animals – rabbits. Behavior – misbehavior. Books, reading. Etiquette.

Watterson, Carol. *An edible alphabet: 26 reasons to love the farm* ill. by Michela Sorrentino. Tricycle, 2011. ISBN 978-1-58246-421-3 Subj: ABC books. Farms.

Weatherford, Carole Boston. *The Beatitudes: from slavery to civil rights* ill. by Tim Ladwig. Eerdmans, 2010. ISBN 978-0-8028-5352-3 Subj: Ethnic groups in the U.S. – African Americans. Prejudice. Religion. Slavery. U.S. history.

Webster, Sheryl. *Noodle's knitting* ill. by Caroline Pedler. Good Books, 2010. ISBN 978-1-56148-694-6 Subj: Activities – knitting. Animals – mice.

Weiss, Ellen. *The taming of Lola: a shrew story* ill. by Jerry Smath. Abrams, 2010. ISBN 978-0-8109-4066-6 Subj: Animals – shrews. Behavior – misbehavior. Emotions – anger. Family life – cousins. Family life – grandmothers.

Weitzman, Jacqueline Preiss. *Superhero Joe* ill. by Ron Barrett. Simon & Schuster, 2011. ISBN 978-1-4169-9157-1 Subj: Character traits – bravery. Emotions – fear. Imagination.

Wells, Robert E. *Why do elephants need the sun?* ill. by author. Whitman, 2010. ISBN 978-0-8075-9081-2 Subj: Animals – elephants. Science. Sun.

Wells, Rosemary. *Hands off, Harry!* ill. by author. HarperCollins, 2011. ISBN 978-0-06-192112-4 Subj: Behavior – misbehavior. Problem solving. Reptiles – alligators, crocodiles. School.

Love waves ill. by author. Candlewick, 2011. ISBN 978-0-7636-4989-0 Subj: Activities – working. Animals – rabbits. Emotions – love. Family life – parents. Rhyming text.

Max and Ruby's bedtime book ill. by author. Penguin Group (USA), 2010. ISBN 978-0-670-01141-4 Subj: Animals – rabbits. Family life – brothers & sisters. Family life – grandmothers.

Yoko's show-and-tell ill. by author. Hyperion/Disney, 2010. ISBN 978-1-4231-1955-5 Subj: Behavior – misbehavior. Ethnic groups in the U.S. – Japanese Americans. Gifts. School. Toys – dolls.

Wewer, Iris. *My wild sister and me* ill. by author. NorthSouth, 2011. ISBN 978-0-7358-4003-4 Subj: Activities – playing. Emotions – envy, jealousy. Family life – brothers & sisters.

Wheeler, Lisa. *Dino-baseball* ill. by Barry Gott. Carolrhoda, 2010. ISBN 978-0-7613-4429-2 Subj: Dinosaurs. Sports – baseball.

Dino-basketball ill. by Barry Gott. Carolrhoda, 2011. ISBN 978-0-7613-6393-4 Subj: Dinosaurs. Rhyming text. Sports – basketball.

Ugly pie ill. by Heather Solomon. Houghton Harcourt, 2010. ISBN 978-0-15-216754-7 Subj: Activities – baking, cooking. Animals – bears. Food.

Whelan, Gloria. *The boy who wanted to cook* ill. by Steve Adams. Sleeping Bear, 2011. ISBN 978-1-58536-534-0 Subj: Activities – baking, cooking. Careers – chefs, cooks. Family life. Foreign lands – France. Restaurants.

White, Becky. *Betsy Ross* ill. by Megan Lloyd. Holiday House, 2011. ISBN 978-0-8234-1908-1 Subj: Flags. Rhyming text. Sewing. U.S. history.

White, Kathryn. *Ruby's school walk* ill. by Miriam Latimer. Barefoot, 2010. ISBN 978-1-84686-275-5 Subj: Activities – walking. Family life – mothers. Imagination. Rhyming text. School.

White, Linda. *Too many turkeys* ill. by Megan Lloyd. Holiday House, 2010. ISBN 978-0-8234-2084-1 Subj: Birds – turkeys. Farms. Gardens, gardening.

Wick, Walter. *Can you see what I see? toyland express* ill. by author. Scholastic, 2011. ISBN 978-0-545-24483-1 Subj: Picture puzzles. Toys.

Can you see what I see? treasure ship ill. by author. Scholastic, 2010. ISBN 978-0-439-02643-7 Subj: Boats, ships. Picture puzzles. Rhyming text. Riddles & jokes.

Wiesner, David. *Art and Max* ill. by author. Clarion, 2010. ISBN 978-0-618-75663-6 Subj: Activities – painting. Art. Careers – artists. Reptiles – lizards. Self-concept.

Wild, Margaret. *Harry and Hopper* ill. by Freya Blackwood. Feiwel & Friends, 2011. ISBN 978-0-312-64261-7 Subj: Animals – dogs. Death. Emotions – grief.

Hush, hush! ill. by Bridget Strevens-Marzo. Little Hare, 2010. ISBN 978-1-92-127286-8 Subj: Animals – hippopotamuses. Bedtime.

Itsy-bitsy babies ill. by Jan Ormerod. Little Hare, 2010. ISBN 978-1-921541-36-0 Subj: Babies. Rhyming text.

Willems, Mo. *City dog, country frog* ill. by Jon J Muth. Hyperion, 2010. ISBN 978-1-4231-0300-

4 Subj: Animals – dogs. Friendship. Frogs & toads. Seasons.

Knuffle Bunny free: an unexpected diversion ill. by author. HarperCollins, 2010. ISBN 978-0-0619-2957-1 Subj: Activities – traveling. Animals – rabbits. Behavior – lost & found possessions. Character traits – bravery. Toys.

Williams, Karen Lynn. *A beach tail* ill. by Floyd Cooper. Boyds Mills, 2010. ISBN 978-1-59078-712-0 Subj: Activities – drawing. Ethnic groups in the U.S. – African Americans. Sea & seashore – beaches.

Williams, Laura E. *The can man* ill. by Craig Orback. Lee & Low, 2010. ISBN 978-1-60060-266-5 Subj: Character traits – generosity. Homeless.

Williams, Treat. *Air show!* ill. by Robert Neubecker. Hyperion/Disney, 2010. ISBN 978-1-4231-1185-6 Subj: Airplanes, airports.

Willis, Jeanne. *I'm sure I saw a dinosaur* ill. by Adrian Reynolds. Andersen, 2011. ISBN 978-0-7613-8093-1 Subj: Dinosaurs. Rhyming text. Sea & seashore – beaches.

That's not funny! ill. by Adrian Reynolds. Andersen, 2010. ISBN 978-0-7613-6445-0 Subj: Animals. Animals – hyenas. Humorous stories.

Wilson, Karma. *Bear's loose tooth* ill. by Jane Chapman. Simon & Schuster, 2011. ISBN 978-1-4169-5855-0 Subj: Animals – bears. Rhyming text. Teeth.

The cow loves cookies ill. by Marcellus Hall. Simon & Schuster, 2010. ISBN 978-1-4169-4206-1 Subj: Animals – bulls, cows. Farms. Food. Rhyming text.

Hogwash! ill. by Jim McMullan. Little, Brown, 2011. ISBN 978-0-316-98840-7 Subj: Activities – bathing. Animals – pigs. Character traits – cleanliness. Farms. Rhyming text.

Mama, why? ill. by Simon Mendez. Simon & Schuster, 2011. ISBN 978-1-4169-4205-4 Subj: Animals – polar bears. Bedtime. Character traits – questioning. Rhyming text. Sky.

What's in the egg, Little Pip? ill. by Jane Chapman. Simon & Schuster, 2010. ISBN 978-1-4169-4204-7 Subj: Animals – babies. Birds – penguins. Eggs. Family life – new sibling.

Wing, Natasha. *How to raise a dinosaur* ill. by Pablo Bernasconi. Running Press, 2010. ISBN 978-0-7624-3342-1 Subj: Dinosaurs. Format, unusual – toy & movable books. Pets.

Winter, Jeanette. *Biblioburro: a true story from Colombia* ill. by author. Simon & Schuster, 2010. ISBN 978-1-4169-9778-8 Subj: Animals – donkeys. Books, reading. Foreign lands – Colombia. Libraries.

The watcher: Jane Goodall's life with the chimps ill. by author. Random House, 2011. ISBN 978-0-375-86774-3 Subj: Animals – chimpanzees. Careers – scientists. Foreign lands – Tanzania. Nature.

Winter, Jonah. *Here comes the garbage barge!* ill. by Red Nose Studio. Random House, 2010. ISBN 978-0-375-95218-0 Subj: Boats, ships. Careers – sanitation workers.

Winters, Kay. *This school year will be the best!* ill. by Renée Andriani. Penguin Group (USA), 2010. ISBN 978-0-525-42775-4 Subj: School – first day.

Wishinsky, Frieda. *Where are you, Bear? a Canadian alphabet adventure* ill. by Sean L. Moore. Owl Kids, 2010. ISBN 978-1-897349-91-5 Subj: ABC books. Foreign lands – Canada.

You're mean, Lily Jean! ill. by Kady MacDonald Denton. Whitman, 2011. ISBN 978-0-8075-9476-6 Subj: Activities – playing. Family life – sisters. Friendship.

Witte, Anna. *Lola's fandango* ill. by Micha Archer. Barefoot, 2011. ISBN 978-1-84686-174-1 Subj: Activities – dancing. Birthdays. Ethnic groups in the U.S. – Hispanic Americans. Family life – mothers.

Wiviott, Meg. *Benno and the night of broken glass* ill. by Josée Bisaillon. Lerner/Kar-Ben, 2010. ISBN 978-0-8225-9929-6 Subj: Animals – cats. Foreign lands – Germany. Holocaust. Jewish culture.

Wolfe, Myra. *Charlotte Jane battles bedtime* ill. by Maria Monescillo. Houghton Harcourt, 2011. ISBN 978-0-15-206150-0 Subj: Bedtime. Pirates.

Wood, Audrey. *Piggy Pie Po* ill. by Don Wood. Houghton Harcourt, 2010. ISBN 978-0-15-202494-9 Subj: Animals – pigs. Rhyming text.

Wood, Douglas. *Aunt Mary's rose* ill. by LeUyen Pham. Candlewick, 2010. ISBN 978-0-7636-1090-6 Subj: Death. Family life – aunts, uncles. Flowers – roses. Gardens, gardening.

No one but you ill. by P. J. Lynch. Candlewick, 2011. ISBN 978-0-7636-3848-1 Subj: Nature. Senses.

Where the sunrise begins ill. by K. Wendy Popp. Simon & Schuster, 2010. ISBN 978-0-689-86172-7 Subj: Nature. Sun.

Woodhull, Anne. *The buzz on bees: why are they disappearing?* (Rotner, Shelley)

Woodson, Jacqueline. *Pecan pie baby* ill. by Sophie Blackall. Penguin Group (USA), 2010. ISBN 978-0-399-23987-8 Subj: Babies. Ethnic groups in the U.S. – African Americans. Family life – new sibling. Family life – single-parent families.

Wooley, David Freeman. *Little Man* (Warwick, Dionne)

Wortche, Allison. *Rosie Sprout's time to shine* ill. by Patrice Barton. Random House, 2011. ISBN 978-0-375-86721-7 Subj: Behavior – boasting. Emotions – envy, jealousy. Gardens, gardening. Plants. School.

Wright, Maureen. *Sneeze, Big Bear, sneeze* ill. by Will Hillenbrand. Marshall Cavendish, 2011. ISBN 978-0-7614-5959-0 Subj: Animals – bears. Rhyming text. Seasons – fall. Weather – wind.

Sneezy the snowman ill. by Stephen Gilpin. Marshall Cavendish, 2010. ISBN 978-0-7614-5711-4 Subj: Clothing. Snowmen.

Wright, Michael. *Jake goes peanuts* ill. by author. Feiwel & Friends, 2010. ISBN 978-0-312-54967-1 Subj: Food. Rhyming text.

Wu, Faye-Lynn. *Chinese and English nursery rhymes: share and sing in two languages* ill. by Kieren Dutcher. Tuttle, 2010. ISBN 978-0-8048-4094-1 Subj: Foreign languages. Nursery rhymes.

Yaccarino, Dan. *All the way to America: the story of a big Italian family and a little shovel* ill. by author. Random House, 2011. ISBN 978-0-375-86642-5 Subj: Careers – authors. Ethnic groups in the U.S. – Italian Americans. Immigrants. U.S. history.

Lawn to lawn ill. by author. Random House, 2010. ISBN 978-0-375-85574-0 Subj: Animals. Moving.

Yahgulanaas, Michael Nicoll. *The little hummingbird* ill. by author. Greystone, 2010. ISBN 978-1-55365-533-6 Subj: Birds – hummingbirds. Character traits. Ecology. Folk & fairy tales. Foreign lands – South America.

Yamaguchi, Kristi. *Dream big, little pig!* ill. by Tim Bowers. Sourcebooks, 2011. ISBN 978-1-4022-5275-4 Subj: Animals – pigs. Character traits – ambition. Character traits – persistence. Sports – ice skating.

Yamashita, Haruo. *Seven little mice go to school* tr. by Missy Debs; ill. by Kazuo Iwamura. NorthSouth, 2011. ISBN 978-0-7358-4012-6 Subj: Animals – mice. Character traits – cleverness. Family life – mothers. School – first day.

Seven little mice have fun on the ice ill. by Kazuo Iwamura. NorthSouth, 2011. ISBN 978-0-7358-4048-5 Subj: Animals – mice. Family life – mothers. Seasons – winter. Sports – fishing.

Yankovic, Al. *When I grow up* ill. by Wes Hargis. HarperCollins, 2011. ISBN 978-0-06-192691-4 Subj: Careers. Rhyming text. School.

Yates, Louise. *Dog loves books* ill. by author. Random House, 2010. ISBN 978-0-375-86449-0 Subj: Animals – dogs. Books, reading.

Yeh, Kat. *The magic brush: a story of love, family, and Chinese characters* ill. by Huy Voun Lee. Walker, 2011. ISBN 978-0-8027-2178-5 Subj: Activities – storytelling. Activities – writing. Death. Ethnic groups in the U.S. – Chinese Americans. Family life – grandfathers. Foreign languages.

Yezerski, Thomas F. *Meadowlands: a wetlands survival story* ill. by author. Farrar, 2011. ISBN 978-0-374-34913-4 Subj: Ecology. Nature.

Yolen, Jane. *All star! Honus Wagner and the most famous baseball card ever* ill. by Jim Burke. Penguin Group (USA), 2010. ISBN 978-0-399-24661-6 Subj: Sports – baseball.

Creepy monsters, sleepy monsters: a lullaby ill. by Kelly Murphy. Candlewick, 2011. ISBN 978-0-7636-4201-3 Subj: Bedtime. Monsters. Rhyming text.

The day Tiger Rose said goodbye ill. by Jim LaMarche. Random House, 2011. ISBN 978-0-375-86663-0 Subj: Animals – cats. Death.

An egret's day: poems photos by Jason Stemple. Boyds Mills, 2010. ISBN 978-1-59078-650-5 Subj: Birds – herons. Poetry.

Elsie's bird ill. by David Small. Penguin Group (USA), 2010. ISBN 978-0-399-25292-1 Subj: Birds – canaries. Emotions – loneliness. Moving. U.S. history – frontier & pioneer life.

Hush, little horsie ill. by Ruth Sanderson. Random House, 2010. ISBN 978-0-375-85853-6 Subj: Animals – horses, ponies. Bedtime. Rhyming text.

My father knows the names of things ill. by Stéphane Jorisch. Simon & Schuster, 2010. ISBN 978-1-4169-4895-7 Subj: Family life – fathers. Rhyming text.

Not all princesses dress in pink by Jane Yolen and Heidi E. Y. Stemple; ill. by Anne-Sophie Lanquetin. Simon & Schuster, 2010. ISBN 978-1-4169-8018-6 Subj: Character traits – individuality. Gender roles. Rhyming text. Royalty – princesses.

Sister Bear: a Norse tale ill. by Linda Graves. Marshall Cavendish, 2011. ISBN 978-0-7614-5958-

3 Subj: Animals – bears. Folk & fairy tales. Holidays – Christmas. Mythical creatures – trolls.

Yolleck, Joan. *Paris in the spring with Picasso* ill. by Marjorie Priceman. Random House, 2010. ISBN 978-0-375-83756-2 Subj: Art. Foreign lands – France. Parties.

Yoon, Salina. *At the beach* ill. by author. Feiwel & Friends, 2011. ISBN 978-0-312-66303-2 Subj: Format, unusual – board books. Sea & seashore – beaches.

Yorinks, Arthur. *The invisible man* ill. by Doug Cushman. HarperCollins, 2011. ISBN 978-0-06-156148-1 Subj: Careers – storekeepers. Character traits – being different.

You and me ill. by Rachel Fuller. Child's Play, 2010. ISBN 978-1-84643-277-4 Subj: Family life – new sibling. Format, unusual – board books.

Youme. *Mali under the night sky: a Lao story of home* ill. by author. Cinco Puntos, 2010. ISBN 978-1-933693-68-2 Subj: Foreign lands – Laos. War.

Young, Amy. *The mud fairy* ill. by author. Bloomsbury, 2010. ISBN 978-1-59990-104-6 Subj: Character traits – being different. Fairies. Frogs & toads.

Young, Cybèle. *A few blocks* ill. by author. Groundwood, 2011. ISBN 978-0-88899-995-5 Subj: Behavior – resourcefulness. Family life – brothers & sisters. Imagination.

Ten birds ill. by author. Kids Can, 2011. ISBN 978-1-55453-568-2 Subj: Birds. Counting, numbers. Problem solving.

Young, Ned. *Zoomer* ill. by author. HarperCollins, 2010. ISBN 978-0-06-170088-0 Subj: Activities – playing. Animals – dogs. Imagination.

Zoomer's summer snowstorm ill. by author. HarperCollins, 2011. ISBN 978-0-06-170092-7 Subj: Animals – dogs. Imagination. Weather – snow.

Yu, Li-Qiong. *A New Year's reunion* ill. by Cheng-Liang Zhu. Candlewick, 2011. ISBN 978-0-7636-5881-6 Subj: Activities – working. Family life – fathers. Foreign lands – China. Holidays – Chinese New Year.

Yum, Hyewon. *There are no scary wolves* ill. by author. Farrar, 2010. ISBN 978-0-374-38060-1 Subj: Animals – wolves. Emotions – fear. Imagination.

The twins' blanket ill. by author. Farrar, 2011. ISBN 978-0-374-37972-8 Subj: Behavior – sharing. Character traits – individuality. Family life – sisters. Multiple births – twins.

Zalben, Jane Breskin. *Baby shower* ill. by author. Roaring Brook, 2010. ISBN 978-1-59643-465-3 Subj: Dreams. Parties. Pets.

Zekauskas, Felicia. *One foot two feet: an exceptional counting book* (Maloney, Peter)

Zelch, Patti R. *Ready, set . . . wait! what animals do before a hurricane* ill. by Connie McLennan. Sylvan Dell, 2010. ISBN 978-1-60718-072-2 Subj: Animals. Weather – hurricanes.

Zenz, Aaron. *Chuckling ducklings and baby animal friends* ill. by author. Walker, 2011. ISBN 978-0-8027-2191-4 Subj: Animals – babies.

Zia, F. *Hot, hot roti for Dada-ji* ill. by Ken Min. Lee & Low, 2011. ISBN 978-1-60060-443-0 Subj: Activities – baking, cooking. Ethnic groups in the U.S. – East Indian Americans. Family life – grandfathers. Food.

Ziefert, Harriet. *Bunny's lessons* ill. by Barroux. Blue Apple, 2011. ISBN 978-1-60905-028-3 Subj: Animals – rabbits. Behavior. Emotions. Friendship. Toys.

Counting chickens ill. by Flensted. Blue Apple, 2010. ISBN 978-1-60905-033-7 Subj: Counting, numbers. Format, unusual.

Grandma's wedding album ill. by Karla Gudeon. Blue Apple, 2011. ISBN 978-1-60905-058-0 Subj: Family life – grandparents. Weddings.

My dog thinks I'm a genius ill. by Barroux. Blue Apple, 2011. ISBN 978-1-60905-059-7 Subj: Activities – painting. Animals – dogs.

Wiggle like an octopus ill. by Simms Taback. Blue Apple, 2011. ISBN 978-1-60905-072-6 Subj: Animals. Format, unusual – board books. Participation. Rhyming text. Sea & seashore.

Zoehfeld, Kathleen Weidner. *Where did dinosaurs come from?* ill. by Lucia Washburn. HarperCollins, 2011. ISBN 978-0-06-029022-1 Subj: Dinosaurs.

Zuffi, Stefano. *Art 123: count from 1 to 12 with great works of art.* Abrams, 2011. ISBN 978-1-4197-0100-9 Subj: Art. Counting, numbers. Rhyming text.

Title Index

Titles appear in alphabetical sequence with the author's name in parentheses, followed by the page number of the full listing in the Bibliographic Guide. For identical title listings, the illustrator's name is given to further identify the version. In the case of variant titles, both the original and differing titles are listed.

C

D

I

M

Y

Z

Illustrator Index

Illustrators appear alphabetically in boldface followed by their titles. Names in parentheses are authors of the titles when different from the illustrator. Page numbers refer to the full listing in the Bibliographic Guide.

C

E

G

M

About the Author

REBECCA L. THOMAS recently retired as an elementary school librarian, Shaker Heights City Schools, Ohio. She is the author of numerous reference books, including the *Popular Series Fiction* set for Libraries Unlimited (2009) and *Across Cultures* (Libraries Unlimited, 2007).